Backgrounds to Eighteenth-Century Literature

Chandler Publications in

BACKGROUNDS TO LITERATURE

Richard A. Levine, EDITOR

Backgrounds
to
Eighteenth-Century
Literature

∿

Kathleen Williams

University of California, Riverside

cp

CHANDLER PUBLISHING COMPANY

An Intext Publisher · Scranton / London / Toronto

Previously published and copyrighted materials are reprinted with the permission of authors, publishers, or copyright owners as listed below:

George Boas, "In Search of the Age of Reason," from *Aspects of the Eighteenth Century*, ed., Earl R. Wasserman. © The Johns Hopkins Press 1965. Reprinted by permission.

Bertrand H. Bronson, "When Was Neoclassicism?" from *Facets of the Enlightenment*, Berkeley and Los Angeles: University of California Press, 1968. Reprinted by permission of the author.

Paul Fussell, "What Is Humanism?" from *The Rhetorical World of Augustan Humanism*, New York: Oxford University Press, 1965. Reprinted by permission of the Clarendon Press, Oxford. (The text used here is from the Oxford University Press paperback edition, 1969.)

Meyrick Carrè, "The Empirical Philosophy," from *Phases of Thought in England*, London: Oxford University Press, 1949. Reprinted by permission of Clarendon Press, Oxford.

Ernst Cassirer, "The Mind of the Enlightenment," from *The Philosophy of Enlightenment* by Ernst Cassirer, trans., Fritz C. A. Koelln and James P. Pettegrove (copyright 1051 by Princeton University Press; Princeton Paperback 1968), pp. 3–36. Reprinted by permission of Princeton University Press.

William Powell Jones, "The Background of Science and Ideas," from *The Rhetoric of Science*, Berkeley and Los Angeles: University of California Press, 1966. Reprinted by permission of The Regents of the University of California.

Roland N. Stromberg, "Religion and Social Reform," from *Religious Liberalism in Eighteenth-Century England*, London: Oxford University Press, 1954. Reprinted by permission of the Clarendon Press, Oxford.

F. B. Kaye, "The Influence of Bernard Mandeville," from *Studies in Philology*, vol. XIX, no. 1, January, 1922, University of North Carolina Press. Reprinted by permission.

J. H. Plumb, "Political Man," from *Man Versus Society in Eighteenth-Century Britain*, ed., James L. Clifford, Cambridge: Cambridge University Press, 1968. Reprinted by permission.

A. R. Humphreys, "Literature and Religion in Eighteenth-Century England," from *The Augustan World*, London: Methuen and Company, Ltd., 1954. Reprinted by permission.

"Retrospect" from *The Beautiful, The Sublime, and The Picturesque in Eighteenth-Century British Aesthetic Theory* by Walter John Hipple, Jr. Copyright © by Southern Illinois University Press. Reprinted by permission of Southern Illinois University Press.

Northrop Frye, "Towards Defining an Age of Sensibility," from *ELH*, vol. 23, no. 2, June 1956, pp. 144–52. © The Johns Hopkins Press. Reprinted by permission.

R. S. Crane, "Suggestions Toward a Genealogy of the 'Man of Feeling,'" from *ELH*, vol. 1 (1934), pp. 205–30. © The Johns Hopkins Press. Reprinted by permission.

Contents

༺

Acknowledgements

❦

In addition to the acknowledgments on the copyright page, I wish to express my gratitude to Richard Levine, general editor of the series, for his guidance during the preparation of this volume, and to my colleagues Robert Gleckner and David Hansen for their generous advice. I should like also to thank Frances Fry for her competent help in preparing the manuscript.

University of California, Riverside   Kathleen Williams

Backgrounds to Eighteenth-Century Literature

Introduction

❦

The selection of essays for this volume has proved to be a difficult task, in part because of the immense quantity of material from which to choose. But there is another reason too. All periods doubtless seem very full and complex to those who have occasion to write about them, but the eighteenth century is certainly a time in which a great deal happened in many fields, most of it relevant to the literature of an age when so many writers deliberately kept close to the conditions of actual life. There were changes in political practices and ideas, the industrial revolution was making great strides, Britain was establishing its empire, the social scene was changing, new movements such as Methodism were springing up in religion. And there was a formidable series of philosophers who contributed not only to English but to European thought. But in the space at my disposal all these matters cannot be dealt with in anything like an exhaustive way. Instead, I have tried to select chiefly wide-ranging essays which point to the variety that existed in these areas and to those general changes in thought which took place during the eighteenth century.

The eighteenth is not the only century which has a claim to be the beginning of the modern world. According to one's point of view, the sixteenth and seventeenth centuries may make the claim too. But certainly many far-reaching changes took place within the period. In literature, for example, the earliest writers have an affinity with those of the seventeenth century, in which many of them were born; by the end of the period Romanticism has already begun with the publication of the *Lyrical Ballads*. One of the most interesting and difficult tasks for an eighteenth-century scholar is to trace the minute gradations by which this change took place and the influences—or perhaps they are only

1

concurrent changes—which can be detected alongside it. Criticism alters likewise from that of "nature" and "the rules" to that of taste and sensibility. This is the period within which aesthetics develops, through the concentration of various writers on such categories in nature and art as sublimity, beauty, and the picturesque. Science again, developing rapidly since the seventeenth century, had its effect on the subjects and the imagery of literature. Excellent detailed works have been written on all these subjects, and many of them are included in the bibliography to this volume.

In the early part of the century particularly, literature was closely allied to politics, and such major figures as Swift, Pope, Defoe, and Addison, to say nothing of a host of minor writers, were in part political figures, whose works contributed to party differences even when they were not political pamphlets. Critics often took their positions on party lines rather than literary ones, and it is surprising for a modern reader to whom *Gulliver's Travels*, for instance, is an important investigation of the nature of man to see how largely it was for Swift's contemporaries a political satire. Ideally, a book of backgrounds would include an account of the often exciting politics and political intrigues of the late Stuart and Hanoverian periods; but then ideally it would have much else that it has not been found possible to include. Many matters deserve detailed treatment, but unfortunately space does not allow it. But at least one can attempt to show the complications and diversities of a period in which so much activity and so much thought of the first importance took place, and the relevance of these diversities to literature, and that is what this collection attempts to do. The eighteenth century used to be thought a monolithic one for most of its length: the neoclassic age, in which writers accepted concepts like "nature" and "reason" and standards like "correctness," all quite simply understood, and wrote according to them. "The Age of Reason" has for some time ceased to seem an acceptable summing-up of the period, unless it is heavily qualified, and recent work is still showing how inadequate it is, how many senses the word "reason," like "nature," can express and how many relations literature can have to such concepts. In fact just as critics have been

asking "when was the Renaissance" so have others been looking for the age of reason and neoclassicism. How useful is it to divide up our literature in this arbitrary way? How misleading can our labels become, distorting our vision of what is actually there?

It is because it seemed wise to begin with an emphasis on the variety of the period and the inadequacy of our old labels that I have opened the volume with "In Search of the Age of Reason" by George Boas and "When was Neoclassicism?" by B. H. Bronson. (A different approach to the matters dealt with by these two critics may be found in "Augustinianism and Empiricism" by Donald Greene, an article cited in the bibliography to this volume.) Perhaps one may point to the theme of the first article by quoting two sentences. After an examination of the many things that went by the name of "reason" Professor Boas concludes

If one may call doctrines of these sorts rationalism, then the eighteenth century is the Age of Reason only in the sense that the word was frequently used at that time.

and again, stressing the fact that an age is made by the men who live in it, and that the men are not made by some abstraction called an "age," he writes

In short, we may as well say, however dogmatically, that when one is in search of an age, one ends with human beings.

And human beings in any given period are going to be considerably different from one another, even if they live in an age in which some put forward a theory about the uniformity of human nature, and even if they can in certain respects be placed together under a heading. As Professor Boas points out, the ideas of Johnson and Hume, both Tories, could scarcely have been more different from one another, and the great friends Johnson and Burke differed violently about the American revolution. Indeed several of the best writers of the age seem particularly concerned to show that all labels are misleading, and even to break down the idea of "man" into that of a multitude of very different and individual persons.

There were, of course, strong positions held on a number of subjects—philosophical, political, religious, literary—in the eighteenth century, but they were not always consistent enough to constitute a school, and there was usually opposition to them from other groups. Even French classicism, commonly thought of as a singularly consistent and coherent group of ideas, has been shown by Henri Peyre to have been unsystematic enough. And so it goes. Opinions are expressed, and opposing opinions are set up to refute or to modify them. Words like "nature" and "reason" shift as different persons use them and alter radically in the course of the century. The difference between the "nature" of the *Principia Mathematica* and the "nature" of Wordsworth's poetry is a case in point; and "reason," in France and Germany as well as in England, had a variety of meanings. This is not to say that there were no systems or movements of thought—other essays in this volume are concerned with some of them—but that there were many movements, and that these movements were not monolithic within themselves.

Along similar lines, Professor Bronson suggests that our notion of a straightforward progression from an age of classicism to one of Romanticism is altogether too simple. From the earliest time that we think of as classical, anti-classical attitudes, that we have accustomed ourselves to think of as pre-Romantic, exist, and Professor Bronson brings evidence not only from literature but from music, landscape gardening, and painting to suggest an alternative view to the old one that classicism "declined into a debility from which the arts were saved by the Romantics." May not the eighteenth century be seen, he asks, as "a period when the spirit of classicism steadily *refined* its values, grew increasingly *assured* in its declaration of them, and never knew better their true and vital meaning and importance than when on the verge of losing them?" He makes, too, the interesting point that the various arts are at their most classical at different points of time in the century.

The term "classical" is abandoned altogether in Paul Fussell's "What is 'Humanism'?", the first chaper of his book *The Rhetorical World of Augustan Humanism: Ethics and Imagery from Swift to Burke*. This essay deals with, among other things, a sit-

uation which has disconcerted many a beginning student of the
eighteenth century, that some of the greatest writers of the period, including Swift, Pope, and Johnson, do not seem to fit with
our general theories of the way the century thought, or with our
view of a dominant classicism gradually defeated by an emergent
Romanticism. When one tries to enclose Swift, for instance,
within the term "classical," one encounters difficulties; Professor
Fussell prefers to see the confrontation of traditions in the period
less as an opposition between "classicism" and "Romanticism"
than as "a continuation clear through the century of the old
Renaissance battle of the Ancients and the Moderns." Paradoxically enough, those writers whom we commonly think of as most
representative of the eighteenth century are the most conservative, strongly opposed to certain developing tendencies of the
Enlightenment, inheritors of the Renaissance tradition of humanism and admirers of those passages in the great writers of
the past (Shakespeare and Milton are Mr. Fussell's chief examples) which most fully embody humanistic values. The Augustan humanists believe passionately in great literature, as
humanists always had done; and to them great literature is what
concerns itself with the essential nature of men, necessarily faulty,
complicated, and mixed, yet capable of nobility. Man's primary
task is moral evaluation and moral action, and forms of knowledge or of achievement which do not relate to this task seem to
the humanist to be of minor importance. Pope, Swift, and Johnson, and in some ways Burke, were already somewhat old-
fashioned in their day; the Christian-classical tradition on which
their values were based was faced by more modern and more
optimistic attitudes, valuing science and commerce, nature (as
natural scenery) and individualism. It is not surprising that the
eighteenth-century humanist was also often a satirist. This view
of the period is surely a useful one in guiding us through its
complications and contradictions. It stresses the continuity with
the past, the continuing opposition of attitudes which had appeared or had begun to appear before the century began.

But if it is important, as it seems to me to be, to point first to
the manysidedness of the eighteenth century and to its inheritance
from the past, it is also important to establish what is new in its

way of thinking. It is a great age in English philosophy, and though even here it necessarily builds in part on the achievement of the seventeenth century, it is the eighteenth which sees the full development of what is known as the Enlightenment. Old philosophic certainties were broken down, to be replaced either by certainties of another kind or by scepticism. It would have been desirable, if space allowed, to include an essay on each of the outstanding philosophers of the time, but as it is I have put in a chapter from Meyrick H. Carré's *Phases of Thought in England* in which he deals concisely with the English empirical philosophy of the eighteenth century, beginning as one must with the "tutelary geniuses" Locke and Newton, whose great work was done at the end of the preceding century. The work of these men formed the starting point for their successors, and the influence of Locke's *Essay Concerning Human Understanding* (1960), with its emphasis on establishing what the human mind is or is not able to deal with, can hardly be overestimated. Moreover two other developments of the seventeenth century, the dualism of mind and matter originating with Descartes and the influence of the new science, shape the thinking of the period, and the mind is conceived of as comparable to the physical world as the new science saw it. In Mr. Carré's words, "The system of knowledge depends upon a few laws of attraction between ideas, comparable to the laws that rule the behaviour of physical particles."

The emphasis on the sensory origin of all knowledge and on the importance of the association of ideas, and the denial of the existence of universals apart from the mind, dominated philosophy during the period, and became part of the background of assumptions among educated people, influencing the subjects, attitudes, and methods of poetry and prose. The tendency of both Newton and Locke was to discourage speculation about ultimate causes, and so to reinforce that emphasis on practical morality which is found also in the works of divines of the period. Berkeley and Hume made their own deductions from the empirical philosophy of ideas, and as Mr. Carré says, by the end of the century the way of ideas had led "to mentalism, to scepticism, and to determinism," but for most of the age it was

the attitudes inculcated by Locke and Newton that influenced the educated public.

While Mr. Carré analyses the contributions made to philosophy by particular thinkers, Ernst Cassirer, in a chapter taken from his *The Philosophy of Enlightenment,* deals rather with the general principles which inform the thought of the period in England and in France. He too stresses a scientific influence; the ideal of the Enlightenment mode of thinking was related to the pattern of contemporary science, which attempted to extend the boundaries of truth and philosophy, rather than to the pattern of seventeenth century philosophy, which aimed at the construction of a philosophical system complete in itself and starting from an intuitively grasped certainty. Eighteenth century "reason" is not a body of truths but "a kind of energy, a force which is fully comprehensible only in its agency and effects." It dissolves and analyses the merely factual and the traditional, and builds a new structure from them. In this essay the application of reason in various spheres—the material and psychological worlds, the theory of the state—and such subjects as the relation of philosophy to mathematics are treated, and a general picture emerges of the century's mode of thinking. It goes without saying that the relation of the literature of the time to these general principles of thought is by no means simple. Some writers embody in their work in various ways resistance to rather than agreement with the general philosophical tendencies of the period.

As the essays already discussed make evident, no account of the background relevant to eighteenth century literature would be complete without a study of the flourishing new science and its reception by the literary mind, and this is provided in the essay by William P. Jones. It is Professor Jones's claim that in the late seventeenth and most of the eighteenth century the hostility which was later to grow up between the attitudes of the literary artist and those of the scientist did not exist, and this is doubtless generally true, though one must allow for certain exceptions among Mr. Fussell's Augustan humanists. Swift and Johnson, for example, had intellectual, moral, and practical objections to the scientific activities of the Royal Society, if not

to science itself, while Pope on the other hand makes considerable use of imagery drawn from contemporary science. As Marjorie Nicolson has demonstrated in detail, the new realms revealed
by the microscope and the telescope appealed to the imagination
of writers, and even Swift makes use of the idea of looking at
man through a microscope as part of his presentation of the
relativity of our standards in *Gulliver's Travels*. For others of
less satiric bent the new instruments show forth more clearly the
boundless wisdom of God and the fertility of nature, the minute-
ness of the links in the chain of being.

Similarly Newton's discoveries contributed to the sense of an
all-embracing harmony and providential care in the universe,
with its laws extending from the limitlessness of space to the
infinitely small. Pope and Thomson refer to Newton, and so do
a number of lesser poets; the newly revealed universe was to
many a source of excitement and inspiration. Prose writers too
celebrated the world of order the new science had opened out to
them, a world not only wonderful in itself but expressive of the
power and goodness of its creator. William Derham's *Physico-
theology*, originally a series in the Boyle Lectures, delivered in
1711-1712, is perhaps the most famous of a number of works
which demonstrated the attributes of God from the works of
creation, but the idea appears too in Shaftesbury and in Blackmore's ambitious *Creation* and was ably popularised by Addison
in the *Spectator*. Not until the end of the century, when Blake
used Newton as well as Bacon and Locke to symbolise the opposition of materialism and an analytic habit of mind to the
imaginative world, did hostility develop between science and
literature. The abundant nature poetry of the eighteenth century
was written by men whose attention was turned to the wonders
of nature at least in part by the excitement the new science
aroused.

Another development usually associated with the eighteenth
century is the growth of philanthropy, as a natural result of
some of the attitudes discussed here in the various essays on
the thought of the period. Certainly there is much written in
the period about the feeling heart, touched by the miseries of
others, and R. S. Crane's essay, to be discussed later, investigates

the provenance of such sentiments. Professor Stromberg, however, is concerned to see how far the reputation of the period
as one of philanthropy is justified in terms of practical achievement. He examines the records of the different churches and of
deism in the actual practice of social reform, and finds that
despite the frequency of noble sentiments about social brotherhood and despite the charitable efforts of a small group of people
at the beginning of the century, the actual achievement was slight
enough, for there was little spirit of systematic reform of social
conditions until the middle of the century, notably in the Unitarians. The charity-schools, instituted early in the century, rapidly degenerated, and were always subject to political hostility
from those who believed it to be in their own interest to keep
the poor still poor and still uneducated. Bernard Mandeville
attacked the degeneracy of the charity-school movement in 1723,
when he added his "Essay on Charity and Charity-Schools" to
The Fable of the Bees. The interest in charity-schools was so
great as to attract attention for the first time to the *Fable* itself
and the ideas it contained, and from this time on *The Fable of
the Bees* was notorious; it was attacked, defended, and above all
used.

I have included F. B. Kaye's article on Mandeville because of
the importance of Mandeville's influence, which is sometimes
overlooked, and because without the development traced by
Professor Kaye our picture of the century would be incomplete.
A knowledge of Mandeville's views and a recognition of their
formidable nature is visible in both Pope and Swift, and Johnson, Adam Smith, and Voltaire also knew his work. Mandeville
was to the eighteenth century what Hobbes had been to an
earlier period, and the frequent execration of his works gave
them ever greater publicity. In the end his influence on ethics
and economics was considerable. Professor Kaye's essay discusses
the principles underlying Mandeville's famous phrase "Private
Vices, Publick Benefits" in such a way as to refer to much of the
moral theory of the time, and so is doubly useful. But central
to Mandeville's importance is his contribution, through the response to him of such men as Adam Smith, Hume, Bentham,
and Godwin, to the growth of utilitarianism. The laissez-faire

theory can also be traced in Mandeville, and his influence in ethics and economics extended to France as well as England.

From economics one may turn to politics, and to J. H. Plumb's essay on "Political Man" in the eighteenth century. I have not thought it necessary in this collection to enter upon current differences of opinion about the party system of the early part of the century or to include essays concentrating on historical fact or on the discussion of particular issues or figures. Mr. Plumb's essay is a general one, admirably conveying what it was like to be a man with political powers or even merely with political interests in the eighteenth century. As I have remarked earlier, the literate public of the period was passionately concerned with politics, ready to concentrate always on the political aspect of works which appear to us to have far more than political significance. On the other hand, the political aspect did exist in such works, and Professor Plumb's examination of the politically active nature of the general public, and the widespread interest in national and party issues, makes it easier to understand the involvement in such matters of the major literary figures of the age. The British were proud of their constitution, still recently established and extravagantly admired by liberal elements in Europe; and they jealously guarded those parts of it which seemed most important, differing passionately about what mattered most and about how best to sustain it. Through political activity ideals of human behavior and organization could be put into practice. For such Tories as Swift, Pope, Bolingbroke, and their circle the landed gentry formed the basis of old English virtue and strength, and power should continue to be vested in that group. For the Whigs, with Walpole long at their head, the new moneyed interest was paramount, and power should be centered there for the good of the nation. Addison embodies the two sides in the squire Sir Roger de Coverly and the Whig merchant Sir Andrew Freeport, each presenting a different kind of value, different strengths and weaknesses. Such political positions bore a relation to moral and religious beliefs, and in such a situation few issues can be regarded as "merely" political, as we can see from the writings and activities of such men as Swift and Addison himself.

In the seventeenth century a comparatively large parliamentary electorate had been created, and in the early part of our period general elections were frequent. Many gentlemen, freeholders, and burgesses thus had an opportunity to make political choices relatively often. According to Mr. Plumb, "the issues were clear, and understood by thousands of voters, if not all, and men in the heart of borough politics watched closely and with passion what was happening at Westminster." Political knowledge and concern were not confined to London, and local politicians "were keenly aware of the twists and turns of party tactics." After all, such large issues as war and peace, toleration, the succession to the crown, the position of the church, were at stake, and these affected many people's lives. But as the century advanced the party leaders made efforts of various kinds to lessen the power of the voter. Bribery direct or indirect was rife, influence was exerted, freemen were no longer made, and property which carried a vote was brought up. Election contests in large constituencies became so expensive that they were less frequently held, and settlements were made without them.

But although the electorate was diminished and was functioning comparatively rarely, by the middle of the century the literate politically-minded public continued to grow, to read pamphlets and newspapers, to discuss and argue, to form political clubs. Even with a sharply reduced electorate the public could still make its wishes known by demonstration, letters to newspapers, and addresses to parliament; in some cases, like that of Wilkes, it could influence votes by such means. For the most part however such demonstrations serve to show the growing conflict between what Mr. Plumb calls "the political establishment and the political nation," a conflict which becomes evident in the later part of the century in increasing radicalism and demand for parliamentary reform. In an age when some of the finest writing is political it is of some importance to be aware of the general interest in public affairs, extending, according to the Swiss César de Saussure who visited England in 1726, to the shoe-blacks who followed the foreign news in the papers. The political experience of some even quite humble people in eighteenth-century England seems to have been unique in Europe.

If the general public was more active politically during this period than has always been recognized in the past, the same generalisation will hold good for its interest in religion. Professor A. R. Humphreys opens his essay on "Literature and Religion in Eighteenth-Century England" with the observation that our views on the religion of the period have changed substantially since Victorian times. "Where the Victorians saw on the whole only apathy and even cynicism, their successors have found that the sober goodwill, rising at times to a luminous devotion, which characterises much Hanoverian worship still makes its appeal." Yet the false notion of the intellectual sloth of the church has still not wholly died, though it was disproved by scholars as long ago as the late nineteenth century, and the charge of spiritual sloth is only now being countered. With a few colourful exceptions the religious scene within and outside the church still has the reputation of dullness, but in its quiet way the century did occupy itself with considerations of religion and piety. Nor was piety wholly unconcerned with charitable effort. Professor Stromberg's essay points to such men as Butler, Law, Cowper, and Wesley who dispensed charity freely as part of their religious duty. Organised effort was perhaps slow to develop, after some largely abortive attempts early in the century, but there must have been many individual persons less well known who thought it their duty to be charitable.

The essays so far considered taken as a whole suggest that there were in the eighteenth century groups of related tendencies leading gradually towards change in many directions. One such group, developing from the beginning of the century, is treated in the last three essays in this volume. This group of tendencies is of course by no means unrelated to the philosophical, religious, political, social, and other matters treated in the earlier essays. Indeed one of the problems of selecting among the numerous significant articles which exist has been that of avoiding a repetitiveness which is in the end to some degree inevitable, so closely are the various strands of thought, feeling, and action intertwined with one another. But the last group of tendencies to be treated in this volume, the development of aesthetics and of the fostering of feeling and sensibility, is perhaps especially relevant to

literature and the other arts, and the essays by Professors Hipple, Crane, and Frye provide aspects of the "backgrounds" to the eighteenth century which are of a more specifically literary and artistic nature. The contribution by Professor Hipple is the final chapter of his exhaustive work *The Beautiful, the Sublime, and the Picturesque in Eighteenth Century British Aesthetic Theory.* The subject is clearly too vast and far-reaching to be dealt with fully in a single chapter, even one so lengthy and yet so concise as this. But Professor Hipple achieves a fine overview of the growth of British aesthetic speculation, drawing together the chief figures of the century in terms of their common interests, or perhaps rather noting "Those sets and systems of ideas which were then crystallized" and reflected through a number of thinkers, "to examine their facets, to compare their lusters, and to note the various refractions of the same light as it is transmitted through them."

The chief feature which all aestheticians of the period share, and which suggests a concern parallel to that of contemporary philosophy, is that they regard their subject as psychological. Where the neo-classical tradition in discussing the arts was structured by such intellectual concepts as general and particular nature, the aestheticians were concerned with the discrimination of feelings, the isolating of those qualities of the mind which yielded such feelings, and the impressions by which they were produced. They turn inward upon the responses of the man who reads or regards a work of art, rather than upon the nature of the reality to which the work of art should correspond. They are in fact concerned primarily with "taste," so that in a sense they may be seen as developing from a rudimentary form the tenets of that "school of taste" for which Pope strove to find room in his amalgam of contemporary critical approaches, *The Essay on Criticism.* Addison, an important early figure in the history of aesthetics, put forward the basic position of the practioners in his statement in the *Spectator,* quoted by Professor Hipple, that the arts were "to deduce their Laws and Rules from the general Sense and Taste of Mankind, and not from the Principles of those Arts themselves." Hutcheson, who in the tradition of Shaftesbury examines morals in terms of a discriminating inner

sense, uses the phrase "internal sense" for what is essentially a
kind of taste. Gerard and Hume both write essays on taste, the
treatises of Burke, Kames, Blair, Reid, Alison, and Knight all
discuss it, and in general it is the premise from which the aestheticians begin. Their "Analyses" and "Inquiries" work towards
the breaking down of complex ideas and feelings to combinations of the primary materials of original impressions. In this
they are, as Mr. Hipple remarks, akin to the philosophers proper,
the empirical thinkers of eighteenth-century England, and indeed some philosophical knowledge, in practice generally a
knowledge of associationist philosophy, is necessary to those
whose aim is "to extract and refine the sublime and beautiful
whenever they are imbedded in nature or in art" rather than to
comment on the value of individual works. "Taste" moreover
obviously relates primarily to the perceiving mind of the observer
or reader, rather than to the creating mind of the painter or
writer. It is of some interest to relate this to Professor Frye's
thesis in "Towards Defining an Age of Sensibility."

The aesthetic tradition is closly associated not only with contemporary philosophy but with other phenomena such as the
period's growing interest in nature in the sense of natural scenery.
It is in connection with nature, simpler than art and prior to it,
that those data are found upon which depend the answers to
such problems as the meanings of the terms "beautiful" and
"sublime" and the difference between them. The word "picturesque" is particularly closely related to the consideration of natural scenery and of the relations between nature and art that
become visible in landscape gardening, an important physical
feature of eighteenth-century Britain and one that has left a
lasting mark upon the countryside, and in the natural descriptions of the poets. The interest in aesthetics touches also upon
various other aspects of the period, and as befits so broad and
shifting a subject it does not develop consistently towards one
position. Rather than a straightforward development Professor
Hipple sees a broad common method within which exists "a
scattered variety of particular systems," varying according to the
different purposes of the authors. Yet one can say that though
aesthetic theory does not advance systematically, as time goes on

it does become more dominant. It exists, certainly, in the early years of the century in the important essays of Addison, but it is with the second half of the century that we associate a spate of writings on the differentiation of the sublime, the beautiful, and the picturesque. There are clearly ways in which the later part of the century differs in method and attitude from the earlier years; there is some novelty and still more change of emphasis, and this is true of literature proper as well as of the history of thought. There is a sense in which "classicism" or "Augustanism" strengthens and refines itself during the period, as Professor Bronson suggests, but it is also time that alongside the later representatives of Augustanism there exist writers of another kind, which includes those once known as "pre-Romantic."

This misleading term has, I think deservedly, fallen into ever greater disrepute in recent years, and Northrop Frye gives it the coup de grace in his "Towards Defining an Age of Sensibility." Professor Frye's position is that the literature of the second half of the century, or at least of certain writers of that time, is to be defined not negatively by its relation to Augustanism or Romanticism but positively by observation of the specific characteristics which differentiate it from either. For "pre-Romantic" he substitutes the title "age of sensibility," and he sees as its distinctive quality its view of literature as process. Throughout the history of literature, he suggests, there are two opposed views of literature, that of literature as product and that of literature as process. Parallel to the age's interest in the workings of the mind and feelings, as seen for example in the investigation of the individual's response to nature and art, there appear works of prose and poetry characterized by an interest in the process of writing rather than by a "sense of literature as a finished product." This interest is seen sporadically much earlier, particularly in essayists, Montaigne being an outstanding example, but in the later eighteenth century it is more developed and more widely spread. Sterne, who leads us not "into a story, but into the process of writing a story," is the chief example among the novelists, and the sense of literature as process is perhaps especially visible in prose fiction. But Professor Frye demonstrates its effects also in poetry. He shows how Pope's couplets

give us "a sense of continually fulfilled expectation" whereas in the poets typical of the age of sensibility we meet unpredictable assonances, alliterations, and other sound effects. Ossian, the extreme example, is repetitive and diffused; his long poems are dreamlike because the poet's interest is in "the poetic process as distinct from the product"; he is at that primary stage of composition where sound, rather than sense, links the words together. Hence clear syntax, wit, concentrated "sense" and a regular metre give way to repetition and irregular sound-patterns. Ossian is a special as well as an extreme case, for the typical example of poetry as process is naturally enough to be seen in the lyric, so suddenly widespread in the age of sensibility. Professor Frye's thesis embraces too the typical emotions expressed in and aroused by the poems of Blake, Cowper, Smart, and Collins. Where there is a sense of literature as process, he suggests, pity and fear are not detached from the beholder and directed towards objects, as in Aristotelian theory; instead "pity and fear become states of mind without objects, moods which are common to the work of art and the reader, and which bind them together psychologically instead of separating them aesthetically." In fact the notion of a particular "age of sensibility" convincingly embraces many of the characteristics of later eighteenth century poetry, and distinguishes it as sharply from Romanticism as from Augustanism. For the Romantics like the Augustans saw literature as product not process, though to them it was the product of the creative imagination; and the kinship Professor Frye sees is between the later eighteenth century and contemporary poetry, which "is still deeply concerned with the problems and techniques of the age of sensibility."

The emotion of pity which is so often an element in the poetry of the later part of the century can also be considered from another though related aspect, that stress on benevolent feeling as an ethical force and a source of personal pleasure which becomes so marked during this period. From the 1730s to the 1790s writers of all kinds wrote about, or embodied in their invented characters, the humanity and goodness of the cultivation of sensibility, a feeling response to the misfortunes of our fellow men. Sensibility should be cultivated for our own sake as well as for the

sake of those we benefit, for nothing can give us greater pleasure. The growth of this attitude clearly shows the influence of Shaftesbury and his follower Hutcheson, but R. S. Crane, in his "Suggestions toward a Genealogy of the 'Man of Feeling'," demonstrates that the origins of the movement can be traced back beyond the time of Shaftesbury's writings to the "Latitude-men" of the late seventeenth century. These Latitudinarian divines were deliberately opposing themselves to the Puritan stress on divine sternness, natural human evil, and the worthlessness of good works. Men like Barrow, South, and Tillotson, and later Gilbert Burnet and Samuel Clarke, stress moral goodness rather than doctrine; and with their sense of the importance of good works they naturally lay great emphasis on the social virtues, exhorting above all to charity, benevolent feelings and actions directed towards all men. They were opposed not only to the darker aspects of Puritanism but to the tenets of Stoicism, so fashionable in the seventeenth century, and here again their opposition was wholly conscious and deliberate. They insisted that the Stoic elimination of the passions could never produce a positive and vigorous goodness, since "Our Reason is a cold and heavy principle, that moves us but slowly to our Work; but Passion puts an eagerness into our Desires, and a warmness into our Prosecutions"; the passions therefore, duly moderated and regulated, contribute to a good life. Especially these divines attack the Stoic dictum that a good man, though he should relieve distress, should not allow himself to be personally affected by it; the Latitudinarians believe that it is an emotional response to the miseries of others that is most likely to produce actions directed towards relieving such miseries.

Hence benevolent feeling, what was later to be called sensibility, was being presented as a moral good before the eighteenth century, and it was also seen as natural to man. Whichcote, who was praised as a "Preacher of Good-nature" by Shaftesbury himself, was not alone in putting forward this view. Such an optimistic attitude to human nature was prompted not only by opposition to Puritanism but by opposition to Thomas Hobbes, whose view of man was as gloomy as that of the Calvinists. Here again the Latitudinarian attack was deliberate and articulate;

dislike of Hobbes's position leads them to emphasise the natural-
ness, moral goodness, and pleasantness of benevolence. A quotation from a work of Samuel Parker, printed as early as 1681,
already brings together the whole philosophy of the "man of
feeling" as that is seen in the literature of the eighteenth century.
Professor Crane proves his case fully by sharply relevant documentation. By showing so clearly and circumstantially the contribution made to this kind of thinking by the "anti-Puritan,
anti-Stoic, and anti-Hobbesian divines of the Latitudinarian
school" he makes the cult of the man of feeling more intelligible
in that it arose in part at least through an understandable, and
it might now seem almost inevitable, response by concerned
churchmen to the influence of Puritan, Stoic, and Hobbesian
views in the later seventeenth century.

It will be evident that this collection of essays is not intended
to present any single interpretation of the kind of period the
eighteenth century was. Rather it is hoped that the collection will
suggest the many approaches—through politics, philosophy, social
comment, aesthetics, an examination of the literature itself—
which can be fruitful in helping us to an understanding of this
period in which so much of the past and so much of the future
existed together. Conceptions typical of earlier periods were by
some still accepted and by some opposed; dichotomies already
visible in the seventeenth century were carried further or, by
others, reconciled; views and conditions which we associate with
the nineteenth century were already coming into being. As with
all centuries, the eighteenth when one regards it closely appears
much less unified than it does from a distance. Almost any generalization that one might make about it comes to seem dubious,
except perhaps the generalization that it is a period of differences
and growth. One is reminded of one of the greatest literary figures
in the age itself, Alexander Pope, who writing on the characters of
men found that the only general explanation which would hold
was one that allowed for the maximum of variety. What all men
have in common, he concludes, is that they are governed by a ruling
passion, which differs from person to person and is further modified in each case by its relation to lesser passions and to the
reason. Only some such loose generalization, flexible enough to

make for differentiation rather than for uniformity, will suffice when applied to the eighteenth century in England, where unifying concepts such as "nature" and "reason" were so often broken down by the empirical bent of a people given to the practical examination of theories. It is hoped that these essays, chosen from the considerable quantity of "background" books and articles which has appeared over the past few decades of intensive scholarly examination of the eighteenth century, will do justice to the variety of the period and to its creativity both in dealing with the legacy of the past and in evolving new attitudes which were to come to fruition in the future.

In Search of the Age of Reason

ᗡᎡᏅ

GEORGE BOAS

Though it seems to be convenient to divide history into ages and periods and times, it is questionable whether the practice has not been abused. We have pretty nearly got rid of the Renaissance by splitting it up into the Early Renaissance, the High Renaissance, and the baroque, which breathed its last as the rococo. We have also found that there were proto-Renaissances occurring in what used to be the Middle Ages, the Carolingian Renaissance and the Renaissance of the twelfth century being the most important. Something similar has happened to the Romantic Period, which has been pushed forward into the twentieth century and backward at least to the time of Racine; whereas in my youth it was ushered in by the publication of the *Lyrical Ballads* (1798) and came to an end with the death of Scott (1832), which was also the date of the death of Goethe. This sort of thing was trouble enough, but added to the problem of chronological termini was that of determining the so-called spirit of such ages and movements. Nowadays we seldom use the term *Zeitgeist,* but we have little hesitation in using its equivalents. Thus terms like the Spirit of the Age, the Intellectual Climate, and the Time or Times have become common usage. As rough statistical generalizations denoting the modal interests of a chronological division, these words are harmless. But there is genuine harm when they are put to explanatory uses. There

From Aspects of the Eighteenth Century, *ed., Earl R. Wasserman (Baltimore: The Johns Hopkins Press, 1965), pp. 1–19.*

can be no denying the similarity of purpose among, for instance, the members of the group known as Encyclopedists, though no two of them agreed about everything. They agreed that education was a good, indeed the best, instrument for improving society, and d'Alembert agreed with Diderot that the manual and liberal arts were of equal importance. On most other points they disagreed. However to say that they all shared the belief that education would give men certain blessings because the Age or the Times demanded these blessings—or because they were expressing the Spirit of the Times or were influenced by the intellectual climate—is sheer mythology if said seriously.[1] I can see how one can be influenced by an idea, either influenced in its favor or against it, but how one can be influenced by a time is too mysterious to be treated rationally.

Historians who are given to this sort of investigation have found that the eighteenth century was characterized by a strange variety of traits. It is a period which has been called rationalistic, sentimentalistic, optimistic and pessimistic, melancholy, necrophilic, contented with itself, and fond of nature. It has of course also been called the Enlightenment, the *siecle des lumieres*, and the *Aufklärung*. But if the Spirit of the Times did not suffer from divided personality, these traits should not turn out to be fairly general, and none of them do. And if its *Geist* is divided against itself, one had best find out how many *Geister* existed simultaneously. That is what my paper is hinting at, for to examine the matter in detail would require a book. Since one of the most popular labels for this century is the Age of Reason, I should like to see how far it is justified.

But first we must take up the premise on which such practices seem to be built—the premise that a time is existentially different from the people who live in it. The time presumably causes people to think in a certain way, to express their thoughts in certain ways, and to value certain things more than others. But in the first place, how is one to discover what a time is without studying the men who lived in it? Take away Voltaire, Diderot, d'Alembert, d'Holbach, Helvétius, and their friends from the middle eighteenth century in France and what is left of the spirit of that time? Take away Johnson, Reynolds, Gold-

smith, Garrick, Sheridan, Burke, Hogarth, and even Boswell from the latter half of the same century in England, and what would happen to the Age of George III?

Second, if something is to cause something else, it must be different from that something, and, if it is not, the effect is self-caused. At the risk of announcing truisms as if they were profundities, I should like to suggest that men are not made by the age in which they live but that, as far as cultural history is concerned, they make it. Our conception of their times comes from them, and there is no time, except on the calendar, save that found in and through them. We have not denied that groups of men may agree about certain matters. And if a group were found whose members agreed about everything within a given field, it might be said that they established an Age. But what one finds is that even when they do agree, they also disagree and that their disagreements are frequently about essential doctrinal matters. Samuel Johnson and David Hume, for instance, were both Tories. But Johnson not only disliked Hume personally, he disagreed with his ideas. He said at one time (Boswell's *Life of Johnson*, 1763, Everyman edition, I, 275), that "Hume and other sceptical innovators, are vain men, and will gratify themselves at any expence. Truth will not afford sufficient food for their vanity; so they have betaken themselves to error." And fourteen years later, when Boswell reported to him that Hume had no fear of death, he replied,

It was not so, Sir. He had a vanity in being thought easy. It is more probable that he should assume an appearance of ease, than so very improbable a thing should be, as a man not afraid of going . . . into an unknown state, and not being uneasy at leaving all he knew. And you are to consider, that upon his own principle of annihilation he had no motive to speak the truth." (*Ibid.*, II, 114)

Burke was one of Johnson's best friends. He was called by him a "great man of nature" (*ibid.*, I, 320), an "extraordinary man" whose "stream of mind" was "perpetual" (*ibid.*, I, 619). This appreciation was reciprocated by Burke. Yet Johnson did not hesitate to disagree with Burke on the question of the American

Revolution. We all know what Burke's sentiments were, but to his friend the Americans were "a race of convicts and ought to be thankful for any thing we allow them short of hanging" (*ibid.*, 1775, I, 526). Unfortunately his pamphlet *Taxation No Tyranny* is too long to be quoted and analyzed here, but anyone looking into it will see that his alliance with Burke did not lead to sharing his opinions *in toto*. In fact, as late as 1778 he shouted at Boswell, "I am willing to love all mankind, *except an American*," and, Boswell adds, "his inflammable corruption bursting into horrid fire, he 'breathed out threatenings and slaughter'; calling them, 'Rascals—Robbers—Pirates'; and exclaiming, he'd 'burn and destroy them'" (*ibid.*, II, 209). This sort of disagreement can be exemplified in any period.

In the third place, one sometimes forgets that philosophical positions, like political, religious, and even aesthetic positions, are taken because of a man's opposition to another position. If everyone had been a Tory, there would have been no Whigs, though there might have been splits within the Tory party caused by special questions. Two men might believe in monarchial government in England and yet violently disagree about the legitimacy of the rule of William III. Though Burke, again, was enchanted by the beauty of Marie-Antoinette and deplored her fate in one of the most fulsome pieces of oratory ever declaimed, he was not enchanted by absolute monarchy. His famous remarks about the French Revolution were made in opposition to a historical event and were based, to be sure, on a political philosophy that he had never before had occasion to articulate with such vehemence and eloquence. In short, it is as important to discover what a man is against as it is to discover what he is for. The preface to the *Lyrical Ballads* is admittedly a manifesto of one side of the Romantic aesthetics. But it is also a protest against traditional poetic diction and a protest which would not have made any sense had the poetic tradition not been fairly influential at the time of its publication. Its strength for that matter can be seen in the early poems of Byron, if any evidence of its survival is needed. Similarly, in seventeenth-century France, there were of course Cartesians, but there were also very outspoken anti-Cartesians, and what one group said was said in

rebuttal to what the other proposed. Professor Henri Peyre has clearly demonstrated how unsystematic was that group of ideas which are called French classicism, and it requires a special purgation of inconsistencies to turn them into a doctrine. I do not deny that by selecting certain figures as typical, one can trace the history of the geometrical method in philosophy, just as by emphasizing certain of its aspects and supposed implications one can find it in Racine and even in Poussin. But neither Racine nor any other poet, Poussin nor any other painter, ever started out by drilling himself in the *Discours de la méthode.* Their Cartesianism is very dilute, as it was bound to be if it was to turn into an aesthetic doctrine.[2]

I think it will be found that in all the ages of which we have records, opinions and practices were responses to other opinions and practices when they were set forth in books and manifestos. This is true even of the thirteenth century, hailed as the most unified of times. For though Aquinas, following Albertus Magnus, is nowadays thought of as its spokesman, there existed alongside of him the figure of Duns Scotus, and beside the two of them the equally influential figure of Bonaventura. It is just as important to unearth the clashes in opinion of these men as it is to insist upon their agreements. It would be absurd to deny that they were Catholics, but even an elementary history of medieval philosophy is forced to expound the differences among Catholic philosophers. There seems in fact always to be a Jefferson for every Hamilton, a Piccini for every Gluck, a Tennyson for every Browning, a Delacroix for every Ingres, as there was a Poussin to balance Rubens, a Roscellinus to balance William of Champeaux, and a Hippias to balance Socrates. I am not saying this because I believe in some historical law or a metaphysical principle of polarity. It need be nothing of the sort. The simple fact is that no one so far has appeared in human society whose opinions seem sound to all of his contemporaries, and, when opinions appear to be weak, someone is always there to say so. After all, even in the days of great papal authority there were heretics, and the heretics felt the need of speaking their minds, though they risked being burned alive and knew it. It took about 150 years for the Copernican Theory to be generally accepted, and the

kinetic theory of heat, suggested by Bacon in the seventeenth century, was not accepted until the nineteenth. In scientific cases a theory makes its way by a man's dogged belief in it, by his attempting to refute one by one all of his opponents' refutations. In aesthetic matters the problem is more easily solved, for the factor of fatigue enters in.

Nor are there only two opposing groups in any period. Quite the contrary. Few men disagree with everything someone else has to say, and if Dr. Johnson disagreed with Voltaire's deism, he agreed with his attack on optimism. His refutation of Soame Jenyns is as strong as anything either in *Candide* or the poem on the Lisbon Earthquake. There was very little in Rousseau with which Diderot agreed, but he is in hearty agreement with Rousseau's individualism. So it went then as it goes now. Rather than absorb men into specimens of an ideology, would it not be better to admit that ideologies are composed of opinions that may or not be held by any given man, regardless of the label which has been pasted on him by historians? For no man is all of a piece. The Horace Walpole of the *Castle of Otranto* does not seem to me to be the Horace Walpole of, for instance, the letters to Mme du Deffand, though I would not maintain that there was no similarity between them. One might compare the presentation which Macaulay makes of his character with that of F. L. Lucas[3] to realize how the complexities of human nature defeat classification. If one were to think of Walpole as merely the inventor of the Gothic novel, one would be hard put to it to understand why he took care of Tonton after the death of Mme du Deffand. But similarly, if one knew Rousseau only as the author of *La Nouvelle Héloise,* one would never guess him to be the author also of the *Contrat social.* Who would guess that the Voltaire of the *Dictionnaire philosophique* had dedicated one of his tragedies to Pope Benedict XIV, as the *chef de la véritable religion*? If these suggestions were not plausible, little would be left for historians to do. What would be the grounds for all our reinterpretations if the men whose ideas we reinterpret were consistent?

In the fourth place, though certain catchwords become popular at certain times, it is clear that they are nothing more than catch-

words and not the names of a pervasive interest. This appears with special clarity in such a book as Basil Willey's *Eighteenth Century Background*. It will be recalled that the catchword in this case is "nature," and, though Mr. Willey points out that an American scholar, otherwise unidentified, has distinguished many meanings of that term, yet he ventures to discuss nature as the prevailing interest of his period. The question immediately arises of whether there is such a thing as nature, which we all recognize, about which the eighteenth century had a number of opinions, or whether we are reading about the history of a word. And when the book is finished, one learns that he has been reading an amazing and erudite bit of historical semantics. For the word "nature," he says, meant the subject matter of science as opposed to the subject matter of theology and religion; it meant the state of nature as opposed to custom; it meant the true, i.e., the universal, as opposed to the false, the particular. In that form of meditation known as natural theology, the term meant whatever is described in natural science, mainly astronomy and physics, or what Mr. Willey neatly calls "Physico-theology." But here another assumption is introduced, and nature becomes good rather than evil, and the optimism of an Alexander Pope is inferred from natural theology. And it may not be superfluous to remind ourselves that before the book is ended, nature becomes the rural scene of Wordsworth, anticipated by such poets as Cowper, and is no longer the integrated system of moving bodies which formed the subject matter of the *Principia Mathematica*. The vernal woods, the lonely reapers, the primroses by the river's brim are not and cannot be made to be the Law of Gravitation.

Hence I say what Mr. Willey has given is not the history of an idea but the history of a word, of its changing detonations and connotations. And he has made an enviable job of it. But when one man says that the life according to nature is the life according to the dictates of the senses and another says that it is the life of reason, they are clearly not talking about the same thing, even though they declare that nature is the norm of good behavior. Two ideas are here expressed by the same term. The meaning of a term is not an idea which could possibly be true or false or even debated, except by men who insist that words have what

they call real meaning as distinguished from those given by usage. The meaning of a term is a rule, an imperative, and, if you will, a statement of intention. When one uses "nature" in opposition to "art," or the natural in opposition to the supernatural, one undoubtedly has some idea in the back of one's mind which sets up an *argumentum ad hominem* to be utilized in ethical and aesthetic debates. For to those who believe that a life in accordance with nature is better than one which is dominated by custom, "nature" becomes a term denoting something factual and connoting something valuable. Thus if "nature" is defined as that set of harmonious laws decreed by God, no one will probably maintain that nature is inferior to, for example, art or custom. But if "nature" is defined as man's animal instincts, then fewer people will agree that it is better to follow nature than to elevate oneself above it. In attempting to describe the character of a period in terms of general or pervasive ideas or of its modal desires and aversions, one always has to go behind the sacred words which are fashionable during the period being studied to try to discover what those words actually denoted. Their connotation can be studied later.

Let me now turn to that popular label of the eighteenth century, *The Age of Reason*. Rationalism, as a word, according to the *NED*, began by denoting a doctrine of theology and proliferated into meaning also a doctrine of women's clothing. From the reason embodied in God's laws exemplified in astrophysics to the reason embodied in costume is a long distance to travel. But when one realizes that both Voltaire and Joseph de Maistre found the source of all truth in the reason, one sees that another problem has arisen. To abbreviate matters, let us say that by the close of the eighteenth century in France the clash in opinion was not only rationalism versus sentimentalism, but the reason of the individual versus the reason of the group, alias, tradition. De Maistre and Bonald were convinced that all truth was rational, a conviction which was to be reinforced by Pius IX in his encyclical *Qui pluribus* (1846). But the rationality in question was that of the race as a whole expressed in language and, as I said, tradition. This, except for the religious element, was analogous to the doctrine of Reid, known as the philosopher of

common sense. It can be shown, I think, to go back to the medieval belief in the natural light *(lumen naturale)*, and it was therefore a revival rather than an innovation. Now neither Voltaire nor any of his associates, as far as I know, denied that if every man were rational, all men would agree, though the conclusion did not necessarily follow. But in the use of reason every man was independent of every other, nor was there any impulsion to seek agreement with something called tradition.

In this, however, the rationalistic individualist was more in accord with the sentimental individualist, like Rousseau and even Robespierre, than with the rationalistic traditionalist. And at the same time De Maistre was more in accord with Voltaire than he was with Rousseau or, for that matter, with Chateaubriand. Therefore, to label the eighteenth century the Age of Reason is either simply to say that the word "reason" was popular in certain circles as "nature" was or to overlook the ambiguities of the doctrine itself. For besides the two interpretations mentioned above, there was also the doctrine that opposed reason to the heart, or in Germany to the *Verstand*. The *Verstand* meant the processes used in reaching scientific conclusions; the *Vernunft*, though translated into English as "reason," denoted some higher and more glorious kind of insight.[4] Then there was that form of rationalism which denied the efficacy of faith or, indeed, of its need. If one may call doctrines of these sorts rationalism, then the eighteenth century is the Age of Reason only in the sense that the word was frequently used at that time.

If now one means by rationalism doctrines which depend on purely dialetical methods of reaching the truth, one has to go back to the seventeenth century to find them. It is men like Descartes and Spinoza and Leibniz who are the traditional rationalists, and the only thinkers of that sort in the eighteenth century are their disciples, the outstanding one being Wolff. By laying down supposedly self-evident or otherwise indubitable premises and deducing from them their consequences, one built a system of philosophy, psychology, ethics, and, in one case (that of Baumgarten), aesthetics, which was believed to be incontrovertible. This was reasoning *more geometrico* and, though it was a method pursued in some of the schools well into the eighteenth

century,[5] it was precisely that method which the outstanding eighteenth-century philosophers rejected. The rejection was initiated by John Locke, who died in 1704; it was zealously adopted by his successors, Berkeley and Hume, and the one warrant for calling their philosophies empirical, as the histories do, is their belief, far from justified, that their first principles were garnered from experience. Even the Platonists of the eighteenth century in England thought they were basing their systems on experience, not on abstract rational principles. And when we come to France, we find that the two great names among the Encyclopedists and their friends were Bacon and Locke. It is true that the *Encyclopédie* dates from 1750, but even as early as Bayle, who died in 1706, we find a repudiation of the rationalistic method. Bayle was not more interested in logical inconsistency than he was in factual inconsistency, by which I mean inconsistency with the established facts of experience. His skepticism was aimed at authority as a source of truth and at uncriticized traditions. If, however, by reason we mean the use of our reasoning powers, then all ages are ages of reason, from that of Thales down to that of Sartre.

A moment's reflection will also justify calling this period the Age of Sentiment. In England we have men like Shaftesbury (died in 1713) and Hutcheson (died in 1746) whose ethical theories were founded on nothing more than feeling. And what is English hedonism if not a sentimental philosophy? The vogue of the word "sentimental" was such that we find the *NED* quoting Lady Bradshaugh writing to Richardson in 1749, "What in your opinion is the meaning of the word *sentimental,* so much in vogue among the polite. . . . I am frequently astonished to hear such a one is a *sentimental* man; we were a *sentimental* party; I have been taking a *sentimental* walk." And of course we all know about a famous sentimental journey that extended the use of the term until at least 1768. Nor must it be forgotten that the discipline known as aesthetics was elaborated by Baumgarten in 1739, and, if it was called *aesthetic,* it was because its inventor situated the basis for our judgments of beauty in our senses and feelings. It is unlikely that Carey in his *Namby-Pamby* (1725) would have written a parody of Philip's *Distrest Mother,* unless

people were moved by it.[6] This was also the period, as we all know, when melancholy, tombstone poetry, weeping willows, the sublime and the awful were stylish, not the clarity and calm of a Boileau.[7] One could sustain the thesis that sentimentalism in all its forms was a reaction against the seventeenth-century cult of simplicity, logicality, and stoicism. But, I admit, this would be as unbalanced as its antithesis.

For I suspect, though I cannot prove, that for every senti-mentalist in the eighteenth century there is an anti-sentimentalist. Think of Rousseau. A generation later his thesis in the fourth book of *Emile* passed into technical philosophy in the works of Immanuel Kant. But at the time Rousseau was writing, he found powerful antagonists among his compatriots, and he himself felt constrained to leave the circle of the Encyclopedists because of incompatibility of doctrine as well as of temperament. As for his love of solitude, we have the famous passage from Johnson, as given by Boswell, in which he thunders—or should I say ful-minates?—"If man were a savage, living in the woods by himself, this might be true; but in civilized society we all depend upon each other, and our happiness is very much owing to the opinion of mankind" (*Life*, I, 272). And in 1766, when Boswell told him he had been seeing Rousseau "in his wild retreat," Johnson said,

I think him the worst of men; a rascal, who ought to be hunted out of society, as he has been. Three or four nations have expelled him; and it is a shame that he is protected in this country. . . . Rousseau, Sir, is a very bad man. I would sooner sign a sentence for his transportation, than that of any felon who has gone to old Bailey these years. (*Ibid.,* I, 317)

As for melancholy, sublimity, the picturesque, the wild, we have Addison's delight, in his *Remarks on Italy,*[8] at seeing a plain after seeing the Alps. But we also have J. Forrester on Whitehall:

> That true politeness we can only call,
> Which looks like Jones's fabrick at Whitehall . . .
> It fills the mind with rational delight,
> And pleases on reflection, as at sight.[9]

Gray wrote to his mother in 1739 from Italy, "The country of Lombardy, hitherto, is one of the most beautiful imaginable; the roads broad and exactly straight, and on either hand vast plantations of trees, chiefly mulberries and olives."[10] Hume says about beauty, "In painting . . . a figure which is not justly balanced is disgraceful . . . the principal part of personal beauty is an air of health and vigour and such a construction of members as promises strength and activity."[11] Walpole wrote to West in 1739, "The last four [days] in crossing the Alps. Such uncouth rocks, and such uncomely inhabitants! My dear West, I hope I shall never see them again."[12] And need I mention that Warton wrote an *Ode to Health* in 1746 and Collins' one to simplicity? One could go on and make an impressive inventory of pieces ridiculing melancholy, the Gothic ruins, the awfulness of cascades and forests; but one could also make such an inventory of pieces in praise of them.

After all, this is the period of Chardin's painting of children and domestic interiors, all quiet and simple, of Boucher's happy mythologies which turn Venus into a *cocotte* or a royal mistress, of Gabriel du Saint-Aubin and of L-L. Boilly who continued the tradition well into the nineteenth century. But the moment we see the eighteenth-century spirit objectified in such painters, we come upon the melancholy of Watteau and the wistfulness of some of Fragonard. We have the *Carceri* of Piranesi balanced by the sunny ruins of his friend, Hubert Robert. If in Spain Goya was painting his *Disasters of War* and his *Caprichos*, in Venice Guardi was painting his spirited and delightful scenes of fashionable life, while in England Reynolds was at work glorifying the ladies of the nobility and the stage. Goldoni was not only a contemporary of Carlo Gozzi and Metastasio, but also of Alfieri. The eighteenth-century, along with its Voltaire, Diderot, and d'Holbach, also had its mystics, like Pasqualis Martinez, Swedenborg, Lavater, and Saint-Martin; its adventurers and rogues—Casanova, the Comte de Saint-Germain, and Cagliostro—who may have used their reason but were hardly rationalists; its Bernardin de Saint-Pierre, its Marquis de Sade, its Choderlos de Laclos, its Restif de la Bretonne, none of whom were on the rationalistic side of

the barriers.[13] Cowper's *The Task* came out in 1785, four years before the storming of the Bastille, Blake's *Songs of Innocence* four years later. David was the official painter of the Revolution. Could he be merged with the School of Greuze?

Another feature of the eighteenth century which is easily overlooked by students of literature is the contribution made at this time to natural science. Surely men like Réaumur, Lavoisier, Lagrange, Coulomb, Buffon, Volta, Spallanzani, Galvani, Haller, Cavendish, Herschel, Black, Priestley, Rumford, Jenner, Edwards the ornithologist, and Linnaeus are as important in determining the temper of a period as are poets, philosophers, and painters. Each of these men made discoveries which were far-reaching in their effects. As a group they annihilated what was left of alchemy, astrology, and traditional therapeutics, to select only the best known of their achievements. The eighteenth century saw the birth of modern biology, modern medicine, and modern chemistry, and it saw this because its scientists had rejected the rationalistic methods of the past in favor of observation and experimentation. And while all this was going on, phrenology, physiognomonics, and applications of what was known as animal magnetism were also popular.

Again, it was the eighteenth century during which an attempt was made to understand the historical origins of modern society, an attempt weakened by speculation, to be sure, but which in its independence of clerical authority laid the foundation for a philosophy of history. And no account of this period is complete without some mention of men like Vico, Herder, and Condorcet. Whatever may be said against the kind of evidence which they utilized, their naiveté, if you will, they did make one new assumption in common, that the past was not like the present. History to them was just a repetition of universal and eternal human traits, but as times changed they believed that men's minds and ways of thinking and living changed too. Changes in history went deeper than modifications in clothing and speech. The laws which were formulated and the correlations which were made between geography and climate on the one hand and psychology on the other were faulty of course. But then the very fact that a search for law was made, as well as an attempt to under-

stand the varieties of human nature, was something to be remembered.

It is unfortunately true that these three figures were those mainly responsible for giving us the idea of ages and times, a gift of dubious value. The concept itself goes back, as everyone knows, to Hesiod. But the inhabitants of his ages disappeared at the ends of their periods, and new starts were made. The story of the Hesiodic ages and those like them has been told elsewhere and requires no repetition here. The Christian writers had at first only two ages, that before the Fall and that after, but later on the matter became more complicated. In St. Augustine[14] we find seven ages corresponding to the seven days of creation. But the differentia of each age was exclusively moral. In Vico, the three ages he called the mythological, the heroic, and the human differed in customs, language, jurisprudence, authority, reasoning, judgment, and general culture. By use of the comparative method Vico thought he could identify the occurrence of an age in any of the cultures which he knew, and it must be said that, though his evidence is both ambiguous and at times fictitious, Vico is no worse off in that respect than some of our own contemporaries, such as Spengler. He granted that in the later ages there were survivals from the earlier and hence was realistic enough to see that an age is made up of people and not of abstractions. In fact, of the three philosophers of history I have mentioned, he strikes me as the most sober. A reading of the *Scienza Nuova* should convince any fair-minded reader that in spite of certain fantastic details, his study of ancient jurisprudence had disciplined Vico's mind. But aside from this, two features stand out, the relative homogeneity of each age and the presence of its distinctive traits in all of its activities.

It is these two assumptions which gave birth to cultural history and which have led later scholars to look for unity rather than diversity, to neglect those traits which are inharmonious with their hypotheses as minor or exceptional, and above all to deal almost exclusively with the thoughts and doings of those whom they call representative men. And if Kant is right in thinking of the Enlightenment as "man's release from self-imposed tutelage," then the notion of the Enlightenment goes back to Vico. For

Vico pointed out that as the human or third stage develops, it increases in its clarity of ideas. This is not happiness; it is simply illumination, understanding. Like Herder later, Vico speaks of human development under the metaphor of the biological growth. Having accepted this as fundamental, it was inevitable that he include senility and death in his narrative. In his 66th Axiom he says, "Men first feel needs, then look for the useful, then observe the fitting, then delight in pleasure, whereupon they become dissolute in luxury and finally turn to folly and waste their substance." This depressing picture of human history is not explained through any relation of man to God, as it would have been in St. Augustine. The one general principle which is clear is that history is human history and is a story of progress from bad to better only in the sense that clear ideas are better than nebulous ones, that true and general ideas are better than false and limited ones, and that the derivation from such ideas of philosophic laws is better than fables and myths. This is a straightforward assertion of the terminal or inherent value of knowledge. In short, for Vico knowledge in itself is better than ignorance, science is better than myth, regardless of pleasure or comfort.

If my interpretation of Vico is correct, one has here an idea of enlightenment which is closer to that of Kant than to that of Herder or the Encyclopedists. For Herder, it is true, something called Humanity was the goal of human history, and moreover it grew as a plant grows. Otherwise there were important differences between the two men. For reason in Herder's eyes is a tool which serves to liberate man from his linkage to the physical environment. Its full actualization was to be in the form of religion. Reason (*Vernunft*) was superior to understanding (*Verstand*), in spite of the fact that the latter proves the existence of God and the necessity of the former. Enlightenment, if I may paraphrase Herder, comes from the realization of all men's potencies, those which are expressed in the arts as well as in the sciences. Hence it should not be identified with the reason that was the special interest of the Encyclopedists. To Diderot and d'Alembert reason was the *Verstand*, scientific reasoning, based on facts furnished men by observation and closely related to the

manual arts. It was, moreover, something which would provide human beings with the means of being happy, in the terrestrial sense of enjoying life. The moral improvement which it would induce through education was welfare, giving men food, clothing, physical and spiritual satisfaction. This was a much more *terre à terre* program than any envisioned by Herder. And when one examines the motives guiding these men, one sees that the freedom which enlightenment was to produce according to the Encyclopedists was freedom from ecclesiastical authority, whereas for Herder it was freedom from Mediterranean culture, as far as the Germans were concerned, and freedom for every nation to be itself. That nations had selves was not emphasized by the French, though variations in national character had long been a subject of remark.[15] Their cultural history and language went back to Rome; their religion to Saint Dionysius the Areopagite; their art to Latin Gaul. But it was difficult for Herder to take such a point of view. Germany as a nation did not exist in 1784; the popular mythology was not that of Hesiod and the other ancient mythographers; the dominant religion was Protestant and dated only from the sixteenth century; and the only monarch to whom they could all pretend to be loyal was either a local princeling or the Holy Roman Emperor. In practical terms what Herder was doing was what Fichte was to attempt later and with more success, namely to create in the minds of his readers a sense of their participation in a German soul that owed nothing to a Latin soul.

It is such novel problems which characterize a period as much as the ways in which they are solved. For example, in the fourth book of Rousseau's *Emile* we find the Savoyard Vicar maintaining that the results of natural science would deprive us of a belief in God, freedom, and immortality. His way out of this difficulty was to turn to feeling as a justification of such beliefs. He did not say that any feeling whatsoever was as good a witness to the truth as any other. But he did say that what he called the heart bore witness to these three rules. Now Europeans had for centuries been educated to believe in them. Their belief involved accepting certain assertions of fact which require no documentation here. They were promulgated by an institution that was protected by the state and had a monopoly on education. To deny

their truth was to risk imprisonment and even death. But for our purposes it is enough to point out that the problems discussed were given to French thinkers by tradition, in exactly the same way as the problem of squaring the circle or that of the ultimate constitution of matter. They were not suddenly invented by someone who had a fertile imagination. The rise of new problems is in itself a historical problem which so far has not been solved. But in this case the problem was to find acceptable answers to questions based on beliefs that the majority of men sustained. Rousseau was right in maintaining that if one accepted the principles of scientific method as then interpreted, one would come neither upon God nor an immortal soul nor a free will. These ideas did not follow from the indestructibility of matter or universal determinism. He was probably wrong in thinking that feeling could supply premises that would be generally accepted, for it is too well known that men vary in what they feel to be true. But when feelings have been directed by religious instruction, they probably become general by the time men reach the age of putting them into words. Unfortunately we are too unwilling to assume that men were once children in the hands of teachers. We talk about them as adults with pure untrained and unindoctrinated minds. So in the eighteenth century, as in our own time, writers had a tendency to look for an aboriginal man who was common to all men. They all had a tendency to believe that variations in belief or even in customs, likes, and dislikes were accidents of a homogeneous substance called Humanity. If it occurred to any of the philosophers of the period that if you removed the accidents the substance would disappear, I have not come upon his books. Oddly enough they were willing to grant this in the case of material objects, but not in the case of men. Man before the Fall, man in a state of nature variously described, was the substance; man as he is here and now the problem.

It was not until the end of the century that the search for essential humanity took a new turn, though there were intimations of the development earlier. By the time of Bonald and de Maistre it appeared that reason was not the social cement which had been sought for so long, if one was thinking of the

reason of individuals. It was now, as we have said, the reason of the race as found in tradition, expressed in language, which would give us the clue to truth. In short, mankind was thought of as a collective unity, and, since one could not put one's hands on it by the usual techniques of that period, one turned to something that was recorded and whose duration had been long enough to be impressive. That was Catholicism. No one item in it could be held in isolation from all the others. But as a whole it was truth itself. One must not, as de Maistre said, rely on the authority of evidence, but on the evidence of authority. Authority is not capricious; it expresses the rationally consistent knowledge of the race as a whole.

The notion that men were cells in the body politic was of course anticipated. The works of both Vico and Herder were based on that premise. It was, moreover, one of the most influential metaphors of our period. As early as 1750 Turgot had outlined a course of intellectual history in three stages which, except for the words he used, were identical with those that Comte was to promulgate in 1822 and thereafter.[16] Turgot's speech was not printed until 1808, but it was heard much earlier, and we may believe that coming from such a source, it was not without effect. In any event the habit of thinking of all culture as passing through progressive stages of growth could not have been as startling an idea as it might seem, inasmuch as some of its details had already been discussed. What was startling was the pervasiveness of change.

However one defines the Age of Reason, however revolutionary and anti-authoritarian one estimates its spirit to have been, it should be noted that neither the Roman Catholic nor the Anglican nor the Lutheran communions ceased their ministrations in 1750. Moreover, in England, men like Burke and Johnson and Goldsmith, as much earlier Pope and Addison, continued to believe in the religion and philosophy of their forefathers. In spite of Voltaire the Church was not crushed, and as soon as Napoleon became Emperor, the short-lived educational program of the *Idéologues* was ended. If rationalism in the sense of the analysis of ideas was the platform of the French Enlightenment, it proved a very shaky one indeed. At most it survived for about

ten years.[17] In Germany the *Aufklaerung* of Herder and Jacobi, of Hamann, if he is to be considered an *Aufklaerer*, was really anti-intellectualistic. None of them would have advocated acting under the guidance of those principles bestowed upon us by natural science rather than by insight. Lessing's *Education of the Human Race* (1780), like Mendelssohn's *Phaidon* (1767), was soon swamped by the more mysterious writing of the early Romantics.

In short, we may as well say, however dogmatically, that when one is in search of an age, one ends with human beings. And if the history of philosophy contributes anything to the investigation, it is that two men may interpret the same idea in their own individual ways. We see this happening today in the case of Marxism, psychoanalysis, existentialism, and surrealism, to mention only four programs. All existentialists, for instance, may say that existence is prior to essence, but that does not turn Professor Tillich into Jean-Paul Sartre. Similarly, all psychoanalysts may say that unconscious determinants of overt behavior are more potent than conscious, but two of Freud's immediate associates, Jung and Adler, disagreed on how and why experiences are repressed. I conclude, then, with what the most naive reader would have realized at the outset, namely that the eighteenth century, like all others, was made up of men, not of over-individual spirits, and that movements and ideas can be understood only as they are represented and manifested in men.

NOTES

[1] Egon Priedell's *A Cultural History of the Modern Age*, trans. Charles Francis Atkinson (New York, 1931), will provide dozens of examples of explaining what individuals did as an effect of the spirit of their times. This is very much influenced by the type of philosophy which appeared in Spengler's *Decline of the West*, which in turn has Hegelian overtones. But it may be more profitable to cite one or two less prominent examples of this. See Lewis Mumford on the baroque in *The Culture of Cities* (New York, 1938), p. 77, where he writes, "The concept of the baroque, as it shaped itself in the seventeenth century, is particularly useful because it holds in itself the two contradictory elements of the age. First: the mathematical and mercantile and methodical side, expressed to perfection in its rigorous street plans, it formal city layouts, and its geometrically ordered landscape designs. And at the same time, in the

painting and sculpture of the period, it embraces the sensuous, rebellious, anti-classical, anti-mechanical side, expressed in its clothes and its sexual life and its religious fanaticism and its crazy statescraft. Between the sixteenth and the nineteenth century these two elements existed together: sometimes acting separately, sometimes held in tension within a larger whole." The idea named in the verb "to express" is never clarified in this very interesting book, and the supposed conflict is common to all times. All that is said in ordinary terms is that the various types of interest existed contemporaneously. But one finds analogous expositions in books which lay down no formal principles of historical explanation. Wilfrid Mellers, for instance, in *The Sonata Principle* (London, 1957), after saying (p. xiii) that "No work of art can be 'explained' by reference to its historical connotations," immediately adds, "Every artist self-evidently 'reflects' the values and beliefs of his time; he has no choice in the matter, even though he may, like Swift, express them largely in negative terms. At the same time, any truly creative artist is also making those beliefs. It is true that we cannot fully understand Beethoven without understanding the impulses behind the French Revolution. It is equally true that we cannot fully understand the French Revolution without some insight into Beethoven's music. We can see in his music those elements which are conditioned by his time (for they could not be otherwise) and yet are beyond the topical and local." Then (p. 7) after speaking of the rise of democratic ideas in Europe, he says, "The growth of eighteenth century sonata style is the musical expression of this new democracy. Indeed, the symphony orchestra itself reflected a new democratic ideal; Joseph von Holzmeister, in a speech delivered on the occasion of Haydn's admission to the Masonic Order, pointed out that Haydn had created a new order in the orchestra, 'for if every instrument did not consider the rights and properties of the other instruments, in addition to its own rights, if it did not often diminish its own volume in order not to do damage to the utterance of its companions, the end—which is beauty—would not be attained.'" Cf. Paul Henry Lang, *Music in Western Civilization* (New York, 1941), pp. 533, 570, 571. But we also come upon this sort of thing in histories of philosophy, where it is much more serious. I refer merely to J. H. Randall, Jr., *The Career of Philosophy* (New York, 1962), where we find that (p. 66), "Italian Aristotelianism was able to lead the European schools in the fifteenth and sixteenth centuries is due to ... the settled commercial prosperity the Italian cities had now achieved"; that (p. 121) "when with the rise of industrialism social experience changed from an economy of thrift and scarcity to an economy of consumption, Protestant ethic shifted easily from its initial this-worldly asceticism to an ethic of pleasure and enjoyment and humanitarianism." I have expatiated on this in my review of *The Career of Philosophy* that appeared in the *Journal of the History of Ideas*, XXIV (1963), 287–92. Though it is easy to read Hegel's philosophy of history into this type of exegesis, it comes more directly from Marx. For Hegel himself, as a reading of these sections of the *Phenomenology* that deal with the Enlightenment will show, was setting up an ideal conceptual model of a type of thinking which he implied might

under certain conditions be exemplified in history. See Lanson's edition, pp. 383ff. May I add that one historian is outstanding in his rejection of this technique. I refer to Paul Hazard's *La Pensée europiéenne au XVIIIᵉ siècle* (Paris, 1946) , where no attempt is made to fuse all the men of this period into one over-soul, though a great variety of individuals and interests are organized under specific headings, with due regard to their main preoccupations. Cf. James W. Johnson, "The Meaning of 'Augustan,' " *Journal of the History of Ideas,* XIX (1958), 507ff.

2 For a discussion of the influence of Cartesianism on the arts, see Emile Krantz, *Essai sur l'esthétique de Descartes* (Paris, 1882) .

3 See F. L. Lucas, *The Art of Living: Four Eighteenth Century Minds* (London, 1959) , pp. 79ff., esp. pp. 104ff., which discuss Macaulay's comments on Walpole. Mr. Lucas has the advantage over many of his contemporaries in retaining his good sense even when dealing with men in whom it was conspicuously lacking.

4 See A. O. Lovejoy, *The Reason, the Understanding, and Time* (Baltimore, 1961) .

5 I have in my library a MS that dates from the end of the eighteenth century and which was probably written by a pupil in a seminary in Angoulême. It consists of lectures which are presumably taken down, as the custom was, from dictation, and the thought is straight Cartesianism.

6 E. F. Carritt, *A Calendar of British Taste* (London, n.d [1948?]), p. 166. Cf. the quotation from Steele which immediately follows.

7 See F. Baldensperger, *Études d'histoire littéraire* (Paris, 1907) , the essays on "Young et ses 'nuits' en France" (p. 54), for the vogue of this melancholy poem in France.

8 Carritt, *A Calendar of British Taste,* p. 139.

9 *Ibid.,* p. 210.

10 *Ibid.,* p. 218. Cf. Gray's ridicule of the poetry of melancholy in his famous letter to Walpole (1739) , in *Elegant Epistles, being a Copious Collection of Familiar and Amusing Letters* (London, 1803) .

11 Carritt, *A Calendar of British Taste,* p. 218.

12 *Ibid.,* p. 221.

13 A list of eighteenth-century rogues and adventurers would include at least Talvia, Schwerin, Saint-Germain, Casanova, Cagliostro, Trenck, and certainly the Chevalier d'Eon. For a partial bibliography, see Hazard, *La Pensée européenne au XVIIIᵉ siècle,* III, 102. Cf. Stefan Zweig, *Master Builders* (New York, 1939) , Pt. 3, pp. 564ff. The eighteenth century also continued the magical traditions of the sixteenth and seventeenth centuries. See especially E. M. Butler *Ritual Magic* (New York, 1959), pp. 225ff. and Kurt Seligmann, *The Mirror of Magic* (New York, 1948), pp. 453ff.

14 For the legend of the ages in a medieval setting, see George Boas, *Essays on Primitivism and Related Ideas in the Middle Ages* (Baltimore, 1948) , pp. 177ff.

15 Though this in all probability goes back to the distinction between

Greeks and barbarians, and reappears here and there in the Middle Ages and the Renaissance, it certainly was a preoccupation of some of the eighteenth-century writers. For this period, see especially Adrien Baillet, *Jugemens des savans, revus, corrigés, et augmentés, par M. de la Monnoye* (Paris, 1722), Vol. I, Ch. vii, pp. 122ff. See also the Abbé Yart as quoted in Baldensperger, *Etudes d'histoire littéraire*, p. 60. But this type of thing continued into our own times. The young Vernon Lee, in her delightful *Studies in Eighteenth Century Italy* (2nd ed.; Chicago, 1908), p. 276f., in describing the court of Charles VI, mentions French elegance and levity, German coarseness and heaviness, oriental splendor and misery, and Italian pride and love of display. This was written in 1881 and retained in the edition of 1907. National characters were sometimes, at least in Italy, split up into local characters, as in France the Normand and the Auvergnat and Gascon were thought of as having special traits not generally French. So we have Pulcinella, Pantaleone, Meneghino, the *Dottore,* Brighella, and Truffaldino standing for certain cities. In the fixing of national types, cf. Hazard, *La Pensée européenne au XVIIIᵉ siècle*, II, 226 and 235.

[16] See George Boas, *French Philosophies of the Romantic Period* (Baltimore, 1925), pp. 263ff., for the development of Turgot's schema.

[17] See F. Picavet, *Les Idéologues* (Paris, 1891), pp. 32ff., for the foundation and fortunes of the *Ecoles Normales and Centrales.*

When Was Neoclassicism?

∽

B. H. BRONSON

Chambers, in his provocative book *The History of Taste*, pointed out that when the greatest monuments of classic art— the Parthenon, the Athena Parthenos, and other glories of Periclean Athens came into being, no appreciation of these masterpieces was expressed in writing. No literary evidence survives to show that the aesthetic consciousness of that golden day had reached a level more sophisticated than that of admiring "gold-and-glitter."[1] Art, to be sure, had value, but it was prized for irrelevant reasons, reasons potentially inimical to a free development of the artistic impulse. The reasons were moral, idealistic, or civil: concerned, that is, with useful instruction, or regulative norms, or polity. Art was always to serve some ulterior, public purpose. The artist was of little account or interest in himself but the impersonal objects in view was important. Thus the name of Ictinus, and his part in designing the Parthenon, were only of local and immediate concern and were soon forgotten. Pericles could propose divesting the Athena Parthenos of her gold, should the city need the money. The vandalism of such an act he ignores, as he ignores the name of the sculptor, Phidias, his friend. But piety, he allows, would of course require restitution to the goddess. Likewise Herodotus, a world traveler exactly contemporary, estimates the weight of the gold he has seen and carefully inquired about, in famous temples and statues, but says

From Bertrand H. Bronson, Facets of the Enlightenment *(Berkeley and Los Angeles: University of California Press, 1968), pp. 1-25.*

42

nothing about the aesthetic properties—unless mere size be such —of the works he describes. Thus, for instance: "there was in this temple the figure of a man, twelve cubits high, entirely of solid gold." Or again, Thucydides, on any question of beauty, is equally noncommittal.

Plato, we remember, judges art as the excellence of a *copy* thrice removed from the original, and justifies it only so far as it instructs. Aristotle, in the *Poetics*, also bases the arts on imitation, and our pleasure in them in recognition—that is, of the object represented, whether actual, probable, or ideal ("such as it was or is, such as it is supposed, or such as it ought to be").[2] Led by the Sophists, eventually we approach an art appreciation loosened from the tether of pedagogy and religion, and flowing toward the Hellenistic Renaissance and the consequent Alexandrian efflorescence of patron, collector, connoisseur, antiquary, and dilettante—*id genus omne*. In due course, Rome abandons her earlier puritanic asceticism, is drawn into the Hellenistic current, and imbibes culture and corruption from the vanquished. By the time of Augustus, Rome has little more to learn, though the process continues "as streams roll down, enlarging as they flow."

Classicism, then, as a conscious theory of art, as doctrine defensible and defended, was, in the ancient world, Hellenistic, not Hellenic. May we not proceed to hazard the generalization that there can hardly be such a phenomenon as a primary, original classicism? For by the time we meet conscious formulations of aesthetic principle, it is always Neoclassicism that we confront. The doctrinal motivation is always traditional, invoking established norms, and to these the artist's individuality is subservient. Subservient, but not servile nor suppressed by them—rather, inspired—for the attitude is one of worshipful acceptance. Tradition is Law, in fullest realization of which lies the artist's supreme satisfaction. When this frame of mind has become self-conscious and deliberate, with allegiance acknowledged, we are in the presence of Neoclassicism.

Thus, the Augustan classicism of the first century B.C. was an integral part of the Hellenistic cultural renaissance: it was a neoclassical movement, consciously recreative of older and purer

models. Terence remembered Menander, Catullus Sappho, Vergil Homer and Theocritus. Similarly, of course, the Italian Renaissance is a gradual recovery of the values and ideals of antiquity. Brunelleschi, Alberti, Vignola, Palladio, Lomazzo were neoclassicists in the fullest sense, votaries of ancient order and system, profound students of the Vitruvian precepts. In the following century, the learned genius of Poussin, the encyclopedic labors of Junius, and the poetical treatise of Dufresnoy led to the crystallization of the classical code by the French Academy, establishing the example of the Ancients as "one clear, unchanging, universal light." Under these auspices, English Neoclassicism is launched; and here begins *our* more particular field of inquiry.

The elder of us were bred up in the critical conviction that the eighteenth century was one century we needn't worry about: we knew precisely where it stood, and what it stood for. It was fixed in its appointed place, and there it would always be when we cared to look again. We understood its values, and they bored us. The interesting thing was to see how the human spirit struggled out of that straightjacket into new life. As students of English literature, we knew that its tenets had reached their probably ultimate exemplification in the work of Pope, and that what followed in his track was only feebler and more arid imitation, while the buds of fresh romantic promise were beginning here and there to peep out timidly. That this view, or something like it, is still current is suggested by a front-page article on Christopher Smart in the *Times Literary Supplement*, entitled "Lucky Kit?" "To us," we read, "Smart seems one of the first rebels against the rational behaviour and rationalist thought which have come down like a bad debt from his century to ours."[3] One might have thought that a statute of limitation could ere now have been invoked in such a case.

However the debt may lie, certain it is that the century no longer looks so placid as formerly, whether because we have done more reading, or because events of recent decades have affected our eyesight, or because the newer telescopic lenses have altered the range of visibility and brought things into sharper focus. More seems to have been going on formerly than we had suspected. The painstaking and systematic research of our minute

topographers has left seemingly few corners of the eighteenth-century terrain unscrutinized. The net result of this turning over of all such reading as was never read—well, hardly ever—has been to reveal a region of the most baffling complexity and self-contradiction, in which can be found almost anything we choose to seek. Wherever we pause, we are bewildered by the diversity that surrounds us: not alone in the conflict of opinion but shot through the very texture of every considerable author's or artist's work. Of even the chief spokesmen this is probably true. Pope is no exception. The difficulty of making a consistent pattern of Johnson's thinking is notorious. Yet when we look at the authoritative surveys of critical historians, such is not the impression we receive. Their momentum bears us stoutly forward, and at any point they tell us where we are, how many miles we have traveled, how far we have still to go. Best safety lies perhaps in maintaining our speed; but there might be something deceptive in this sense of undeniable progress: "The rough road then, returning in a round, / Mock'd our impatient steps, for all was fairy ground."

All the authoritative guides tell us—and we believe them, do we not?—that the road sets out from "Neoclassicism" and in due course arrives at "Romanticism," taking roughly a century to cover the distance. As we trace it, the landscape visibly alters: it grows less cultivated, more picturesque, wilder. The vegetation is ranker, the hills are higher and more precipitous; the road begins to wind, first in graceful curves (the "line of beauty") ; then, adapting itself to the ruggeder country, skirting torrents overhung with jagged rock and blasted old trees, becomes ever more irregular and full of surprises. The wayfarer is at first likely to be struck with solemn awe; later, he finds himself almost breathless and gasping with fearful joy; and at last, in self-surrender, now with streaming eyes, now with shouts of apolaustic abandon, identifies himself with the spirit of what he beholds—or rather, perhaps, identifies what he beholds with his own exalted and pathetic state.

But we have been snatched aloft on the wings of metaphor. Let us decline from the resulting oversimplification and try to regain our composure. And first, returning to Neoclassicism, let

us acknowledge that, if regarded as a distinct phase of Art, separate in time and visible effects, in England it never really existed. Or, if it ever took palpable shape, that was only in the pages of certain bloodless theorists, whose formulations, when themselves regarded as efforts of the imagination or works of art, are the sole extant examples of its wholehearted enforcement. Conceptually, it exists as a theoretical terminus that was not and could not be reached in practice, a *reductio ad absurdum* of valid and defensible ideals.

We observed that Classicism, wherever it achieves self-conciousness, in works of art or in underlying doctrine, is always retrospective and therefore essentially neoclassical. Now we have declared that in actual fact a truly neoclassical work of art, as the term is usually employed, was never created in England. The solution of this apparent contradiction is that for practical purposes the troublesome term Neoclassicism is otiose and expendable. It pretends to a distinction without a difference, for the difference is only in degree, not in kind, while the instances of it are hypothetical. The simple term Classicism, then, with occasional inflections, will answer all our needs, and the tautological *neo-* may be dismissed unlamented.

We know pretty clearly what we mean by Classicism, and therefore need not be overelaborate in definition. Briefly to recapitulate: Man, being endowed with ratiocination, has as his birthright the key to proper conduct. What he does ought to be in conformity with the best use of the faculty that so far as he can tell distinguishes him from all other living things. If he so employs it, he may arrive at reasonable inferences about his relation to the universe, and his limitations; about his responsibilities and obligations to himself and to society — "Placed on this isthmus of a middle state." He ought thereby to be led to the recognition of those ideals of truth, morality, order, harmony, which he shares with his fellow man.

In Art, the classical ideals follow from these premises. All the arts—the nobler ones especially—imitate nature, in the sense that they search for a norm, or an ideal, that shall perfectly fulfill and express the natural capabilities or potentialities of the entities, or class of entities, represented: not for the worse but for

the essentially typical, or for the better. Analysis has ranked the categories and genres from high to low, has differentiated their characteristic excellences and shown their special objectives. It has noted the appeal of simplicity, the charm of variety within perspicuous unity, the desirability of balance and proportion. And it has discerned a large number of proprieties great and small which can be drawn up and codified at will under the general head of Decorum. The latter are what provide the Dick Minims with their chief exercise and they are, to be sure, the readiest subjects for discussion and debate.

From the ancient classical world we have by a miracle of good fortune inherited a body of literature in many kinds, a large amount of sculpture and sufficient remains of architecture to serve as enduring models of such shining merit that they can hardly be surpassed. They establish the moral and rationally ideal bases of art, teach virtue, and provide inexhaustible illustration of aesthetic beauty and truth . . . So much may suffice by way of summary.

Whatever date may be chosen to mark the beginning of the new age of classicism, in England the emotional state of the last decades of the seventeenth century, like the political situation, is in equilibrium highly precarious. Everywhere the dominant impression is one of instability and insecurity, of which the Stuarts in their brilliant undependability are almost the paradigm. A music characteristically of poignant, nostalgic sweetness, frequent change of tempo, brevity of movement. An architecture eclectic and experimental in its major examples, inclining to the theatrical and grandiloquent. A poetry incapable of broad definition, containing Milton, Butler, Marvell, the pyrrhonism of Rochester, the sweep of Dryden: in over-all summary uncommitted and capable of anything from the sublime to the obscene. Classic·control is an ideal then but seldom exemplified and, in a society standing in need of the strong purgatives of Swift's satire, most often perceptible only through a screen of negative images. On the heels of the brittle artificiality of Restoration comedy, and subsiding from the stratosphere of Dryden's heroic drama, the tumultuous rant of Nat Lee, the passionate distresses of Southerne, and the pathos of Otway, the last decade of the cen-

tury sees the rise of sentimental comedy and the stage is committed to the new era with irresistible parting tenderness, tears of welcome, abundance of fine feeling and flown phrasing. " 'Tis well an old age is out, And time to begin a new." The air is heavy with *un*restrained emotion. John Dennis, the foremost dramatic critic of the new decade, and no contemptible judge when all is said, puts Otway next to Euripides for "a Faculty in touching the softer Passion"[4]—a rating which will be repeated when, much later, Joseph Warton exalts him among "sublime and pathetic poets."[5]

Sublimity is constantly in the thought of Dennis and his contemporaries, made vividly aware of Longinus by Boileau. With consequent editions, translations, and commentaries arriving post with post, Longinus in the front of the eighteenth century is a name to conjure with, in the defense of irregular genius and unbounded Nature. The critics invoke him with a fervor not often accorded the tame Quintilian, who "the justest rules and clearest method joined." The six lines devoted to Longinus in that handbook of Augustan orthodoxy, Pope's *Essay*, are a timely corrective of too rigid notions of that school:

> Thee, behold Longinus! all the Nine inspire,
> And bless their Critic with a Poet's *Fire*.
> An *ardent* Judge, who *zealous* in his trust,
> With *warmth* gives sentence, yet is always just;
> Whose own example strengthens all his laws;
> And is himself that great Sublime he draws.
>
> (ll. 675–80)

Pegasus spurns the common track, takes a nearer way, and all his end at once attains. Here Pope cites an interesting analogy:

> In prospects [i.e., natural scenery] thus,
>   some objects please our eyes,
> Which out of nature's common order rise,
> The shapeless rock, or hanging precipice.
> Great Wits sometimes may gloriously offend,
> And rise to faults *true* Critics dare not mend.
>
> (ll. 156–60)[6]

A quarter of a century earlier, Dennis, crossing the Alps, called Longinus to mind. Walking, he says, "upon the very brink . . . of Destruction," he was moved to introspection:

. . . all this produc'd . . . in me . . . a delightful Horrour, a terrible Joy, and at the same time, that I was infinitely pleas'd, I trembled . . . Then we may well say of her [Nature] what some affirm of great Wits, that her careless, irregular and boldest Strokes are most admirable. For the Alpes are works which she seems to have design'd, and executed too in Fury. Yet she moves us less, where she studies to please us more.[7]

This passage, penned in the very year when Pope was born, and published in 1693, must surely have lain in the poet's mind, to produce the same comparison between "great wits" and wild Nature at the opportune moment. But the coincidence failed to sweeten the personal relations of the two men.

Along with frank emotional outbursts, preoccupation with the appearance of Nature is one of the traditional signals, as all know who gladly teach and all who docilely learn, of the rising tide of Romanticism. Yet here at the outset of the century, in the very Citadel of the Rules, we observe these full-fledged extravagancies. Loving description of a gentler Nature fills early pages of Pope, in the 1704 half of *Windsor Forest*, in the *Pastorals* — recall the extremes of empathetic trees and blushing flowers: these springing under the footfall of beauty, those crowding into a shade. Pathetic tenderness, heightening to overwhelming passion, suffuses the *Elegy* and the amazing *Eloisa to Abelard*. And later, of course, praise of Nature and of God in Nature finds supreme expression in the first Epistle of the *Essay on Man*. Already, however, by the date of the latter, Thomson had published the most extended paean to Nature in all her moods that his century, or probably any century, was to see in verse. But, as we shall increasingly observe, it is significant of a trend that, as the years passed, Thomson tried to intellectualize his spontaneous overflow of powerful emotion by injecting more and more sociological, philosophic, politico-economic, and other filler: "untuning the sky," to borrow a phase from an elder poet, by cerebration.

During these same decades external Nature was receiving tribute in other art forms as well as in poetry. By this time, a great tonal poet, Handel, had written work that both in quantity and quality sets him high among those artists of all time who have made Nature an important part of their subject matter. I do not speak metaphorically but with literal truth. To illustrate, an example may be cited, convenient because brief and universally familiar, though all but unrecognized in such a connection. In the opera *Serse*, there is an aria mistakenly called the "Largo from *Xerxes*," or more popularly, "Handel's Largo." As we know, Handel was a dramatic composer, which means that his creative imagination went hand in hand with textual idea. This is not to say that the process of translating consisted of choosing particular notes to represent named objects — though, in its place, he did not disdain particular imitation of that kind. His genius, however, lay in finding musical equivalents for moods, emotions, scenes coming to him in verbal form. Thus, in the aria mentioned, he is calling up the musical image of a tree: a tree which has grown with the seasons, in the favoring sun and air, and has put forth spreading branches that provide a cool, rustling delight in which to respire and be thankful, "Annihilating all that's made / To a green thought in a green shade." The verbal statement is perfectly explicit about this:

Recitative: Fair, soft, leafy branches of my beloved sycamore, for you may fate shine brightly. Let thunder, lightning, and storm never outrage your precious peace, nor desecrate you with violence.

Larghetto (not *Largo*) : Never gave tree a dearer, sweeter, more lovely shade. (Ombra mai fù di vegetabile cara ed amabile soave più.)

The world, of course, has taken that larghetto to its heart for a talisman against mischance in all weathers. But when we return to the stated literal meaning, could (we ask) that total experience, sensuous, sensible, spiritual, be more satisfyingly evoked?

Nature in Handel's music is a topic large enough for extended study. *L'Allegro ed Il Penseroso,* for example, contains abundant responses, from the obvious sound effects of the chirping cricket, the fluting bird song, the ringing round of the merry bells, and the "bellman's drowsy charm," to the subtle impressionism of the "whisp'ring winds soon lull[ing] asleep" in a D minor cadence hushed with twilight, and the rising moon evoked by a voice-line that climbs slowly for an octave and a half. Our total sense of the work, to quote Winton Dean, "is not a matter of pictorial embellishment, but of a creative sympathy transfusing the entire score, a sympathy with English life and the English scene which is perhaps the profoundest tribute Handel ever paid to the land of his adoption." [8] But on the larger subject of Handel's intense susceptibility to nature's more permanent features, Dean declares, with a just disregard of irrelevant temporal considerations: "There is something Wordsworthian in Handel's view of nature, and a strong element of Hellenic pantheism; a consciousness of the immanence of some superhuman power, aloof yet omnipresent, is often combined with a sense of mystery and awe." [9]

To understand Handel's music as description inevitably requires a little concentrated study. Our contemporary notions of the true and proper functions of music are so opposite to the traditions out of which his art grew that at first it seems almost belittling to suggest that he intended his compositions to be understood so literally. But it will not do to ignore the fact, or to laugh off the theory behind it as the midsummer madness of an era now happily outgrown. The problems of imitation in the arts are basic to all classical theory and practice. It is especially important for us to realize that the kind of imitation involved in Handel's work is not a mere invitation to free subjective reverie on the listener's part, the uncontrolled Träumerei, beginning anywhere, to which the latter-day concertgoer is all too prone. If we wish to converse in this tongue, we must learn it. Simply to follow it at all, we have to know its scope and purpose.

The musicians of that period believed that music could and should be a kind of sound-language, precise in the expression of ideas, emotional states, conceptions. But they always started from

verbal language, and built an accompanying system of tonal equivalents. Motion swift or slow, rough or even, unbroken or interrupted, was easy enough, given the verbal clue; so too were onomatopoetic concepts, ideas of sound or sound-producing agents, water, wind, animal noises — as exemplified, for instance, in Vivaldi's *Seasons*. Place relations like high or low, near or far, found ready musical equivalents — again if words confirmed them. Handel's contemporary and boyhood friend, Johann Mattheson, who developed this language with extreme elaboration (1739), made a useful classification.[10] He divided the "figures" or *loci topici* into two sorts, *loci notationis* and *loci descriptionis*. The first were the abstract technical devices of music, like inversion, repetition, imitation in its compositional sense. The second were the devices with nonmusical implication, emblematic in meaning, allegorical, metaphorical, of pictorial similitude. In practice, of course, the two kinds were mutually collaborative and consubstantial. The metaphysical and ethical significance of Music had not yet faded from memory. Music had once been next to Divinity in importance because on earth it was the image of celestial order, harmony, and proportion: the Higher mathematics, in fact, with a capital H. It *must* therefore have intellectual meaning, and there ought to be no unbridgeable gap between the physical and metaphysical in music. To give it ideational significance and coherency was not merely right but almost an obligation. As Bukofzer admirably stated the case: "Music reached out from the audible into the inaudible world; it extended without a break from the world of the senses into that of the mind and intellect ... Audible form and inaudible order were not mutually exclusive or opposed concepts ... but complementary aspects of one and the same experience: the unity of sensual and intellectual understanding."[11] *Die Affektenlehre,* then, was not the quaint, Shandean aberration it is commonly reported to be. It strove to bring a little more of the unknown within the bounds of the knowable; to introduce evidences of order at the frontiers of rational experience. It became absurd only when it was pushed to extremes — as happened also to rules vainly imposed on other forms of aesthetic expression.

One of its benefits was to describe and objectify emotions in such a way that our private feelings could be shared — identified, experienced, and made generally available in a recognizable musical shape. This, I take it, is the impulse behind all allegory. The process of personifying the passions in *descriptio,* by means of rhythm, tonality, modes, and keys with an established significance, renders music continually allegorical and thereby intellectually viable. This is the rationale of Handel's music, and, basically, it embodies a profoundly classical ideal. Let us not be intimidated by the term Baroque, which in music is a neologism of perhaps mainly negative utility. So universal a man as Handel will not be contained in a narrow room, and we must be wary of trying to impound him. But one thing is certain: it is not for being a revolutionary that he was exalted in his own century. Nor, on the contrary, when in the days of Mannheim and Vienna the classical forms of that great musical age were reaching perfection, was it for being reactionary that Handel's towering genius was arriving at full recognition. From the middle of the century on, whatever school was in the ascendant in England, his fame never ceased.

To emphasize Handel's firm classic alignment is not to do him any injustice. Apart from external nature, the themes that seldom fail to strike fire in his imagination, from *Acis and Galatea* and *Esther* to the very end, were drawn from two sources, the Old Testament and Greek myth. His chief formal innovation lay in the use he made in the oratorios — but not the operas — of the chorus, where his debt is to Greek tragedy via Racine's imitative handling of it. In him appears a similar deployment of choral participation on two levels: that is, both within and above the dramatic action. The chorus concentrates the issues and sums them up; and they rise in and out of that involvement and not as a moral tag superimposed from without. This important insight I owe again to Winton Dean. "With Handel," Dean declares, "as with the Greeks, the force of such pronouncements varies in proportion with their dramatic motivation. The central themes of *Saul, Belshazzar, Hercules,* and *Jephtha,* round which the whole plot revolves, are envy, *hubris,* sexual jealousy, and

submission to destiny — all favorite subjects of the Greeks — and it is no accident that those works are conspicuous both for the grandeur of their choruses and for the overriding unity of their style. Handel in this temper reminds us again and again of Aeschylus."[12]

Without leaving problems of imitation, and still pursuing the classical ideals, we may shift now to the subject of landscape gardening, wherein the mid-century is seen to have defined its sympathies and characterized itself in especially typical fashion. Not the least characteristic fact here is the confluence of contradictory impulses that blur the purpose and direction of changes taking place. Are we watching the gradual repossession of England by Nature with the approach of the Romantic Age, or is the motivation behind this movement quite another thing? Which, it may be asked, is the more romantic, in the deepest sense, the appeal to the eye or the appeal to the mind which "creates, transcending these, / Far other worlds and other seas?"

Several kinds of imitation are involved here, of which we may distinguish two or three in what may have been the order of their emergence. Under the guidance of Sir William Temple, who led away from the stiff, geometrical garden patterns in vogue at the end of the seventeenth century, with their radiating or parallel straight walks, clipped hedges, trees shaped in balls, cones, pyramids symmetrically balanced, the century opened with a strong impulse toward the "Sharawadgi," the supposed sophistication of oriental irregularity. Pevsner has shown the political overtones of English "'liberty'" in this movement. Shaftesbury's declared approbation of the "horrid graces of the wilderness" indicates British restiveness under too strict control, and also reflects anti-Gallic sentiment in opposition to the rule of Lenôtre.[13] The English Constitution was a *natural* growth, was it not?

This tendency soon broadened and blended with Augustan ideas of classical attitudes toward Nature. The great Roman poets were all poets of nature, assuming the pastoral frame of mind, reveling in country philosophizing, cultivating the natural delights of their rural retreats. The mood was inherited from the Hellenistic development of natural parks and gardens, associated

with the Muses and philosophical discussion, and carried on in the Sicilian pastoral tradition and its Alexandrian sequel. Country life in the sumptuous villas of the later Roman nobles, statesmen, generals, not to mention emperors, had much of what the English landed gentry emulated in their great estates; and similar attitudes toward the natural scene seem to have been generated in both worlds.

Even before William Kent came the experiments of Vanbrugh and Bridgman at Castle Howard, Blenheim, and Stowe in romantic gardening. H. F. Clark observes:

The triumph of the irregular occurred during the rise of Palladianism in architecture. Both were derived from classical sources filtered through the work of Italian Renaissance scholarship ... Irregular gardens were as classical and correct as the buildings of the Burlington group ... [Sir Henry Wotten's precept that] "as fabrics should be regular, so gardens should be irregular," was a truth which classical authority was found to have practiced ... [This, it was asserted] was "the method laid down by Virgil in his second *Georgic*." Addison, whose vogue as a leader of taste was enormous, brought the weight of his authority to the side of change by claiming that his own taste was Pindaric, that in his garden it was difficult to distinguish between the garden and the wilderness.[14]

Chiswick Park, began after Burlington's first visit to Italy, was one of the first of the new irregular gardens, in which, it appears, Pope himself had a hand along with Bridgman. Kent continued it, and Pope theorized the work in his Epistle to Burlington.

Nothing is clearer than that these designers painted primarily to the mind's eye, and aimed at presenting to the observer temporal vistas. "What an advantage," exclaims Shenstone,

must some Italian seats derive from the circumstance of being situate on ground mentioned in the classicks! And, even in England, wherever a park or garden happens to have been the scene of any event in history, one would surely avail one's self of that circumstance, to make it more interesting to the imagination. Mottoes should allude to it, columns, &c. record it; verses moralize upon it.[15]

Like the poets with their bejeweled incrustations of literary quotation, they enriched the scene by setting up as many echoes as possible, by every variety of associated device that might stimulate the imagination and excite emotion. Urns and obelisks, statues and temples evoked the classical nostalgia on three levels: through the recollection of actual classical scenes; through such scenes idealized in the idyllic canvases of Poussin and Claude; and by recalling images and sentiments from the ancient poets with whose work so much of their literary experience was impregnated. This art, then, was an imitative art not only in a pictorial sense but also in its close kinship to literature.

The art of music and the art of gardening are alike in the fact that specific meaning in both must be introduced from another medium. Music, we have seen, expresses ideas by developing a metaphorical language that must depend on verbal assistance for correct interpretation of any but the most rudimentary conceptions. But modes and keys acquire independent meaning from repetitional use; and conventional rhythms, meters, and musical figures will convey an accepted sense without the help of intermediaries. Obviously, we must have been tutored in order to understand: it is not enough to be sensitive to musical impressions. Similarly, now, gardening developed its own *Affektenlehre*. The language of flowers has always been a very arbitrary one that had to be memorized; but the toughness and durability of oaks, the dark foliage of yews, the cadent habit of willows, have supplied an obvious symbolism that by association is generally known and acknowledged.

It may be that in some parts of the Orient the language of vegetation has been pursued to such a degree of cerebral sophistication that complex ideas can be formulated by its means alone. If so, it would of course presume in the recipients equal study, knowledge of conventions, and fastidious discrimination in their use. Among the English, poets have been the earliest interpreters and moralizers of natural phenomena. Topographical poetry was already in vogue by the time the landscape artists began to elaborate the extrasensory content of nature in their pictorial compositions. "So," writes Dyer in "Grongar Hill,"

So we mistake the future's face,
Ey'd thro' hope's deluding glass,
As yon summits soft and fair,
Clad in colours of the air,
Which, to those who journey near,
Barren, brown, and rough appear . . .
Thus in nature's vesture wrought
To instruct our wand'ring thought.
(ll. 121–26, 99–100)

The landscape designers determined to make equally certain, by the employment of adventitious means, by architecture, sculpture, inscriptional mottoes, artful scenic punctuation,[16] and control of point of view, that the significance of their statements should be rightly understood. Indeed, it sometimes seems as though they resent the pulse of life and would fix the scene in a single moment of time, like the garden in Chaucer's dream, where the sun was always temperate and never set, and change of seasons was unknown. "To see one's urns, obelisks, and waterfalls laid open," Shenstone reflects, "the nakedness of our beloved mistresses, the Naiads and the Dryads, exposed by that ruffian Winter to universal observation: is a severity scarcely to be supported by the help of blazing hearths, chearful companions, and a bottle of the most grateful burgundy."[17]

But, as the decades passed, purposes were clarified, subtler meaning was directed to a wider "literate" public, and taste altered. Imitation grew more sophisticated and in a sense more philosophical. The classical idea of what nature herself intended in an imperfect realization of purpose in any given local effort, struggling with intractable elements, became the overriding concern. The genius of place held the secret, and it was the duty of the artist to consult this genius and liberate it into perfect expression. The art, however, lay in ridding it of local idiosyncrasy and domestic encumbrances, which were like bad personal habits, the uncouth awkwardness of village speech, dress, or manners. It was a generalized, ideal beauty that was sought, the perfect classical statement that did not imply stereotyped repetition or dull platitude but became a fresh and living realization of uni-

versal truth. "Great thoughts," Johnson said, "are always general."

To reconstitute the face of nature in this way was to compose three-dimensional paintings not from devotion to the charms of nature but according to an intellectual conception as classical as the modeling of antique sculpture. Truth to an ideal beauty, essentialized from a myriad of imperfectly beautiful particulars, was the object here as there: to be real but not realistic, natural but not naturalistic—"the artifice of eternity," the mind's embodiment. "Objects," Shenstone wrote, "should indeed be less calculated to strike the immediate eye, than the judgment or well-formed imagination." To be sure, there are natural proprieties, rules derived from Nature's own practice, "discovered, not devised." "The eye should always look rather down upon water." "The side-trees in vistas should be so circumstanced as to afford a probability that they grew by nature." "Hedges, appearing as such, are universally bad." "All trees" (that is, species of them) "have a character analogous to that of man . . . A large, branching, aged oak is perhaps the most versatile of all inanimate objects."[18]

It must be apparent, then, that what we have been tracing is not the development of a more and more romantic love of an external Nature uncontaminated by the hand of man; but rather a more and more subtly refined Art, working with natural phenomena as its plastic elements, on the same classical principles that had been operative in literary art, sculpture, architecture, and were now coming to new and vigorous life in English painting, and, soon after, in the classical revival in France. How, then, is it permissible to use this art of landscape gardening as proof of the continual progress toward Romanticism? Brown's notorious "capabilities" were basically a classical theory — a point too seldom acknowledged.

So far as concerns the cult of the Picturesque, it may be fair to say that it is the belated psychologizing stepchild of the much earlier cult of irregularity, via the theories of Burke at the mid-century and concerned to rationalize, not to retreat into, wilderness. It set up "savage" Rosa, who had not lacked earlier admirers — note Walpole's outburst, going over the Alps with Gray in 1739: "Precipices, mountains, torrents, wolves, rumblings, Salva-

tor Rosa!"[19] — on a higher pedestal than Claude, partly in conscious protest against a late classicism that it felt had become too pure. The asymmetry of the older Baroque tradition, continued on the Continent in the Rococo, no doubt also helped to familiarize sensitive spirits with these "Gothic" tastes.

The connection between the landscape gardener's and the painter's point of view was patent to all. Shenstone pronounced: "Landskip [which he distinguishes from 'prospects,' or distant views] should contain variety enough to form a picture upon canvas; and this is no bad test, as I think the landskip painter is the gardiner's best designer. The eye requires a sort of balance here; but not so as to encroach upon probable nature."[20] But there was as yet no school of English landscape painters to provide models, and of course Shenstone was looking toward Italy. Not until the seventh decade, when Richard Wilson translated the English scene into classical terms, was the need supplied. Hitherto, no painter of the English natural scene had appeared who could hold a candle to Claude or the Poussins. And, in fact, when we look for classicism of any sort among *early* eighteenth-century British painters, it is very hard to find. The sequence of names, Holbein, Van Dyck, Lely, Kneller, covers in symbolic outline much of the earlier history of British art. Against this long tradition of foreign lawgivers, and the current snobbery of the Connoisseurs, Hogarth fought with every weapon he could find or invent. He managed to loosen the soil for a British planting. He was no traditionalist and neither by precept nor practice did his influence tell in the direction of Classicism. It was not, however, ancient art he was tilting against but snobbery and pseudo-connoisseurs.[21] But neither would anyone be likely to attach a Romantic label to him. Although he was a theorist, he was by temperament an improviser more interested in facts than in formulas. His masterpieces, e.g., Captain Coram's portrait, his Mrs. Salter, the sketches of the Shrimp Girl, and his Servants, do not set up for "ideal nature," though the Coram has been called one of the great original landmarks of British portraiture.

Ellis Waterhouse dates the beginning of the classical age in British painting precisely at 1760, with the accession of George III and the first public exhibition of the newly incorporated Society

of Artists.[22] To this exhibition Reynolds contributed his "Duchess of Hamilton as Venus." The following year Hogarth sent his ill-starred "Sigismonda"; in 1764, Benjamin West entered his first classical history picture. But matters were already getting out of hand because the rules were so permissive that anything sent in was eligible to be shown — even paper cutouts; and the Academy was inaugurated in 1768 to introduce some needful measures to control rights of entry.

Thenceforward, after the establishment of the Royal Academy, throughout Reynold's presidency, in spite of shortcomings and backslidings, the principles of the Grand Style predominated. During the decade of the seventies, Reynolds made his most determined effort to emulate the old Renaissance masters. This was also the time of his greatest influence. From the late seventies through the early eighties, Barry was doing his big work ("Progress of Human Culture") for the Royal Society of Arts, the logical fulfillment, if not the triumph, of the doctrine. The history picture, in full panoply and classical costume, stood up for the main, and West, with crown patronage, Gavin Hamilton, Copley, Opie, Northcote, and Reynolds as well, strove to realize the ideal. But other winds were blowing, and the mesmerism of Raphael and Michelangelo lost compulsion with the passing years. By 1790, the history piece had been, if not declassicized, then refurbished in modern guise, and "ideal nature" in the Grand Style, though still a noble ideal, no longer compelled assent — at least in England.

Nonetheless, with the presidential addresses of Reynolds, we are given the *first* great *literary* statement of the classical ideal in painting. Professor Bate goes even further, declaring that "Reynolds' *Discourses* comprise perhaps the most representative single embodiment in English of eighteenth-century aesthetic principles."[23] The *Discourses* were delivered over a very long span — from January 1769 to December 1790 — and were first published complete in 1794. They had a cumulative power; and it is beyond contradiction that eighteenth-century classical *doctrine* reaches its climactic formulations in the last decades of the age.

As for Reynold's own enormous achievement on canvas, it is very difficult to confine. "Damn him," exclaimed Gainsborough

in grudging acknowledgment, "how various he is!" At the end of his life, Reynolds simply and regretfully confessed that Michelangelo's example had been too lofty for imitation: "I have taken another course, one more suited to my abilities, and to the taste of the times in which I live."[24] Nevertheless, this clear and uplifted spirit, this "very great man," as Johnson justly called him, did incontrovertibly succeed, without violating the bond of individual portraiture, in typifying and idealizing for all time a class, a portion of society, a way of life, in dozens of his numberless subjects. In the abundant best of his canvases, we seem to have been shown, not merely so many named personages, but a great deal of the age in which they lived. In a subtle way, he reconciled the individual portrait to the generalized, ideal history piece, a marriage most fully exemplified in his monumental *Family of the Duke of Marlborough*, but demonstrated as well in many of his more informal works.

If there were stirrings against the classical teaching of Reynolds in the art of painting, the doctrine was hardly questioned when applied to sculpture. Reynolds devoted his Tenth Discourse to this subject. In it, he rebukes all attempts to include elements of the picturesque, or such pictorial effects as flying drapery or wind-swept hair, or contrasts of light and shade, or imbalance, as a child against a full-size figure, or a stooping figure as companion to an upright one. The delight of sculpture, he declares, is an intellectual delight in the contemplation of perfect beauty, in which the physical pleasure has little part. This art only partly represents nature. "Sculpture," Reynolds pronounces, "is formal, regular, and austere; disdains all familiar objects, as incompatible with its dignity, and is an enemy to every species of affectation. . . . In short, whatever partakes of fancy or caprice, or goes under the denomination of Picturesque . . . is incompatible with that sobriety and gravity which is peculiarly the characteristic of this art."[25]

It is plain that the work of the previous generation of sculptors, even the great Roubillac in his funerary monuments, would not have been approved by Reynolds, because their work was semidramatic, and aimed to make a theatrical statement. But the new members of the Royal Academy, Nollekens, Flaxman,

Banks, and Bacon, received the doctrine *con amore*. Nollekens persisted, after his years in Rome, in modeling even Johnson without benefit of wig, evoking (it is said) Johnson's growling protest: "Though a man may for convenience wear a cap in his own chamber, he ought not [in a bust] to look as if he had taken physic." Flaxman's work is filled with the distillation of eighteenth-century ideas of "the just designs of Greece."[26] He worked in Rome 1787–1790. Bacon's statue of Johnson, in St. Paul's, in toga and cropped head, perfectly fulfills Reynold's notion of "ideal nature." Indeed, Katherine Esdaile, the historian of British sculpture, is filled with indignation at the lamentable triumph achieved by classicism over the native tradition of good homely realism. It is certain that in this art, if naturalism means the tendency toward Romantic individualism, the last two decades of the eighteenth century were a palpable retrogression from its arrival.

A kindred spirit is visible in architecture. The Burlingtonian tradition, carried past 1750 by Isaac Ware, James Paine, and Sir Robert Taylor, was reinvigorated, reoriented, and achaeologized, in part through the excitement over Pompeii at the mid-century, and by investigation all the way from Paestum, Sicily, Athens, as far eastward as Palmyra. The fifties were a decade of strenuous field work by both English and French in Greek and Roman antiquities. Soufflot and Leroy, the Comte de Caylus, Stuart and Revett, William Chambers, Winckelmann, Clérisseau, were some of the best known, and Piranesi, who published three sets of Roman engravings by 1754 — not to mention the official volumes on Herculaneum beginning to appear in 1757. Robert Adam's first tour lasted from 1753 to 1758. He filled notebook after notebook with archaeological studies. His brother James followed his example in 1760. James Stuart's and Nicholas Revett's *Antiquities of Athens*, published in 1762, was based on their investigations of the previous decade. Lord Anson's London house, in the Greek style, was the first conspicuous result. Between the two stricter modes, the Palladian and Athenian, falls the revolutionary Adam work, more various, freer, but classical in inspiration, and enormously successful, influential, and fashionable. Fiske Kim-

ball, in fact, our most painstaking authority on the Rococo, credits Adam's vogues with being responsible for the demise of that style even in France, its originator.[27] Sir William Chambers likewise throws his weight solidly behind the classical tradition (apart from sowing his wild oats in Chinese gardens) ; so did the Woods of Bath; and even James Wyatt, although flirting occasionally with the Gothic, began and continued throughout his career with classically designed buildings. Fashions in architecture are not easily overturned. But the Adam brothers were thoroughgoing, and did really change the looks of things. And their regulation, of course, affected all the interior appointments, from carpet to ceiling, wall decoration, furniture, and lighting. Wedgewood, who belongs to the same decades, with his Etruscan and classical pottery adorned with charming antique luting modeled by Flaxman, fitted in beautifully here. Moreover, thanks to the practical improvements of Caslon in type-founding, and the fanatical perfectionism of Baskerville in the middle decades, fine printing was moving on a parallel course. Along with the extreme beauty and refinement of his Roman type, Baskerville was learning how to manipulate the white space on his page, until his Latin titles sprang out three-dimensional, like antique urns and pedestals standing in the 'open air, bearing classical inscriptions. His example was not lost on his immediate successors, and in the hands of the Foulis brothers, of Bensley, and Bulmer — with the aid of such designers as Wilson, Fry, the Martins, and Figgins — printing became more classically splendid right to the end of the century. It would be hard to conceive of any piece of furniture more thoroughly at home in the library of an Adam house than some of the magnificent quartos and folios that were published in the years when those great houses were built or remodeled: Syon, Osterly, Kedleston, Kenwood, Luton Hoo, Mellerstain, Newby Hall, and many others. Appropriately, some of the most sumptuous volumes were works of the line of architects already named, Burlingtonians and Classicists both: Campbell's *Vitruvius Britannicus*, Burlington's *Fabbriche Antiche*, Chamber's *Treatise*, Stuart's and Revett's *Antiquities of Athens*, Robert Adam's *Ruins of Diocletian's Palace* and the Adams brother's

Works in Architecture are only a few of the most distinguished. They had, moreover, an international circulation and international influence.

If, in summarizing our impressions of the latter decades of the century we recall that Goldsmith then showed in his two great essays in decasyllabic couplets how freshly the Augustan music could be reembodied in the hands of a master of that tradition; if we add to Reynold's *Discourses* Johnson's *Lives of the Poets* (1779–1781) : we shall be in no danger of attributing to Classicism an early demise. If we set beside these masterpieces Gibbon's magnificent elegiac monument to ancient Rome (1776–1787), a supreme embodiment of the Augustan Spirit — an epic, as Lewis Curtis demonstrates, reared to celebrate Wisdom and Moral Virtue guiding Power, and warning against surrender;[28] and if, moreover, we remember Burke's nobly conservative defense of the principle of continuity and tradition: we shall not imagine that the Classical Age dwindled or died from anemia and decay. Classicism is a faith, and, being a faith, therefore never fully realized but demanding constant effort from its devotees to attain the values it essentially embodies: the humane ideals of rational truth, moral virtue, order, and beauty expressive of these goods. The community of artists and thinkers with whom we are here concerned, whatever their individual variance, ardently professed and diligently sustained these convictions in art and in life. Burke's *Letters to a Noble Lord* (1796) is not the least splendid expression of that spirit, and George Sherburn's sentence upon it is finely appropriate: "The echo from Virgil may serve to remind us that Burke's art came from the ancients, and that with the figured and fervent mood of his last works eighteenth-century prose goes out in a blaze of noble artifice."[29]

In studying the past, we have grown so habituated to our progressive way of anticipating the future in its earliest premonitory signs that we seldom allow a moment's reflection to the oversimplification and really gross distortion of the historical truth of any actual moment of the past which this practice entails. To the people who are living in it, the present seldom looks like the future. Very few have the leisure for prophecy — except of calamity — or the power of disinterested observation

and detachment. The present is always a confused muddle of conflicting values and doubtful issues, and the battle never ceases.

Much earlier, I quoted a dubious couplet: "The rough road then, returning in a round, / Mock'd our impatient steps, for all was fairy ground." It would not be surprising if no one recognized the lines, which intrinsically are hardly memorable. They are part of Johnson's crafty demonstration that in Pope's celebrated onomatopoetic description of the labors of Sisyphus—

> With many a weary step, and many a groan,
> Up a high hill he heaves a huge round stone;
> The huge round stone, resulting with a bound,
> Thunders impetuous down, and smoakes along the ground.

—"the mind governs the ear and the sounds are estimated by their meaning."[30] They do not make very good sense; but I intended to impose on them a kind of symbolic sense, to suggest that the looks of the road and the speed of the passage were highly subjective matters, largely dependent upon—or at least radically affected by—the purpose and preoccupations of the passenger. I have wished in this paper to spend an hour looking at the eighteenth century as if it were a spatial rather than a temporal panorama. For a while I was tempted to take as my title, "From Romantic to Classic," thinking thereby to point the moral in a ready and easy way. The pretty paradox seemed to provide a sort of compass or a means of escape from the bewildering complexities wherein I was stumbling. And indeed it was a help, though insufficient, by its inherent magnetic property of lifting by attraction one sort of matter from the indiscriminate mass.

But, in the end, it had to be rejected because the truth is that, as historians, we are not obliged to travel the road either in one direction or in the other. Both ends of the panorama are equally open to our elevated, timeless vision. A topographical map does not itself move: it lies open to inspection. It is not like Rabelais's Island of Odes, "où les chemins cheminent, comme animaux." Its roads, on the contrary, stay exactly where they are laid down.

It is worthwhile, I think, and corrective of the distortions arising from our obsession with interpretation *ex post facto*, to try to
look at an Age in the richness of its complexities and contradictions. If we did not know—or if we could awhile forget—that the
Age of Romanticism followed on the heels of the Age of Enlightenment, should we not quite naturally be seeing the eighteenth
century in quite another than the customary view: as in fact
a period when the spirit of Classicism steadily *refined* its values,
grew increasingly *assured* in its declarations of them, and never
knew better their true and vital meaning and importance than
when on the verge of losing them?

> This thou perceiv'st, which makes thy love more strong,
> To love that well which thou must leave ere long.

Hence, I have been concerned to call to mind the emotional
ferment, the resistance to rule, the communion with external
nature, all those signs and signals of "Romanticism" that com-
plicate the *opening* of the Age of Reason; next, the irregular
and disconcertingly rhythmless horizon line where at unpredictable intervals the different arts thrust up their temporal peaks;
and, toward the close of the century, the passion for order, the
lofty vision of a timeless beauty, the powerful affirmations of
faith in man's ability to define and by strenuous effort to approx-
imate it by the rational use of his human endowment, his shared
inheritance, native and natural: the persistent and lasting devotion to the Classical Ideal.

NOTES

[1] Frank P. Chambers, *The History of Taste* (New York, 1932), pp. 273ff.

[2] *Poetics* 146ob 10.

[3] *Times Literary Supplement*, December 29, 1961, p. 921.

[4] "Remarks upon Mr. Pope's Translation of Homer" (1717), *Critical Works,*
ed. Edward Niles Hooker (Baltimore, 1943), II, 121.

[5] Joseph Warton, *An Essay on the Genius and Writings of Pope* (London,
1756), I, dedication. Otway was demoted in later editions.

[6] Ed. Warburton, 1744. Earlier editions place the last couplet at II. 152–53;
Warburton returned to that order in 1764.

[7] *Miscellanies in Verse and Prose* (1693), ed. Edward Niles Hooker, II, 380–81.

8 Winton Dean, *Handel's Dramatic Oratorios and Masques* (London and New York, 1959), p. 320.

9 *Ibid.*, p. 63.

10 Johann Mattheson, *Der volkommene Capellmeister* (Hamburg, 1739).

11 Manfred Bukofzer, *Music in the Baroque Era* (New York, 1947), p. 369.

12 Dean, *Handel's Dramatic Oratorios and Masques*, p. 41.

13 Nikolaus Pevsner, "The Genesis of the Picturesque," *The Architectural Review*, November 1944; also the same author's *The Englishness of English Art* (London, 1956), p. 156.

14 H. F. Clark, *The English Landscape Garden* (London, 1948), pp. 12–13.

15 William Shenstone, "Unconnected Thoughts on Gardening" in *Works* (1768 ed.) II, 113.

16 The neat word is A. R. Humphreys's in *William Shenstone* (Cambridge, 1937), p. 100.

17 Shenstone, "Unconnected Thoughts," II, 121.

18 *Ibid., passim.*

19 Horace Walpole to Richard West, September 28, 1739.

20 Shenstone, "Unconnected Thoughts," II, 115.

21 J. T. A. Burke, "Classical Aspect of Hogarth's Theory of Art" in *England and the Mediterranean Tradition* (Oxford, 1945).

22 Ellis K. Waterhouse, *Painting in Britain, 1530–1790*, Pelican History of Art (Baltimore, 1953), p. 157.

23 Walter Jackson Bate, *From Classic to Romantic* (Cambridge, Massachusetts, 1946), Chapter III, §6, p. 79.

24 Conclusion of the Fifteenth Discourse, December 10, 1790.

25 Conclusion of the Tenth Discourse, December 11, 1780.

26 An offshoot of this impulse is to be observed in the sudden flood of Homeric illustration after 1750, reaching its classical climax about 1790. See Dora Wiebenson, "Subjects from Homer's Iliad in Neoclassical Art," *Art Bulletin*, XLVI (March 1964), 23–37.

27 Fiske Kimball, *The Creation of the Rococo* (Philadelphia, 1943), pp. 207ff.

28 "Gibbon's Paradise Lost" in *The Age of Johnson: Essays Presented to Chauncey Brewster Tinker,* ed. F. W. Hilles (New Haven, 1949), pp. 73ff.

29 George Sherburn, "The Restoration and Eighteenth Century" in *A Literary History of England,* ed. Albert Baugh (New York, 1948), p. 1094.

30 Johnson, Life of Pope, paragraph 332 (*Lives of the Poets, ed.* G. Birkbeck Hill [Oxford, 1905], III, 231).

What Is "Humanism"?

ᕦ〜ᕤ

PAUL FUSSELL

Next to terms like 'classic' and 'romantic', there is apparently no word invoked in interpretations of English thought and expression more barren of precise meaning at the present time than 'humanism'. Its use in our day by the literary old-fashioned is a common occasion of either smiles or yawns. During its vogue of over three hundred years the term has been employed as an emotive sign for practically anything valued by the speaker, from piety to scepticism, from aristocracy to egalitarianism, and from indifferentism to humanitarianism. Those people in universities who profess something that is neither science nor social science are today often called 'humanists', although, alas, very few of them are in the sense in which the word means something when applied to a group of major eighteenth-century authors. Used as it often is to describe emotional and intellectual phenomena of the sixteenth and seventeenth centuries, 'humanism' suggests a sort of wise and broad piety, a rich, civilized amalgam of Christian devotion and pagan wisdom—or even worldly wisdom; in our century the term, as used at least by the British Humanist Association, denotes something entirely different: it suggests what the eighteenth century was fond of calling 'freethinking', that is, religious scepticism founded on purely anthropocentric premises. This latter meaning comes close to Coleridge's sense of the term: he defines it as 'Belief in the mere

From Paul Fussell, The Rhetorical World of Augustan Humanism *(New York: Oxford University Press, 1965). The text used here is from the paperback edition, 1969, pp. 3–27.*

humanity of Christ'. Matthew Arnold's conception of the meaning of 'humanism' brings us nearer to the meaning I have in mind. 'Milton was born a humanist', writes Arnold, 'but the Puritan temper mastered him'.

In Johnson's *Dictionary* (1755) the word had not yet assumed its late-nineteenth-century suggestions of broad wisdom. Johnson defines a humanist as 'A philologer; a grammarian: a term used in the schools of Scotland'. And yet, as even this definition reminds us, the term once suggested a devotion to the texts of the ancients and, hopefully, an acquaintance as well with the conception of man embodied in Greek and Roman literature. The term thus tends to suggest the opposition of the 'humanist' to anything narrowly individualist, subjective, exclusive, relativistic, Puritan, or parochial. As Santayana has said, the humanist seeks out everywhere 'the normalities of human nature'.

Perhaps the best way to suggest how the term is descriptive of what can be called the 'orthodox' ethical tradition in the eighteenth century is simply to list certain postulates and characteristics generally shared by conservative writers of the period:

(1) The humanist either possesses or affects such broad and historical awareness of actual human nature as to justify grave doubts about the probability of any moral or qualitative 'progress'. This is not to say that a humanist like Johnson denies the reality of experiential or material progress; as he remarks in his *Life of Butler,* where he puzzles over the motive of Butler's satire on the Royal Society, 'The most zealous enemy of innovation must admit the gradual progress of experience, however he may oppose [as Johnson does] hypothetical temerity'. Any humanist, Johnson included, knows that a sedan-chair beats walking and that the world is the 'better' for the extirpation of the bubonic plague. What makes the humanist suspicious is facile analogizing between material and moral 'improvements'. The humanist tends to believe that, in all the essentials, human nature is permanent and uniform, quite unchanged by time or place. It is this idea in the eighteenth century that sanctions the orthodox conception of the permanence of the literary genres, each of which is thought to address itself to one unchanging element of the human consciousness. And because the fundamental nature

of man is uniform, both historically and geographically, the impulse towards 'innovation' in important matters becomes naturally ludicrous:

> BOSWELL. *So*, Sir, you laugh at schemes of political improvement.
> JOHNSON. Why, Sir, most schemes of political improvement are very laughable things.
>
> (BLJ, ii, 102)

And as Gibbon puts it, in the first chapter of his *Autobiography*, 'The satirist may laugh, the philosopher may preach, but Reason herself will respect the prejudices and habits which have been consecrated by the experience of mankind'. These 'habits' express a fundamental, permanent human nature to Gibbon, and this conviction informs his satire on the early Christians in Chapters XV and XVI of *The History of the Decline and Fall of the Roman Empire*. As he observes of the Roman Christians in Chapter XVI: 'They dissolved the sacred ties of custom and education, violated the religious institutions of their country, and presumptuously despised whatever their fathers had believed as true or had reverenced as sacred.' Gibbon's quasi-religious awareness of the dignity and value of long-practised, 'consecrated' human habits is re-experienced at the very end of the century by Burke in the *Reflections on the Revolution in France*. All this is to say that the humanist is necessarily a historian and that he derives his values always from the study of human history.

(2) The humanist believes that most human 'problems' cannot be solved, 'failures and defects', as Johnson says in *Rambler* 43, 'being inseparable from humanity'. And yet at the same time the humanist will argue passionately on behalf of the nobility of human nature, for he finds that man's paradoxical 'dignity' is in part the result of his being the only creature whose consciousness apprehends—or contrives—problems too complicated for solution.

(3) The humanist assumes, as Burke does, that it is both the index and the privilege of the human consciousness to be largely a construction of man's own imaginative making, and that,

therefore, the mind and the imagination—what perhaps can be called the symbol-making power—are the quintessential human attributes. This is to insist that man becomes fully human, or properly realized, only when he uses his mind in a uniquely human way. Sir Joshua Reynolds thus establishes his aesthetics on man's observed capacity to 'raise' his nature by contemplating heroic images; like other humanists, Reynolds begins with and returns constantly to 'human nature, whence arts derive the materials upon which they are to produce their effects' (*Thirteenth Discourse*). The humanist emphasis on the symbol-making power as the focus of man's uniqueness is reflected in the humanist veneration for the practice of literature, for in literature as in no other human experience the mind is exercised—to the humanist, 'ennobled'—by a constant oscillation between things and symbols, between actualities and metaphors of actualities. One sign of the humanist, whether of the Middle Ages, the Renaissance, or the eighteenth century, is an apparently immoderate love of 'humane learning' (that is, literature). To Johnson's Imlac, in Chapter XXX of *Rasselas,* 'learning and ignorance . . . are the light and darkness of thinking beings'. The humanist, as Herschel Baker has observed, is likely to be 'a schoolmarm at heart'.[1]

(4) The humanist betrays so habitual and profound a concern with the act of evaluation that it often grows into what can be described as 'the evaluative obsession'. This 'vertical' cast of mind seems impelled to order everything in rank, whether the elements of animated nature which it delights to contemplate as a vertical scale of being, or the social stations in a society, or the various studies in a curriculum. This *libido aestimandi* is naturally accompanied by hierarchical rather than egalitarian expectations about society and politics; about literary genres and techniques, some of which are conceived to be in the nature of things 'better' than others; about periods of history, some of which are assumed to be more 'noble' than others; and even about the assumed elements of the human psyche, which is still imaged by the eighteenth-century humanist in a very seventeenth-century way — with 'will' in a position of almost military 'command' at the top, 'reason' or 'judgment' in the middle, and the senses or

'passions' as servants at the bottom. Pope exemplifies this evaluative habit of mind while subjecting it to irony at the same time:

> Tho' the same Sun with all diffusive rays
> Blush in the Rose, and in the Diamond blaze,
> We prize the stronger effort of his pow'r,
> And justly set the gem above the Flow'r.
>
> *(Epistle to Cobham,* 97–100)

(5) The humanist is pleased to experience a veneration,
which often approaches the elegiac, for the past, a feeling
accompanied by a deep instinct for the tested and the proven in
the history of human experience. This reverence for the experience of the past is inseparable from the humanist belief in
the historical uniformity of human nature. Burke is characteristic in the way he looks with satisfaction, in the *Reflections,* on
'the powerful prepossession towards antiquity, with which the
minds of all our [British] lawyers and legislators, and of all the
people whom they wish to influence, have always been filled'.

(6) The humanist assumes that ethics and expression are
closely allied. It is this assumption that makes possible Johnson's
unique fusion of biographical, ethical, and aesthetic criticism in
The Lives of the Poets. Like Swift exhibiting the 'modern' moral
squalor of his Grub-Street *persona* in *A Tale of a Tub* by a corresponding structural and stylistic incoherence, the humanist finds
it easy to believe that when a man has himself in order, when
he has become a proficient at what Adam Smith calls 'self-
command', the man's writing will naturally reflect his internal
clarity and coherence. Good writing becomes thus, as it does to
the Pope of the *Epistle to Dr. Arbuthnot* or *The Dunciad,* an
index of moral virtue.

(7) The humanist is convinced that man's primary obligation is the strenuous determination of moral questions; he thus
believes that inquiries into the technical operation of the external world ('science') constitute not only distinctly secondary
but even irrelevant and perhaps dangerous activities. Johnson
stresses the primacy of man's moral nature by insisting, in the
Life of Milton, that 'We are perpetually moralists, but we are

geometricians only by chance'. That is, our nature in itself does not oblige us to function as geometricians—or patriots, or Tories, or consumers, or other kinds of exclusive specialists—but it does oblige us to function as moral adjudicators. The English humanist is thus obsessed by ethical questions. He sees man not primarily as a maker or even as a knower, but rather as a moral actor. Prescription rather than description is the humanist's business. We may almost define a humanist as one who finds it impossible to leave serious moral subjects alone. This is why Thomas Gray, although a conservative, is not really a humanist; this is why Horace Walpole, for all his interest in human nature, is not a humanist. The humanist takes an almost sensual pleasure in the image of moral virtue, especially the image of self-restraint triumphing over temptation, and his pleasure in this spectacle is similar to the pleasure taken by the Epicurean in images of erotic or gustatory delights. Only occasionally does the humanist's moral impulse decline into the moralistic, as it does in Swift's *A Project for the Advancement of Religion and the Reformation of Manners* (1709), which anticipates the tone of the mere Victorian 'moralist' in its exhortation to the Queen to put down drunkenness, deep play, and vice.

(8) The humanist is convinced that human nature, for all its potential dignity, is irremediably flawed and corrupt at the core. If the eighteenth-century humanist is oriented towards the Christian tradition, he will often conceive of this flaw by means of the myth of the Fall of Man. If the humanist's Christian impulse is weak or non-existent, he will often conceive of this flaw by means of the myth of the Decay of Nature. But whatever mythology or imagery he invokes, he will generally assume that man's dignity arises in part from his very perception of the human flaw. Self-distrust thus becomes a central humanist experience, and satire becomes a central literary action. The awareness which prompts Swift to satirize the self-sufficient spider in *The Battle of the Books* is identical with that which moves Johnson to assert that 'Man's chief merit consists in resisting the impulses of his nature'. Frances Reynolds, who records this remark of Johnson's, is careful to explain just what he means: 'Not what may be call'd his second Nature, evil

habits, &c., but his Nature originally corrupted from the fall'
(*JM*, ii, 285).

(9) The humanist tends to assume that the world of physical
nature is morally neutral and thus largely irrelevant to man's
actual—that is, his moral—existence. Whether 'scenery' is conceived of as static or as organic, the humanist images man as
positioned against it rather than inside it. In some ways, indeed,
as can be seen in the tenth and eleventh books of *Paradise Lost,*
physical nature participates in man's corruption. To the humanist, therefore, physical nature can 'teach' man little that is
morally useful; if it ever does speak to man, it speaks not to his
moral centre. When Bolingbroke in a primitivist mood asserted
that nature is man's nature, Burke rejoined vigorously with
'Art is man's nature'. The moral world of man and the natural
world of plants and trees and oceans are perpetually sundered
by the unblinkable fact that man possesses an imagination which,
willy nilly, persists in functioning by means of moral images.

(10) The humanist tends to be suspicious of theories of
government or human nature which appear to scant the experienced facts of man's mysterious complexity. To the humanist, man's most dangerous temptation is his lust to conceive
of his nature as simpler than it is. And this temptation often
prompts man to conceive of his nature, erroneously, as entirely
'rational'. Perhaps the Gulliver of the end of the Fourth Voyage
can serve as a case study of this anti-humanist syndrome. The
humanist insists on the element of the unpredictable in man.
Thus Johnson on 'social science' and conceptions of history based
on simplistic cause-and effect premises:

> It seems to be almost the universal errour of historians to suppose it
> politically, as it is physically true, that every effect has a proportionate
> cause. In the inanimate action of matter upon matter, the motion pro-
> duced can be but equal to the force of the moving power; but the
> operations of life, whether private or publick, admit no such laws. The
> caprices of voluntary agents laugh at calculation.
>
> (*Thoughts on the Late Transactions respecting Falkland's Islands*)

(11) The humanist assumes that, because of man's flaw and
his consequent need of redemptive assistance, man's relation to

literature and art is primarily moral and only secondarily aesthetic. The eighteenth-century humanist is given to uttering and re-uttering the classical commonplace that the office of literature is to teach, but to teach through the agency of aesthetic delight. Johnson on pastoral poetry is typical: a man will not, he asserts, 'after the perusal of thousands [of pastorals], find his knowledge enlarged with a single view of nature not produced before, or his imagination amused with any new application of those views to moral purposes' (*Rambler* 35). Only if man were not flawed could the humanist justify a literary aesthetic of pure pleasure.

(12) Finally, the humanist believes that man is absolutely unique as a species. This is the belief from which all the others seem to depend. The humanist scorns analogies between men and dogs, even though both salivate similarly; between men and lower animals, even though both breed similarly; and between men and insects, even though both tend to organize societies similarly. The humanist suspicion of analogies between men and other creatures assumes that there is no help for man but within himself, within his own moral universe imaginatively conceived, in which unremitting self-conscious volition is the active principle. Despite his devotion, as we shall see, to received modes of metaphor as a technique of expression, the humanist tends to distrust analogy as a mode of thought. As Thomas R. Edwards observes in connexion with Pope's *Essay on Man,* 'Analogy is not a solution; to know something by analogy is painfully unlike knowing it by experience'.[2] To the humanist, analogy may be conceived of as imposing a 'system' on the will, which, in the humanist view of things, must be regarded as entirely free. Swift's mockery throughout *A Tale of a Tub* of the intellectual technique of ready and complacent analogy is suggestive of one major thrust of the whole eighteenth-century humanist enterprise. Man's dignity depends on his belief that he has a free power of choice sufficient to overcome the apparent determinisms of environment and physical nature, for as Joseph Wood Krutch and other humanistic revivalists have argued in our own time, human nature is an 'independent reality, not merely a product'.[3] If man cannot attain an improved physical

circumstance through the operation of his will, he does always have it in his power to will a different attitude toward his circumstance. 'Acceptance', and thus 'happiness'—that primary eighteenth-century objective—is always within his own power. This is the eighteenth-century humanistic version of the conclusion of Socrates in the *Apology* that 'no evil can happen to a good man, either in life or after death'.

This, then, is the general humanist code. As Krutch sums up the definition:

> ... a humanist is anyone who rejects the attempt to describe or account for man wholly on the basis of physics, chemistry, and animal behavior. He is anyone who believes that will, reason, and purpose are real and significant; that value and justice are aspects of a reality called good and evil and rest upon some foundation other than custom; that consciousness is so far from being a mere epiphenomenon that it is the most tremendous of actualities; that the unmeasurable may be significant; or, to sum it all up, that those human realities which sometimes seem to exist only in the human mind are the perceptions rather than merely the creations, of that mind.[4]

It seems clear that the humanist code constitutes a more or less diminished and secularized version of the Christian humanism of the English Renaissance, although the Christian element in eighteenth-century humanism is very hard to measure. Swift, for example, in his sermon on *The Excellency of Christianity,* directed to unsophisticated listeners, rejects pagan wisdom as gravely inferior to Christian revelation. And yet, in his *Letter to a Young Gentleman Lately Entered into Holy Orders,* where, playing the role of a wise and experienced person of quality, he is at pains to warn his addressee against a stylish contempt of classical learning, he appears to value ancient ethics very highly indeed. He says 'nothing can justly be laid to the Charge of the [ancient] Philosophers further, than that they were ignorant of certain Facts which happened long after their Death. But I am deceived, if a better Comment could be any where collected upon the moral Part of the Gospel, than from the Writings of those excellent Men'.

Except in Johnson and perhaps in Swift, the proportion of

Christianity to classical wisdom in eighteenth-century humanism is roughly what it is in the following account in the *Gentleman's Magazine* for 1733 of the funeral of Mr. John Underwood,
of Whittlesea, in Cambridgeshire:

the six gentlemen who followed [the coffin] to the grave sang the last
stanza of the 20th Ode of the second book of Horace. No bell was
tolled, no one invited but the six gentlemen, and no relation followed
his corpse; the coffin was painted green, and he laid in it with all his
clothes on. Under his head was placed Sanadon's Horace, at his feet
Bentley's Milton; in his right hand a small Greek Testament . . .; in his
left hand a little edition of Horace . . . and Bentley's Horace, *sub podice*.
After the ceremony was over, they went back to his house, where his
sister had provided a cold supper; the cloth being taken away, the
gentlemen sang the 31st Ode of the first book of Horace, drank a chearful glass, and went home about eight.

One interesting thing about Augustan humanism is that it may
make as little use of a religious dimension as John Underwood
and his friends, and yet still locate its absolutes as readily as the
Christian humanism of the Renaissance. And what Herschel
Baker has said of Erasmus and the Northern humanists is true of
the Augustan humanists as well: 'they were not original thinkers . . . Erasmus and his friends hankered for what was safe
and settled: . . . the Faustus-mood of radical individualism
passed them by'.[5] An entry made by the eight-year-old Samuel
Johnson in his diary seems to symbolize the persistence of this
strain of Renaissance humanism into a new age: proudly
recording the accession of a new book, the boy Johnson writes,
'I got an English Erasmus'. The illustrative citations in Johnson's *Dictionary* attest abundantly to Johnson's devotion to the
Renaissance English humanists, especially Richard Hooker,
whose *Laws of Ecclesiastical Polity* Johnson knew intimately.
When the eighteenth-century humanist looked back to the preceding century, he was likely to be more impressed by the judi-
ciousness of a Hooker or the seriousness of a Milton than by the
passion of a Marlowe or even a Donne. The Renaissance
admired by the eighteenth-century humanist was likely to be a
serious world of intellectual order and 'correspondences' rather

than a gay theatre of exhuberant individualism or neo-pagan hedonism.

Because it is characteristic of humanism to look at the central rather than the peripheral, it will not surprise us that the main seventeenth-century literary 'sources' of Augustan humanism appear to be *Hamlet, King Lear,* and *Paradise Lost.* And what seems to excite the Augustan humanist in these works is the tenderness and penetration of their version of man's condition as a unique creation in a largely foreign world of mere organic vitality. It is passages like those in *Hamlet* which stress man's obligations as man that the humanist recalls most vividly: Hamlet's observation on the haste of Gertrude's second marriage, for example,

> O God! a beast that wants discourse of reason
> Would have mourn'd longer;
>
> (I, ii, 150–1)

or his recollection of his father:

> *Horatio.* I saw him once. He was a goodly King.
> *Hamlet.* He was a man, take him for all in all.
>   I shall not look upon his like again.
>
> (I, ii, 186–8)

or his scheme of the ideal internal psychic hierarchy in which man's will is liberated from mechanism and released for its glorious work of choice and command; as Hamlet tells Horatio,

> blest are those
> Whose blood and judgment are so well commingled
> That they are not a pipe for Fortune's finger
> To sound what stop she please. Give me that man
> That is not passion's slave, and I will wear
> Him in my heart's core, ay, in my heart of heart
> As I do thee.
>
> (III, ii, 73–79)

To see Johnson in 1775 playing an aging Hamlet to Boswell's

recidivist Horatio is to appreciate the power of such scenes to persist deep in the conservative consciousness throughout the eighteenth century. Johnson writes to Boswell, 'Never, my dear Sir, do you take it into your head that I do not love you; you may settle yourself in full confidence of my love and my esteem; I love you as a kind man, I value you as a worthy man, and hope in time to reverence you as a man of exemplary piety. I hold you as Hamlet has it, "in my heart of heart" . . .' (*LSJ,* ii, 83) . The allusion here just sufficiently hints Boswell's obligations to liberate himself from his slavery to passion and 'Fortune'. If we know Boswell, we are fully aware that too often he was unable to follow Johnson's moral injunctions. But even in the midst of his backslidings Boswell himself recovers *Hamlet* for his own purposes. As readers of his *London Journal* (1763) will recall, the actress Louisa Lewis finally consents to grant Boswell the ultimate favour. But Boswell is destined for an ironic fall from felicity. Eight days after the triumphal night which has brought him his happiness he perceives that he has been severely poxed. 'Too, too plain was Signor Gonorrhea', he laments in his journal. Since he is convinced that Louisa has been aware of her condition all along, he conceives that a manly confrontation is in order, but he is momentarily perplexed about the way it should be conducted. What if he should appear ridiculous before Louisa? One way of appearing ridiculous, he imagines, would be to upbraid her with an hysterical severity: 'Enraged at the perfidy of Louisa', he writes, 'I was resolved to go and upbraid her most severely; but this I thought was not acting with dignity enough.' Momentarily baffled in his search for a literary model for the forthcoming 'scene', he consults his memory and takes a hint from his recollection of Hamlet's 'I will speak daggers to her, but use none'. Now firm in his sense of role, Boswell proceeds: 'So I would talk to her cooly and make her feel her own unworthiness'.

I then went to Louisa. With excellent address did I carry on this interview, as the following scene, I trust, will make appear. . . .

BOSWELL. Do you know that I have been very unhappy since I last saw you?

LOUISA. How so, Sir?

BOSWELL. Why, I am afraid that you don't love me so well, nor have such a regard for me, as I thought you had.

LOUISA. Nay, dear Sir! (Seeming unconcerned.)

BOSWELL. Pray, Madam, have I no reason?

LOUISA. No, indeed, Sir, you have not.

BOSWELL. Have I no reason, Madam? Pray think.

LOUISA. Sir!

The dramatic situation here, that of the abused and deceived youth reproaching the guilty older woman in her closet; the formal tone; the youth's archness in posing his questions; the rapid, almost stichomythic repetitions in lines of similar length near the end of the interchange—these particulars all suggest *Hamlet* IV, iii, where, at the beginning of the closet scene, Hamlet confronts Gertrude and proceeds to 'set . . . up a glass / Where you shall see the inmost part of you'. Boswell's pleasure in playing Hamlet here must have been enhanced by knowing that Louisa herself had played Gertrude in a production of *Hamlet* at Covent Garden the year before (*LJ*, 84–85, n. 4).

If *Hamlet* permeates the Augustan humanist consciousness because of its dramatization of man's offices as man, *King Lear* is laid under contribution, especially by Burke, because of its continuous definition of man as non-animal and non-mechanical, a definition conducted through imagery as often as through literal precept or dramatic situation. The principle of hierarchy as natural to the human imagination is insisted upon in *King Lear*. As the fool tells the King,

> When thou clovest thy crown i' the middle and gav'st away both parts, thou bor'st thine ass on thy back o'er the dirt.
>
> (I, iv, 174–6)

The imagery of *King Lear* asserts likewise that, as Swift seems to recollect in *A Tale of a Tub,* a man is not to be made by his tailor; and it insists throughout that a man is not in his nature analagous with a rat, a vulture, a dog, a goose, a wolf, an owl, a bear, a lion, a hog, a fox, a pelican, a worm, a horse, or a fly. Surrounded and attacked, as he imagines, by the savage brutes of Jacobinism, and abandoned now by his colleagues of the

Foxite persuasion, Burke astonishes the House of Commons in the spring of 1791 by quoting Lear's puzzled observation on his own altered condition:

> The little dogs and all,
> Tray, Blanch, and Sweetheart, see, they bark at me.
>
> (III, vi, 65–66)

And as we shall see, the heart of Burke's impassioned argument against the oversimplified version of man embraced by the Jacobins derives both substance and figure from Lear's.

> Allow not nature more than nature needs,
> Man's life is cheap as beasts'.
>
> (II, iv, 269–70)

Augustan memories of *Hamlet* and *King Lear* thus provide a multitude of general humanist motifs and images which are recovered and exploited by conservatives throughout the eighteenth century. But of *Paradise Lost* the main Augustan use can be more precisely located. Although the Augustan humanist values highly the Miltonic myths of human frailty and of both external and psychological hierarchy, his moral imagination luxuriates especially in recalling one particular scene. The humanist mind in the eighteenth century returns again and again to Book VIII of *Paradise Lost* and to the dialogue between Raphael and Adam about what we would call 'science'. As the 'Argument' to Book VIII sums it up: 'Adam inquires concerning celestial Motions, is doubtfully answer'd, and exhorted to search rather things more worthy of knowledge'. In the preceding book, Raphael, narrating to Adam the events of Creation, has concluded by inviting Adam to inquire further about his condition:

> if else thou seek'st
> Aught, not surpassing human measure, say.
>
> (639–40)

As Book VIII opens, Adam humbly accepts Raphael's invitation and ventures to wonder why God has contrived so many

visible planets and stars, many of them apparently more impressive than Earth. Raphael first replies—humanistically—that

> Great
> Or Bright infers not Excellence,
>
> (90–91)

and goes on to suggest that the pursuit of virtue and wisdom, rather than the quest for astronomical knowledge, is the primary duty incumbent upon such a creature as man:

> be lowly wise:
> Think only what concerns thee and thy being;
> Dream not of other Worlds. . . .
>
> (173–5)

Adam, apparently 'clear'd of doubt', now becomes the spokesman of Milton's point:

> not to know at large of things remote
> From use, obscure and subtle, but to know
> That which before us lies in daily life,
> Is the prime Wisdom.
>
> (191–4)

Adam's use of the term 'remote' here reminds us of the Swiftian exploitation of this motif in the Third Voyage of *Gulliver's Travels*, where the Laputians, like creatures who have chosen not to hear Raphael's warning, have elected the quantitative life of stargazing and mathematics and as a result have lost the use of both their memories and their senses. Pope, in the *Essay on Man*, treats the same Miltonic point, speaking like a kind of sardonic Raphael, skilled in sarcasm, to the reader's naive Adam:

> Go, wond'rous creature! mount where Science guides,
> Go, measure earth, weigh air, and state the tides;
> Instruct the planets in what orbs to run,
> Correct old Time, and regulate the Sun; . . .

> Go, teach Eternal Wisdom how to rule—
> Then drop into thyself, and be a fool!
>
> (II, 19–22; 29–30)

And we think also of the astronomer in *Rasselas,* whose researches have served only to disorder his intellect to the point where *post hoc* and *propter hoc* have become hopelessly confused.

Modern readers of Johnson's *Life of Milton* easily remember Johnson's interesting hostility to Milton's politics and his curious pietistic reaction to *Lycidas*. But they remember less readily something which is probably more important, Johnson's extraordinary admiration for the wisdom embodied in the anti-scientific colloquy between Raphael and Adam. It would be hard to find an occasion where Johnson, who often rebuked Mrs. Thrale for her bad habit of loose and irresponsible commendation, paid higher praise to anything merely human; he writes, 'Raphael's reproof to Adam's curiosity after the planetary motions, with the answer returned by Adam, may be confidently opposed to any rule of life which any poet has delivered'. Johnson's rare hyperboles and absolutes here—'any rule of life which any poet has delivered'—are almost shocking. And they become the more startling when we recall Johnson's final estimate of *Paradise Lost*, which he pronounces 'not the greatest of heroic poems, only because it is not the first'. It is, in short, second only to the *Iliad,* and superior to the *Odyssey,* the *Aenid,* and the epics of the Italian Renaissance.

This Johnsonian low assessment of scientific knowledge would seem to indicate more accurately his real feelings on the subject than any inferences drawn from his trivial interest in home-made chemical experiments, the condition of dried orange peelings, or the rate of growth of his own fingernails. Commenting on Milton's ideal scheme of education, Johnson further observes:

the truth is, that the knowledge of external nature, and the science which that knowledge requires or includes, are not the great or the frequent business of the human mind. Whether we provide for action or conversation, whether we wish to be useful or pleasing, the first

requisite is the religious and moral knowledge of right and wrong; the next is an acquaintance with the history of mankind, and with those examples which may be said to embody truth, and prove by events the reasonableness of opinions. Prudence and justice are virtues and excellencies of all times and of all places.

What all this is leading up to is the famous next sentence about our being moralists essentially but geometricians only adventitiously. And he proceeds, reminding us of the humanist prayer of Erasmus, '*Sancte Socrates, ora pro nobis*': 'I have Socrates on my side. It was his labour to turn philosophy from the study of nature to speculations upon life; but the innovators whom I oppose are turning off attention from life to nature. They seem to think, that we are placed here to watch the growth of plants, or the motions of the stars. Socrates was rather of opinion, that what we had to learn was, how to do good, and avoid evil.'

Johnson seems never to lose contact with the Raphael-Adam conversation; he treats it in *Rambler* 180 and returns to it in *Adventurer* 107. And in his admiration for the wisdom of Milton's Book VIII he is in distinguished company. John Locke himself, in his *Essay Concerning Human Understanding* (1690), that book which attained an authority almost scriptural during the eighteenth century, puts it this way: 'Our business here is not to know all things, but those which concern our conduct' (I, i, 6). And later in the *Essay* Locke reveals the way his empiricism lends support quite naturally to the humanist tradition in learning:

since our faculties are not fitted to penetrate into the internal fabric and real essence of bodies ..., it will become us ... to employ those faculties we have about what they are most adapted to, and follow the direction of nature, where it seems to point us out the way. For it is rational to conclude that our proper employment lies in those inquiries, and in that sort of knowledge which is most suited to our natural capacities, and carries in it our greatest interest, i.e. the condition of our eternal estate. Hence I think I may conclude, that *morality* is *the proper science and business of mankind in general.*

(IV, xii, 11)

Milton's and Locke's point is echoed frequently by Burke, who scorns the chemists and mathematicians who constitute the revolutionary National Assembly because, as he says, '*Hominem non sapiunt*'; the contrivers of the new French system of parliamentary representation, he writes,

have much, but bad, metaphysics; much, but bad, geometry; much, but false, proportionate arithmetic. . . . It is remarkable, that in a great arrangement of mankind [i.e. a rearrangement into new, geometrically shaped departments, communes, and cantons], not one reference whatsoever is to be found to any thing moral or any thing politic; nothing that relates to the concerns, the passions, the interests of men.

And Gibbon reacts similarly to the implications of the new science. In his *Autobiography* he recalls his youthful experience with the study of mathematics and remembers the delight with which he turned away from it; 'nor can I lament', he says, 'that I desisted before my mind was hardened by the habit of rigid demonstration, so destructive of the finer feelings of moral evidence, which must, however, determine the actions and opinions of our lives'. Gibbon's emphasis here on the 'finer feelings' and on 'moral evidence' resembles Burke's later stress on the moral incapacity of the mere scientist. He writes in his *Letter to a Noble Lord*: 'The geometricians and the chemists bring, the one from the dry bones of their diagrams, and the other from the soot of their furnaces, dispositions that make them worse than indifferent about those feelings and habitudes which are the supports of the moral world.'

The insistence that man is made not for inquiry into 'celestial motions' but for moral decision is thus a central literary action of the Augustan humanists, who, brought up as they were on *Paradise Lost* and *An Essay Concerning Human Understanding*, would be wholly astonished by something like C. P. Snow's recent suggestion in *The Two Cultures and the Scientific Revolution* that not to know the second law of thermodynamics is as grave an intellectual want as not to be steeped in a given work of traditional—that is, moral—literature. The distance we have

drifted from the world of the Augustan humanists can be gauged by the fervour with which Snow's formulation has been embraced by many 'humanists' in American and British universities. Perhaps we catch an echo of Samuel Johnson's conversational tone of voice in F. R. Leavis's vigorous characterization of Snow: 'he is intellectually as undistinguished as it is possible to be'.[6]

The dependence of the Augustan humanists on Shakespearian and Miltonic figures and motifs bespeaks their close alliance with a conservative literary past, a literary past which is perhaps as justly termed 'Renaissance' as 'classical'. Their cause was beginning to look thoroughly old-fashioned even by the early years of the eighteenth century, and by Johnson's time the English humanist found it quite natural to conceive of himself as a small fortified city besieged by Goths.

Modern scholars and critics are perceiving increasingly that the Augustan humanists, far from being 'representative' of the general tendencies of their time, constitute actually an intensely anachronistic and reactionary response to the eighteenth century. Their rhetorical careers conduct a more or less constant warfare with the 'official' assumptions of their age, assumptions held by most of their contemporaries. It is certainly true that Samuel Johnson enjoyed arguing for the fun of it, but it is also true that he had plenty to argue about; his recorded conversation indicates how frequently he found it necessary to oppose the progressivist or sentimental truisms of his own time: 'The woman's a whore, and there's an end on't!' Joseph Wood Krutch is one who had perceived the reliance of Augustan humanism on seventeenth-century habits of thought and feeling. Commenting on Johnson's contrast between man's roles as moralist and geometrician, he observes that 'When Johnson wrote that passage he was defending what was already beginning to look like a lost cause'.[7] Earl R. Wasserman likewise has perceived that 'Pope's mind, like Swift's, was the product of a body of learning that was fading, or had already faded, by the end of the seventeenth century. To this degree, Pope and Swift, like Milton earlier, were anachronisms . . .' .[8] And Thomas R. Edwards, explicating Pope's moral and economic notions in the *Epistle to Bathurst,* reminds us that in his own time Pope's posi-

tion was 'ultraconservative, appealing to an aristocratic ethic, firmly rooted in classical and medieval traditions of conduct, which by the 1730's had become obsolete except as a literary ideal'.[9] Ezra Pound, perhaps pre-eminent among twentieth-century readers of literature, is another who has apprehended Johnson's profound dislocation from his own times; Pound says of Johnson that he is ' "fuori del mondo", living in the seventeenth century, so far as Europe is concerned'.[10]

The vigour of the assertion and embodiment of seventeenth-century ideas by the eighteenth-century humanists is a measure of their severe moral discomfort in a world rapidly turning 'modern' all about them. Indeed, the power and, in Burke especially, the fury of the Augustan humanist expression suggests ideas of actual wartime conditions. And the enemies are fairly clear: they are the mechanism, relativism, and 'Rationalism' ascribed to the influence of Hobbes and Descartes; the new system of finance capitalism, whose 'bubbles' can be observed bursting through the eighteenth century; the 'new science', especially in its role as midwife to the new industrialism; the new sentimentality attributed to Shaftesbury and Hutcheson; the newly sanctified commercial and acquisitive ethic, visible not merely in Grub Street and the City, but, to Pope's and Swift's horror, in Westminister and the West End as well; the new conception of art as an end-product of self-expression, a conception issuing from the pleasing premise—among others—that man is by instinct virtuous and that he comes equipped with an inborn 'moral sense'; the new lower-middle-class prudential religious 'enthusiasm', with its built-in threat to authority and traditional usages; and what can be called the new utopian flippancy in works like Soame Jenyn's *A Free Inquiry into the Nature and Origin of Evil* (1757). The continued resuscitation of Renaissance moral ideas is the Augustan humanists' response to what Edwards has seen as 'the breakdown of the public images of heroism and piety in the politics of the seventeenth century'.[11]

It is characteristic of the humanist attitude, wherever in history we encounter it, that it relishes the opportunity to make large and clear choices. The humanist attitude, indeed, is as

easily defined by its rejections as by its acceptances. Geoffrey Scott, discoursing on classical architecture, sees a similar sort of 'great rejections' at the heart of the humanist architectural enterprise: 'Great architecture, like great character, has been achieved not by a too inclusive grasp at all values, but by a supreme realisation of a few. In art, as in life, the chief problem is a right choice of sacrifices. In life, and in the arts, civilisation blends a group of compatible values into some kind of sustained and satisfying pattern, for the sake of which it requires great rejections'.[12]

Once we perceive the fundamental unity of the ethical tradition articulated by Swift and Pope and transmitted to Johnson and Reynolds, to Gibbon, and finally to Burke, we are in a position to measure its 'great rejection' of what is sometimes thought of as 'the eighteenth century'. Against the humanist tradition running from Swift to Burke we must place the optimistic tradition bounded on one end by Defoe and on the other by Burns and Blake, and including writers like Addison and Steele, James Thomson, Samuel Richardson, Edward Young, Robert Blair, Mark Akenside, William Shenstone, Oliver Goldsmith, Thomas Chatterton, and William Cowper. This other tradition, although it may draw some strength from classical literature, tends to operate as if the classics are largely irrelevant to the modern experience; regardless of its occasional quarrels with industrialism, it tends to draw its real strength from the new industrial and commercial evidence of the validity of the idea of progress. It is notable that the very few writers of the century whose infant minds escaped subjection to a severe course in classical literature are to be found in this group: it is here that we find Defoe, Chatterton, Burns, and Blake. The replacement of the classics by the new evangelical materials is happily expressed by Blake in his Preface to *Milton*: 'We do not want either Greek or Roman models if we are but just and true to our own Imaginations, those Worlds of Eternity in which we shall live forever, in Jesus our Lord'. This other tradition is generally friendly to religious evangelicism and often looks on the mercantile revolution with a feeling very like satisfaction. It feels delight rather than horror at the prospect of innovation and change. It takes pleasure in conceiving of man as a creature

who, far from being flawed by some sort of original defect, exhibits an almost unwavering 'goodness of heart'. Where the humanists are devoted to prescribing and proscribing, the spokesmen for the newer morality tend towards an amiable mitigation of the orthodox moral rigour. The difference between human life conceived as 'action' (as it is by Johnson) and human life conceived as 'behaviour' (as it is by Sterne) is one important point at issue between these two ethical and expressive traditions. When the non-humanist writer does aspire to the moral, he often deviates, like Edward Young or William Cowper, into the merely moralistic. We can see the opposition between humanist and 'modern' in the eighteenth century re-enacted in later literature if we juxtapose the tradition passed from Conrad and James to Fitzgerald and Faulkner against the tradition represented by, say, Steinbeck, Thornton Wilder, and the self-parodic Hemingway of *The Old Man and the Sea.*

One hallmark of the non-humanist tradition is the decay of satire in its hands. In Addison, for example, satire turns gentle and optimistic; frequently it softens to a sort of mild kidding, suggesting that human corruption is only skin-deep within a fundamentally benign and almost automatically redemptive new world of trade, compromise, and general benevolence. By contrast, the satire in Pope and Swift, even in works so apparently cheerful as *The Rape of the Lock* or the *Compleat Collection of Genteel and Ingenious Conversation,* suggests always the presence just off-stage of dark threats and of immitigable primeval dangers. But in works like Cowper's *Task* satire becomes increasingly conceived of as at best a waste of time and at worst an indication of bad taste:

> Disgust concealed
> Is oft-times proof of wisdom, when the fault
> Is obstinate, and cure beyond our reach.
>
> (III, 38–40)

One of Cowper's more significant transitions in *The Task,* a work in which transition can be said to be the primary subject-matter, is: 'But truce with censure'. This injunction can stand

almost as the motto of the new tradition as if proceeds systematically to abdicate ethical rigour and seriousness. We are already
light-years away from the moral universe of 'great rejections':
we have only to recall the conception of satire held in common
by Swift, Pope, and Johnson — 'O sacred Weapon! left for
Truth's defence'—to perceive the extremity of the collapse of
satire under the soft assaults of sentimentalism, mercantilism,
and egalitarianism.

Johnson's inability to take seriously benign characters from
Fielding's fictions like Squire Allworthy in *Tom Jones* and
Thomas Heartfree in *Jonathan Wild* suggests why we should
place a writer like Fielding just outside the humanist tradition.
Characters like these—and we can include as well the Reverend
Dr. Primrose, the saintly vicar of Wakefield—belong, as Johnson perceives, in romances rather than in novels: their appearance in novels, where they are surrounded by all the seductively
lifelike empirical data of actual contemporary experience, constitutes an ethically dangerous, sentimentalist falsification of the
conditions of life and choice. And William Blake's similar distance from the humanist centre can be measured by the degree
of his impulse towards philosophic monism. The humanistic
tradition happily accepts a dualistic conception of man, of
which Pope's related oppositions 'Wit' and 'Judgment',
'Passion' and 'Reason', help define the terms. The boundaries
between unequal entities, insisted upon by the humanists, it is
Blake's ambition to obliterate for the sake of energetic totality.
We end with witty, novel injunctions—Proverbs, it is true, of
Hell—like this:

Exuberance is Beauty.

Blake's interesting quarrel with Reynolds in the margins of
the first eight of the *Discourses on Art* also reveals his distance
from the humanist position. Reynold's sober, Lockean account
of the real as the humanist 'norm' of external objects Blake
confronts with this quasi-evangelistic remark suggestive of the
utterance of one of Swift's comical Puritans: 'Knowledge of
Ideal Beauty is not to be Acquired. It is Born with us. . . . The

Man who says that we have No Innate Ideas must be a Fool &
Knave, having No Con-Science or Innate Science.'

Although Blake's quarrel with Reynolds seems to be about
the validity of Locke's account of the mind, it is actually as
much about the humanist premise of the natural depravity of
human impulse. Here is an example of the sort of perpetual re-
enactment of seventeenth-century oppositions which we see
throughout the century. Here Blake takes the unwitting role of
Swift's hysteric spider in the *Battle of the Books* and plays out
the traditional quarrel with Reynolds's serene bee.

Douglas Bush has written of the Renaissance, 'The complex
literary and philosophic tendencies of the Renaissance can be
best understood if we regard the humanistic tradition as the
central road and the other more or less antagonistic movements
as departures from that road'.[13]

Although this view stacks the cards perhaps needlessly, there
is a sense in which it is applicable to eighteenth-century literary
history. Without necessarily insisting that the humanist tradition constitutes the pristine highway and the heterodox tradition
the dirty divagations, we can suggest that the contrast between
humanist orthodoxy and its opposition offers perhaps a more
meaningful way of sensing the shape of literary history than
the customary chronological opposition of one 'period' to another. This kind of contrast offers for contemplation perhaps
more important distinctions—moral rather than predominantly
technical—than the more traditional way of regarding the relation between the eighteenth century and its chronologically
neighbouring complexes. This kind of contrast throws into
relief the important opposition between the 'aristocratic orthodoxy'—the phrase is Bush's—of the line Hooker–Milton–Johnson–
Coleridge–Arnold–Eliot and the progressivist heterodoxy of
the line Bacon–Defoe–Benjamin Franklin–Darwin–John Dewey.
Seen in this way, the confrontation of these two traditions in
the eighteenth century becomes less an opposition between 'classicism' and 'romanticism' than a continuation clear through the
century of the old Renaissance battle of the Ancients and the
Moderns. Swift's quarrel with conventicle and Grub Street, his
satiric attack on innovators in the allied worlds of devotion and

discourse, is re-enacted eighty-six years later in Burke's assaults on Dr. Richard Price's tabernacle sedition and on the National Assembly's mechanical clichés about the Rights of Man. Both Swift's and Burke's battles are against the same enemy, a simple-minded Puritan utopianism which has seized the arguments of the seventeenth-century party of the Moderns and applied them, with a superficially persuasive admixture of the new sentimentalism, to the same old reality, a reality as complex and unmanageable as ever.

The case of James Boswell is instructive here. In his interesting psychic career we find projected with almost unique poignancy this confrontation of Ancient and Modern in the eighteenth century. Boswell is urged both backwards and forwards: he can be considered a highly representative man standing ill-at-ease between the two worlds, the world of medieval and Renaissance faith and heroism, on the one hand, and, on the other, the modern 'industrial' world of prudence, materialism, 'consumption', simple hedonism, and pragmatism. By his lust for a ripe and gaudy religious faith, and by his desire to conceive of himself as a feudal hero and to engage, thus, in meaningful symbolic actions, he betrays his loyalty to what he imagines as the old world. And by his frequent painful awareness of his own triviality and worthlessness, his desire to becomes less eccentric and better 'adjusted', he reveals his identification with the new. It is a very Renaissance Boswell who, upon taking his leave of Edinburgh for the infinitely more 'modern' and stylish London, writes in 1763: 'As I passed the Cross, the Ladies and chairmen bowed and seemed to say, "God prosper long our Noble Boswell".' The poignancy of Boswell's whole experience is suggested by the phrase '*seemed* to say'. What he is imitating in this action is, of course, the first line of the ballad of 'Chevy Chase', a poem which had been recommended to him as an instance of the noble by Addison in *Spectator* 70 and 74. The interesting thing is that the world of 'Chevy Chase'—a world in which one could croon 'God prosper long our noble King' without any consciousness of the character and person of George III—is the world of the fifteenth not the eighteenth century. In this way Boswell is like one

of our contemporaries, who, while caught up in the premises of the twentieth century, hunger to chat with Christopher Marlowe—imaged perhaps as Dylan Thomas—or to tote canteens across a decorative battlefield to Sir Philip Sidney. Boswell's consciousness of the conflict between his two worlds, the confrontation of these two implicit views of man's nature and possibility, is one of the causes not only of his neurosis but also of his unremitting—and highly productive—curiosity about the nature of Boswell as man. Underneath his lust for drink, popularity, and escape, underneath his quest for moments of crude sexual forgetfulness, his obsession is with the question, 'What is Boswell, and art Thou mindful of him?' To see him saying merely hours apart 'I have indeed a noble soul' and 'I am a miserable, sarcastical Scots dog' is to sense his tentative awareness of his plight. Much of what he was eternally searching for, in his grotesque attachments to Hume, Paoli, Burke, Reynolds, Rousseau, Voltaire, and Johnson, is a kind of large, rare Renaissance wisdom which, transmitted in the form of 'sincere' homilies and letters, could help him anchor himself in values other than the prudential and utilitarian official values of his time. In fact, it may not be entirely wrong to say that what he really wanted was to live in the age of Shakespeare and Hooker and Milton, for everything that he genuinely admires is there. His perpetual anxiety about the threat of determinism, his pathetic impulse to believe that his dignity—and that of his teachers—reposes squarely upon the absolute freedom of the will, indicates something of the force with which the humanist invitation extended itself to him. And although his approaches to a confirmed humanist position were erratic, we are touched and perhaps instructed to see that, for all his hopeless comedy and even farce, when he was most the humanist, even the humanist-*manqué*, he was the most admirable.

NOTES

[1] *The Dignity of Man: Studies in the Persistence of an Idea* (Cambridge, Mass., 1947), p. 270.

[2] *This Dark Estate: A Reading of Pope* (Berkeley and Los Angeles, 1963), p. 34.

[3] *Human Nature and the Human Condition* (New York, 1959), p. 170.

4 *Human Nature and the Human Condition,* p. 197.

5 *Dignity of Man,* p. 272.

6 *Two Cultures? The Significance of C. P. Snow* (New York, 1963), p. 28.

7 *Human Nature,* p. 200.

8 *Philological Quarterly, xi* (July 1962), 617.

9 *This Dark Estate,* p. 52.

10 *ABC of Reading* (Norfolk, Conn., 1951), p. 186.

11 *This Dark Estate,* p. 17.

12 *The Architecture of Humanism* (2nd ed.: London, 1924), p. 163.

13 *The Renaissance and English Humanism* (Toronto, 1939), p. 39.

KEY TO THE REFERENCES

The following abbreviations are used for references in the text:

BLJ: Boswell's Life of Johnson, ed. George Birkbeck Hill, rev. L. F. Powell (Oxford, 1934-50, 6 vols).

JM: Johnsonian Miscellanies, ed. George Birkbeck Hill (New York, 1897, 2 vols).

LJ: Boswell's London Journal: 1762-1763, ed. Frederick A. Pottle (New York, 1950).

LSJ: The Letters of Samuel Johnson, ed. R. W. Chapman (Oxford, 1952, 3 vols).

The Empirical Philosophy

ᒼᕬᕉ

MEYRICK CARRÉ

I

'The celebrated Lord Bacon struck out new light in an age of general ignorance and corruption, and prepared the way for those subsequent discoveries and advances in every branch of science which have rendered the last century so distinguished in the annals of time. Newton and Boyle pursued the track which he had marked out for unfolding the system of nature, whilst Locke applied the hints he had given, to the investigation and analysis of the human mind.' In such terms and in association with four great English names, a writer in the *Monthly Review* for April 1771 epitomized the achievements of thought during the age of enlightenment. The first motions of the modern phase, the period commanded by Bacon and Boyle, have been sketched; it remains to observe the later career of the new philosophy in England, and here the tutelary geniuses are indeed Locke and Newton; though we cannot accept the belief in the dependence of these philosophers upon Bacon. We have seen that before the close of the seventeenth century the main current of speculation was running in channels shaped by the new sciences of nature. And it was already animated by the impuse to introduce the experimental method of reasoning into moral subjects, into the comprehension of man's mind as well as of the world. In the year 1685 Newton achieved the masterly

From Meyrick Carré, Phases of Thought in England *(London: Oxford University Press, 1949), pp. 280–304.*

synthesis by which the immense and complex motions of the
solar system were deduced from a cardinal principle, the principle that every particle of matter attracts every other particle
with a force proportional to the product of its mass and inversely
proportional to the square of the distance between them. The
movement of bodies from the fall of a block of stone to the orbits
of the moon and the planets were brought together in one
mathematical design and accurate observations and measure-
ments, terrestrial and celestial, were found to corroborate the
theoretical deductions. The printing of the *Philosophiae Natu-
ralis Principia Mathematica* by the Royal Society in 1687 was
the culminating point of the labours of the society, and the triumphant vindication of the methods of the new philosophy.

In his preface to the *Essay concerning Human Understanding*,
published in 1690, John Locke described his inquiries as being
those of 'an under-labourer in clearing the ground a little' leaving the task of extending knowledge to 'a Boyle or a Sydenham',
'the great Huyghensius' and 'the incomparable Mr. Newton'.
The *Essay* was the most searching attempt of the age to render
explicit the main assumptions of the new outlook on experience.
Locke's investigations into human knowledge were qualified by
the close association that he had enjoyed at Oxford with the band
of experimental observers who worked there, and he himself
became a member of the Royal Society in 1668; the dominant
influence on his thought was that of Boyle. The *Essay* controlled the direction and procedure of subsequent speculation.
It rapidly became the standard text-book of general philosophy
and many abridgements of it were published in the eighteenth
century. It determined men's thinking for generations and all
the leading developments in the theory of experience flowed
from it.

The *Essay* formulated systematically much of the underlying conceptions of the natural philosophy of the seventeenth
century, but it gave a change of direction to ultimate inquiries
by stating the main problem in terms of knowing rather than
in terms of what is known. The main issue is confined to the
question of the extent and validity of human knowledge. This
diversion from metaphysical investigations to epistemological

problems is a tribute to the success of natural science and to its
independence of metaphysics. Holding before them the new
physics as standards of what can be known and as guides to
the way of attaining knowledge of anything, Locke and his
numerous disciples conceived their task to be that of examining
knowledge in the light of physical science. Philosophy in the
strict sense became a criticism of human abilities in order to
'see what objects our understandings were, or were not, fitted
to deal with'. But the inquiry was guided by the metaphysical
assumptions that had grown up with the new natural philosophy, and these were confidently accepted owing to the explicit
repudiation of metaphysical notions by the leaders of the new
science of matter. The new science had carried with it from
its birth, as we have seen, certain beliefs about knowledge and
reality; in England these beliefs sprang in part from the basic
dualism of mind and matter which had been the main working hypothesis of the new philosophy of nature, and in part
from the decided empirical qualities of English physics in
the seventeenth century. The general outline of the psycho-
physical dualism has been noticed in the previous chapter.
With differences in detail the Cartesian dichotomy had become
the settled background of the scientific view of things; it assumed a material universe of spatio-temporal relations facing
a world of thinking substances. The fabric of knowledge is
woven on the one hand of scientific realities described in
mathematical terms, on the other hand of qualities in which
the sentient organs of human beings are entangled, the qualities of colour, sound, taste, and smell. These qualities are
excluded from the domain of physical reality. The mind perceives itself and its ideas immediately, it knows material things
through the mediation of ideas. The ideas with which it is
occupied represent the true character of things so far as they
are concerned with the mechanical conceptions of Newtonian
physics; they distort it so far as they are concerned with the
sensory qualities of the world. From the experimental and
analytic character of natural philosophy there grew the tendency to seek the ultimate constituents of knowledge in simple
ideas, and these were conceived as mental effects of impressions

accepted from the spatio-temporal order. The governing norms of explanation are analysis, composition, and mechanical connexion. The primary units of knowledge are impressions or sensations. The philosophers of nature constructed the physical realm from the determined relations of moving corpuscles; the investigators of mind devoted themselves to fabricating knowledge and thought from sensory atoms united by natural laws. The system of knowledge depends upon a few laws of attraction between ideas, comparable to the laws that rule the behaviour of physical particles.

The explicit parallel assumed between the mental laws of association and the grand generalization of natural philosophy can be illustrated by utterances made at an early and at a later stage of this phase of speculation. Edmund Law, in a passage published in 1747, pronounced his conviction that the principle of association 'will not appear of lesser extent or influence in the Intellectual World than that of Gravity is found to be in the Natural'. And John Stuart Mill wrote in 1865 that the laws of association are to psychology what the law of gravitation is to astronomy.[1] The consequences of this theory of mental processes was that all the factors that are implied in the connexion and stability of the world of experience, all relations and metaphysical notions such as substance, causation, similarity, difference, time, space, were traced to the action of association. Since all knowledge has its source in the sequence and coexistence of ideas the mind possesses no knowledge of formal principles. It cannot treat conceptions that have arisen in the course of the integration of separate perceptions and ideas as though they had an independent origin and nature. The categories of substance and of causation, for example, are merely the recognition of the way in which sensations and the ideas that survive sensations occur in sequence or union with one another. And the sensationalist foundation of this method naturally supported nominalist theories of universals. Abstract terms are amalgamations of concrete particular references; they are rendered universal by convention. Concepts are words which by being substituted for selected elements of concrete ideas arrest

our attention on these elements. They refer to nothing apart from the concrete ideas.

Such are some of the capital positions of the philosophy that dominated speculation in England from the end of the seventeenth century to the latter portion of the nineteenth, from the writings of Boyle and of Locke to those of Bain and Spencer. Its logic reflects the methods of experimental science and it is interesting to observe how the successive theories of mental analysis echo developments in physical theory; Locke is influenced by the corpuscular doctrine, Hartley is affected by the discussions of his time on the nature of sound, Priestley carries over recent chemical principles to his psychology, Bain's view of mind is imbued with the physiological discoveries of his day. Our preliminary view of the classic position ignores many important differences among the procession of philosophies during this phase of our thought. All the components of the empirical outlook underwent development, the doctrine of the elements of experience, the theory of the association of ideas, the belief in the representative quality of ideas, the view of abstract ideas and the conclusions relating to the scope of metaphysical knowledge. During the earlier sections of the movement there were borne forward from the past many conceptions that consorted ill with the empirical standards that it asserted. Locke employed scholastic principles at important points of his argument, the notions of essence and of eminent causation, for example. And despite his destruction of beliefs in all classes of 'innate ideas' he upheld in several passages Cartesian and even Platonic views of knowledge. This rational intuition is especially prominent in the theological controversies which agitated the times of Pope and Swift. Orthodox defenders of the Church as well as the critics of revealed religion professed belief in certain infallible and universal dictates intuitively apprehended by all normal men. Reason could perceive by its own light the essential truths touching the being and character of God and the duties of men. Rational religion had always existed and the religion of the Gospel is the true original religion of reason and nature. By reason the theologians

meant the original light of truth that had been corrupted by the
Fall; by nature they meant the eternal laws of things and fundamental constitution of man's mental fabric. This rationalism
was accordingly composed of several strains. Much of it was
derived from the persistence of ancient propensities, Augustinian and Neo-Platonic idealism, and the Stoic conceptions of
common notions that had been recalled to life in the seventeenth century. But these dispositions mingle with recent
Cartesian and mathematical principles and with the dazzling
prospect of all-embracing natural law. Yet by the middle of
the eighteenth century the profession of natural religion founded
upon abstract reason was yielding to the current of empiricism
and scepticism. It became common to reject completely the
claims of self-evident reason in religion, and, like the fourteenth-
century thinkers, theologians turned to arguments from probability and from the external evidences of Christianity.

Let us now observe some of the principal moments in the
career of this system. We have to recall its first authoritative
formulation at the end of the seventeenth century and the
bearing of the grand advances in physical theory upon its
construction. We must touch on the strange conclusion to
which its doctrine was soon pressed, the conclusion that nothing
exists but ideas and spirits. The sceptical tendencies that
accompanied the empirical outlook from the beginning of its
course moved next to the front of the intellectual scene and they
were closely followed by applications of the empirical premises
that reduced mental activity to material operations controlled
by chemical laws. Of these disturbing applications it was the
doctrine that the human mind is material and determined that
raised the most serious concern in the eighteenth century.
Berkeley's thesis that the world is composed of sensations in
the mind was received with polite incredulity and had small
influence on the trend of reflection. And Hume's brilliant
exposure of the difficulties to which the initial assumptions of
the scientific doctrine of knowledge led was not fully appre-
ciated. His few important critics, such as Thomas Reid and,
later, Thomas Brown, themselves accepted some of the chief
principles of the theory which they attacked; a manifestation

of the hold that the classic theses had obtained over the minds of thoughtful men. Throughout the eighteenth century it was the *Essay* of Locke that dominated philosophical opinion. It was the bible of cultured discussion in metaphysical matters, and writers such as Reid and Josiah Tucker were severely admonished for venturing to question its teaching. Fresh conceptions derived from German thought began to penetrate philosophical debate early in the eighteenth century, but the main tide of English speculation returned with confidence to the principles of the eighteenth century.

The analysis of knowledge brought forward by Locke and his successors illustrates one of the recurrent tendencies of which the history of our thought gives abundant evidence. Their account of knowledge vividly recalls in many passages the descriptions of the nominalists of the fourteenth century. Their doctrine of signs, their view of judgement, their criticism of the postulates of causation and substance, often reproduce verbally the discussions of the Ockhamists; and the theological basis of Berkeley's philosophy resembles the emphasis placed by Ockham on the omnipotence of God. What they were attacking resembles also the Augustinian realism criticized by the terminists. But now the time was more favourable to the development, in association with these conceptions of knowledge, of a positivist outlook on experience. One strange voice was uplifted on behalf of 'the ancient philosophy that continued to the days of Mr. Cudworth'. But Lord Monboddo's *Ancient Metaphysics or the Science of Universals* in six quarto volumes was received with indifference by readers for whom the doctrine of intelligible forms had long been exploded.

II

In tracing the familiar outlines of the tradition we must begin with the two men who stand at its head, Isaac Newton and John Locke. Newton's work united on a fresh plane the experimental and mathematical logic of the proceeding period. He built upon the researches of Boyle and Barrow, of Flamsteed and Wallis, and upon the labours of the great natural philosophers of the Continent, such as Galileo and Huyghens. The

purpose of the experimental observations is to discover those characters in things that can be mathematically handled. Mathematical formulae are generalizations of the perceived facts. The ideal to be aimed at is to express experimental physics in mathematical form, 'but geometry is founded in mechanical practice'.[2] The conspicuous note of the method is its emphasis on perception. Newton insists constantly on the necessity for the experimental verification of hypotheses and mathematical calculations. In many passages he spurns the employment of hypotheses in physical inquiries, but by hypotheses he means speculations that cannot be brought to the test of perception and experiment. He refuses, for example, to indulge in theories concerning the real nature of gravitational attraction. He allows that the atoms that constitute the basis of matter are moved by 'certain active principles', but he immediately adds that these principles must not be understood as occult qualities, nor as specific forms, but as general laws of nature, that is to say, as descriptions of ways in which material bodies are found to behave. It is not the business of natural philosophy to discuss the metaphysical causes of these manifest operations. 'To derive two or three general Principles of Motion from Phaenomena, and afterwards to tell us how the Properties and Actions of all corporeal things follow from these manifest Principles, would be a very great step in Philosophy, though the Causes of those Principles were not yet discovered.'[3] Newton accomplished the great step. He succeeded in deriving the two or three general principles of motion from phenomena and in applying them to the elucidation of many aspects of the physical universe, from the rise and fall of the tides to the behaviour of light. His cardinal scientific discoveries and generalizations are not at present our concern. In relation to the new phase of speculation in England the interesting feature of his thought is its empirical quality. He was anxious to keep apart the sphere of metaphysics or general philosophy and that of science or natural philosophy. Natural philosophy treats only of secondary causes, not of the real or primary causes of phenomena.

This cautious attitude towards theories of reality encouraged the tendencies that had been characteristic of the new philosophy in England since the days of the Oxford meetings, and had determined the attitude of its leaders to the rational deductions of Descartes and of Hobbes. Under the authority of Newton the term hypothesis became applied, at the turn of the century, not only to the speculation of the Cartesians, but also to the principles of the schools; and forms and essences, genera and species are now frequently dismissed under the opprobrious name of hypothesis. Nevertheless, the sweeping span of the new mechanics of nature inevitably overshadowed general beliefs relating to the truth of things. And despite the avowed disconcern with metaphysics the Newtonian prospect of the universe carried forward to modern times a number of philosophical principles that had been acccpted by the natural thinkers of the previous age. It assumed the dualism of mind and matter. The world of mathematically determined matter is divided abruptly from the realm of mental life. It assumed that knowledge of the world is indirect. Immediate apprehension takes place at a point in the brain, to which point motions are conveyed by external and mathematical objects to sense-organs and nerves. We perceive only the distorted representations of things. This view of knowing presumes that sense qualities, such as colours and sounds, do not exist in the real objects that constitute the frame of nature. The awareness of colour, the green of grass, for example, is the result of vibrations propagated through the fibres of the optic nerve to the brain, and the shade that is perceived depends upon the size of the vibrations. In a word, sensory qualities are subjective. Those entities that are discussed by mathematical physics are the solely objective entities, extension, inertia, mass.

The revulsion from debates concerning ultimate causes and real natures that characterized the philosophers of the Royal Society is no less apparent in Locke's *Essay on Human Understand*. The spirit of the *Essay* is wholly in accord with the current distaste for vain speculation, and its purpose is to warn men from seeking to extend their inquiries beyond their

faculties and allowing their thoughts to wander into those depths where they can find no sure footing.[4] The philosophy of knowledge that springs from naturalism is anxious to impress a practical lesson upon men, that they should subordinate speculation to conduct. 'Our business here is not to know all things, but those which concern our conduct.' 'Morality is the proper science and business of mankind in general.' It was a lesson that the modern type of earnest Englishman was ready to embrace. The advice that it is futile to pursue questions which human understanding is unfitted to answer discouraged metaphysical inquiries in England and promoted the growing preference for moralization over speculation. It was the age of *Robinson Crusoe,* of the middle-class virtues of industry, thrift, sobriety, and caution.

But the attempt to proscribe the limits of knowledge involved many declarations of positive belief. The current definitions of matter are accepted, and approval is given to the corpuscularian theory. The Platonic or Cartesian features that had entered naturalism are carried into the new empirical structure. Locke related that he had been attracted to philosophy by the works of Descartes, and though he declared his disagreement with the Cartesian outlook, the presence of that outlook in the doctrines of the *Essay* is manifest.[5] The dichotomy that rules the Cartesian perspective is assumed throughout; the world of material extended things faces the world of immaterial mental substances. The mind is aware primarily of ideas, secondarily of material things and accordingly the representative view of consciousness, frequently expressed by the earlier English physicists, is adopted. Material substances affect the mind by indirect impact, and the ideas so generated represent or correspond to the real qualities of objects. The qualities are faithfully represented in the case of the mechanical ideas, 'solidity, extension, figure, motion or rest, and number', while colour, sound, and other sensible ideas do not represent qualities in the material things as they are in themselves but are produced by the mechanical qualities in the mind. Locke followed his friend Boyle in naming these two classes of ideas primary and secondary. In neither class are we in direct contact with things; ' 'tis

evident that the mind knows not things immediately but only by the intervention of the ideas it has of them.'[6]

In this distinction the quantitative or mathematical view of things is taken for granted; in the object there is nothing in reality but the determined interaction of its minute parts. The new physics are assumed. But the Cartesian influence on the empirical view of knowledge appears most vitally in the ideal of knowledge that informs the *Essay*. Locke seeks, as Descartes sought, the ground of certainty; and the type of genuine knowledge he found where Descartes found it, in mathematics. The science of mathematics and especially the science of geometry, furnished the ideal form of knowledge in the light of which all other claims to knowledge were to be tested. Genuine knowledge consists in the intuition of irresistible truths, 'and this kind of knowledge is the clearest and most certain that human frailty is capable of'.[7] Demonstrative knowledge consists of a chain of necessary connexions between intuitive truths. The mathematical criterion of thought that had developed in association with the exploration of phenomena in the seventeenth century dominates the new theory of knowledge. The abstract modes and relations in which things appear are *aeternae veritates,* and the illustrations of necessary ideas in the *Essay* are drawn from arithmetic and geometry.

But this mathematical view of knowledge is set in an empirical frame. In accordance with the experimental and observational methods of Locke's friends the foreground of knowledge is occupied with data given by experience. Guided by the 'physiological' methods of analysis the new theory of thought seeks by 'a plain historical inquiry' the original, primary, and simple elements that provide the basis of experience. The original components of ideas are natural occurrences that underlie the processes of knowing as the material atoms underlie the processes of the physical world. These elementary constituents are 'simple ideas' of sensation and reflection, presenting the external and internal primary data of experience. From these elements complex ideas arise by combination, the combination being the work of mind which unites and separates simple ideas at will. This analysis of experience into elements and com-

pounds influenced the psychology and theory of knowledge in England for two hundred years; but acute critics in Locke's own day pointed out that he himself failed to preserve the distinction between simple and complex ideas, and that he allowed ideas to be given originally in complex as well as in simple modes. Nevertheless, the repudiation of all notions that are not derived from external and internal sensations is the cardinal doctrine of the *Essay*. The mind is a *tabula rasa* upon which the characters are first written by outer and inner sensations. 'In all that great extent wherein the mind wanders in those remote speculations it may seem to be elevated with, it stirs not one jot beyond those ideas which sense or reflection have offered for its contemplation.'[8] This inductive position leads to a conceptualist view of universals. Mental operations begin with particulars and particular ideas are taken as representative of all ideas of the same kind. Our knowledge is not knowledge of real universal species, for it is dependent upon sensory experience. The universals of natural philosophy do not exist apart from the mind; they are formed by the mind from observation of those phenomena that are found to 'go together'. We attain only the nominal essences of things, not their real essences. Subjective activity is especially present in mathematical reasoning. Mathematical ideas do not refer to existence, nor are they fundamental forms of reality apprehended by the pure intellect. They are creations of the mind, though they exhibit necessary relations between ideas. Thus, the empirical outlook of this theory of knowledge prevails over the Cartesian elements that are associated with it. Mathematical reasoning remains the criterion of knowledge, but owing to the sensory constitution of our minds it consists of abstractions. Certain knowledge lies in the perception of the relation between ideas, in 'the perception of the connexion and agreement, or disagreement and repugnancy, of any of our ideas'.[9] But these ideas are not the objects of the pure intellect according to the Augustinian and Cartesian outlook. They do not represent real objects; they comprise a necessary system of *ideas*.

The sensory origin of human thought severely restricts the extent of our knowledge of the external world. 'I am apt to doubt that how far soever human industry may advance useful and experimental philosophy in physical things, scientifical will still be out of our reach; because we want perfect and adequate ideas of those very bodies which are nearest to us and most under our command.'[10] The coarseness of our senses prevents us from perceiving the underlying corpuscular nature of things. We cannot penetrate to the essential connexions of qualities; we can only record coexistences, such as that yellow and dissolubility in Aqua Regia are found with the object we name gold. The sceptical trend of English philosophical thinking at the end of the seventeenth century is strikingly manifest in the famous discussion concerning substance. The idea of substance as that which supports the several qualities of things apprehended by the senses is a necessary idea. But our ideas are ideas of particular qualities and since substance is not a particular quality we can have no idea of it. Material substance is the unknown substratum of simple ideas. When we perceive a horse or a stone, we perceive a collection of several simple ideas, of simple qualities that we find are united in the thing called horse or stone. But we can have no clear idea of this unity.[11] And similar considerations apply to mental and spiritual substance; it is the unknown substratum of the 'operations which we experiment ourselves within'. It may for aught we know be material. Two certain items of knowledge are admitted. We possess indubitable knowledge of the existence of the self and from this knowledge we can demonstrate the existence of God. These two objects exhaust our knowledge of existence; the rest is belief or opinion. In all this the parallel with the fourteenth-century critics is striking.

During Locke's own lifetime the doctrines of the *Essay* were attacked and defended in a score of books. The attacks reveal the continued virility of older principles and also the lively fear of materialism. Locke's unlucky remark that for aught we know thought may be a property of material substance was singled out for warm condemnation and the debate on this issue

raged long after his death. It opened the way to the physical psychology of Hartley and Priestley. The most celebrated instance of conflict between traditional metaphysics and the new mode of thought occurred in the course of the long controversy between Bishop Stillingfleet and Locke. The Bishop maintains the realist, the Anselmian, position. There must be common natures or universals in things. The common nature man must reside in individual men and must be one and the same thing despite their individual differences. Otherwise there would be nothing but particulars and thought and language would be impossible. The universal essences of things must be the fundamental realities. Locke's account of abstract ideas is irreconcilable with the articles of the Trinity and Incarnation.[12] Thus the new nominalism was confronted with the same combination of realism and orthodoxy that had condemned the nominalism of Berengar in the eleventh century and of Ockham in the fourteenth. Locke was charged by many prelates with Hobbism, scepticism, and infidelity. But in his discussion of religious faith he led the tendency to rely upon the external signs and testimonies recorded in the Bible for evidence of Christian truth. This line of defence ran parallel to the appeal to natural reason in the eighteenth century, and a stream of books pursued the evidence for miracles and prophecies.[13]

The most striking outcome of the way of ideas was a stricter interpretation of its empiricism. A more consistent adherence to the sensory origins of experience quickly resulted in a radically mental philosophy of knowledge. This type of idealism merged with a current of thought based on principles utterly opposed to the new way of ideas. The Platonic school of thinkers had sharply distinguished sense-perception from reason. What we apprehend immediately are not physical objects but the sensations produced by them. When I touch a coal of fire it is not the fire I feel but the pain. I infer the fire by reason.[14] For the disciples of Malebranche the function of sensation was what it was for St. Augustine, to excite our minds to discern the intelligible ideas that are the grounds of things. Norris deemed Locke's way of ideas as 'lame and defective as any that can well be'. Yet certain thinkers derived from the study of Male-

branche and of Norris the conclusion which others were infer-
ring from the study of Locke, that the external world possesses
no existence apart from the mind. Arthur Collier is representative of this development. Relying on arguments drawn from
Descartes and the Platonists he shows that the exterior world
of objects assumed by the philosophers is otiose, for it is invisible and unknowable. It is 'the same thing to us as if there
were no such thing at all'. The belief in the external world is
full of contradictions. For example, philosophers tell us it is
both finite and infinite, divisible and indivisible, motionless and
moving. The antinomies cannot refer to anything actual. The
external world has no independent existence. The argument of
Clavis Universalis (1713) attracted little attention; it was not
aided by the scholastic definitions and divisions by which it was
advanced; such methods were now out of fashion. But similar
conclusions were being offered from an empirical point of departure. In 1710 George Berkeley of Trinity College, Dublin,
published his *Principles of Human Knowledge.* His inquiries
were animated by the old desire to vanquish the materialism
that lurked in the new philosophy of nature, for he felt, with
the Platonic school, that the belief in the mathematical substance of things was a danger to morality and revealed religion.
He hoped that his account of experience would be welcomed by
moralists, divines, politicians, and experimental philosophers,
and he saw his opponents in 'mathematicians and natural philosophers (I mean only the experimental gentlemen)'.[15] He offered
a view of knowledge in which a strict empiricism, nominalism,
and a contingent account of natural science are united with
Locke's way of ideas so as to recommend an immaterial system
of reality. All knowledge is knowledge of particulars. The
general relations and ideas assumed in natural philosophy,
matter, substance, cause, power, are usages of words by which
names are made to stand for similar groups of particular
phenomena. Terms such as force, gravity, and attraction refer
to nothing real, for they cannot be perceived. The notions
of absolute space and absolute motion are unintelligible and
the mathematical hypotheses employed in mechanics do not
designate genuine causes in the world. The only real causation

known to us is that which is experienced in conscious volition. Here Berkeley's speculations join the current of reflection that flowed from the philosophy of Malebranche and that had in turn descended from the teaching of Duns Scotus and William of Ockham. The sole motive power in nature is the will of God.

But the arresting doctrine that Berkeley proposes is that the objects of knowledge have no existence apart from the mind that knows them. Not only are the qualities that are apprehended by the senses, colours, sounds, textures, and tastes, nothing but sensations in the minds of the perceivers, but the qualities asserted by the Newtonians to form the real nature of the physical world are also mental sensations or ideas. Extensions, motion, substance, and figure are ideas, and no idea can exist outside the mind. For the same arguments which prove that the secondary qualities cannot exist apart from the mind prove that the primary qualities are in the same position. Extension, motion, and solidity are apprehended in the same manner as the sensory qualities; they vary according to the state of the perceiver, they are dependent upon the sense-organs, in short they cannot be conceived apart from the secondary and sensory qualities. The belief that knowledge is indirect since it is the result of sensations generated by effects proceeding from scientific realities is contemptuously dismissed. The world of real things is composed of items that are immediately perceived, and these are sensations in the mind. The order and objectivity of the world is contained in an infinite and omnipresent spirit. 'Men commonly believe that all things are known or perceived by God, because they believe the being of a God; whereas I, on the other side, immediately and necessarily conclude the being of a God, because all sensible things must be perceived by Him.'[16]

The immaterialism of Berkeley was widely discussed but few were prepared to defend it. Samuel Clarke, who was regarded as an oracle, refused to discuss a theory so inept, and most of the writers on first principles in the period sharply reject Berkeley's conclusions. Two later expressions of opinion concerning the Bishop of Cloyne's 'ingenious sophistry' may be taken as representative of the prevailing attitude. Abraham

Tucker refers to Berkeley's scheme 'that bodies subsist only in our idea, and are, or cease to be, according as our ideas fluctuate. So that when everybody goes out of the room, the tables, the chairs, the pictures they left behind, become instantly annihilated; and upon the company's return, become as instantly re-existent.'[17] James Beattie refutes the doctrine by a declamatory appeal to common sense. 'Where is the harm of my believing', he asks, 'that if I were to fall down younder precipice, and break my neck, I should be no more a man of this world? My neck, Sir, may be an idea to you, but to me it is a reality, and an important one too'; and much more to the same effect. He admits that he has known many who could not answer Berkeley's arguments, but he has never known one who believed his doctrine. It is contrary to common belief and leads to universal scepticism.[18]

These consequences of Locke's premisses were received with incredulity. More popular was a philosophy that, discarding all the intellectual notions that had been surreptitiously incorporated into the *Essay*, reached a position of sensory phenomenalism. The mind at birth is a *tabula rasa* and all knowledge enters through the five senses. Knowledge has no further origin than simple ideas of sensation which in respect to all conceptions of the mind may be compared to the first particles of matter of the natural philosophers in respect to compound substances. These simple sensations are immediate, direct, and clear. They are passively received by the mind and lodged in the imagination. There are no purely intellectual ideas as the Platonists assert. All of our notions of spiritual beings are drawn by analogy from the observation of material and sensory things. The teaching of Descartes and of Locke that we have direct knowledge of ourselves cannot be admitted; it is as true to say that the body is in the spirit as to say that the spirit is in the body. Such are the opinions of Peter Browne, Provost of Trinity College, Dublin, at the beginning of the century. Nominalism is necessarily a feature of such a philosophy. But the salient consequence that is derived from the principles of Locke and Newton is the extreme depreciation of the search for real causes. 'All the real true knowledge we have of Nature is

entirely experimental, insomuch, that how strange soever the assertion seems we may lay this down as the first fundamental inerring rule in Physics, that it is not within the compass of human understanding to assign a purely speculative reason for any one phaenomenon in Nature; as why grass is green or snow white? Why fire burns or cold congeals?' He defines a speculative reason as the true and immaterial efficient cause *a priori*. Observation and experiment show us that certain effects are produced, but any attempt to go beyond the facts is precarious.[19]

Other teachers reverted more nearly to the framework of Locke. But we have now to notice the most remarkable consequence of this philosophy. Before the middle of the eighteenth century the principles of Boyle, Locke, and Newton had been pressed to completely sceptical conclusions. No rational basis for human knowledge can be discovered, and we are obliged to believe by natural propensities of the mind the notions upon which common sense and science rely. The way to this sceptical conclusion was opened by Francis Hutcheson (d. 1746) whose theory of knowledge closely adhered to the scheme of Locke. He reproduces the familiar circle of doctrines. All the materials of thought are traced to external and internal sense; the mind compares the elements thus received, discerns their relations, and inquires into their causes.[20] *A priori* notions are explicitly rejected, though a number of non-sensory ideas are allowed to accompany simple sensations. Hutcheson upholds the distinction between primary scientific qualities and secondary sensible qualities; our ideas of sensible qualities resemble nothing in objects themselves, but our ideas of primary qualities, duration, number, extension, motion, and other mechanical factors, correspond to the real natures of things.[21] But he accepts the orthodox conception of the limits of our knowledge. We cannot grasp the essences of things. We are assured of the reality of the external world only by natural instinct; the substance of both body and mind is unknown. For the rest, Hutcheson's metaphysics reproduce the Cartesian division between mind and body and other features of the philosophy of naturalism. His strength lay in ethical and aesthetic investigations. But the significant note in his application of the naturalist philos-

ophy is the recourse to instinctive belief. He develops Locke's opinion relating to the ordinary confidence in the reality of the world of objects; it is a confidence founded upon the practical requirements of our nature, not upon theoretical conviction. Hutcheson refers this problem and other problems raised by philosophical inquiry to the natural propensities of man. We are led to embrace a number of important principles in dogmatic philosophy not through arguments and reasons drawn from the intelligible nature of things but rather by a kind of internal sense, habit, and impulse or instinct of nature.[22]

These suggestions had already been expressed by Hutcheson in earlier works on moral theory published in 1725 and 1728 and they had deeply influenced the strenuous reflections of a brilliant young man whose mind was possessed with ethical problems. David Hume's *Treatise of Human Nature, being an Attempt to introduce the Experimental Method of Reasoning into Moral Subjects,* appeared in three volumes in the years 1739 and 1740 when the author was twenty-eight. The doctrine of moral sense propounded by Shaftesbury and Hutcheson had led him to distrust accounts that attributed the source of moral activity and understanding to reason. He had rejected the rationalist theory of the Platonists, embraced also by Locke, 'which establishes eternal rational measures of right and wrong' and had become convinced that moral perception is a mode of feeling, 'so that when you pronounce any action or character to be vicious, you mean nothing, but that from the constitution of your nature you have a feeling or sentiment of blame from the contemplation of it'.[23] But could not the principle of natural propensity be ascribed equally to knowledge? Hume's attempt to apply it to the fundamental assumptions of knowledge constitutes part of his great contribution to English speculation. But the principle of natural instinct is associated with the standard positions of the experimental philosophy instituted by Locke, Newton, and Berkeley. The other side of Hume's signal achievement is the rigorous and comprehensive way in which he applies their conceptions. All perceptions of the human mind resolve themselves into impressions and ideas, the latter being faint images of the former; all our ideas are

particular and separate from one another; the bond of union between them is supplied by modes of mechanical association that display a kind of attraction comparable to the law of gravitational attraction in the physical world. From these bases he conducts a penetrating analysis of the beliefs that are presupposed in knowledge, the result of which is to show that the orderly connexion assumed to exist between particular items in the world of objects cannot be rationally proved. The belief in the continued existence of objects apart from our ideas 'is soon destroyed by the slightest philosophy, which teaches us, that nothing can ever be present to the mind but an image or perception' and these cannot give us any intimation of any thing beyond nor, since the impressions are separate, can they rationally provide us with the notion of continued existence. The idea of substance is nothing but a collection of simple ideas, the notion of the self no more than a bundle of different perceptions. Of all the relations upon which science is founded the central relation is that of causation or necessary connexion of phenomena. Hume submits the idea to a searching investigation. The rational principles upon which the scientific analysis of phenomena was presumed to rest, power, force, energy, efficacy, productive quality, and others are shown to represent nothing in reality. 'All our ideas are derived from, and represent impressions. We never have any impression that contains any power or efficacy. We never therefore have any idea of power.[24] Our notions of spirits and of the Deity are derived from impressions and cannot give us ideas of force or efficacy; the arguments of Malebranche and of the Cartesians must be dismissed. In the manner of Newton the ultimate force and efficacy of nature is declared to be unknown to us. After examining the natural belief he concludes that our universal confidence in the principle of necessary connexion arises from an internal propensity of the mind constituted by custom. A number of conjunctions between impressions produces through the natural forces of association a prevailing belief that the conjunctions are necessary. When we are accustomed to see two impressions associated, the appearance or idea of the one immediately carries us to the idea of the other. Our experiences present us with constant conjunctions of phenomena and we

suppose a general rule as a result of these experiences, but the assurance of necessity arises from our imaginations. We cannot penetrate into the reason for the conjunctions. Our minds are determined by custom which induces a lively expectation that the same causes will be followed by the same effects. The belief in the uniformity of nature is not founded on arguments of any kind but springs from a habit of mind. No reason can take us beyond the particular impressions or connexions that we have experienced, for all experiences are distinct and have no union but in the mind. Necessity 'is nothing but an internal impression of the mind, or a determination to carry our thoughts from one object to another.' Reverting to the cardinal notion offered by Hutcheson, Hume asserts that our ineradicable beliefs relating to the objectivity and rational order of the world are more properly acts of the sensitive than of the cogitative part of our natures. He refers them to 'a kind of instinct or natural impulse' that no philosophy can destroy. Philosophical inquiry shows 'the whimsical condition of mankind, who must act and reason and believe; though they are not able, by their most diligent inquiry to satisfy themselves concerning the foundation of those operations, or to remove the objections which may be raised against them'.[25] Our intellectual postulates are dependent upon propensities of which we are not masters.

This annihilating criticism of the fundamental assumptions of natural philosophy excited a few incredulous comments from Hume's contemporaries. To some of the misrepresentations of his position Hume was able to reply. He protested, for example, against the charge that he had asserted that a thing could be produced without a cause.[26] But the *Treatise,* as its author confessed, fell dead-born from the press, and twenty-five years passed before serious examination of its arguments was undertaken. The *Enquiry concerning Human Understanding* (1748), in which the scepticism of the earlier work is modified, received scarcely more attention from philosophers. It was among the theologians that the conclusions of Hume were discussed and the polite public became vaguely aware of the doctrine of the *Treatise* through its association with the author of the notorious essay 'Of Miracles'.

The deductions of Berkeley and of Hume from the empirical

philosophy of ideas did little to deflect the course of that philosophy. The outlook of Locke and Newton continued to rule the educated opinion. Yet there are signs of the effects of Hume's destructive inquiry upon thoughtful men. The effects appear in a shrinking from the investigation of first principles common among leaders of opinion in the latter part of the century. Dr. Johnson was averse to philosophical discussions and Burke expressed a dislike of metaphysics. Beattie, in a letter to a friend written in 1767, declares his 'conviction of the insignificance of metaphysics and scepticism' — the two are for him one—and in a later epistle he describes the philosophy of Hume as 'a frivolous, though dangerous, system of verbal subtility, which it required neither genius, nor learning, nor taste, nor knowledge of mankind, to be able to put together; but only a captious temper, an irreligious spirit, a moderate command of words, and an extraordinary degree of vanity and presumption'.[27] The Rev. Mr. Knox of Tunbridge School was kindled to similar heat at 'the new infidelity'. And there was acclamation when the doctrine of the *Treatise* was refuted by Thomas Reid and by Beattie upon the commodious principles of common sense.

Meanwhile there had appeared a further development of the scientific conception of knowledge that had a powerful influence on subsequent thought in England. David Hartley, a physician who practised in London and Bath, published in 1749 his *Observations on Man* in which he put forward a theory of experience derived from certain suggestions of Newton in the *Optics* relating to the connexion between vibration and sensations of colour. Hartley combined this theory with the account of the association of ideas that was added by Locke to the fourth edition of the *Essay*. He acknowledged also the work of John Gay, a fellow of Sidney Sussex College, Cambridge, who had discussed the psychological doctrine in a *Dissertation* introducing Edmund Law's translation of the 'Origin of Evil' by Archbishop King (1731). According to Hartley's view of the physical aspect of the process, material changes in the nerves and brain are produced by physical impulses entering the body from external objects. The material changes consist of vibrations set up in the infinitesimal particles of the medullary substance of the brain. When the exciting causes, the external objects, have

been removed, the vibrations persist in the brain, and this persistence is the cause of sensations. The order and arrangement of the sensations reflect the order and arrangment of the original impulses that excited the vibrations. A mechanical and atomic theory of the association of ideas is elaborated upon this basis. The succession of physical vibrations and the psychological association of sensations are two aspects of the same phenomenon. The complex associations of affections in the nerves and brain excite corresponding complex perceptions and ideas. The difference in the degree, kind, place, and direction of the vibrations correspond to the differences in the sensations and in the simple ideas that are the traces or vestiges left by the sensations. Now when several vibrations occur simultaneously in the brain or when they follow one another, a single vibration may in time excite the other vibrations that accompanied it. The chief condition that causes this reproduction of the original vibrations is repetition; a further condition is the strength of the excitement. The physical phenomena correspond to the mental. When sensations are frequently or vividly associated, one element in the group will call up other members of the group; 'thus the names, smells, tastes and tangible qualities of natural bodies suggest their visible appearances to the fancy, i.e. excite their visible ideas'.[28] These simple ideas become united and merge into unique complex ideas the original factors of which cannot be easily distinguished, just as the various ingredients in Venice treacle cannot be separately tasted. This psychology is applied in detail to each of the sensations, to the formation of complex ideas and trains of ideas, to muscular habits, to memory, and to imagination. Hartley brings out the cardinal part played by words and phrases in exciting ideas.[29] The empirical basis of his view of mathematical ideas is manifest in the following passage. 'Now the cause that a person affirms the truth of the proposition, twice two is four, is the entire coincidence of the visible and tangible idea of twice two with that of four, as impressed upon the mind by various objects. We see everywhere that twice two and four are only different names for the same impression. And it is mere association which appropriates the word truth, its definition, or its internal feeling to this coincidence.'[30] He approves of 'the ingenious

bishop Berkeley's' denial of abstract ideas and maintains that
the propositions of science are derived from experiments performed a sufficient number of times, and from the observations
of scientifical persons of 'the constancy and tenor of nature'.
Here, and in many other passages, he takes much for granted.
In his concluding remarks on the mechanism of the human mind
he defends his doctrine against the philosophical theory of free
will. He holds the view that actions result 'from the previous
circumstances of body and mind in the same manner and with
the same certainty, as other effects or from their mechanical
causes'.[31] But he declares that this position has the merit of
making us dependent upon the grace of God.

These practical consequences of the theory attracted immediate attention and Hartley was charged with denying personal
responsibility for action. But the hypothesis of Hartley was
soon pressed to materialist conclusions. The belief in the two
independent orders of mind and matter that had descended in
its modern form from Descartes was abandoned. The whole
man is composed of a uniform substance and his mental powers
are the result of the organic structure of the brain. Mind is
a kind of matter; but this conclusion is reached through re-
defining matter in terms of attraction and repulsion. Matter is
not solid, it has penetrative properties. This materialism draws
upon recent experimental work in physics and chemistry, and
asserts that the new conceptions of matter as a system of activities is not incompatible with the phenomena of sensation and
thought. These processes are never found apart from brains
and sense-organs and the distinction between ideas and their
objects cannot be maintained. Reversing the idealist argument
this philosophy declared that ideas must possess extension and
parts if they represent objects.[32] No arguments from the exquisite subtlety and complexity of mental powers can prove
their immateriality, for the affections of matter are as subtle and
as complex as those that are called mental affections. Hartley's
theory of mind is a practical answer to all objections of this
kind.[33] Theological difficulties were boldly met by Priestley and
those who agreed with him. For instance, the materialist hypothesis entailed the belief that the mind perished with the
body. But Priestley held that God would reassemble the ma-

terial and therefore the mental elements of the dead at the last day. A fierce controversy arose over the necessitarian consequences of the doctrine. Priestley stoutly defended a rigorous determination, a 'mechanism of the mind, depending upon the certain influences of motives to determine the will; by means of which the whole series of events, from the beginning of the world to the consummation of all things, makes one connected chain of causes and effects, originally established by the Deity'. Hobbes was the first to discover this great truth; it was promoted by Collins and Hartley. Abraham Tucker and Lord Kames are also cited in support of it. The will is determined by certain invariable laws depending upon the previous state of mind, but this view does not imply fatalism nor Calvinist predestination, for our own determinations and actions are necessary links in the chain of causation.[34] A rain of pamphlets descended on Priestley's head. Joseph Berington, a Roman Catholic, attacked him in a series of 'Letters on Materialism' (1776), in which it was pointed out at length that the powers of consciousness are incompatible with a matter composed of exclusive parts, a point which the author acutely pressed also against Hume's doctrine of association. A full and frank correspondence between Priestley and Richard Price on philosophical necessity appeared in 1778; and exchanges on the same question occurred between the great controversialist and the Rev. John Palmer. A swarm of other combatants rushed into print against the man who appeared to subvert the doctrine of a future state and to deny all moral responsibility. A few defended his theory of volition; no one was prepared to support in public the view that the animation of the body depended, not upon an immaterial principle, but upon a certain arrangement of matter.

NOTES

[1] *Metaphysical Tracts of the 18th Century*, edited by Dr. S. Parr, London, 1837, p. lvii; J. S. Mill, *Auguste Comte and Positivism*, London, 1865, p. 53.

[2] *Principia*, Preface.

[3] *Opticks*, iii. I.

[4] *Essay*, i. I, 17.

[5] J. Gibson, *Locke's Theory of Knowledge*, Cambridge, 1931, chapter ix.

[6] *Essay*, iv. iv. 3.

[7] Ibid. ii. i. Prof. R. I. Aaron (*John Locke*, Oxford, 1937, p. 218) suggests that Locke found the doctrine in the *Regulae ad Directionem Ingenii* of Descartes, which was being circulated among Cartesians during his sojourn in France.

[8] *Essay*, ii. i. 24.

[9] Ib. iv. i. 2.

[10] Ib. iv. iii. 26.

[11] Ib. ii. xxiii. 4.

[12] Edward Stillingfleet, *Works*, London, vol. iii, p. 511 f. The Augustinian position is affirmed in *Origines Sacrae*, vol. ii, p. 232, where an idea is said to be the objective being of a thing.

[13] Charles Leslie, *A Short and Easy Way with the Deists* (1698), and Thomas Sherlock, *Tryal of the Witnesses of the Resurrection of Jesus* (1729), are prominent examples.

[14] John Norris, *Essay on the Ideal and Intelligible World*, London, 1701–4, p. 199.

[15] Berkeley, *Life and Letters*, ed. A. Campbell Fraser, Oxford, 1871, p. 420.

[16] Berkeley, *Three Dialogues between Hylas and Philonous* (1713), ii.

[17] *Man In Quest of Himself* (1763), by Cuthbert Comment (Abraham Tucker), Metaphysical Tracts, ed. S. Parr, London, 1837, p. 190.

[18] James Beattie, *An Essay on Truth*, Edinburgh, 1776 ed., pp. 179 f.

[19] Browne, *The Procedure, Extent and Limits of Human Understanding* (1728), bk. ii, iv. Browne's argument that the notion of spirit is reached by analogy from sensible experience was used by the critics of the deistical view that the notion of God is an innate common notion. Cf. Philip Skelton, *Ophiomachus or Deism Revealed*, London, 2nd ed., 1751, vol. ii, p. 65.

[20] Hutcheson, *System of Moral Philosophy*, published posthumously, 1755, bk. i. i.

[21] *Synopsis Metaphysica* (1742), ii, i.

[22] Ib. 3.

[23] *Treatise*, bk. iii, pt. i, sect. i.

[24] Ib. i. 3. 14.

[25] *Enquiry concerning Human Understanding*, xii, Part ii.

[26] The charge, typical of the general failure to understand the argument of the *Treatise*, was made by Prof. John Stewart of Edinburgh. The correspondence on the subject is given in N. K. Smith, *The Philosophy of David Hume*, London, 1941, pp. 411 f.

[27] *Life of Beattie*, by Sir William Forbes, Edinburgh, 1807, vol. i, p. 168.

[28] *Observations on Man*, part i, chap. i, sect. 2.

[29] Ib., chap. iii, sect. i.

[30] Ib., sect. 2.

[31] Ib., Conclusion.

[32] Joseph Priestley, *Disquisitions relating to Matter and Spirit*, 2nd ed., Birmingham, 1782, vol. i, p. 58. The first edition appeared in 1777.

[33] Ib., p. 113.

[34] Priestley, *The Doctrine of Philosophical Necessity Illustrated* (vol. ii of *Disquisitions*).

The Mind of the Enlightenment

෴

ERNST CASSIRER

I

D'Alembert begins his essay on the *Elements of Philosophy* with a general portrait of the mind of the mid-eighteenth century. He prefaces his portrait with the observation that in the intellectual life of the last three hundred years the mid-century mark has consistently been an important turning-point. The Renaissance commences in the middle of the fifteenth century; the Reformation reaches its climax in the middle of the sixteenth century; and in the middle of the seventeenth century the Cartesian philosophy triumphantly alters the entire world picture. Can an analogous movement be observed in the eighteenth century? If so, how can its direction and general tendency be characterized? Pursuing this thought further, d'Alembert writes:

"If one examines carefully the mid-point of the century in which we live, the events which excite us or at any rate occupy our minds, our customs, our achievements, and even our diversions, it is difficult not to see that in some respects a very remarkable change in our ideas is taking place, a change whose rapidity seems to promise an even greater transformation to come. Time alone will tell what will be the goal, the nature, and the limits of this revolution whose shortcomings and merits will be better known to posterity than to us.... Our century is called, accordingly, the century of philosophy par excellence. ... If one considers without bias the present state of our knowledge, one cannot deny that philosophy among us has shown

From Ernst Cassirer, The Philosophy of Enlightenment *(Princeton: Princeton University Press, 1951), pp. 3–36.*

progress. Natural science from day to day accumulates new riches. Geometry, by extending its limits, has borne its torch into the regions of physical science which lay nearest at hand. The true system of the world has been recognized, developed, and perfected. . . . In short, from the earth to Saturn, from the history of the heavens to that of insects, natural philosophy has been revolutionized; and nearly all other fields of knowledge have assumed new forms. . . .

"The study of nature seems in itself to be cold and dull because the satisfaction derived from it consists in a uniform, continued, and uninterrupted feeling, and its pleasures, to be intense, must be intermittent and spasmodic. . . . Nevertheless, the discovery and application of a new method of philosophizing, the kind of enthusiasm which accompanies discoveries, a certain exaltation of ideas which the spectacle of the universe produces in us—all these causes have brought about a lively fermentation of minds. Spreading through nature in all directions like a river which has burst its dams, this fermentation has swept with a sort of violence everything along with it which stood in its way. . . . Thus, from the principles of the secular sciences to the foundations of religious revelation, from metaphysics to matters of taste, from music to morals, from the scholastic disputes of theologians to matters of trade, from the laws of princes to those of peoples, from natural law to the arbitrary laws of nations . . . everything has been discussed and analyzed, or at least mentioned. The fruit or sequel of this general effervescence of minds has been to cast new light on some matters and new shadows on others, just as the effect of the ebb and flow of the tides is to leave some things on the shore and to wash others away."[1]

These are the words of one of the most important scholars of the age and of one of its intellectual spokesmen. Hence they represent a direct expression of the nature and trend of contemporary intellectual life. The age of d'Alembert feels itself impelled by a mighty movement, but it refuses to abandon itself to this force. It wants to know the whence and whither, the origin and the goal, of its impulsion. For this age, knowledge of its own activity, intellectual self-examination, and foresight are

the proper function and essential task of thought. Thought not only seeks new, hitherto unknown goals but it wants to know where it is going and to determine for itself the direction of its journey. It encounters the world with fresh joy and the courage of discovery, daily expecting new revelations. Yet its thirst for knowledge and intellectual curiosity are directed not only toward the external world; the thought of this age is even more passionately impelled by that other question of the nature and potentiality of thought itself. Time and again thought returns to its point of departure from its various journeys of exploration intended to broaden the horizon of objective reality. Pope gave brief and pregnant expression to this deep-seated feeling of the age in the line: "The proper study of mankind is man." The age senses that a new force is at work within it; but it is even more fascinated by the activity of this force than by the creations brought forth by that activity. It rejoices not only in results, but it inquires into, and attempts to explain, the form of the process leading to these results. The problem of intellectual "progress" throughout the eighteenth century appears in this light. Perhaps no other century is so completely permeated by the idea of intellectual progress as that of the Enlightenment. But we mistake the essence of this conception, if we understand it merely in a quantitative sense as an extension of knowledge indefinitely. A qualitative determination always accompanies quantitative expansion; and an increasingly pronounced return to the characteristic center of knowledge corresponds to the extension of inquiry beyond the periphery of knowledge. One seeks multiplicity in order to be sure of unity; one accepts the breadth of knowledge in the sure anticipation that this breadth does not impede the intellect, but that, on the contrary, it leads the intellect back to, and concentrates it in, itself. For we see again and again that the divergence of the paths followed by the intellect in its attempt to encompass all of reality is merely apparent. If these paths viewed objectively seem to diverge, their divergence is, nevertheless, no mere dispersion. All the various energies of the mind are, rather, held together in a common center of force. Variety and diversity of shapes are simply the full unfolding of an essentially homogeneous formative power.

When the eighteenth century wants to characterize this power in a single word, it calls it "reason." "Reason" becomes the unifying and central point of this century, expressing all that it longs and strives for, and all that it achieves. But the historian of the eighteenth century would be guilty of error and hasty judgment if he were satisfied with this characterization and thought it a safe point of departure. For where the century itself sees an end, the historian finds merely a starting-point for his investigation; where the century seems to find an answer, the historian sees his real problem. The eighteenth century is imbued with a belief in the unity and immutability of reason. Reason is the same for all thinking subjects, all nations, all epochs, and all cultures. From the changeability of religious creeds, of moral maxims and convictions, of theoretical opinions and judgments, a firm and lasting element can be extracted which is permanent in itself, and which in this identity and permanence expresses the real essence of reason. For us the word "reason" has long since lost its unequivocal simplicity even if we are in essential agreement with the basic aims of the philosophy of the Enlightenment. We can scarcely use this word any longer without being conscious of its history; and time and again we see how great a change of meaning the term has undergone. This circumstance constantly reminds us how little meaning the terms "reason" and "rationalism" still retain, even in the sense of purely historical characteristics. The general concept is vague, and it becomes clear and distinct only when the right "differentia specifica" is added. Where are we to look for this specific difference in the eighteenth century? If it liked to call itself a "century of reason," a "philosophic century," wherein lies the characteristic and distinguishing feature of this designation? In what sense is the word "philosophy" used here? What are its special tasks, and what means are at its disposal for accomplishing these tasks in order to place the doctrines of the world and of man on a firm foundation?

If we compare the answers of the eighteenth century to these questions with the answers prevailing at the time when that century began its intellectual labors, we arrive at a negative distinction. The seventeenth century had seen the real task of

philosophy in the construction of the philosophical "system." Truly "philosophical" knowledge had seemed attainable only when thought, starting from a highest being and from a highest, intuitively grasped certainty, succeeded in spreading the light of this certainty over all derived being and all derived knowledge. This was done by the method of proof and rigorous inference, which added other propositions to the first original certainty and in this way pieced out and linked together the whole chain of possible knowledge. No link of this chain could be removed from the whole; none was explicable by itself. The only real explanation possible consisted in its "derivation," in the strict, systematic deduction by which any link might be traced back to the source of being and certainty, by which its distance from this source might be determined, and by which the number of intermediate links separating a given link from this source might be specified. The eighteenth century abandons this kind of deduction and proof. It no longer vies with Descartes and Malebranche, with Leibniz and Spinoza for the prize of systematic rigor and completeness. It seeks another concept of truth and philosophy whose function is to extend the boundaries of both and make them more elastic, concrete, and vital. The Enlightenment does not take the ideal of this mode of thinking from the philosophical doctrines of the past; on the contrary, it constructs its ideal according to the model and pattern of contemporary natural science.

The attempt to solve the central problem of philosophic method involves recourse to Newton's "Rules of Philosophizing" rather than to Descartes' *Discourse on Method,* with the result that philosophy presently takes an entirely new direction. For Newton's method is not that of pure deduction, but that of analysis. He does not begin by setting up certain principles, certain general concepts and axioms, in order, by virtue of abstract inferences, to pave the way to the knowledge of the particular, the "factual." Newton's approach moves in just the opposite direction. His phenomena are the data of experience; his principles are the goal of his investigation. If the latter are first according to nature ($\pi\rho\acute{o}\tau\epsilon\rho\text{ov}\ \tau\tilde{\eta}\ \phi\nu\acute{o}\epsilon\iota$), then the former must always be first to us ($\pi\rho\acute{o}\tau\epsilon\rho\grave{o}\nu\ \pi\rho\text{o}\varsigma\ \acute{\eta}\mu\tilde{\alpha}\varsigma$). Hence the

true method of physics can never consist in proceeding from any arbitrary *a priori* starting-point, from a hypothesis, and in completely developing the logical conclusions implicit in it. For such hypotheses can be invented and modified as desired; logically, any one of them is as valid as any other. We can progress from this logical indifference to the truth and precision of physical science only by applying the measuring stick elsewhere. A scientific abstraction or "definition" cannot serve as a really unambiguous starting-point, for such a starting-point can only be obtained from experience and observation. This does not mean that Newton and his disciples and followers saw a cleavage between experience and thinking, that is, between the realm of bare fact and that of pure thought. No such conflicting modes of validity, no such dualism between "relations of ideas" and "matters of fact" as we find in Hume's *Enquiry concerning Human Understanding,* is to be found among the Newtonian thinkers. For the goal and basic presupposition of Newtonian research is universal order and law in the material world. Such regularity means that facts as such are not mere matter, they are not a jumble of discrete elements; on the contrary, facts exhibit an all-pervasive form. This form appears in mathematical determinations and in arrangements according to measure and number. But such arrangements cannot be foreseen in the mere concept; they must rather be shown to exist in the facts themselves. The procedure is thus not from concepts and axioms to phenomena, but vice versa. Observation produces the datum of science; the principle and law are the object of the investigation.

This new methodological order characterizes all eighteenth century thought. The value of system, the *"esprit systématique,"* is neither underestimated nor neglected; but it is sharply distinguished from the love of system for its own sake, the *"esprit de système."* The whole theory of knowledge of the eighteenth century strives to confirm this distinction. D'Alembert in his "Preliminary Discourse" to the French *Encyclopedia* makes this distinction the central point of his argument, and Condillac in his *Treatise on Systems* gives it explicit form and justification. Condillac tries to subject the great systems of the

seventeenth century to the test of historical criticism. He tries to show that each of them failed because, instead of sticking to the facts and developing its concepts from them, it raised some individual concept to the status of a dogma. In opposition to the "spirit of systems" a new alliance is now called for between the "positive" and the "rational" spirit. The positive and the rational are never in conflict, but their true synthesis can only be achieved by the right sort of mediation. One should not seek order, law, and "reason" as a rule that may be grasped and expressed prior to the phenomena, as their *a priori*; one should rather discover such regularity in the phenomena themselves, as the form of their immanent connection. Nor should one attempt to anticipate from the outset such "reason" in the form of a closed system; one should rather permit this reason to unfold gradually, with ever increasing clarity and perfection, as knowledge of the facts progresses. The new logic that is now sought in the conviction that it is everywhere present on the path of knowledge is neither the logic of the scholastic nor of the purely mathematical concept; it is rather the "logic of facts." The mind must abandon itself to the abundance of phenomena and gauge itself constantly by them. For it may be sure that it will not get lost, but that instead it will find here its own real truth and standard. Only in this way can the genuine correlation of subject and object, of truth and reality, be achieved; only so can the correspondence between these concepts, which is the condition of all scientific knowledge, be brought about.

From the actual course of scientific thinking since its revival in modern times the Enlightenment derives its concrete, self-evident proof that this synthesis of the "positive" and the "rational" is not a mere postulate, but that the goal set up is attainable and the ideal fully realizable. In the progress of natural science and the various phases it has gone through, the philosophy of the Enlightenment believes it can, as it were, tangibly grasp its ideal. For here it can follow step by step the triumphal march of the modern analytical spirit. It had been this spirit that in the course of barely a century and a half had conquered all reality, and that now seemed finally to have

accomplished its great task of reducing the multiplicity of natural phenomena to a single universal rule. And this cosmological formula, as contained in Newton's general law of attraction, was not found by accident, nor as the result of sporadic experimentation; its discovery shows the rigorous application of scientific method. Newton finished what Kepler and Galileo had begun. All three names signify not only great scientific personalities, but they have also become symbols and milestones of scientific knowledge and thought. Kepler pushes the observation of celestial phenomena to a degree of precision never achieved before his time. By indefatigable toil he arrived at the laws which describe the form of the planetary orbits and determine the relation between the revolution periods of the individual planets and their respective distances from the sun. But this factual insight is only a first step. Galileo envisages a more general problem: his doctrine of motion marks an advance to a broader and deeper stratum of the logic of scientific concepts. It is no longer a question of describing a field of natural phenomena, however broad and important, a general foundation of dynamics, of the theory of nature as such, has now to be evolved. And Galileo is aware that direct observation of nature cannot accomplish this task, and that other cognitive means must be invoked. The phenomena of nature present themselves to perception as uniform events, as undivided wholes. Perception grasps only the surface of these events, it can describe them in broad outline and in the manner of their taking place; but this form of description is not sufficient for a real explanation. For the explanation of a natural event is not merely the realization of its existence thus and so; such an explanation consists rather in specifying the conditions of the event, and in recognizing exactly how it depends on these conditions. This demand can only be satisfied by an analysis of the uniform presentation of the event as given in perception and direct observation, and by its resolution into its constitutive elements. This analytical process, according to Galileo, is the presupposition of all exact knowledge of nature. The method of formulation of scientific concepts is both analytical and synthetic. It is only by splitting an apparently simple event into its elements and by reconstruct-

ing it from these that we can arrive at an understanding of it. Galileo has given us a classical example of this process in his discovery of the ballistic parabola. The path of a projectile could not be described directly from observation; it could not simply be abstracted from a great number of observations. Observation gives us to be sure certain general characteristics; it shows us that a phase of ascent is followed by a phase of descent, etc. But observation fails to produce any precise determination of the path of a projectile. We arrive at a truly mathematical conception of an event by tracing the phenomenon itself back to its peculiar conditions, by isolating each set of conditions simultaneously affecting the event, and by investigating these sets of conditions with respect to their laws. The law of the parabolic path of the projectile may be found, and the increase and decrease of velocity may be exactly recorded once the phenomenon of projection has been shown to be a complex event, the determination of which depends on two different forces, that of the original impulse and that of gravity. In this simple example, as in a preliminary sketch, we have the whole future development of physics and its complete methodological structure. Newton's theory retains and substantiates all those features which are clearly recognizable here. For it is founded on the interdependence of the analytical and synthetic methods. Taking the three laws of Kepler as its point of departure, Newton's theory is not content merely to interpret them as expressing the factual results of observation. It seeks to derive these results from their presuppositions and to show that they are the necessary effect of the concurrence of various conditions. Each of these sets of conditions must be investigated by itself and its function known. Thus the phenomenon of planetary motion, which Kepler had regarded as a simple entity, is proved to be a complex structure. It is reduced to two fundamental forms of natural law: to the laws of freely falling bodies and to the laws of centrifugal force. Both forms of law had been investigated independently by Galileo and Huygens and precisely determined; now it was a question of reducing these discoveries to one comprehensive principle. Newton's great achievement lay in this reduction; it was not so much the discovery of hitherto unknown facts or the

acquisition of new material but rather the intellectual transformation of empirical material which Newton achieved. The structure of the cosmos is no longer merely to be looked at, but to be penetrated. It yields to this approach only when mathematics is applied and it is subjected to the mathematical form of analysis. In as much as Newton's theory of fluxions and Leibniz's infinitesimal calculus provide a universal instrument for this procedure, the comprehensibility of nature seems for the first time to be strictly demonstrated. The path of natural science traverses indefinite distances; but its direction remains constant, for its point of departure and its goal are not exclusively determined by the nature of the objective world but by the nature and powers of reason as well.

The philosophy of the eighteenth century takes up this particular case, the methodological pattern of Newton's physics, though it immediately begins to generalize. It is not content to look upon analysis as the great intellectual tool of mathematico-physical knowledge; eighteenth century thought sees analysis rather as the necessary and indispensable instrument of all thinking in general. This view triumphs in the middle of the century. However much individual thinkers and schools differ in their results, they agree in this epistemological premise. Voltaire's *Treatise on Metaphysics,* d'Alembert's *Preliminary Discourse,* and Kant's *Inquiry concerning the Principles of Natural Theology and Morality* all concur on this point. All these works represent the true method of metaphysics as in fundamental agreement with the method which Newton, with such fruitful results, introduced into natural science. Voltaire says that man, if he presumes to see into the life of things and know them as they really are in themselves, immediately becomes aware of the limits of his faculties; he finds himself in the position of a blind man who must judge the nature of color. But analysis is the staff which a benevolent nature has placed in the blind man's hands. Equipped with this instrument he can feel his way forward among appearances, discovering their sequence and arrangement; and this is all he needs for his intellectual orientation to life and knowledge. "We must never make hypotheses; we must never say: Let us begin by inventing prin-

ciples according to which we attempt to explain everything. We should say rather: Let us make an exact analysis of things. . . . When we cannot utilize the compass of mathematics or the torch of experience and physics, it is certain that we cannot take a single step forward."[2] But provided with such instruments as these, we can and should venture upon the high seas of knowledge. We must, of course, abandon all hope of ever wresting from things their ultimate mystery, of ever penetrating to the absolute being of matter or of the human soul. If, however, we refer to empirical law and order, the "inner core of nature" proves by no means inaccessible. In this realm we can establish ourselves and proceed in every direction. The power of reason does not consist in enabling us to transcend the empirical world but rather in teaching us to feel at home in it. Here again is evident a characteristic change of meaning in the concept of reason as compared with seventeenth century usage. In the great metaphysical systems of that century—those of Descartes and Malebranche, of Spinoza and Leibniz—reason is the realm of the "eternal verities," of those truths held in common by the human and the divine mind. What we know through reason, we therefore behold "in God." Every act of reason means participation in the divine nature; it gives access to the intelligible world. The eighteenth century takes reason in a different and more modest sense. It is no longer the sum total of "innate ideas" given prior to all experience, which reveal the absolute essence of things. Reason is now looked upon rather as an acquisition than as a heritage. It is not the treasury of the mind in which the truth like a minted coin lies stored; it is rather the original intellectual force which guides the discovery and determination of truth. This determination is the seed and the indispensable presupposition of all real certainty. The whole eighteenth century understands reason in this sense; not as a sound body of knowledge, principles, and truths, but as a kind of energy, a force which is fully comprehensible only in its agency and effects. What reason is, and what it can do, can never be known by its results but only by its function. And its most important function consists in its power to bind and to dissolve. It dissolves everything merely factual, all simple data

of experience, and everything believed on the evidence of revelation, tradition and authority; and it does not rest content
until it has analyzed all these things into their simplest component parts and into their last elements of belief and opinion.
Following this work of dissolution begins the work of construction. Reason cannot stop with the dispersed parts; it has
to build from them a new structure, a true whole. But since
reason creates this whole and fits the parts together according
to its own rule, it gains complete knowledge of the structure of
its product. Reason understands this structure because it can
reproduce it in its totality and in the ordered sequence of its
individual elements. Only in this twofold intellectual movement can the concept of reason be fully characterized, namely,
as a concept of agency, not of being.

This conviction gains a foothold in the most varied fields of
eighteenth century culture. Lessing's famous saying that the real
power of reason is to be found not in the possession but in the
acquisition of truth has its parallels everywhere in the intellectual history of the eighteenth century. Montesquieu attempts to
give a theoretical justification for the presence in the human soul
of an innate thirst for knowledge, an insatiable intellectual curiosity, which never allows us to be satisfied with any conception
we have arrived at, but drives us on from idea to idea. "Our
soul is made for thinking, that is, for perceiving," said Montesquieu; "but such a being must have curiosity, for just as all
things form a chain in which every idea precedes one idea and
follows another, so one cannot want to see the one without
desiring to see the other." The lust for knowledge, the *libido
sciendi,* which theological dogmatism had outlawed and branded
as intellectual pride, is now called a necessary quality of the
soul as such and restored to its original rights. The defense,
reinforcement, and consolidation of this way of thinking is the
cardinal aim of eighteenth century culture; and in this mode
of thinking, not the mere acquisition and extension of specific
information, the century sees its major task. This fundamental
tendency can also be traced unambiguously in the *Encyclopedia,*
which became the arsenal of all such information. Diderot himself, originator of the *Encyclopedia,* states that its purpose is

not only to supply a certain body of knowledge but also to bring about a change in the mode of thinking—*pour changer la façon commune de penser.*[2a] Consciousness of this task affects all the minds of the age and gives rise to a new sense of inner tension. Even the calmest and most discreet thinkers, the real "scientists," are swayed by this movement. They do not dare as yet to specify its final aim; but they cannot escape its force, and they think they feel in this trend the rise of a new future for mankind. "I do not think that I have too good an idea of my century," writes Duclos in his *Thoughts on the Customs of this Century,* "but it seems to me there is a certain universal fermentation whose progress one could direct or hasten by the proper education." For one does not want simply to catch the contagion of the time and to be driven blindly on by whatever forces it may contain. One wants to understand these forces and control them in the light of such understanding. One does not care merely to dive into the eddies and whirlpools of the new thoughts; one prefers to seize the helm of the intellect and to guide its course toward definite goals.

The first step which the eighteenth century took in this direction was to seek a clear line of demarcation between the mathematical and the philosophical spirit. Here was a difficult and intrinsically dialectic task, for two different and apparently contradictory claims were to be equally satisfied. The bond between mathematics and philosophy could not be severed, or even loosened, for mathematics was the "pride of human reason," its touchstone and real guarantee. Yet it became increasingly clear that there was also a certain limitation inherent in this self-contained power of mathematics; that mathematics to be sure formed the prototype of reason, and yet it could not with respect to content completely survey and exhaust reason. A strange process of thinking now develops which seems to be motivated by diametrically opposed forces. Philosophical thinking tries at the same time to separate itself from, and to hold fast to, mathematics; it seeks to free itself from the authority of mathematics, and yet in so doing not to contest or violate this authority but rather to justify it from a new angle. In both its efforts it is successful; for pure analysis is recognized in its

essential meaning as the basis for mathematical thinking in the modern era; and yet at the same time, precisely because of its universal function, such analysis is extended beyond the limits of the purely mathematical, beyond quantity and number. The beginnings of this trend are already discernible in the seventeenth century. Pascal's work *Of the Geometric Spirit* seriously attempts to draw a clear and distinct line between mathematical science and philosophy. He contrasts the "geometric spirit" with the "subtle spirit" (*esprit fin*) and tries to show how they differ both in structure and in function. But this sharp line of demarcation is soon obliterated. "The geometric spirit," says, for instance, Fontenelle in the preface to his work *On the Usefulness of Mathematics and Physics,*[3] "is not so exclusively bound to geometry that it could not be separated from it and applied to other fields. A work on ethics, politics, criticism, or even eloquence, other things being equal, is merely so much more beautiful and perfect if it is written in the geometric spirit." The eighteenth century grapples with this problem and decides that, as long as it is understood as the spirit of pure analysis, the "geometric spirit" is absolutely unlimited in its application and by no means bound to any particular field of knowledge.

Proof of this thesis is sought in two different directions. Analysis, whose force had hitherto been tried only in the realm of number and quantity, is now applied, on the one hand, to psychological and, on the other, to sociological problems. In both cases it is a matter of showing that here too new vistas open up, and that a new field of knowledge of the highest importance becomes accessible to reason as soon as reason learns to subject this field to its special method of analytic dissection and synthetic reconstruction. But psychological reality, concretely given and immediately experienced, seems to elude any such attempt. It appears to us in unlimited abundance and infinite variety; no element, no form, of psychological experience is like any other, and no content ever recurs in the same way. In the flux of psychological events no two waves exhibit the same form; each wave emerges, as it were, out of nothingness, and threatens to disappear into nothingness again. Yet, accord-

ing to the prevailing view of psychology in the eighteenth century, this complete diversity, this heterogeneity and fluidity, of psychological content is illusory. Closer inspection reveals the solid ground and the permanent elements underlying the almost unlimited mutability of psychological phenomena. It is the task of science to discover those elements which escape immediate experience, and to present them clearly and individually. In psychological events there is no diversity and no heterogeneity which cannot be reduced to a sum of individual parts; there is no becoming which is not founded in constant being. If we trace psychological forms to their sources and origins, we always find such unity and relative simplicity. In this conviction eighteenth century psychology goes one step beyond its guide and master, Locke. Locke had been content to indicate two major sources of psychological phenomena; in addition to "sensation" Locke recognizes "reflection" as an independent and irreducible form of psychological experience. But his pupils and followers attempt in various ways to eliminate this dualism and to arrive at a strictly monistic foundation of psychology. Berkeley and Hume combine "sensation" and "reflection" in the expression "perception," and they try to show that this expression exhausts both our internal and external experience, the data of nature and those of our own mind. Condillac considers his real merit and his advance beyond Locke to be that, while retaining Locke's general method, he extended it into a new field of psychological facts. Locke's analytical art is effective in the dissection of ideas, but it goes no farther. It shows how every idea, be it ever so complex, is composed of the materials of sensation or reflection, and how these materials must be fitted together in order to produce the various forms of psychological phenomena. But, as Condillac points out, Locke stops with his analysis of psychological forms. He limits his investigation to these forms but does not extend it to the whole realm of psychological events and activity, or to their origin. Here then is a province for research hitherto scarcely touched and of untold riches. In Locke the different classes of psychological activity were left alone, as original and irreducible wholes like the simple data of sense, the data of sight, hearing, touch, mo-

tion, taste, and smell. Observing, comparing, distinguishing, combining, desiring, and willing are looked upon by Locke as individual independent acts existing only in immediate experience and not reducible to anything else. But this view robs the whole method of derivation of its real fruits. For psychological being remains an irreducible manifold which can be described in its particular forms but can no longer be explained and derived from simple original qualities. If such derivation is to be taken seriously, then the maxim which Locke applied to the realm of ideas must be applied to all operations of the mind. It must also be shown that the apparent immediacy of these ideas is an illusion which does not withstand scientific analysis. Individual acts of the mind, when analyzed, are in no sense original, but rather derivative and mediate. In order to understand their structure and true nature, one must examine their genesis; one must observe how, from the simple sense data which it receives, the mind gradually acquires the capacity to focus its attention on them, to compare and distinguish, to separate and combine them. Such is the task of Condillac's *Treatise on Sensation.* Here the analytical method seems to celebrate a new triumph in the scientific explanation of the corporeal world, a triumph not inferior to its performance in the realm of natural science. The material and mental spheres are now, as it were, reduced to a common denominator; they are composed of the same elements and are combined according to the same laws.[4]

But in addition to these two spheres of reality there is a third which, similarly, must not be accepted as consisting of simple sense data, but which must be traced to its origins. For we can only succeed in reducing this reality to the rule of law and reason by an inquiry into its sources. The third sphere of reality is that which we find in the structure of the state and of society. Man is born into this world; he neither creates nor shapes it, but finds it ready-made about him; and he is expected to adapt himself to the existing order. But here too passive acceptance and obedience have their limits. As soon as the power of thought awakens in man, it advances irresistibly against this form of reality, summoning it before the tribunal of thought

and challenging its legal titles to truth and validity. And society must submit to being treated like physical reality under investigation. Analysis into component parts begins once more, and the general will of the state is treated as if it were composed of the wills of individuals and had come into being as a result of the union of these wills. Only by virtue of this basic supposition can we make a "body" of the state and subject it to that method which had proved its fruitfulness in the discovery of universal law in the physical world. Hobbes had already done this. The fundamental principle of his political theory, that the state is a "body," means just this: that the same process of thought which guides us to an exact insight into the nature of physical body is also applicable without reservation to the state. Hobbes's assertion that thinking in general is "calculation" and that all calculation is either addition or subtraction also holds for all political thinking. Such thinking too must sever the bond which unites the individual wills, in order to join them again by virtue of its own special method. Thus Hobbes resolves the "civic state" into the "natural state"; and in thought he dissolves all bonds of individual wills only to find their complete antagonism, the "war of all against all," remaining. But from this very negation is derived the positive content of the law of the land in its unconditional and unlimited validity. The emergence of the will of the state from the form of the covenant is set forth because this will can only be known by, and founded in, the covenant. Here is the bond which connects Hobbes's doctrine of nature with his doctrine of the state. These doctrines are different applications of Hobbes's logical basic assumption, according to which the human mind really only understands that which it can construct from the original elements. Every true formulation of a concept, every complete definition, must therefore start from this point; it can only be a "causal" definition. Philosophy as a whole is understood as the sum total of such causal definitions; it is simply the complete knowledge of effects from their causes, of derivative results from the totality of their antecedents and conditions.

The eighteenth century doctrine of the state and society only rarely accepted without reservations the content of Hobbes's

teaching, but the form in which Hobbes embodied this content exerted a powerful and lasting influence. Eighteenth century political thought is based on that theory of the contract whose underlying assumptions are derived from ancient and medieval thought, but it develops and transforms these assumptions in a manner characteristic of the influence exerted by the modern scientific view of the world. In this field too the analytic and synthetic method is henceforth victorious. Sociology is modeled on physics and analytical psychology. Its method, states Condillac in his *Treatise on Systems,* consists in teaching us to recognize in society an "artificial body" composed of parts exerting a reciprocal influence on one another. This body as a whole must be so shaped that no individual class of citizens by their special prerogatives shall disturb the equilibrium and harmony of the whole, that on the contrary all special interests shall contribute and be subordinated to the welfare of the whole.[5] This formulation in a certain sense transforms the problem of sociology and politics into a problem in statics. Montesquieu's *Spirit of the Laws* looks upon this same transformation as its highest task. The aim of Montesquieu's work is not simply to describe the forms and types of state constitutions—despotism, constitutional monarchy, and the republican constitution—and to present them empirically, it is also to construct them from the forces of which they are composed. Knowledge of these forces is necessary if they are to be put to their proper use, if we are to show how they can be employed in the making of a state constitution which realizes the demand of the greatest possible freedom. Such freedom, as Montesquieu tries to show, is possible only when every individual force is limited and restrained by a counterforce. Montesquieu's famous doctrine of the "division of powers" is nothing but the consistent development and the concrete application of this basic principle. It seeks to transform that unstable equilibrium which exists in, and is characteristic of, imperfect forms of the state into a static equilibrium; it attempts further to show what ties must exist between individual forces in order that none shall gain the ascendancy over any other, but that all, by counterbalancing one another, shall permit the widest possible margin for freedom. The ideal

which Montesquieu portrays in his theory of the state is thus the ideal of a "mixed government," in which, as a safeguard against a relapse into despotism, the form of the mixture is so wisely and cautiously selected that the exertion of a force in one direction immediately releases a counterforce, and hence automatically restores the desired equilibrium. By this approach Montesquieu believes he can fit the great variety and diversity of the existing forms of the state into one sound intellectual structure within which they can be controlled. Such a basic arrangement and foundation is Montesquieu's primary aim. "I have established principles," he points out in the preface to the *Spirit of the Laws,* "and I have observed how individual cases, as if by themselves, yielded to these principles, and I have seen that the histories of all nations are but sequences, and that each individual law is connected with another law or depends on a more general law."

The method of reason is thus exactly the same in this branch of knowledge as it is in natural science and psychology. It consists in starting with solid facts based on observation, but not in remaining within the bounds of bare facts. The mere togetherness of the facts must be transformed into a conjuncture; the initial mere co-existence of the data must upon closer inspection reveal an interdependence; and the form of an aggregate must become that of a system. To be sure, the facts cannot simply be coerced into a system; such form must arise from the facts themselves. The principles, which are to be sought everywhere, and without which no sound knowledge is possible in any field, are not arbitrarily chosen points of departure in thinking, applied by force to concrete experience which is so altered as to suit them; they are rather the general conditions to which a complete analysis of the given facts themselves must lead. The path of thought then, in physics as in psychology and politics, leads from the particular to the general; but not even this progression would be possible unless every particular as such were already subordinated to a universal rule, unless from the first the general were contained, so to speak embodied, in the particular. The concept of the "principle" in itself excludes that absolute character which it asserted in the great metaphysical

systems of the seventeenth century. It resigns itself to a relative validity; it now pretends only to mark a provisional farthest point at which the progress of thought has arrived—with the reservation that thought can also abandon and supersede it. According to this relativity, the scientific principle is dependent on the status and form of knowledge, so that one and the same proposition can appear in one science as a principle and in another as a deduced corollary. "Hence we conclude that the point at which the investigation of the principles of a science must stop is determined by the nature of the science itself, that is to say, by the point of view from which the particular science approaches its object. . . . I admit that in this case the principles from which we proceed are themselves perhaps scarcely more than very remote derivations from the true principles which are unknown to us, and that, accordingly, they would perhaps merit rather the name of conclusions than that of principles. But it is not necessary that these conclusions be principles in themselves; it suffices that they be such for us."[6] Such a relativity does not imply any skeptical perils in itself; it is, on the contrary, merely the expression of the fact that reason in its steady progress knows no hard and fast barriers, but that every apparent goal attained by reason is but a fresh starting-point.

Thus it is evident that, if we compare the thought of the eighteenth century with that of the seventeenth, there is no real chasm anywhere separating the two periods. The new ideal of knowledge develops steadily and consistently from the presuppositions which the logic and theory of knowledge of the seventeenth century—especially in the works of Descartes and Leibniz—had established. The difference in the mode of thinking does not mean a radical transformation; it amounts merely to a shifting of emphasis. This emphasis is constantly moving from the general to the particular, from principles to phenomena. But the basic assumption remains; that is the assumption that between the two realms of thought there is no opposition, but rather complete correlation—except for Hume's skepticism which offers an entirely different approach. The self-confidence of reason is nowhere shaken. The rationalistic postulate of unity dominates the minds of this age. The concept of unity

and that of science are mutually dependent. "All sciences put together," says d'Alembert repeating the opening sentences of Descartes' *Rules for the Conduct of the Understanding,* "are nothing but human intelligence, which always remains one and the same, and is always identical with itself, however different the objects may be to which it is applied." The seventeenth century owed its inner solidarity, particularly as exemplified in French classical culture, to the consistency and rigor with which it clung to this postulate of unity and extended its application to all the spheres of knowledge and living. This postulate prevailed not only in science, but in religion, politics and literature as well. "One king, one law, one faith"— such was the motto of the epoch. With the advent of the eighteenth century the absolutism of the unity principle seems to lose its grip and to accept some limitations and concessions. But these modifications do not touch the core of the thought itself. For the function of unification continues to be recognized as the basic role of reason. Rational order and control of the data of experience are not possible without strict unification. To "know" a manifold of experience is to place its component parts in such a relationship to one another that, starting from a given point, we can run through them according to a constant and general rule. This form of discursive understanding had been established by Descartes as the fundamental norm of mathematical knowledge. Every mathematical operation, according to Descartes, aims in the last analysis to determine the proportion between an unknown quantity and other known quantities. And this proportion can only be strictly determined when the unknown and the known participate in a "common nature." Both elements, the unknown and the known, must be reducible to quantity and as such they must be derivable from the repetition of one and the same numerical unit. Thus the discursive form of knowledge always resembles a reduction; it proceeds from the complex to the simple, from apparent diversity to its basic identity. Eighteenth century thought holds firmly to this fundamental method, and attempts to apply it to broader and broader fields of knowledge. The very concept of "calculus" thus loses its exclusively mathematical meaning. It is not merely applica-

ble to quantities and numbers; from the realm of quantities it invades the realm of pure qualities. For qualities too may be placed in such a relationship to one another that they are derivable from one another in a strict order. Whenever this is possible, the determination of the general laws of this order enables us to gain a clear view of the whole field of their validity. The concept of "calculus," therefore, is co-extensive with that of science itself; and it is applicable wherever the conditions of a manifold of experience can be reduced to certain fundamental relations and thus completely determined. Condillac, who first clearly formulated this general scientific concept in his essay *The Language of Calculus,* attempted in his psychology to give a characteristic sample and a fruitful application of the concept. For Condillac, who supports the Cartesian concept of the immateriality and spirituality of the soul, there can be no doubt that a direct mathematical treatment of psychological experience is impossible. For such a direct application of the concepts of quantity is valid only where the object itself consists of parts and can be constructed from these parts; and this can take place only in the realm of corporeal substance, which is defined as pure extension, but not in the realm of thinking "indivisible" substance. However, this fundamental and unalterable opposition between body and soul is no insurmountable barrier for the pure function of analytical knowledge. This function ignores material differences for, by virtue of the purity of its form and the formal nature of its operation, it is bound by no presuppositions regarding content. Even if psychological experience cannot like corporeal experience be divided into parts, yet in thought it can be analyzed into its constitutive elements. To this end it is only necessary that the apparent diversity of such experience be resolved by showing that it is a continuous development from a common source of all psychological phenomena. As proof, Condillac introduces the famous illustration which he places at the center of his psychology. Assuming a marble statue, he describes how it progressively comes to life and acquires an increasingly rich spiritual content because the individual senses engrave their special qualities on the marble. Condillac tries to show that the continuous series of "impres-

sions" and the temporal order in which they are produced are sufficient to build up the totality of psychological experience and to produce it in all its wealth and subtle shadings. If we succeed in producing psychological experience in this manner, we have at the same time reduced it to the quantitative concept. Now everything that we call psychological reality and that we experience as such proves to be fundamentally a mere repetition and transformation of a certain basic quality which is contained in the simplest sense perception. Sense perception forms the borderline between the marble as dead matter and a living being endowed with a soul. But once this borderline has been passed, there is no need of any further assumptions or of any essentially new creations. What we commonly regard as the "higher" powers of the mind, contrasting these powers with sensation, is in reality only a transformation of the basic element of sense perception. All thinking and judging, all desiring and willing, all powers of the imagination and all artistic creation, qualitatively considered, add nothing new, nothing essentially different to this fundamental element. The mind neither creates nor invents; it repeats and constructs. But in this repetition it can exhibit almost inexhaustible powers. It extends the visible universe beyond all bounds; it traverses the infinity of space and time; and yet it is unceasingly engaged in the production of ever new shapes within itself. But throughout its activities the mind is concerned only with itself and its "simple ideas." These constitute the solid ground on which the entire edifice constructed by the mind, both in its "external" and in its "internal" aspects, rests—and from which the mind can never depart.

Condillac's attempt to show that all psychological reality is a transformation, a metamorphosis, of simple sense perception is continued by Helvetius in his book *On the Mind (De l'Esprit)*. The influence which this weak and unoriginal work exerted on the philosophical literature of the eighteenth century is explicable in that the epoch found here a basic element of its thought expressed with pregnant clarity, and indeed with an exaggeration which parodies this thought. In Helvetius's exaggeration the methodological limitation and danger of this mode of thinking is clearly presented. The limitation consists in a

leveling process which threatens to deny the living wealth of human consciousness and to look upon it merely as a disguise. Analytical thinking removes this disguise from psychological phenomena; it exposes them, and in so doing reveals their naked sameness rather than their apparent diversity and inner differentiation. Differences in form as well as in value vanish and prove to be delusions. As a result, there is no longer a "top" and "bottom" or a "higher" and a "lower" in the realm of psychological phenomena. Everything is on the same plane— equal in value and in validity. Helvetius develops this line of thought especially in the field of ethics. His main intention was to sweep away all those artificial differentiations which convention had erected and was trying hard to maintain. Wherever traditional ethics spoke of a special class of "moral" sensations, wherever it thought it found in man an original "feeling of sympathy" which rules over and restrains his sensual and egotistical appetites, Helvetius tries to show how poorly such a hypothesis corresponds to the simple reality of human feeling and action. Whoever approaches this reality without prejudice will find none of that apparent dualism. He will find everywhere and always the same absolutely uniform motivation. He will see that all those qualities which we refer to as unselfishness, magnanimity, and self-sacrifice are different only in name, not in reality, from the elementary impulses of human nature, from the "lower" appetites and passions. No moral greatness rises above this plane. For no matter how high the aims of the will may be, no matter what supernatural values and supersensible goals it may imagine, it remains nonetheless confined within the narrow circle of egotism, ambition, and vanity. Society does not achieve the suppression of these elemental impulses, but only their sublimation; and in so far as society understands its own function, this is all it can ever expect or ask of the individual. Consideration of the theoretical world should be guided by the same viewpoint. According to Helvetius there are neither fundamental gradations in the scale of ethical values nor radical gradations of theoretical form. On the contrary, all such distinctions boil down to the same undifferentiated mass of sensation. The so-called faculties of judgment and cognition,

imagination and memory, and understanding and reason, are by no means specific original powers of the soul. Here again we have been subject to the same delusion. We think we have transcended the sphere of sense perception when we have only slightly modified its appearance. The criticism which explains away this modification also applies to theoretical distinctions. All operations of the mind can be reduced to judgment, and judgment consists only in grasping similarities and differences between individual ideas. But the recognition of similarity and difference presupposes an original act of awareness which is analogous to, or indeed identical with, the perception of a sense quality. "I judge or I perceive that of two objects the one I call 'fathom' makes a different impression on me from the one I call 'foot,' and that the color I call 'red' affects my eyes differently from the color I call 'yellow.' Hence I conclude that in such a case to judge is simply to perceive."[7] Here, as one sees, both the edifice of ethical values and the logically graded structure of knowledge are demolished. Both structures are, as it were, razed to the ground because it is thought that the only unshakable foundation of knowledge lies in sensation.

It would be erroneous to consider the fundamental viewpoint represented by Helvetius as typical of the content of the philosophy of the Enlightenment, as has often been done; and it is equally erroneous to regard it as typical of the thought of the French Encyclopaedists. For the sharpest criticism of Helvetius's work was exercised by precisely this school of thought; and this criticism originated among the best minds in French philosophical literature, as, for instance, Turgot and Diderot. But one thing is undeniable, namely, that in Helvetius as well as in Condillac a certain methodology appears, a methodology characteristic of and decisive for the entire eighteenth century. Here was a form of thinking whose positive achievement and immanent limitations, whose triumphs and defeats, were so to speak predetermined.

2

Thus far we have considered eighteenth century thought principally in its connection with the development of the ana-

lytical spirit, especially as it evolved in France. France was the
birthplace and the truly classical land of analysis, for Descartes
had based his revolutionary transformation of philosophy on
analysis. After the middle of the seventeenth century the Cartesian spirit permeates all fields of knowledge until it dominates not only philosophy, but also literature, morals, political
science, and sociology, asserting itself even in the realm of
theology to which it imparted a new form.[8] But neither in
philosophy nor in general intellectual history does this influence
remain unchallenged. With the philosophy of Leibniz a new
intellectual power emerges. Leibniz not merely alters the content of the prevailing world picture, but he also endows thinking
in general with a new form and a new basic direction. At first,
to be sure, it seemed as if Leibniz were merely continuing the
work of Descartes, as if his intention were simply to free the
forces latent in that work in order to bring about their complete
development. Just as Leibniz's mathematical achievement, his
analysis of the infinite, stems directly from Descartes; just as
this is merely a consistent continuation and a systematic completion of Descartes' analytical geometry, so the same appears to
hold for Leibniz's logic. For this logic begins with the science
of permutations and combinations, and it attempts to develop
this to a general science of the forms of thought. And Leibniz
is convinced that the progress of this theory of the forms of
thought, the realization of the ideal of a *scientia generalis,* as
he imagined it, can only be looked for as a result of the progress
of analysis. From now on all of Leibniz's logical studies are
concentrated on this one point. His goal is to arrive at an "alpha-
bet of ideas," to resolve all complex forms of thought into their
elements, into the last simple basic operations, just as in the
theory of numbers every number can be understood and represented as a product of prime numbers. Thus here again unity,
uniformity, simplicity, and logical equality seem to form the
ultimate and highest goal of thought. All true statements, so far
as they belong to the realm of strictly rational "eternal" truths,
are "virtually identical" and can be reduced to the principle of
identity and contradiction. One can—as Louis Couturat did in
his excellent presentation—try to see Leibniz's logic as a whole

from this viewpoint; or one can go further and include his theory of knowledge, his philosophy of nature, and his metaphysics. In doing the latter one would seem merely to be pursuing Leibniz's own direction, for he always declared that there was no cleavage between his logic and mathematics and his metaphysics, that his entire philosophy was mathematical and had sprung from the innermost core of mathematics.

And yet, if one studies this general and indissoluble connection between the various parts of Leibniz's philosophy, one sees that the tendency hitherto considered basic, however essential it may be to the structure of Leibniz's system, does not exhaust this philosophy as a whole. For the deeper one penetrates into the originality and meaning of the Leibnizian concept of substance, the more distinctly one sees that this concept, both in content and form, represents a new trend of thought. A logic based exclusively on the principle of identity, and considering the whole significance of knowledge to consist in the reduction of diversity to unity, of change to stability, of difference to strict uniformity—such a logic would not do justice to the new concept of substance. Leibniz's metaphysics differs from that of Descartes and Spinoza in that it substitutes for Descartes' dualism and Spinoza's monism a "pluralistic universe." The Leibnizian "monad" is no arithmetical, no merely numerical, unit, but a dynamic one. The true correlate of this unit is not particularity but infinity. Every monad is a living center of energy, and it is the infinite abundance and diversity of monads which constitute the unity of the world. The monad "is" only in so far as it is active, and its activity consists in a continuous transition from one state to another as it produces these states out of itself in unceasing succession. "The nature of the monad consists in being fruitful, and in giving birth to an ever new variety." Thus every simple element of the monad contains its own past and is pregnant with its future. Never is one of these elements just like another; never can it be resolved into the same sum of purely static qualities. Anything we may find in the monad as a whole is self-containing and self-sufficient. The nature and being of the form as a whole is not weakened or divided in the sequence of these distinctions but is contained un-

diminished in each of them. Leibniz sums up this fundamental conception, both conceptually and terminologically, in his concept of *force*. For, according to Leibniz, force is the present state of being in so far as this tends toward a future state or contains that state in itself (*status ipse praesens, dum tendit ad sequentem seu sequentem praeinvolvit*). The monad is not an aggregate but a dynamic whole which can only manifest itself in a profusion, in an infinity, of different effects. In this very infinity it preserves its identity as the same living center of force. This conception, which is no longer based on the concept of being but on that of action, lends an entirely new significance to the problem of the individual entity. Within the limits of analytical logic, of the logic of identity, this problem can only be mastered if the individual entity can be reduced to general concepts and shown to be a special case of these concepts. Such an entity is only "thinkable," can only be clearly and distinctly known, when it can be referred back to general concepts. Taken by itself every individual entity as presented in sense perception or direct intuition must remain an indistinct impression. To be sure, we can ascertain *that* such an impression exists, but we cannot with real precision and assurance say *what* it is. Knowledge of this "what" is reserved for the general concept; it can be gained only from an insight into the nature of the genus or from the definition which offers a general criterion. The individual entity, accordingly, can only be understood when it is included in, and subsumed under, the general concept. Leibniz's doctrine of the concept remains for the most part within this traditional framework yet it was his philosophy that criticized it decisively and implicitly transformed it. For in Leibniz's philosophy an inalienable prerogative is first gained for the individual entity. The individual no longer functions merely as a special case, as an example; it now expresses something essential in itself and valuable through itself. For in Leibniz's system every individual substance is not only a fragment of the universe, it is the universe itself seen from a particular viewpoint. And only the totality of these unique points of view gives us the truth of reality. This truth is not determined by the fact that the various monadological philosophies share certain portions of their content on which

they agree, and these points of agreement form a common core of objectivity. Such truth can be grasped and explained only if every substance, remaining within itself and developing its conceptions according to a law peculiar to its own nature, through this characteristic creation stands in relation to the totality of all other substances and is as it were attuned to their pitch. The central thought of Leibniz's philosophy is therefore to be looked for neither in the concept of individuality nor in that of universality. These concepts are explicable only in mutual relationship; they reflect one another, and in this reflection they beget the fundamental concept of harmony which constitutes the beginning and end of the system. "In our own being," says Leibniz is his essay *Of the True Mystical Theology*, "is contained a germ, a footprint, a symbol of the divine nature and its true image." This means that only the highest development of all individual energies—not their leveling, equalization, and extinction—leads to the truth of being, to the highest harmony, and to the most intensive fullness of reality. This fundamental conception calls for a new intellectual orientation because not only has a transformation in individual results taken place, but the ideal center of gravity of all philosophy has shifted.

To be sure, this inner transformation seems at first to have no immediate, historically demonstrable significance for eighteenth century philosophy. For the whole body of Leibniz's thought does not act immediately as a living and pervading force. At first the eighteenth century knows the Leibnizian philosophy only in a very imperfect, in a purely "exoteric" form. It depends for its knowledge of Leibniz's teachings on a few writings which, like the *Monadology* and the *Theodicy*, owe their existence to external and accidental occasions and hence do not contain these teachings in a strictly conceptual treatment, but only in an abbreviated popular version. The chief work of Leibniz's theory of knowledge, *New Essays on the Human Understanding*, did not become known to the eighteenth century until the year 1765 when it was published by Raspe from the manuscript in Hanover at a time when the evolution and formulation of eighteenth century thought had for the most part already reached completion. The influence of Leibnizian ideas is there-

fore indirect, namely, by way of the transformation they underwent in the system of Wolff. Wolff's logic and methodology
differ from those of Leibniz in that they attempt to reduce the
variety of their deductions to as simple and uniform an arrangement as possible. The idea of harmony, the principle of continuity, and the law of sufficient reason have their specified place
within Wolff's system, but Wolff tries to limit their original
significance and independence and to show that they are inferences and deductions from the law of contradiction. Thus the
concepts and basic tendencies of the Leibnizian system are transmitted to the eighteenth century with certain limitations, and
they appear here, as it were, through a glass darkly. Gradually,
however, a movement gets under way which endeavors to
abolish this barrier to full comprehension. In Germany it is
Wolff's most important pupil, Alexander Baumgarten, who
shows his intellectual independence and originality in this matter also. In his metaphysics, and especially in the outline of his
aesthetics, Baumgarten finds his way back to certain central
conceptions of Leibniz which hitherto had lain fallow. The
development of aesthetics and the philosophy of history in
Germany now leads us back to the original and profound conception of the problem of individuality as first set forth in Leibniz's monadology and in his "system of pre-established harmony." But in eighteenth century French culture too, in which
the Cartesian influence is still predominant, certain basic conceptions and problems of Leibniz appear with increasing fre-
qency. The development does not proceed via aesthetics and
the theory of art, which only with difficulty free themselves
from the spell of seventeenth century classicism; but rather
via the philosophy of nature and the descriptive sciences within
which the rigid concept of form gradually breaks down. Leibniz's conception of evolution now receives more and more stress,
and it gradually transforms from within the eighteenth century
system of nature which had been dominated by the idea of fixed
species. Steady progress can be traced from Maupertuis' revival of the basic idea of Leibniz's dynamics and from his
defense and interpretation of the principle of continuity to
Diderot's physics and metaphysics of the organic and to the

beginnings of a comprehensive descriptive natural science in Buffon's *Natural History*. In *Candide* Voltaire parodies Leibniz's *Theodicy*, and in his essay on the elements of the Newtonian philosophy he charges that in natural science too Leibniz's concepts had been obstacles to progress. "His insufficient reason, his continuity, his plenum, his monads, etc.," writes Voltaire in 1741, "are the germs of confusion from which Mr. Wolff has methodically hatched fifteen quarto volumes which more than ever will put German heads to reading much and understanding little."[9] But Voltaire did not always judge in this manner. When, as in his *Age of Louis XIV*, he wanted to present the intellectual structure of the seventeenth century and to understand this structure in the light of its basic forces, he could not overlook Leibniz; and here in fact he acknowledges without reserve the universal significance of Leibniz's total achievement. This change of opinion becomes even more apparent in the generation after Voltaire, namely, among the French Encyclopaedists. While opposing the principles of Leibniz's metaphysics, d'Alembert shows the deepest admiration for Leibniz's philosophical and mathematical genius. And Diderot's article on Leibniz in the *Encyclopaedia* bestows enthusiastic praise on the philosopher. Diderot agrees with Fontenelle that Germany has gained as much honor through this one mind as Greece did through Plato, Aristotle, and Archimedes together. From such personal expressions of praise to a deeper understanding of the principles of the Leibnizian philosophy is still, to be sure, a long way. Yet if one wishes to grasp the entire intellectual structure of the eighteenth century and see it in its genesis, one must clearly separate the two streams of thought which converge at this point. The classical Cartesian form of analysis and that new form of philosophical synthesis which originates in Leibniz are now integrated. From the logic of "clear and distinct ideas" the way leads to the logic of "origin" and to the logic of individuality; it leads from mere geometry to a dynamic philosophy of nature, from mechanism to organism, from the principle of identity to that of infinity, from continuity to harmony. In this fundamental opposition lay the great intellectual tasks which eighteenth century thought had to ac-

complish, and which the century approaches from different
angles in its theory of knowledge and in its philosophy of nature, in its psychology and in its theory of the state and society,
in its philosophy of religion and in its aesthetics.

NOTES

1 D'Alembert, "Éléments de Philosophie," in *Mélanges de Littérature, d'Histoire, et de Philosophie,* nouvelle édition, six volumes, Amsterdam, 1759, vol. IV,
pp. 3–6.

2 Voltaire, *Traité de Métaphysique,* chs. III and V.

2a Cf. Ducros, *Les Encyclopédistes,* Paris, 1900, p. 138.

3 *Oeuvres,* Paris, 1818, vol. I, p. 34.

4 Cf. Condillac, *Traité des sensations,* and also the "Extrait raisonné" which
Condillac added to later editions of his treatise (ed. Georges Lyon, Paris, 1921,
especially pp. 32 ff.).

5 Condillac, *Traité des systèmes,* part II, ch. XV.

6 D'Alembert, "Éléments des Sciences," *Encyclopédie,* Paris, 1755, V, 493. Cf.
Éléments de Philosophie, IV; *Mélanges de littérature, d'histoire et de philosophie,* IV, 35 f.

7 Helvetius, *De l'Esprit,* Paris, 1759, p. 8.

8 For more detailed information see Gustave Lanson's excellent account
entitled "L'influence de la philosophie cartésienne sur la littérature française,"
in *Revue de métaphysique et de morale,* 1896; now also in *Études d'histoire
littéraire,* Paris, 1929, pp. 58 ff.

9 Cf. Voltaire's correspondence, especially his letters to Mairan (May 5, 1741)
and to Maupertuis (August 10, 1741).

The Background of Science and Ideas

ᖇᕑᕐ

WILLIAM POWELL JONES

I

The conflict between the visionary power of the artist and the analytical method of the scientists has led to the twentieth-century hostility of literature and science. This is what A. N. Whitehead calls 'the discord between the aesthetic intuitions of mankind and the mechanism of science', of which nineteenth-century English poetry is a witness.[1] This hostility did not exist, however, in the late seventeenth and early eighteenth centuries, when poets greeted the advancements of science with enthusiasm. This book tells the story of this enthusiasm, the influence of science on eighteenth-century English poetry, particularly in ideas and imagery.

The transition from the seventeenth-century confidence in science as proof of order in nature to the nineteenth-century hostility to science can be found in the profuse number of poems in the eighteenth century that lent a new rhetoric to science in an overwhelming desire to show the wisdom of God in nature. The subjects used for illustration changed during the century, gradually shifting after 1750 from astronomy and microscopic studies as the chief source of examples to natural history, but the faith in an orderly universe was still there at the end of the century. Before 1800 there was little determined hostility to science, only the continuity of a skeptical attitude that illustrated the limitations of

From William Powell Jones, The Rhetoric of Science (Berkeley and Los Angeles: University of California Press, 1966), pp.1–32.

science because it could not give the answer as to how or why certain phenomena took place in nature.

The change in the attitude of eighteenth-century English poets toward science can be dramatized in the two extremes shown in attitudes toward Sir Isaac Newton, one by James Thomson in 1727 and the other by Blake at the end of the century. In the best of a number of poems on Newton's death, Thomson described Newton's scientific achievements and lavishly praised his ability to 'trace the secret hand of Providence' from the laws of motion. William Blake by 1800 had freely expressed his dislike of science by linking Newton with Bacon and Locke as symbols of materialistic analysis and experiment opposed to the spiritual world of imagination symbolized by Milton, Shakespeare, and Chaucer.

Between Thomson and Blake science had developed so rapidly that natural history became the only branch of science that was easily grasped by the poets. The soaring imagination that had sublimely written about Newton's orderly universe of limitless space and the equally harmonious world under the microscope now found its chief scientific inspiration in realistic description of numerous plants and birds. The story of this slowly developing rhetoric of science may be said to begin about 1700 when the use of telescope and microscope so fired the poetic imagination that science became the chief inspiration of a new kind of Biblical paraphrase and a new interest in sublime descriptions of the physical universe. The real story, however, begins much earlier with Galileo and Bacon in science, and with Donne and More in English poetry.

Modern science began when Galileo and Kepler, with their research in astronomy and mechanics in the late sixteenth and early seventeenth centuries, demonstrated and perfected the theory of the universe which Copernicus had formulated in opposition to the older Ptolemaic system. In England it was Francis Bacon who gave the impetus to scientific research ('experimental philosophy') that bore fruit in the founding of the Royal Society. Bacon had in his writings, especially the *New Atlantis,* promoted the idea that scientists should pool their research, since the vast body of natural knowledge was too much for one man to attempt. The 'Invisible College', composed of devoted English scientists, met weekly in

1645 and as regularly as the confusion of Civil War would allow until 1662, when it received the patronage of the newly restored King Charles II and became the *Royal Society of London for the Promotion of Natural Knowledge.*

Meanwhile such poets as John Donne and John Milton showed the impact of the newer science on the creative mind, while Shakespeare, Spenser, and Sidney wrote with little or no awareness of the ferment around them. As early as 1642 Henry More was using science in his philosophical poetry, and after 1660 Abraham Cowley and John Norris of Bemerton followed his lead. Men of letters were closely associated with the Royal Society— Dryden, Waller, Denham, and Cowley—and conversely, the desire of scientists to simplify the language and make it more universal had a decided effect on changing prose style from the florid and decorative to the simple and straightforward.

Excitement was in the air around 1700 over the limitless possibilities of this new science, an excitement much like that of today when the prodigious discoveries in all fields of science, especially nuclear physics, stagger the imagination. At the end of the seventeenth century in Europe, the celestial universe seemed boundless: each new development in the telescope revealed new stars, and so it was self-evident that still further improvement in observation would show newer suns and systems. Ordinary men, theologians and poets in particular, studied astronomy and let their imagination play among the stars. Space travel was a frequent topic, at least in fantasy, and trips to the moon dominated the science fiction of the time. Speculation was abundant over what creatures inhabited this plurality of worlds revealed by the telescope.

Conversely, the stretching world of micro-organisms revealed by constantly improved microscopes appealed to the imagination. The under side of a leaf or drop of water could hold myriads of living creatures that were just as orderly in their little world as the planets and comets in the celestial universe. If men could see so much with their present knowledge of optics, how much more would they be able to see with new optical improvements. The wisdom of God was apparent, and the boundless fertility of nature was staggering to the imagination.

And there was fear then, too, not that man would destroy himself through science, but that God, who had brought the elements of nature together into an orderly world, might at any moment put the process in reverse and unspin 'the web of nature' as a prelude to the Last Judgment. There was much in 1700 that looks like the 1960's, but there was one great difference: the layman then was an amateur scientist who could follow the new discoveries and even write about them. His imagination was stirred by this science that he called 'natural philosophy', and so it seemed sublime enough for poetry, even if the verse he wrote might not always be sublime or even worthy of being called poetry.

The seventeenth-century scientist himself was far from a specialist in the modern sense of the word. Robert Boyle, discoverer of the famous law of gases, wrote many books on physics and theology as well as chemistry. Sir Isaac Newton was not only mathematician and university science professor but also inventor of a reflecting telescope, efficient Master of the Mint, and author of books on theology and ancient history. Many of the scientists, moreover, were also collectors of many kinds of things, of skeletons, plants, mummies, stuffed crocodiles, and all kinds of natural monstrosities, as well as such cultural things as books, manuscripts, and objects of art. Ironically, they became known to writers and men about town, however, as *virtuosi* or specialists, and so they were ridiculed for not being 'gentlemen'. The pattern is best known in Shadwell's play, *The Virtuoso*, in Pope's *Dunciad*, and in Swift's picture of the Royal Academy of Lagado in Book III of *Gulliver's Travels*. The sequel is also interesting, for the butt of much of this ridicule was Sir Hans Sloane, a wealthy physician who, when he died, left his great collection of books and specimens to become the nucleus of the British Museum.

The new science that had been developing in the late seventeenth century, in spite of this unsympathetic reception by some writers, opened up vast new realms for the play of the imagination that had a tremendous impact on literature. With the improvement of the telescope and the founding of observatories at Paris and Greenwich, such astronomers as Huygens, Flamsteed, and

Halley were able to improve upon the early work of Kepler and reveal a universe in the skies that stretched to new stars which could be shown to be new suns for new systems like the solar system. The earth, which was formerly the center of the universe, became a mere speck in a plurality of worlds, each of which was believed to be inhabited by reasonable creatures, some of them undoubtedly of a higher intelligence than human beings. The earliest fantasies of a world in the moon, an imaginary voyage to which furnished the plot for a number of books,[2] now stretched in poetry to include distant galaxies and systems. Most important of all to the imagination, Newton demonstrated by his laws of motion that this telescopic universe was orderly and harmonious, by proving mathematically that the orbits of planets and stars, and even comets, could be calculated with precision. He became to the poets the symbol of the new science that magically revealed the wisdom of God in creating and setting in motion a world that, though mechanically perfect, still required divine direction. By 1700 the microscope had also been so improved as to reveal, at the other end of the Great Chain of Being, an orderly universe in miniature that showed God's watchful care in the small animals in a drop of pond scum as much as in the vast stretching world in the skies.[3]

II

The new scientific movement symbolized by the formation of the Royal Society in 1662 was dominated by a fervor for experimentation and collecting of data from observation of nature that was inspired by Bacon. At the same time it was keenly interested in philosophical ideas: it rejected the debilitating theory of the decay of nature in favor of the idea of progress; it developed a faith in the method of direct investigation that led to a break with the authority of Aristotle and the ancients and an attack on the scientific ideas of antiquity; and finally it weighed carefully the new ideas, especially Cartesianism, with varying results. The impact of the new philosophy upon thought, and later upon religion and literature, is of the greatest importance to our subject of science and poetry in the eighteenth century. The best account of the rise of the scientific movement in seventeenth-century

England is probably Professor Richard Foster Jones's *Ancients and Moderns,* first published in 1936, and his later books and articles. He emphasizes the fact that the new science of that day not only encouraged discoveries based on experiment and observation but also, unlike that of our own day, ardently preached and defended the controlling ideas.[4]

The English reaction to the new mechanical philosophy of Descartes around the middle of the seventeenth century is an example of this intellectual movement among scientists in England. The dramatic appeal of matter as particles whirling in vortices, of the importance of the mind ('Cogito, ergo sum'), and of the infinity of life in a plurality of worlds (later popularized by Fontenelle) aided an early acceptance of the Cartesian doctrine by English scientists, courtiers, and the Cambridge Platonists. Within a short time, however, the suspicion of atheism arose, aided perhaps by the fact that Thomas Hobbes vigorously supported Descartes, and the writing of such orthodox scientists as Robert Boyle began to attack Descartes's notion of a physical universe that was mechanistically determined and therefore seemed to have no place for God.[5]

Paradoxically, a good example of the early acceptance of Descartes, Henry More's *An Antidote against Atheism* (1652), is also a startling instance of the orthodox praise of science as a means of discovering the uniformity, beauty, and harmony of the natural world, not only in the celestial phenomena of Descartes but also in the more familiar minerals, plants, and animals. Such proofs of a 'knowing principle, able to move, alter, and guide the matter according to his own will and pleasure' revealed to More a God whose 'visible footsteps' could be traced by science. This enthusiasm for science symbolized by Descartes appears in More's summary of the scientific activities of the seventeenth century, written before the founding of the Royal Society:

For there being so many notable objects in the world to entertain such faculties as reason and inquisitive admiration, there ought to be such a member of the visible creation as man, that those things might not be in vain; and if man were out of the world, who were then left to view the face of heaven, to wonder at the transcursion of comets, to calculate

tables for the motions of the planets and fix'd stars, and to take their heights and distances with mathematical instruments; to invent convenient cycles for the computation of time, and consider the several forms of years; to take notice of the directions, stations and repedations of those erratick lights, and from thence most convincingly to inform himself of that pleasant and true paradox of the annual motion of the earth; to view the asperities of the moon through a dioptrick glass, and venture at the proportion of her hills by their shadows; to behold the beauty of the rain-bow, the halo, parelii and other meteors; to search out the causes of the flux and reflux of the sea, and the hidden virtue of the magnet; to inquire into the usefulness of plants, and to observe the wisdom of the first Cause in framing their bodies, and giving sundry observable instincts to fishes, birds, and beasts?[6]

The attacks on Descartes began early in England. In 1663 Boyle proclaimed in *The Usefulnesse of Experimental Natural Philosophy* the combination of religion and experimental science that was later to become the foundation of orthodox physico-theology. In the second essay of this book he made this plain by praising the new science 'on the ground that it incites men to devotion, since experiments and observation, especially with the aid of such instruments as the telescope and microscope, reveal the power, wisdom, and goodness of God as seen in his marvelously contrived creations'. The fourth essay specifically attacks Descartes's theory on the ground that, while it successfully explained the physical universe, the logical inference arising from it was that it left no place for God. In other words Boyle believed what he thought Descartes denied, namely that God created the world, imparted motion to matter, and continued to operate the machine of the world.[7]

Thomas Sprat in his *History of the Royal Society* (1667) and a number of other scientific writers of the Restoration period attacked Descartes for basing his philosophy too much upon conjecture and not enough on experiment. To them the atheistic implications in Cartesian materialism revealed by Hobbes made it necessary to distinguish between their philosophy and Descartes's. All scientists believed in the methods of experimental philosophy, whereas the mechanical philosophy was theory with which they might or might not agree.[8]

These apologists for the new science in the late seventeenth century were devout men of religion who saw no difficulty in reconciling data from observation of nature with natural religion itself. The best example of the continuity of the idea that science furnishes the aptest illustrations from nature for the wisdom of God are to be found in the prose writings of the scientists themselves and in the poetical paraphrases of certain parts of the Bible. Thomas Sprat, Joseph Glanvill, Walter Charleton, John Ray, and Robert Boyle were among the eminent writers on science in the late seventeenth century who tried to show that there is a God demonstrated by nature, whose power and wisdom we should be led to admire from a study of the natural world. They cited parts of the Bible, particularly Job and the Psalms, as models for the praise of God in nature. John Ray led the way for many scientific poems by his famous book, *The Wisdom of God as Manifested in the Works of the Creation,* which appeared in a number of enlarged editions after its first appearance in 1691. Probably no one was more effective in linking science and religion than Boyle, especially in the lectures he endowed to defend Christianity against unbelievers. These lectures, delivered from 1692 to 1722 and later collected under the title, *A Defence of Natural and Revealed Religion* (1739), included summaries of scientific opinion and the latest scientific discoveries by such philosophical writers as Richard Bentley, Samuel Clarke, William Derham, and William Wollaston.[9]

Sir Isaac Newton should be included with these scientists who defended religion. Among the important discoveries of seventeenth-century science was Newton's universal law of gravitation, from which the laws of motion were propounded by which the orbits of celestial bodies could be mathematically demonstrated. Newton was essentially a scientist who said himself that he was able to discover 'the cause of those properties of gravity from phenomena' and therefore he would 'frame no hypotheses'. Yet he too was a religious man like his friend Boyle, and so, though he made no mention of God in the first edition of his famous *Principia* in 1687, he allowed his editor Roger Cotes to add to the second edition in 1713 the belief that there was a First Cause, a Creator who made the laws of motion, put the universe in order,

and has kept it ever since.[10] Though he would have nothing to do with metaphysics, the influence of his own assumptions on subsequent thought was great, leading to ideas that Newton, himself the author of theological treatises, would have rejected.[11]

The growing conflict between the scientist and the man of genuine religious convictions did not affect the othodox views of Newton or of many scientists of his day, and certainly not those of the theologians and poets who followed him and made of his demonstrations of an orderly universe a sort of new religion that took as its main theme a rhapsodic praise of the power, wisdom, and goodness of God.[12] This kind of poetic Newtonianism refused to acknowledge that Newton had shown a mechanical universe that left God with little to do. The poets of the eighteenth century expressed their admiration of Newton with repeated verboseness, the praise that Pope, with his usual conciseness, put into a single couplet:

> Nature, and Nature's Laws lay hid in Night:
> God said, *Let Newton be!* and All was *Light.*

Modern commentators can see the mistake that Newton made in mixing the two levels of discourse, the mechanical and the religious, but the popularizers and the poets, struck by the sublimity of the new conception of the universe, could see no inconsistency.[13]

III

We are not concerned here with understanding or trying to present the scientific data involved in the discoveries of this period, of Gilbert or Harvey or Boyle or Newton, or even of the new discoveries made possible by technical improvements in optics used in telescope and microscope. The historian of science may show that the genius of Newton was that of synthesis, since all the data needed for his laws were already published, and the historian of ideas may show that Newton's theology was outdated and that the unconscious metaphysics arising from the assumptions of his laws of gravitation and motion were to influence later thinking to a degree and in a manner that would have

horrified Newton. Yet in his own day Newton was best known for proving what the poets already believed, that God had created an orderly universe, and for dramatizing the impact upon the imagination already made by the telescope. Now for the first time man could calculate the motions not only of the solar system, the orbits of the moon around the earth and of the earth and other planets around the sun, but also of distant systems and even of seemingly erring comets. The scientific proof of an orderly universe gave a new meaning to the older praise of God in the creation, which they had been chanting in church services for more than a hundred years, and added new metaphors and illustrations from science to Biblical paraphrases of the glory of God declared by the heavens.

Newton's ideas were made available to the general reader around the turn of the century by the various writings of scientists with a theological turn of mind. Most prominent of these before he turned to odd heresies was Newton's successor at Cambridge, William Whiston, especially in *A New Theory of the Earth,* first written in 1696 but revised in several other editions. An example of the usefulness of this book to the poets is the imaginative comment on the fixed stars that follows a summary of the state of knowledge of the subject: 'But then as to the nature of the fix'd stars, 'tis in all probability the same with the sun's; and so each of them may have their respective systems of planets and comets as well as he has. Which things, considering that the number of them is continually found to be greater, according as the telescopes we use are longer and more perfect, do vastly aggrandize the idea of the visible universe; and ought proportionably to raise our admiration of the Great Author of the whole to the highest degree imaginable.'[14]

Another commentator on Newton quoted by imaginative writers is George Cheyne, whose *Philosophical Principles of Natural Religion* (1705), after chapters on the physical laws of nature, on gravity, and the pagan philosophies of nature, includes chapters on the existence of a deity and 'the proofs for the being of a God arising from the contemplation of the humane structure'. In his preface Cheyne acknowledges his debt to Newton, 'that great inventor and improver of most of our modern philosophy and geometry', as well as to Newton's other interpreters,

Roger Cotes and William Derham. Atheism, he concludes, 'may be eternally confounded, by the most distant approaches to the true causes of natural appearances'.

Roger Cotes, the brilliant young Cambridge mathematician who died young, was largely responsible for the improvements made in the second edition of Newton's *Principia.* The correspondence of Newton and Cotes between 1709, when Bentley got Newton's consent to a new edition, and 1713, when the work was published, shows what great labor lay behind Cotes's comparatively brief Latin preface to the edition, in which he summarized the arguments against 'some persons and those of great name, too much prepossessed with certain prejudices' and added the belief, presumably Newton's, that a divine mind was the first cause of the effects discovered by science.

The third edition of the *Principia* (1726), a handsome folio in large type printed by the Royal Society,[15] had the distinction of a poetic eulogy in Latin by Newton's friend and fellow scientist, Edmund Halley. For a summary of the laws of motion by a learned astronomer, the descriptive portion is very concise, beginning

> Intima panduntur victi penetralia caeli,
> Nec latet extremos quae vis circumrotat orbes.

To continue in what is apparently the first English translation, that of Francis Fawkes in 1761, we now know 'what course the dire tremendous comets steer', the seemingly erratic motions of the moon and its effects on tides. Like other poets, Halley makes Newton the favorite of the muses, 'Newton, that reach'd th' insuperable line, The nice barrier 'twixt human and divine.'

The death of Newton in 1727 seemed to inspire a number of popularizations of his works. The first English translation of the *Principia* was published in 1729 by Andrew Motte, younger brother of Benjamin Motte, who was best known as the publisher of *Gulliver's Travels.* Andrew had helped his brother in 1721 edit a three-volume abridgment of the *Transactions of the Royal Society,* 1700–20, and in 1727 had himself written 'an easy and familiar' explanation of the laws of motion. Motte's translation included not only the additions contained in the second and

third editions but also the first English version of the pertinent parts of Cotes's preface. A sample from the conclusion of this famous preface summarizes much of the Newtonian physico-theology that was the main theme of the long scientific poems to follow: 'Without all doubt this world, so diversified with that variety of forms and motives we find in it, could arise from nothing but the perfectly free will of God directing and presiding over all. From this fountain it is that those laws, which we call the laws of Nature, have flowed; in which there appear many traces of the most wise contrivance, but not the least shadow of necessity. These therefore we must not seek from uncertain conjectures, but learn them from observations and experiments.' From Newton's example the close relation between religion and science, that part of natural philosophy which depended on experiment and observation of data, became well established. By the middle of the century it was a commonplace to say that the way to understand God was to study the works of nature.[16]

Yet the full impact of Newton's discoveries on poetry waited for the theologians and popularizers. At first the popular accounts were written by the divines, particularly the inaugural series of Boyle Lectures given by Richard Bentley in 1692 and William Derham's *Astro-theology: or a Demonstration of the Being and Attributes of God, from a Survey of the Heavens* (1751), the sequel to his own Boyle Lectures (*Physico-theology*) on the wisdom of God as shown by man, animals, and other things seen on land. Perhaps the two books of Derham, together with William Wollaston's *The Religion of Nature Delineated* (1722), were the physico-theological writings that most influenced poetry, and so their ideas will be summarized later. But the number of scientific popularizations of Newton increased after his death in 1727.

In 1728 Henry Pemberton's *A View of Sir Isaac Newton's Philosophy* appeared, a work now best known for the first printing of the inept eulogy of Newton in verse by Richard Glover that contains the phrase 'Newton demands the muse'. In 1735 an English translation of W. J. s'Gravesande's Latin lectures at Leyden was published in London as *An Explanation of the Newtonian Philosophy*. In 1737 the youthful Francesco Algarotti, later the friend of Thomas Gray and protege of Frederick the Great, fired by

Voltaire's interest in Newton, printed his popularization of the *Optics* as *Il Newtonianismo per le Dame,* which the learned Elizabeth Carter was to translate in 1739 as *Sir Isaac Newton's Philosophy Explained for the Use of the Ladies, in Six Dialogues on Light and Colour,* her first contribution in a long life devoted to science and scholarship. Newton's Scots disciple, Colin Maclaurin, had prepared his *Account of Sir Isaac Newton's Philosophy* before 1728, but it was not published until 1748. Benjamin Martin included elementary Newtonian physics among the topics in his many science books written for the layman, yet he also wrote *A Panegyrick on the Newtonian Philosophy* in 1749.

Not all the writings on Newton were favorable. The strangest early opponent, John Hutchinson in his *Moses's Principia* (1724), and the later opposition recorded in William Jones's *Essay on the First Principles of Natural Philosophy* (1762) were repeated in the encyclopedias as late as 1842.[17] The serious refutation of Roger North in his science notebook in the British Museum (Add. MS. 32,546), as far as I know, was never published. The ideas arising from Newton's physics were well established, however, by 1750 and continued through the century in the writings of James Ferguson.

IV

Astronomy was only one of the branches of science that contributed to this physico-theology that excited the poets of the early eighteenth century, though it continued, probably because of its sublime setting, to be one of the most influential. Microscopic study, human physiology, and botany were also popular sources of illustrations of divine wisdom in nature, and occasionally minerals, animals, and insects were added. Even Fontenelle's astronomical dialogues for learned ladies, *Conversations on the Plurality of Worlds,* first published in France in 1686 and later widely known in England, included a section on the value of the microscope for exploring the universe.[18] From 1704 encyclopedias began their popularizations of general science in England, with John Harris's *Lexicon Technicum,* followed in 1710 by a supplementary second volume and in 1728 by the two folio volumes of Ephraim Chambers' *Cyclopaedia, or an Universal*

Dictionary of Arts and Sciences.[19] The use of dialogues for instructing amateur scientists was continued in John Harris's *Astronomical Dialogues between a Gentleman and a Lady* (1719) and in the various editions and translations of Pluche's *Spectacle de la Nature,* over half of which was devoted to insects and the rest to birds, animals, fishes, and plants.

The most prolific of the early popularizers of general science was Benjamin Martin, who in the forty years from 1733 published at least forty works, most of them compendiums of science for amateurs of all ages and both sexes. Perhaps his best known work was *The Philosophical Grammar,* published in at least seven enlarged editions after its first appearance in 1735. This compendium describes itself as 'a view of the present state of experimental physiology, or natural philosophy' and includes in its four parts somatology (doctrine of the universal properties of nature), cosmology (celestial bodies), aerology (air, winds, meteorology), and geology (earth, minerals, waters, plants, animals). By 1743 he could say, in his preface to *A Course of Lectures in Natural and Experimental Philosophy, Geography, and Astronomy,* that science is now fashionable and 'to cultivate this study, is only to be in taste, and politeness is an inseparable consequence'. This idea was repeated in his *General Magazine of Arts and Sciences* beginning in 1755, which he reprinted under the title of *The Young Gentleman and Lady's Philosophy,* containing scientific experiments and dialogues illustrated with plates and poetry. In addition to his books and lectures. Martin kept a shop for optical instruments and advertised in his books that he could repeat the numerous microscopic views mentioned and could furnish every experiment in hydrostatics and mechanics. All this is useful, he said, to study religion and poetry, for even insects under the microscope 'loudly declare the wondrous skill and wisdom of their maker'.

The popularizations of science made by Martin illustrate with a cross-section what was going on with other popularizers in England, that the books were written for the instruction and entertainment of amateurs, especially ladies and young people, that the instruction extended to moral and religious applications that included the physico-theological ideas of the poetry of the time, and that the tastes in science were changing even as the subjects

used to illustrate science in poetry were changing. During the early part of the eighteenth century the ladies studied the stars and tried to understand Newton. From 1740 to 1760 the microscope, which had been already much talked about, came into vogue for actual experimentation by amateurs. After 1760 the chief polite branch of science is botany, supplemented by a certain amount of other natural history, especially birds. These shifts in amateur scientific pursuits were not only important to the social history of the times. They also had a profound influence on the poetry of the late eighteenth century that has not been fully recognized. The full documentation of this popular interest in science must wait for a separate study, but the transfer of ideas from science to poetry cannot be explained without knowing something of the impact of the study of microscopic life and natural history on amateurs. Let us begin with the microscope, an instrument designed for scholarly research but used by amateurs for amusement and by poets and theologians for moral teaching.

The discoveries of the little world of nature under the microscope became the amusement of ladies and young people from about 1740.[20] Henry Baker wrote several popular guides to microscopic study, summarizing the research of Hooke and Leuwenhoek, but his work can be shown best in *The Microscope Made Easy* (1743). Dedicated to the President of the Royal Society and designed to make the discovery of truth by means of experiment 'easy, intelligible, and pleasant', this handbook dramatized the fertility of nature by showing in a drop of water creatures so small 'that a million of them are less than a grain of sand', in male semen 'millions of millions of animalcules', and in the internal structure of a gnat or louse a sublime idea of 'the infinite power, wisdom, and goodness of Nature's Almighty Parent'. We should not, Baker reminds us, be ignorant of the 'capitals in nature's mighty volume', which he identifies as 'bears, tigers, lions, crocodiles and whales, oaks and cedars, seas and mountains, comets, stars, worlds and suns', but to understand the basic principles we must also become 'master of the little letters likewise, which occur a thousand times more frequently'.

In 1746 the elder George Adams published *Micrographia Illus-*

trata, a serious handbook with numerous folding plates illustrating experiments with the microscope. Natural philosophy had by that time become so greatly improved, he said, that few persons with liberal education 'are wholly unacquainted with the value of it', but one should avoid the mistake of pursuing only the big and obvious, since the smallest works are perfect in their kind and show infinite wisdom and power as much as the largest. 'The more we enquire into nature, the more excellent she appears', and there is no way better than with the microscope, where beauty of color combines with amazing variety.

John Hill helped greatly to popularize natural history, particularly the microscope, with his *Essays in Natural History and Philosophy, Containing a Series of Discoveries, by the Assistance of the Microscope* (1752) and with his diverting periodical essays called *The Inspector* that appeared from March 1751 in the London *Daily Advertiser.* He wishes, he said, to improve the use of the microscope, which was already much esteemed for the way in which it leads to useful knowledge, pleases the imagination, and 'renders the whole life one continual act of adoration.' There is a pleasing and familiar air about Hill's microscopic experiments: fungus from the American Grove in Goodwood, coral from the bottom of the sea, stagnant water from the pond behind Montague House, sand from Minorca, and an American moth in the Chelsea Apothecaries' Garden. All such experiments, Hill insisted, were brought in, not as digressions but to introduce general principles. Writing as 'The Inspector' Hill introduced diverting scientific expeditions to teach as well as entertain: a conducted nature tour on Primrose Hill, and a study of the aquatic creatures on Hampstead Heath ready to turn into flies. But he was careful to point out the distinction between natural history, with its childish delight in collecting and observing, and natural philosophy which challenges the highest human understanding.[21]

After 1760 the most popular subject for scientific study was natural history, especially botany. The Englishman has always loved flowers and birds and some animals, and he could always justify his use of them in poetry by citing Virgil's *Georgics.* Yet the difference is that in the eighteenth century, as with the celes-

tial bodies and the invisible world of microscopic animals, the poets put new life into their georgics and their Biblical paraphrases by using sharp imagery and apt illustrations from the latest discoveries of science.

Until the middle of the century the birds and flowers and insects and quadrupeds were usually thrown in with other scientific proofs of divine benevolence and omniscience found in astronomy, microscopic research, and human anatomy. Botany, it is true, had developed early as a science in England, partly because of the interest of medicine in establishing various botanic gardens at great expense, and partly because of the perennial interest in gardening for home, kitchen, and parks. Both interests had accelerated considerably with increasing exploration of foreign lands and the consequent knowledge of exotic plants that came from describing them in travel books and actually importing them for English collections.

It was not until the middle of the eighteenth century, however, that natural history, under the impetus of the new classification scheme of Linnaeus, became an established branch of study with amateurs as well as scientists. After 1760 the scientific study of plants, birds, quadrupeds, and even insects became the polite avocation of clergymen, writers, and ladies, and for this study the term 'natural history' came to be used to distinguish collecting and observing from 'natural philosophy', the general term for all science in the earlier years of the century but used in the late eighteenth century to designate the more theoretical branches of physics and chemistry. Popularizers like Benjamin Martin, John Hill, and Thomas Pennant fed the avid followers of Linnaeus with books, articles in magazines, and numerous compendiums devoted to the new developments in natural history. Gilbert White's *Natural History of Selborne,* which later became a sort of Bible for those amateur naturalists who noted the first blossoms of spring and the last appearance of the swallows before winter, was at first a publisher's venture made up of actual letters by a parson in a little Hampshire village describing rural life for the scientists of London. John Aikin helped to show that natural history was a respectable subject for poetry, and Thomson's *Seasons* furnished the model.

Up to 1750, then, natural history got general treatment in the compendiums of science, with very little in zoology and mineralogy and more on botany. Of these popular handbooks the most widely read were probably the two translations of Noël Antoine Pluche's *Spectacle de la nature* and Benjamin Martin's *The Philosophical Grammar*.[22] An example of the changes taking place in the growing popularity of natural history may be seen by comparing two of Martin's publications. *The Philosophical Grammar* (1735), as we have seen, treats plants and animals as merely part of 'geology', which is itself one of four divisions of science. On the other hand, Martin's *General Magazine of Arts and Sciences* (1755–1763), reprinted in several editions after 1759 as *The Young Gentleman and Lady's Philosophy*, devotes one of its three scientific sections to a 'survey of the principal subjects of the animal, vegetable, and mineral kingdoms'.

The magazines began early to cater to the new taste for natural history. In July 1752 the *Universal Magazine of Knowledge and Pleasure* proposed 'to give a compendious system of natural history illustrated with copper plates of the most curious animals, vegetables, and minerals, in their natural colours'. By 1760 at least four magazines had followed suit: the *Grand Magazine of Universal Intelligence*, the *Lady's Magazine*, the *Royal Female Magazine*, and the *Royal Magazine, or Gentleman's Monthly Companion*. And the *Imperial Magazine, or Complete Monthly Intelligencer* announced in its opening number in 1760 that it would give a copper plate of a Chinese pheasant and follow with other curiosities, since of all the employments of man, 'there is none which conveys so much real advantage, as well as solid pleasure to it, as the enquiring into the nature and properties of the things about us'.

The elegant world was furnished with a series of handsome illustrated folios of natural history by Sir John Hill, two of which came before 1760, *A General Natural History* (1748) with sections on fossils, plants, and animals, and *The British Herbal* (1756). In 1759 Benjamin Stillingfleet, who as the original 'bluestocking' did much to interest the learned ladies of London in science, published his *Miscellaneous Tracts relating to Natural*

History, which included translations of Linnaeus and other scientists designed 'to make known more generally how far all mankind is concerned in the study of natural history, and thereby to incite such as are properly qualified . . . and encourage that branch of knowledge'. A sample of the scientific dictionary available to poets after 1760 can be seen in the six volumes of *A New Accurate System of Natural History* written by Richard Brookes, M.D., to supply for the average person 'a complete cheap, and commodious body' of this most certain of all sciences. The inquirer is at first bewildered by 'the multitude of Nature's productions', he begins, but greater study 'points out a similitude in many objects which at first appeared different', and so the mind rises from minutiae to general considerations, until at last 'it finds Nature in almost every instance acting with her usual simplicity'. The compendium ends, as it began, with the philosophical conclusion that 'in proportion as we increase our knowledge of natural causes, the more elevated idea shall we have of him, who is the author of them all'. Yet in the six volumes of detailed science the poet and other amateurs had descriptions and names, not only of the birds and flowers used in their nature poems but also of all other branches of natural history.

In the last four decades of the century popularized natural history appeared in profusion, highlighted by the books of John Hill and William Curtis on botany, of Thomas Pennant and George Edwards on zoology, and of Sir Joseph Banks on the natural wonders of foreign lands.

v

It is now time to take stock of the leading ideas that appear in theological treatises, in popularizations of science, and in literature. The creative writing of the early eighteenth century in England is filled with the praise of God in the creation, illustrating from science the wonders of the universe that show the power, goodness, omniscience, and other attributes of the Supreme Being. This theme and its variations were repeated in poems and essays, developing lyrically what the scientists themselves had said earlier in their efforts to refute the charges of

atheism hurled at them. Paraphrases of the passages of Scripture dealing with the glories of nature became more numerous and more ecstatic as they used the discoveries of the new science to illustrate their various examples of God's wonders. Many 'poetical essays' developed the physico-theological themes, nearly all of them leaning heavily on how science had revealed with new vigor the wisdom of a Creator who could form so vast and yet so orderly a universe. Many long poems on moral subjects used science to illustrate order, providence, and divine wisdom. And even the less pretentious lyrics and shorter poems often included stock scientific illustrations as metaphors in developing other themes. The poets were elaborating what they found in the standard physico-theological handbooks, and so the progression is a natural one, from the ideas formulated by the theologians and scientists in the seventeenth century to the popular compendiums and finally into literature.

The theological writing of the early eighteenth century is so profuse and complex that I shall limit my sample to two writers that are known to reflect the kind of scientific thinking that interested the poets, William Derham and William Wollaston. They were themselves following such scientists as Boyle and Ray, who, as we have seen, took pride in their orthodoxy. Boyle was so anxious to assert the orthodoxy of science that he endowed lectures in defense of Christianity against atheists, 'theists', and other 'notorious infidels'. The first series of Boyle Lectures was given by Richard Bentley in 1692, beginning with two sermons refuting atheism and deism in general, followed by three showing how the structure and origin of human bodies refute atheism, and three entitled 'A Confutation of Atheism from the Origin and Frame of the World', a summary of scientific opinion on the creation of the universe, including Newton's laws of gravitation and motion.

The most popular of the Boyle Lectures was probably the series of sixteen sermons delivered in 1711–12 by William Derham and published separately and widely as *Physico-theology*. Although this work bore the subtitle 'A Demonstration of the Being and Attributes of God, from His Works of Creation', it dealt only with 'a survey of the terraqueous globe'. He promised another work on the heavens, which appeared as *Astro-theology*

in 1715 but in 1726 he admitted in a preface to the fourth edition of *Physico-theology* that, while he had made progress on a further survey of the waters, he had not enough leisure to finish it. The two companion published volumes together served as a sort of science handbook for divines and poets alike, standing for many years as the epitome of what was now to be known as 'physico-theology'. The two books are filled with scientific data, references to voluminous scientific reading, and accounts of Derham's own experiments, but their real purpose appears in the conclusion that scientific inquiry into nature is commendable, since it shows that infidelity is unreasonable and since it excites obedience, gratitude, and adoration of God.

Derham summarized in *Astro-theology* the new discoveries of Newton under such headings as the magnitude of the universe, the number of the heavenly bodies, their situation, their motions, their figures (mostly limited to the solar system because of the power of telescopes), the usefulness of attraction or gravity in maintaining orderly motion, and the qualities of light and heat. Each section concluded with the firm assertion of the wisdom of God, but one example will be enough to show what appealed to the imagination of the poets:

But in this our scheme we have a far more extensive, grand, and noble view of God's works: a far greater number of them; not those alone that former ages saw, but multitudes of others that the telescope hath discovered since; and all these far more orderly placed throughout the heavens, and at duer and more agreeable distances, and made to serve to much more noble and proper ends: for here we have not one systeme of sun and planets alone, and only one habitable globe, but myriads of systems and more, of habitable worlds, and some even in our own solar systeme, as well as those of the fixt stars. And consequently if in the sun and its planets, altho' viewed only here upon the earth at a great distance, we find enough to entertain our eye, to captivate our understanding, to excite our admiration and praises of the infinite CREATOR and Contriver of them; what an augmentation of these glories shall we find in great multitudes of them! in all those systems of fixt stars throughout the universe, that I have spoken of.[23]

When Newton became a sort of symbol of the proof of God's power and omniscience, his new laws of motion and gravity,

demonstrating the regular movements of the planets, stars, and even comets, became the stock examples of the glory of God in numerous poems. This new spirit of mingled science and religious fervor, later known as Newtonianism, can perhaps be seen more clearly summarized in William Wollaston's *The Religion of Nature Delineated* (1722).

The existence of a Deity approaches demonstration, Wollaston said, from the fact that the motions of the heavenly bodies must be accounted for 'either by one mighty Mover, acting upon them immediately, or by causes and laws of His appointment'. Attraction and gravitation are but effects, and we must look for their cause: 'What a vast field of contemplation is here opened! Such regions of matter about us, in which there is not the *least partical* that does not carry with it an argument of God's existence'. The infinite wisdom and power of the Almighty designer are revealed by the grandness of this world, of the sun with its vast magnitude, heat and distance, of the chorus of planets moving about it (some with secondary planets, 'and probably all possesst by proper inhabitants'), of the comets, and of the fixed stars, not made for their feeble light but 'to convince him, that they are rather so many *other suns*, with their several regions and sets of planets about them . . . to shew that if the world be not infinite, it is *infinito similis*; and therefore such a magnificent structure, and work of an infinite Architect'.

With the help of telescopes and microscopes, Wollaston continued, we extend our knowledge of the great variety of nature and are given 'fresh reasons to believe that there are indefinitely still *more and more* behind, that will for ever escape our eagerest pursuits and deepest penetration'. Wollaston cited scientific evidence of design and thought to indicate the Almighty Mind behind the universe prescribing uniform and steady laws so as to form 'a just and geometrical arrangement of things' that could not be the work of chance. This God who has given existence to the world also governs it by His providence. We glibly talk about Nature and take an unaccountable liberty in the use of the word, he concluded, but in no sense can Nature 'supersede the being of a Deity'.

The ideas of Wollaston, centering on the basic conception of a powerful and beneficent God whose wisdom is shown in nature, occur over and over in the writers of the eighteenth century. Even before Wollaston they can be found, expressed most clearly perhaps in the prose essays so popular in that period. It is scarcely a coincidence that in the two years between 1710 and 1712 the same theological interpretation of the new science appeared in many writers of prose essays, some well known and others obscure, but all concentrating on this new message, in the essays of Lady Chudleigh, Shaftesbury, and Needler, and in the periodical essays of Addison and Blackmore, culminating in the ambitious poem, Blackmore's *Creation.* This is the same period as Derham, who stems from Newton, Boyle, and Ray. Shaftesbury is too well known for quotation, but let us see how Lady Mary Chudleigh in 1710 can express herself with the same enthusiasm and with more use of science.

'Of Knowledge' advises courses of study that will impart insight 'into the useful parts of learning', leading us from effects that show power, wisdom, beauty, harmony, and order, to the cause, 'the Divine Original, to the unexhausted Source, the Foundation of all Perfection'. The new science will show the variety of nature, Lady Chudleigh continues, and 'instruct us heedfully to consider all her wonderful productions, and trace infinite wisdom and power thro' the immense space, from the heights above, to the depths below; from the glorious orbs which roll over our heads, to the minutest insect that crawls under our feet'. She amplifies the idea in her essay 'Of Love' by showing how science can reveal the degrees of divine perfection from astronomy to microscopy:

Wherever we cast our eyes, we may see them displaying their charms; by day shining in the glorious fountain of light, by night glittering in ten thousand stars, sparkling in gems, pleasing the sight in gold, delighting the eye in lofty trees, in the admirable colours of fruits and flowers, in the florid green of plants and grass, and in the amazing mechanism of insects and reptils, those surprizing and inimitable finenesses which by the help of glasses are discoverable in their minute bodies, usefully entertaining it with the exact proportion of parts, and the wonderful variety of shapes in birds, beasts, and fishes.

Lady Chudleigh shows how this can be put to religious use by
the praise of contemplation in her essay 'Of Solitude', running
through creation from man to 'the sensitive and vegetative kingdoms' to inanimate things and finally to the glory of the celestial
universe.[24]

The periodical essays helped to popularize the ideas derived
from science, and in this field, as in many others, no paper was
more successful than the *Spectator*. In an early paper (121) Addison called attention to the remarkable manifestation of divine
providence shown in the instinct of common animals like the hen
or mole and wished that the Royal Society would compile a body
of natural history, which would show the wisdom of God even
though it could not possibly be complete: 'Besides that there are
infinitely more species of creatures which are not to be seen without, nor indeed with the help of the finest glasses, than of such as
are bulky enough for the naked eye to take hold of. However,
from the consideration of such animals as lie within the compass
of our knowledge, we might easily form a conclusion of the rest,
that the same variety and goodness runs through the whole creation.' A paper on cheerfulness (387) shows the delights that arise
from contemplation of nature, whether in the beauty of bird-song
and flowing water or the harshness of wild rocks and deserts: 'In
short, the whole universe is a kind of theatre filled with objects
that either raise in us pleasure, amesement, or admiration.'

Nowhere did Addison glorify 'the authors of the new philos-
phy' better than in one of the final papers on imagination (420).
Here he finds the study of 'metals, minerals, plants and meteors'
appealing to the fancy, but the contrasting worlds revealed by the
microscope and telescope lend a sublime touch to the imagination as it rises from the green leaf that swarms 'with millions of
animals, that at their largest growth are not visible to the naked
eye' to the vast space between Saturn and the fixed stars where
the prospect is so immense that it puts the imagination 'upon the
stretch to comprehend it'. Addison concludes that the imagination is defective in not being able to comprehend such extremes,
but before he does so he takes us on a sublime excursion, first into
the unfathomable space beyond the reach of telescopes where,
lost in a labyrinth of suns and worlds, we are 'confounded with

the immensity and magnificence of Nature', and then into the perfection of the little world surrounding 'an animal, a hundred times less than a mite', where we may discover 'a new inexhausted fund of matter, capable of being spun out into another universe'. In nature we see, nevertheless, the best arguments for the existence, of God, and so it becomes a matter of faith and devotion which can only be expressed properly in poetry, as in the verses he added to *Spectator* 420 in praise of God as revealed in nature, beginning 'The spacious firmament on high'.

Addison often used science to illustrate his papers but we have space only for two more that are almost completely given to scientific topics. The first is a rhapsody on the Great Chain of Being (519) that extends from the infinity of little animals on a green leaf, to the 'numberless kinds of living creatures' on the earth, to the inhabitants of the stars. It becomes almost a hymn to plenitude when he pictures 'the exuberant and overflowing goodness' of God in the diversity shown by the almost imperceptible gradations in nature: 'The whole chasm in nature, from a plant to a man, is filled up with diverse kinds of creatures, rising one over another, by such gentle and easy ascent, that the little transitions and deviations from one species to another, are almost insensible.' The last paper on science (543), inspired by the reading of Blackmore's *Creation*, shows how the human body, and the physiology of animals as well, can reveal divine wisdom and providence as well as the more demanding discovery in a 'whole planetary system' made by a Newton 'who stands up as the miracle of the present age'.

Richard Blackmore's *Lay-Monastery* in 1713 devoted many of its periodical essays to science, and some of his papers give scientific examples of how God is to be seen in nature. One essay (5) shows the great fertility of nature under the microscope; since 'every plant and animal breeds numberless insects, every drop of water and piece of earth is a nest of minute living creatures, and a little pepper-corn is crowded like a populous city, with inhabitants, we cannot but conclude that the regions above are equally peopled'. The Divine Author is to be seen in this endless variety combined with 'a regular and beautiful subordination' of the chain of being, illustrated not only by differences in creatures

but in such similarities as that of the cat to the tiger and lion, of the ape and ourang-outang to man. Another paper (19) illustrates God's perfection by the economy of nature with such examples as the life-giving warmth of the sun or the power in a small seed to sprout, grow, and produce new seeds to multiply itself.[25]

The essays and letters of the ill-fated Henry Needler (1690–1718) are full of the way that the scientific study of nature reveals God. He wrote a rhapsody on nature in 1709, two years before Shaftesbury's *Characteristics,* and another after reading Shaftesbury. His 'familiar letters' also contained discussions of Newton and Locke and a letter on spermatic worms that praised the advances in science made possible by the microscope and telescope. The best of his essays, 'On the Beauty of the Universe,' gives his aesthetic justification for poems based on science, not only in depicting the celestial universe but also plants, animals, and even insects as evidence of the wisdom and goodness of God.

The prose rhapsodies of Mary Chudleigh, Henry Needler, and Richard Blackmore, as well as the more famous essays of Addison and Shaftesbury all belong to the same intellectual milieu in which Derham's *Physico-theology* belongs. The fact that Lady Chudleigh and perhaps Needler anticipate the others matters little, for the ideas were already abroad in the writings of Boyle and Ray and the various interpreters of Newton. Pomfret's judgment day poems, Prior's *Solomon,* and John Reynold's scientific poem on death showed that poetry was already feeling its way toward extensive poetical essays on the subject. In this larger picture Shaftesbury appears as one of a number of writers around 1710–12 who, for lack of a better term, might be called Newtonian.

Certainly there is no dichotomy between the influence of Newton and Shaftesbury. The influence of Shaftesbury seems to me to be in the application of Newtonian order and especially benevolence, to the moral world of man. Many moral poems that stem from this aspect of Shaftesbury portray the idea of moral harmony with much more scientific imagery than does Shaftesbury. Even Thomson's *Seasons,* whose very eclectic nature and overcharged sentiment seem often to stem from Shaftesbury, added

much of this element, as well as his special praise of 'generous Ashley', in later revisions of the poem even after the Newtonian science had been well established. For this reason I take it for granted that many poets, especially the writers of moral poems with scientific interest, are consciously following Shaftesbury, often it is true at second hand through Thomson, but that their scientific imagery comes from various scientific sources, the astronomy from Newton, the world of microscopic life, human anatomy, mineralogy, and natural history from many books and experiments, as well as from that careful observation which is the result of the scientific method.

The ideas represented by scientists, theologians, and essayists were repeated in poetry during the eighteenth century with profuse variation. Yet the main theme is that all the works of the Lord praise him and magnify him forever, to use the words of the Book of Common Prayer in the *Benedicite* chanted in the Morning Prayer by the Church of England. First the heavens declared the glory of God as the telescope revealed more and more of what seemed to be an infinite celestial universe. With the improvements in the microscope, however, another world of amazing plenitude showed a similar orderliness at the other end of the Great Chain of Being. Elaborating on the ideas found in the books on physico-theology, the poets saw the element of the sublime in these contrasting worlds and played up the great range of God's power stretching from the most distant star to the minutest insect. Yet their examples from the world of nature are intended to be representative of all things animate or inanimate, on the land, in the waters, in the skies, celestial, earthly, human, brute, plant, bird, insect, or microscopic creature, it mattered not what. The choice of example, in the earlier comprehensive physico-theological poetical essays at least, depended upon the poet's knowledge of science and his enthusiasm for the subject. For this reason it becomes difficult to illustrate any one branch of science in poetry, for most of them, at any rate the longer poems like Blackmore's *Creation* and Thomson's *Seasons*, include a variety of examples, from planet to primrose, from elephant and whale to silkworm and bacteria, from man to nightingale. For this reason, it seems most logical to summarize

here the ideas found in the poems influenced by science and then to show, in rough chronological fashion, how the poems themselves first use science to put new imagery into old themes, and then learn to versify the new science in a new and often sublime way.

Some of the prevailing ideas in the physico-theological poetry in eighteenth-century England may be briefly summarized as a sort of rough guide to the analysis of individual poems. The list is suggestive and not intended to include many variations.

1. *Order*. The universe is orderly and harmonious, set in motion by a divine Creator. The orthodox scientists and most of the English poets believed that God personally watches over the universe and will dissolve it by fiat at the last judgment. The followers of the mechanical philosophy, especially in France, believed that God set the great clock of nature in motion and does not need to watch it. This order is dramatized in the scientific poetry of two contrasting worlds:

a. The telescope has opened up a vast celestial universe that Newton has shown mathematically to be orderly. The orbits of moon, planets, and even comets can be calculated. The fixed stars are suns for new systems like the solar system, and this earth is a mere speck among many such worlds. The moon, planets, and probably other worlds beyond are believed to be inhabited by reasonable creatures, for it is presumptuous of man to assume that God would create such an elaborate universe just for him.

b. The microscope also shows an orderly system but in miniature and reveals God's watchful care in the small as much as in the vast.

2. *Plenitude*. By analogy there must be still more left undiscovered in a universe that seems infinite in both directions. Since God is in personal control, the universe to the orthodox cannot really be infinite, but a plenitude of forms is evident in an incredible variety in nature. Two common metaphors are related:

a. The Great Chain of Being, very influential in the thought of the period,[26] the graded scale of nature ranging from microscopic life to plants and animals to man to God, was interpreted variously by the poets as a symbol of order and design, of complacent conservatism, and of restraint of the pride of man. The poetic interest in misfits or missing links is listed below under scientific puzzles.

b. The book of Nature, a commonplace for plenitude, lies open to all, and in its pages the wisdom and beneficence of God may be read.

3. *Providence.* Discrepancies in nature can be explained only by assuming that God is good and provides what is best in the long run. Evil was necessary to fill out the divine scheme of plenitude,[27] for the very abundance demanded by the Great Chain of Being had to include imperfections as well as good things. This acceptance of partial evils reconciled with universal good led to the early doctrine of optimism that was rejected by Voltaire and other French writers, especially when applied to the Lisbon earthquake of 1755. The most common examples in English poetry of evil or harshness in nature reconciled by Providence are the following:

a. Violence as shown by earthquakes and hurricanes.

b. Inequalities of climate as shown by the frozen north and torrid jungles.

c. Mountains, even before they became a source of aesthetic pleasure, were believed to be the source of much good to man in spite of their harshness.[28] The most common illustration of the usefulness of mountains was as the source of underground streams.

4. *Puzzles of nature.*

a. Instinct in animals paralleling reason in man.

b. Curiosities in the gradations of the Great Chain of Being, such as the resemblances of apes to man or those apparent mixtures of animal and plant, the polyp, the Tartarian lamb, and the sensitive plant.

5. The limitations of science in not being able to answer the fundamental questions as to the cause behind the effects it observes. The picture of Newton and other scientists finding the answers only after death is common in English poetry.[29]

6. Patriotic praise of Britain, a dominant poetic theme in English poetry after the Peace of Utrecht in 1713, appears in many scientific poems. Nature has played a part in England's world position because a temperate climate is virtually free of violent storms and earthquakes and because British commerce is based on the use of winds and scientific aids to navigation.

This chapter has attempted to give a cursory background of the new science that began in the seventeenth century and of the ideas derived from that science, but only as much as seems necessary to understand the English poetry of the eighteenth century influenced by science. It does not pretend to explain the scientific discoveries or even the metaphysics of the basic philosophy of the period, yet it does try to take into account these momen-

tous events as they enlarged the imagination of the poets or influenced the religious and scientific thinking of the age. It does not try to show the close interchange of ideas between England and France. Here much could be shown, it is true, in the way of similarities at the outset: the almost simultaneous founding of the Royal Society and the Academie des Sciences, the influence of Descartes on Hobbes and Newton and the converse influence of Newton on later French thought, the vogue in England of the early popularizations by Fontenelle and Pluche, the widespread vogue of popular science and natural history in France paralleling what we have seen in England.[30] Yet the dramatic manner in which the French thinkers, particularly Voltaire and La Mettrie, accepted the mechanistic assumptions of Newton's discoveries and consequently repudiated the benevolent God and personal providence that was so dear to the English scientists and poets[31]—this makes the chief difference between the thought and literature of the two nations after the middle of the century.

The full story of several other phases of popular science in this period must wait for other studies. In addition to the handbooks, for example, there was a wide use of encyclopedias, periodicals, lectures, and demonstration classes, many of them especially designed for ladies and young people. From about 1760 there was profuse publication of colored plates to illustrate birds, flowers, quadrupeds, insects, shells, and other aspects of natural history, an important combination of art and science. Large collections of natural objects, alive and dead, were amassed by those with means, and the private collections of the *virtuosi*, ridiculed by neoclassical writers, were often very extensive and some became the basis for public museums.

The interest in the natural history of foreign lands that began in the seventeenth century with the scientific sections of travel books led to the extremely profuse importation of exotic plants, was well as some animals when possible, from all parts of the world. At first arranged privately through agents or commercial ships and later through elaborate and expensive expeditions organized for scientific study, the English imported exotic plants and cultivated them in their greenhouses and gardens, the Society of Apothecaries at their 'physic garden' in Chelsea, the royal

household in their great botanic gardens at Kew. Along with the popularization of natural history in England there arose a serious study of science by amateurs with literary bent, and from the accurate observation of nature by writers like Thomas Gray and George Crabbe there came an understanding of nature that was to have a great influence on English literature, even though these two scientist-poets did not introduce much science into their poetry. The influence is best seen in *The Natural History of Selborne*, written by an obscure parson in a Hampshire village to his prominent scientist friends in London, but observed so accurately and written so well that it was to become a sort of Bible for later students of natural history as well as a companion for poets who wrote about nature.

The full story would indeed require more than one book. The present study will put its emphasis on the scientific poetry of the eighteenth century in England, beginning with the sublime excursions into outer space and ending with the primrose by the river's brim, beginning with encyclopedic physico-theology of poetical essays and ending with short lyrics on flowers, birds, and other aspects of the quiet English landscape. All have essentially the same message, that the attributes of the Supreme Being— goodness, power, omniscience, eternity, immensity, and others, all of them asserting wisdom and providence—may be seen in the works of the creation, in the physical world which is, in this study at least, the same as NATURE. And so I shall attempt to show the poetry that does just this, wherever possible by actual quotation of the poems themselves but usually by description and summary.

NOTES

[1] *Science and the Modern World* (New York, 1925), p. 127.

[2] Marjorie Nicolson, *A World in the Moon,* Smith College Studies in Modern Languages, Vol. XVII, 1935–6.

[3] On the relation between science and imagination in the eighteenth century, the most significant work was done by Marjorie Nicolson in several studies reprinted in *Science and Imagination* (Ithaca, N.Y., 1956). Alan D. McKillop, *The Background of Thomson's Seasons* (Minneapolis, 1942), pp. 1–88, summarized many scientific poems and earlier scholarly research, including several good articles by Herbert Drennon. Many other scientific poems are described in other contexts in the first two volumes of Hoxie N. Fairchild, *Religious*

Trends in English Poetry (New York, 1939, 1942) and in Dwight L. Durling, *The Georgic Tradition in English Poetry* (New York, 1935). Bonamy Dobrée, *The Broken Cistern: the Clark Lectures 1952–53* (London, 1954), pp. 52–103, is suggestive in nature, while Douglas Bush, *Science and English Poetry* (New York, 1950) and B. Ifor Evans, *Literature and Science* (London, 1954), have little of value for the eighteenth century. See also John Butt, 'Science and Man in Eighteenth-Century Poetry', *Durham University Journal,* XXXIX (1947), 79–88, and H. H. Rhys (ed.), *Seventeenth Century Science and the Arts* (Princeton, 1961), especially pp. 3–28.

4 R. F. Jones, *Ancients and Moderns: A Study of the Rise of the Scientific Movement in Seventeenth-Century England* (2nd ed., St. Louis, 1961), p. 184. On the changing ideas to 1700, see Victor Harris, *All Coherence Gone* (Chicago, 1949).

5 Cf. Jones, *op. cit.,* p. 185: 'The atomical, the Epicurean, the corpuscularian, the mechanical, and the Cartesian philosophy were terms which possessed in common the fundamental idea that all physical phenomena are the result of matter and motion, matter consisting of minute atoms or corpuscles. This philosophy, as developed by Descartes, was first embraced in England by the Cambridge Platonists, who, however, were animated less by scientific than religious motives, in that, eschewing Bacon's separation of science and religion, they wished to reconcile the two.'

6 2nd. ed. revised and reprinted in *A Collection of the Philosophical Writings of Dr. Henry More* (London, 1662), pp. 37–85. See Paul R. Anderson, *Science in Defense of Liberal Religion* (New York, 1933) , especially chaps. 4 and 5. More's later attacks on Descartes are discussed in Alexandre Koyrè, *From the Closed World to the Infinite Universe* (Baltimore, 1957).

7 Jones, *op. cit.,* pp. 201 ff. For a fuller account of Descartes and his influence on later thought, see E. A. Burtt, *The Metaphysical Foundations of Modern Physical Science,* (rev. ed., New York, 1951), and J. S. Spink, *French Free Thought from Gassendi to Voltaire* (London, 1960).

8 Jones, *op. cit.,* p. 322. 'The mathematical philosophy was merely one explanation, widely accepted, to be sure, and destined to revolutionize opinions of nature, of the data furnished by the experimental philosophy; and ... the collecting of authentic data, which show how nature acts, and which thus enable men to command nature for the satisfaction of their own needs, was more important than the devising of hypotheses as to why nature acts so.'

9 See my article, 'Science in Biblical Paraphrases in 18th Century England', *PMLA,* LXXIV (1959), 41–51, especially pp. 42 f.

10 E. W. Strong, 'Newton and God', *Journal of the History of Ideas,* XIII (1952), 146–67, summarizes previous scholarship on this subject. A good early study is Herbert Drennon, 'Newtonianism: Its Method, Theology, and Metaphysics', *Englische Studien,* LXVIII (1934), 397–409.

11 E. A. Burtt, *Metaphysical Foundations,* p. 236, summarized Newton's influence: 'It was of the greatest consequence for succeeding thought that now the great Newton's authority was squarely behind that view of the cosmos

which saw in man a puny, irrelevant spectator ... of the vast mathematical system whose regular motions according to mechanical principles constituted the world of nature.'

12 For the historical background of the influence of science on religion, see Roland N. Stromberg, *Religious Liberalism in Eighteenth-Century England* (London, 1954), especially pp. 26–33.

13 See John Dillenberger, *Protestant Thought and Natural Science* (New York, 1960), p. 122.

14 *A New Theory of the Earth* (4th ed. rev., London, 1725), p. 33.

15 The copy from the library of George III (BM 31.g.7) is sumptuously bound in red morocco with the royal crest on the cover.

16 See a later Newtonian treatise, Alexander Campbell's *Chain of Philosophical Reasoning* (London, 1754), p. 40: 'Natural philosophy has been always supposed to lay a sure foundation for natural religion, by leading the mind in a satisfactory manner to the knowledge of the Author and Governor of the Universe. To study nature, is to search into God's workmanship, every discovery in which reveals to us a new part of his scheme, whose works are so manifold and hard to be comprehended.'

17 *Annals of Science,* VII (1951), 365–370.

18 The first critical edition of this work, that of Robert Shackleton, Oxford, 1955, gives its history and scientific background.

19 See Arthur Hughes, 'Science in English Encyclopaedias, 1704–1875', *Annals of Science,* VII (1951), 340–70, and subsequent issues.

20 For the earlier history of the microscope and its influence on literature, see Marjorie Nicolson, *The Microscope and English Imagination,* Smith College Studies in Modern Languages, XVI, 1934–5, reprinted in *Science and Imagination,* pp. 155–234.

21 As late as 1787 the younger George Adams, in his own *Essays on the Microscope,* occasionally quoted poetry or came to a philosophical conclusion about the almost infinite number of intermediate degrees in the universal chain that 'unites all beings, connects all worlds, and comprehends all spheres'.

22 For documentation of some early popularizations of science, see Gerald Dennis Meyer, *The Scientific Lady in England 1650–1760* (Berkeley, 1955).

23 *Astro-theology,* pp. 40 f.

24 Mary Chudleigh, *Essays upon Several Subjects in Prose and Verse* (London, 1710), pp. 9 ff., 180 ff., 235 ff.

25 *The Lay-Monastery, Consisting of Essays, Discourse, etc. published singly under the Title of the Lay-Monk* (London, 1714). The essays cited appeared on 25 Nov. and 28 Dec. 1713. Nos. 31, 32, and 40 discuss color as suggested by Newton's *Optics.*

26 A. O. Lovejoy, *The Great Chain of Being* (Cambridge, Mass., 1936).

27 Lovejoy, 'Optimism and Romanticism', *PMLA,* XLII (1927), 921–45, reprinted in revised form in *The Great Chain of Being.*

28 Marjorie Nicolson, *Mountain Gloom and Mountain Glory* (Ithaca, N. Y., 1959).

29 See my fuller study, 'The Idea of the Limitations of Science from Prior to Blake', Rice University *Studies in English Literature*, I, (1961), 97–114.

30 This has been well documented in Daniel Mornet, *Les Sciences de la Nature en France au XVIIIe Siècle* (Paris, 1911).

31 Richard S. Westfall, *Science and Religion in Seventeenth-Century England* (New Haven, 1958), pp. 20 ff., concludes that the English scientists saw no conflict between orthodox Christianity and their mechanical conception of nature; they merely reinterpreted the concept of providence.

Religion and Social Reform

༄

ROLAND N. STROMBERG

We can never estimate the religion of any age or society without observing its attitude towards the poor.

G. G. COULTON, *The Medieval Village*

1

Arthur Young spoke for his age. Despite an occasional shedding of the poet Thomson's 'social tear', too often open to Mandeville's suspicions about its sincerity, there was no real humanitarian movement until the last quarter of the century. There was the beginning of one, the fruit of a religious philanthropy, at the beginning of the century. The men whom Thomson celebrated in verse—Thomas Bray, James Oglethorpe, and the Wesleys, to name the foremost—set going the charity schools, founded the societies for reforming manners and propagating the gospel, established hospitals and ultimately inquired 'into the horrors of the gloomy jail'. They founded the colony of Georgia. Add to them such nonconforming philanthropists and reformers as the celebrated Quaker John Bellers and the unitarian Thomas Firmin.[1] But this impulse had very nearly died by 1730. Although some claim a tradition of religious charity stretching across the century from Robert Nelson to Hannah More, it would seem

From Roland N. Stromberg, Religious Liberalism in Eighteenth-Century England *(London: Oxford University Press, 1954), pp. 150–65.*

187

that this tradition thinned down to the faintest trace between the first decade or two and the last. As Thomson wrote,

Much still untouched remains, in this dark age;

and amid many evils there were remarkably few men to employ 'the patriot's weeding hand'.

Until after 1750 at the earliest, there was no disposition to 'pry into the state of society'. 'It was beyond the range of their mentality to conceive that the poor were poor because Society was an ill-regulated machine.'[2] Bellers and Firmin did, indeed, advocate constructive social projects for the employment of the poor in experimental 'colleges of industry', and thus won a niche for themselves as dim precursors of Owenite socialism. Mid-century is a dividing point beyond which the mind would move towards new concepts of economic science and social determinism. But this, the time of David Hartley and David Hume, is the earliest we can date the origins of a really systematic approach to economic science and to social amelioration. In general, to the eighteenth century humanitarianism means charity, not social engineering.

There was little enough of that, assumed in theory to be the duty of all Christians. The charity-school movement was the finest fruit of early-century humanitarianism: 'the glory of the age we live in', Addison called it in 1712. But after 1723 it deteriorated sadly, until these schools, in most of England, became scandalous, the prototypes of Dickens's Dotheboys Hall. Mandeville did not exaggerate much when he called them just a fashion of the hour.[3] The zeal of the little group that established them was not enough to sustain them against public indifference and political hostility. To the Whigs they were a Tory project, suspected of teaching Jacobitism. But for the reasons why Whigs neglected them (quite often turning them, after 1723, into work-houses) we must turn to the prevailing social philosophy: 'The conviction that the education of the poor was economically unsound and socially destructive was well entrenched.'[4] Would it not unfit them for their role as manual labourers? There was an equivocation in the middle-class philosophy: the theory that

the workers may rise by their own efforts clashed with the conviction that each class ought to keep its place, and the latter was stronger. The real desire of the middle class was for a working class that would be industrious and sober but well disciplined and tractable. Constant complaints about the 'idleness and stubbornness of the poor' appear from 1680 on: they will not work steadily, 'and when they do work they will often mar what they do'.[5] The charity schools were used only to inculcate religious lessons which were economically useful: not to steal from your master, to make dutiful servants, to waste no time at work. This was the only kind of education wealthy people would invest in; and after 1723 even this was neglected. The 'blackguard boys', armies of homeless, lawless, degenerate children, roamed the country. The remedy for them was thought to be the workhouse.

The idea of catechistical instruction in the charity schools had not been favoured by the noblest minds of the earlier period—Bellers, Firmin, and John Locke. They had favoured work projects, where relief might be combined with practical education.[6] It is doubtful if these worthy men would have approved the workhouses as they existed after 1723, becoming as these did in time 'a symbol of dread and despair', classically delineated in Crabbe's *The Village*. Their great merit was that they reduced the rates and drove the poor to work. Philanthropy, on the dominant middle-class view, had nothing to do with the giving of alms. ('Giving Alms No Charity' was the title of a Defoe tract.) Philanthropy consisted in lowering wages. For this would increase commerce and industry, which in turn would provide work for the poor. Defoe, the typical burgher, holds that the only cause of unemployment is the laziness of the poor and the profitableness of begging. He is against workhouses where the poor would be put to work making things, because of the competition with private industry. The right remedy for idleness, he suggests, would be forced-labour battalions for all vagabonds.[7] Possibly respectable Christian employers did not openly subscribe to Bernard Mandeville's cynical view that the poor must be kept poor, otherwise there would be no one to do the dirty work. But they did feel that the poor must be kept poor so that they would be industrious, and would work for low wages (puni-

tive workhouses keeping them from the recourse of idleness), so that trade and industry might prosper. They believed that in augmenting his own fortune with the aid of these low wages a rich employer is 'increasing the riches and power of his country and giving bread to thousands of his industrious countrymen'.[8] It would seem that Mandeville's 'private vices equal public benefits' had won the field; and it soon received, at least partly, the sanction of Adam Smith.

Christian stewardship had manifestly assumed paradoxical forms, if it still existed. The greatest Christians continued to set an example of charity. Butler and Law gave freely of what they had; Cowper lived up to his maxim, 'If you abound, impart.' John Wesley endowed stewardship with meaning, for the Methodists, if their message was in some respects the typically middle-class one of 'work and earn', insisted that the rich must give freely, and enjoined secrecy to avoid the Mandeville accusation that charity was really selfish. Certainly the Christian spirit produced some attention to social evils. 'In sermon after sermon preachers painted the terrible punishments which awaited the uncharitable in the after-world.'[9] However, this view of social evil was sharply limited. It was limited, first, by its own philosophical belief that evils are of divine decree, inherent in an order of things beyond human control or questioning:

> Let poverty or want be what it will,
> It does proceed from God; therefore's no ill.

Therefore there was no thought of social changes, but only of what mitigation private benevolence might provide. More serious than this, the new wealthy had come to hold with Defoe that real charity was not the giving of alms; it was evidently the indulging of their own greed, with the comfortable thought that the more they made the better off the poor were.

In order to influence them towards reform it became necessary to appeal to their self-interest. 'If compassion cannot move you', William Sharp pleaded in 1755, 'let consideration of interest prevail with you.' Bishop Berkeley, in *The Querist*, makes his appeal to the intelligent interest of the upper classes, in a series

notable for trying to think out a national economic programme for depressed Ireland. But the dominant classes did not see their self-interest as lying in such things as education, penal reform, or projects for the unemployed. Betsy Rodgers points out that such middle-class philanthropists as there were usually had 'little sympathy for the objects of their charity'. If they built hospitals it was because they feared under-population (high wages) ; if they made the prisons cleaner they also made them less cheerful. Captain Thomas Coram and Jonas Hanway, founders of hospitals for prostitutes and foundlings, had to overcome severe prejudice and endure the criticism that paupers would not try to improve themselves if they had 'such a commodious access to ease and relief'. Yet some such projects did succeed; and after 1760 the philanthropic movement regained momentum.

The notable late-century movement of social consciousness was created by religious philanthropists, among them Wilberforce, Granville Sharp, Clarkson, Howard, and Miss More. This was mainly a conservative Church of England group, though with a persistent Quaker influence. In contrast with this religious phil-anthropy we should note the cult of benevolence. The pleasures of charity were 'the most lasting, valuable and exquisite'[10] of all. This effort to apply Shaftesbury's ethic of virtue as its own reward deserved, it is to be feared, the sneers of Mandeville, for it does not appear to have produced any zealots of philanthropy or reform, and was more apt to be a fashionable pose. Zeal, indeed, was the enemy of enemies to the neo-classic gentlemanly code Shaftesbury was so closely related to. A 'virtuoso' of reform would have committed the unpardonable sin of enthusiasm. Bishop Gibson was afraid of being thought enthusiastic because he ventured to attack immorality at the Court!

2

The religious liberals, for their part, were scarcely reformers. That numerous evils existed, ripe for the reformer, need not be argued at length. The condition of the poor was 'nasty and scandalous', Henry Fielding conceded.[11] The eighteenth-century historian of the poor laws gives a picture of callousness and cruelty by the workhouse overseers, chiefly concerned to reduce

the rates.[12] There was the harsh penal code, with its death sentence for even petty robbery. The pressing of sailors was defended by so 'liberal' a Whig as John Tutchin.[13] As is well known, the Asiento treaty of 1723 gave England's merchants a lucrative stake in the slave trade; except for some Quakers and a poet, no one protested against the slave trade until after 1770. In brief, English society was afflicted with all those evils that were later to challenge the energies of the evangelical humanitarians and the utilitarian reformers. It is obvious enough that 'much still untouched remained'. How far did those who were radicals in theology partake of radicalism in social, economic, and political reform? The answer would seem to be, scarcely at all.

At least it is hard to find evidence of that 'tremendous interest of most of the deists in the public good' quite commonly alleged.[14] The English deists were neither reformers nor democrats. There is little social significance to be drawn immediately from their writings and activities. 'Drawn from virtually every scale of society . . ., virtually unknown to each other',[15] they formed no such cohesive society as did the French *philosophes,* nor did they ever have such definite social and political goals. Their numbers included aristocratic dilettanti like Shaftesbury and Bolingbroke; university men such as Tindal, Woolston, and Middleton; scribblers on the make, the Tolands and Morgans; self-taught amateur theologians like Annet and Chubb, the latter being a journeyman glovemaker by trade. What seems true of all is a lack of interest in practical projects of reform. Thomas Firmin, the unitarian philanthropist, is the exception.

Perhaps this does the deists an injustice. In a period that produced few new political or social ideas, Bolingbroke, Shaftesbury, Mandeville, and Toland all have a certain social significance, though it is not in a single direction. But between religious radicalism and socio-political radicalism there is no necessary connexion. Americans are familiar with the fact that Washington, Hamilton, and John Adams, as well as Paine and Jefferson, were (roughly) religious deists. The leading 'free-thinker' of the nineteenth century in the United States, Robert Ingersoll, was conservative enough in his political views. The social and political inferences from deism were most ambiguous. To give only

the most obvious example, the two most persistent ethical ideas in deistic thought were the contradictory ones that man is selfish and needs to be tricked by his rulers (Mandeville, leading to Alexander Hamilton) and that man is benevolent (Shaftesbury, leading to Thomas Jefferson) .[16] Again, the Newtonian, deistic assumption of 'the harmonious order of nature' might mean almost anything: a drive to do away with injustices, or the worst sort of *laissez-faire* complacency. The contradictory impulses here are nowhere better shown than in Adam Smith; whether to assume benevolence or self-love, whether to play the reformer or the apologist for economic egoism—this unresolved dilemma is responsible for the ambiguities in the great economist, which make him still a controversial figure.

Doubtless deism had a certain implicit democratic content. First of all, the deists always fought the battle for free speech and for toleration, though they might well draw the line at free speech for Jacobites and toleration for Roman Catholics. Charles Blount, the early deist, led the battle against the Licensing Act, 1679–93; Anthony Collins' plea for freedom of thought was famous, and all heterodox religious thinkers naturally desired freedom for their own views. Toland expressed an advanced and sincere idea of liberty of opinion, though he excluded Roman Catholicism from his range of toleration.

Then too, the philosophy of deism assumed what Professor Lovejoy has called 'intellectual equalitarianism'. Chubb would say that 'Christians stand to each other in the relation of brethren only, and not in relations of master and servant'. 'The gospel which Christ preached to the poor . . . was plain and intelligible, and level to the lowest understanding.'[17] 'Christianity Suited to Plain Men' had been the title of a section in Locke's *Reasonableness of Christianity,* where he declared that 'these are articles that the labouring and illiterate man may comprehend'. No priests are needed; all men have sufficient understanding to know the truth—here was deism's very creed. True or not, it had obvious democratic aspects.

But, with characteristic inconsistency, deism was also marked by a certain intellectual snobbishness. The same Chubb wrote that he expected his writings to appeal only to 'the more intelli-

gent part of our species, who are not interested in popular
opinion'.[18] Bolingbroke spoke of the 'rabble' as 'a monstrous
beast' which 'has passions to be moved, but no reason to be
appealed to'.[19] With Hume and Middleton, as has been noted,
faith in the common understanding of men is abandoned completely—the masses need 'superstition', and 'philosophic' religion
is only for the few.

Voltaire and Diderot had this contempt for the *canaille,* which
did not prevent them from being tremendously significant as
reformers and inciters to social change. One must not forget that
the socially more militant French and American deists went to
school to the English.[20] The reason why the English deists were
far less dynamic may be found partly in the difference between
France and England. The French *philosophes* were bourgeois,
but they struggled against religious intolerance, legal inequality,
privileged and snobbish aristocracy, and obsolete economic practices. In England such feudal objects of middle-class hostility
existed to a far lesser degree. The 'harmonious order of nature'
meant to Voltaire and his fellows a struggle against an obviously
'unnatural' régime; to Tindal, Toland, and theirs it meant more
nearly just the régime that existed, the Whig England which,
indeed, Voltaire himself thought ideal.

John Toland concerned himself with political matters more
than any other English deist save Bolingbroke. Toland had an
excellent education, and a very high opinion of his own talents.[21]
Locke and Leibniz, who were his friends, thought him opinion-
ated, conceited, and probably superficial. His integrity is beyond
question: Harley was his patron, but he withdrew from that
statesman when he turned Tory. Toland liked to think of himself
as independent of parties, and could well claim to be no syco-
phant, despite his poverty and need for attachments. Yet he was
committed wholly to the Whigs, and never went beyond Whig
orthodoxy. His *sine qua non* principles were religious toleration,
the Protestant succession, and civil liberty. Editor of the works
of Harrington and Sydney, author of a life of Milton, he denied
that he was an extreme republican, or that he agreed with what
he called the 'democratical schemes of government' of Milton
and Harrington. Believing in the classical 'mixed' system, he

regarded the nobility as a natural pillar of society; and, as he said, all true 'republicans' admired, 'almost to adoration', the Hanoverian settlement. He was perfectly satisfied with Hanoverian, Whig England, praising it as 'the most free and best constituted in all the world'. He did not attack the Established Church, but agreed with Warburton that 'some public and orderly way of worshipping God, under the allowance, endowment and inspection of the civil magistrate' is necessary to a State. Toland the deist assumed that it belongs to the nature of man to have a religion; therefore it belongs to the nature of a State to have some common religion.[22] He would, however, grant full toleration, within Protestantism—like all deists he was violently anti-Catholic. He does indeed approach a theory of pure religious freedom. Like Pope, he argues that a variety of religious opinions is as natural as a variey of tastes, and is not an evil. The advanced element in his views on tolerance is his argument that there is no final and fixed religious truth, but a constant progress, analogous to the situation in science. His exclusion of Catholics is based on their alleged political subversiveness.

Toland's opinions on free speech, civil liberty, and religious toleration indicate deism's contribution to these causes. However, the deists were far from alone in favouring such things. This was a normal Whig outlook. Toland, enthusiastic but somewhat complacent Whig, self-styled 'fighter for the truth and assertor of liberty' (his self-composed epitaph), hardly original in any opinion but persistent and even courageous in the Whig faith, may perhaps stand as a typical specimen. He indicted the 'spirit of bigotry and persecution', insisted that a government need not have but one religion (though it should have a public church), and castigated the Tories as despots and Papists in disguise. But he never got beyond these ordinary Whig principles. In some of his pamphlets written around 1700 he did show an awareness of the inadequacies of the 1688 Revolution, noting the need for parliamentary reform.[23] But after the Hanoverians came he had no complaints. Disliked for his religious views, he would scarcely have warranted any special comment on account of his political ones, and seems to have had no socio-economic ones beyond a

Whiggish enthusiasm for commerce. He was a rather typical Whig.

It was generally assumed, at least by Tories, that 'free-thinkers' were Whigs, and Tory propaganda liked to associate Whigs and atheists, in which there was of course no truth.[24] The great majority of Whigs repudiated deism, and welcomed the support of the Tindals and Tolands about as much as a modern New Dealer or Socialist welcomes the support of Communists. Walpole Whiggism and deism came closest together, perhaps, in the crude but gusty writings of Thomas Gordon, the popular 'Independent Whig'. Intemperate attacks on the clergy and on the Tories were blended with a cool Erastianism and a crude deism.[25] But Gordon soon proved to be an embarrassment to the Whigs.

However, not all deists were Whigs. Bolingbroke and Hume, the neo-Tories, discovered that their emancipation from religious orthodoxy did not necessarily mean devotion to Robert Walpole or the Duke of Newcastle. One could easily take the conservative side—the side, as Hume put it, that leaned more to authority than to liberty—without taking the devout position. One could, and can—to put it simply enough—believe in Christianity and be a liberal, or a radical, and one can reject religion without rejecting a variety of views on political and social questions which are ordinarily thought of as highly conservative. There had been a strong tendency for Tories to believe in strictly orthodox Christianity because they had identified this with a secure (divine right) monarchy. But that tendency waned as politics drew apart from religion. (Very pious people in the Dissenting tradition had always been Whigs.) It may be noted, and has been, that the sceptic is very apt to be a Tory. Basil Willey has commented on the 'cosmic toryism' of those who held with Pope that 'whatever is, is right'. Hume's scepticism leads to the mood of relying on custom because of a mistrust of reason. Hume, Middleton, and Bolingbroke doubted human wisdom, in the mass, too much to believe very readily in the progress of human society.

If the attack on such evils as the slave trade and noisome jails came mainly from Anglicans and Quakers, the impulse to political reform and democracy came, after about 1770, mainly

from the left wing of Dissent—from the group that included Priestley, Cartwright, Jebb, and Price.[26] Unitarians, apostles of a Pelagianized Christianity, they were not deists strictly speaking, but held, as Priestley was to warn Paine, that it is as dangerous to believe too little as it is to believe too much; nevertheless they were too heterodox to be admitted as Christians by the orthodox. By their time, deism in England was, as such, dead, but some of its elements surely lived on in the drastic Nonconformity of the Priestley group. Deism had never struck any deep roots, had always been disreputable, and had, without establishing any valid philosophy, lived chiefly on sensationalism, which soon lost its appeal. In a society as prosperous and secure as that of England in this period, it was not easy to maintain even a scandalous notoriety very long by making faces at the gods. The gods were too plainly smiling on England (propertied England, at least) to merit such ingratitude.

Deism had not supplemented this religious iconoclasm with any clear, constructive, social or political ideology. It was a middle-class ideology which did not even appeal to the middle class, wherein lies the secret of its failure. Respectable opinion of the deists was always that expressed by a magazine at the height of the movement in 1733: 'a set of men who, from no better motive than vanity, or malicious wickedness, are labouring to subvert society'.[27] The diagnosis was excellent, except that the deists were not really labouring to subvert society, for they had no political or social programme to offer. It is quite true that their radicalism was capricious and based chiefly on personal vanity.

English deism struck fire in France and America, where it was assimilated to social radicalism under different conditions. Such radicalism, it appears, had no opportunity in England—where the middle classes, unlike the French, were content, and where the lower classes, unlike the American, had not yet approached the threshold of power.

The unitarians who from 1768 on exerted a democratic force in England were, as we said, perhaps deistic in the widest sense. Christianity had become worldly; the pursuit of happiness in this world had become its theme. A long review of one of James

Foster's books in 1749 noted that if men were 'cautious and prudent, diligent and industrious', they would be 'crowned with prosperity'.[28] Such a faith was most acceptable to the complacent *bourgeoisie*. But this mild, worldly religion, which served so well for a properous burgher, also suited those who wished secular reforms in society. The 'dying Christian', in Priestley's case, made way for the energetic reformer. Many new things might emerge once religion had been reduced to a 'compartment', to mere vague morality. The real point of departure towards the modern idea of secular progress would appear to be the exclusion of Christian ideas from society. Christianity as increasingly 'Arminianized' was a moral code increasingly indistinguishable from secular behaviour. Christianity was absorbed by, dissolved into, secularism when it ceased to represent anything more than 'prudence'. No longer influencing culture as an independent force, it was in this sense 'compartmentalized'. A secularized and compartmentalized Christianity might be adopted by secular profit-seekers or secular reformers; it no longer had a will of its own.

In America we observe such a figure as Jonathan Mayhew, who was to some orthodox clergymen 'no better a Christian than a Turk', but who certainly considered himself a Christian. His energies were however directed entirely towards secular goals: political freedom, full civil liberties.[29] If Priestley and Mayhew and Cartwright were not deists, they devoted themselves to goals no deist could disapprove: the happiness and freedom of men on earth. But they were beginning to add some positive social ideas to deism's negativism.

The critical moment in the emergence of a positive spirit of reform undoubtedly came later than the deists' heyday, and consisted in the awareness of evil as being social and remediable. It begins about 1750. The religious people who carried it forward most notably were those left-wing Dissenters who began to call themselves unitarians. By the end of the century the identification of unitarian with democrat had become a natural one. The young Coleridge heard it said of himself that 'In religion he is a Unitarian, if not a Deist; in politics a Democrat, to the utmost extent of the word'.[30] But who were the young Coleridge's idols? Hartley, Priestley, and William Godwin. He had, we surmise, scarcely

heard of Toland and Tindal, Collins and Chubb. No doubt their mistake had been in not tying their religious radicalism to a political credo equally advanced and energetic. The early deists should have realized that, if Christianity was fading, the centre of importance would shift from religion to secular faiths.

The failure of deism also profited the Methodists. They alone reached the working classes. For their pains they were denounced in the most immoderate language, as anarchists, enthusiasts, fanatics, revolutionaries. In this denunciation 'liberals' of all sorts joined. Charles Chauncy and Samuel Johnson in America, William Warburton and Conyers Middleton in England, showed sufficiently that all middle-class liberals, whether deist or Arminian, shared a distrust of the mob when stirred by a Whitefield, that 'Jack Cade in a cassock'. In America, it is true, the Great Awakening had some rather striking social, economic, and political aspects.[31] Wesley, however, was very far from being a social or political radical, and certainly never went farther than the idea of making the poor sober and industrious so that they might raise themselves by self-help. In the long run, he doubtless aided capitalism, by disciplining the poor and spreading the gospel of thrift and steady habits. But the democratic ingredients contained in his genuine love and concern for all of God's children, regardless of class, rendered him suspect as a bloody-handed revolutionary. Wesleyanism made it obvious that English free thought had never reached, and never even tried to reach, the lower classes. It was as far beyond the wishes of Bolingbroke or Shaftesbury to do so as it was beyond the talents of Chubb or Annet.[32]

Militant deism, doubtless, did have a certain social role to play—in the French Revolution, with its Jacobin Supreme Being, and at about the same time in America, with the activity of Tom Paine and Elihu Palmer.[33] In a somewhat extraordinary example of a nation influenced by its own ideas as reflected back through foreign sources—an example which is a tribute to the impotence of the earlier English deists—Voltaire and Paine began to reach the English working classes, in some degree, about 1796. These prophets of French and American liberalism had absorbed deistic ideas from the English deists, but not until they had related them

to a social and political ideology did the English masses hear about them. This popular deism was not very important. Paine was effective through *The Rights of Man,* not *The Age of Reason;* if this extreme deist was to become the very 'centre and life' of the 'radical' political movement of the 1790's, it was not because he attacked religion, but because he spoke out against political corruption and inequality.[34] This English radicalism paid relatively little attention to religion. Who could still believe that 'priests' were the chief enemies of man?

What was significant was the reduction of religion to an adjunct of politics, by men of both camps, the conservative and the liberal. Clearly Edmund Burke was a Christian because he was a conservative in politics—because, that is, he saw in the Church a useful tool of political conservatism and because the French radicals were inclined to deism.[35] In like manner Paine, it would appear, was an anti-Christian chiefly because he associated that faith with the aristocracy he hated. Of this degradation of religion we have already spoken. It was, perhaps, the inevitable consequence of a period when religion and politics, while in fact separating, were still linked in men's minds as the Hippocrates' twins of Clarendon; when new economic and social forces were creating new conflicts and struggles which had nothing to do with theologies, but still bore their imprint.

NOTES

[1] Consult L. C. Hartley, *William Cowper, Humanitarian;* Mary G. Jones, *The Charity School Movement;* Betsy Rodgers, *Cloak of Charity: Studies in Eighteenth Century Philanthropy;* V. W. Crane, *The Southern Frontier* (Durham, North Carolina, 1928), chap. xiii; A. Ruth Fry, ed., *John Bellers, 1654–1725.*

[2] M. G. Jones, op. cit., p. 8.

[3] Mandeville's *Essay on Charity and Charity Schools* (1725) is included in *The Fable of the Bees*—see F. B. Kaye's standard edition.

[4] M. G. Jones, op. cit., p. 13. We owe to A. D. Lindsay *(The Modern Democratic State,* New York and London, 1947, i. 135) the observation that as late as 1822 an English clergyman opposed educating the lower classes as 'dangerous to the public peace', while Merle Curti in his *The Social Ideas of American Educators* (New York, 1935) recounts a similar opposition, based on fear of spoiling the workers for their lowly tasks.

[5] Dorothy Marshall, *The English Poor in the Eighteenth Century,* p. 8.

6 Charles Povey, *The Present State of Great Britain,* presents the case for such 'hospitals of industry'.

7 Defoe, *Everybody's Business is Nobody's Business,* 1725. This tract as well as *Giving Alms No Charity* is in his *Works,* edited by John S. Keltie.

8 John Moore, *A View of Society and Manners in Italy* (1790 edition), i. 327–8.

9 Rodgers, op. cit., p. 7.

10 See *Gentleman's Magazine,* August 1732, 'Benevolence'; Robert Eden, *The Harmony of Benevolence.*

11 Fielding, op. cit., pp. 48 ff. An outstanding brief description of the age's social evils may be found in W. C. Sydney, *England and the English in the Eighteenth Century,* ii. 192–5.

12 Richard Burn, *History of the Poor Laws,* 1764.

13 *Observator,* iii, no. 85 (7 Feb. 1705).

14 A. C. McGiffert, *Protestant Thought before Kant,* p. 229.

15 Mossner, *Butler,* p. 45.

16 It is true that Jefferson was the more typical deist. Such works as Adrienne Koch, *The Philosophy of Thomas Jefferson* and D. J. Boorstin, *The Lost World of Thomas Jefferson* indicate the influence on Jefferson of English deistic thought (e.g. Shaftesbury's), much of which came through Joseph Priestley.

17 Chubb, *True Gospel,* pp. 11, 49, 62–63. Also Toland, *Christianity Not Mysterious,* pp. xix, 141.

18 Chubb, *Posthumous Works,* i. 63–65.

19 Letter to Swift, 10 July 1721; see the latter's *Correspondence,* ed. F. E. Ball.

20 Torrey, *Voltaire and the English Deists,* carefully demonstrates Voltaire's debt to the English.

21 Anna Seeber, *John Toland als politischer Schriftsteller,* is an excellent source; see also F. H. Heinemann, 'John Toland and the Age of Reason', in *Archiv für Philosophie,* Sept. 1950. Our analysis of Toland is based on a number of his political pamphlets; see bibliography for titles.

22 See also Bolingbroke's approval of a state church, *Works,* iii. 485 ff.

23 *The Danger of Mercenary Parliaments,* 1700, and *The Art of Governing by Parties,* 1701.

24 Swift, commenting on the appearance of Shaftesbury's *Characteristics,* called it 'free Whiggish thinking' (*Correspondence,* i. 111). See also his attack on Collins.

25 'He that can read, and has a common portion of reason', Gordon thought, 'may find such plain and easy directions in the New Testament, as will instruct him how to find the ready way to Heaven; by which he will avoid the tedious ambiguities of a mercenary guide.' *Independent Whig,* ii. 374. Yet there ought to be a church, and bishops—'I will not presume to determine, whether . . . by a divine or human institution.' Ibid., p. 415.

26 See R. V. Holt, op. cit., chap. iii; Anthony Lincoln, *Some Political and Social Ideas of English Dissent, 1763–1800.* John Jebb was a liberal, unitarian Anglican; nor did Major Cartwright have a nonconformist background.

27 *Weekly Miscellany,* 1 Dec. 1733.

28 *Monthly Review,* i. 368.

29 See *A Discourse concerning Unlimited Submission,* 1750, and other writings by Mayhew.

30 Quoted in E. K. Chambers, *Samuel Taylor Coleridge* (Oxford, 1938), p. 29. On the growth of democratic ideas among the 'rational Dissenters' (who were unitarian in theology but did not admit to deism) see Anthony Lincoln, op. cit.—a thoughtful and scholarly work. The American Revolution was a turning-point in the emergence of an outspoken political radicalism within Dissent (though by no means embracing the majority of Dissenters).

31 John C. Miller's article on 'Religion, Finance, and Democracy in New England' in vol. vi of the *New England Quarterly,* and Oscar Zeichner's *Connecticut's Years of Controversy, 1750–76,* bring out class lines as between the aristocratic Old Lights and the lower-class New Lights, the religious quarrel often blending into the economic and political. See also the excellent social analysis in Wesley M. Gewehr, *The Great Awakening in Virginia, 1740–90,*

32 Bolingbroke, *Works,* iii. 55; Aldridge, *Shaftesbury,* p. 367; both these citations refer to passages in which these free-thinkers dwell on the desirability of keeping free-thought out of the hearing of the 'vulgar', lest it excite them to discontent.

33 G. A. Koch has told, sympathetically enough, the story of the effort to make deism into a popular republican cult in the United States, and the failure of that movement, in *Republican Religion.* John Morley's brilliant essay on 'Robespierre', in *Biographical Studies* (London, 1923), contains a more severe indictment of the French deistic cult.

34 Walter P. Hall, *British Radicalism, 1791–1797,* pp. 85–95.

35 H. G. Schenk, *The Aftermath of the Napoleonic Wars* (London, 1947), chap. i, pp. 5 ff. especially, discusses Burke's religion and the whole ideological basis of the period's return to religion, for political reasons, as a buttress against the forces of change unleashed by the French Revolution. These conservatives felt, as it has been said of Gentz, more strongly about the value of religion than about religion itself.

The Influence of
Bernard Mandeville

∽

F. B. KAYE

Even to scholars Bernard Mandeville's *Fable of the Bees* is now little more than a name and the recollection of a long-dead scandal. Yet the book had an extraordinary effect on the history of thought, an effect international in scope and still felt. Indeed, so great was Mandeville's influence that he can, I believe, be shown to be a major dignitary of eighteenth century thought. To demonstrate this is the aim of the present paper.

After this introduction it may seem a humorous anti-climax to answer the question: What was *The Fable of the Bees?* but the way in which history has slighted the work renders such an answer necessary. The book opens with a twenty-page rhymed allegory called *The Grumbling Hive,* first published by itself in 1705. This hive is described as made up, like any human state, of the elements of selfishness, pride, ambition, viciousness, and dishonesty. Yet all this evil is the stuff out of which is made the complicated mechanism of a great and prosperous state with

> Millions endeavoring to supply
> Each other's Lust and Vanity (*Fable,* I, 3).[1]

Indeed, it is precisely this lust and vanity, as it shows itself in the desire for power, the love of splendor, the round of fashions, and

From Studies in Philology, vol. XIX, no. 1, January, 1922 *(University of North Carolina Press), pp. 83—100.*

the give-and-take of prodigality and avarice, that is the motive force of the whole commonwealth.

> Thus Vice nurs'd Ingenuity,
> Which join'd with Time and Industry,
> Had carry'd Life's Conveniences,
> Its real Pleasures, Comforts, Ease,
> To such a Height, the very Poor
> Liv'd better than the Rich before (*Fable,* I, 11).

The bees, however, are not satisfied to have their viciousness mixed with their prosperity. All the cheats and hypocrites disclaim about the state of their country's morals, and pray the gods for honesty. This raises the indignation of Jove, who unexpectedly grants them their wish.

> But, Oh ye Gods! What Consternation,
> How vast and sudden was th' Alteration! (*Fable,* I, 13)

> As Pride and Luxury decrease,
> So by degrees they leave the Seas . . . .
> All Arts and Crafts neglected lie;
> Content, the Bane of Industry,
> Makes 'em admire their homely Store,
> And neither seek nor covet more (*Fable,* I, 21).

In this way, through the loss of its vices, the hive at the same time loses all its greatness.

Now comes the moral:

> *Then leave Complaints: Fools only strive*
> *To make a Great an Honest Hive.*
> *T' enjoy the World's Conveniences,*
> *Be fam'd in War, yet live in Ease,*
> *Without great Vices, is a vain*
> EUTOPIA *seated in the Brain.*
> *Fraud, Luxury and Pride must live,*
> *While we the Benefits receive . . . .*
> *So Vice is beneficial found,*
> *When it's by Justice lopt and bound;*
> *Nay, where the people would be great,*

> As necessary to the State,
> As Hunger is to make 'em eat (*Fable*, i, 23–4).

In 1714 Mandeville republished *The Grumbling Hive* with a prose commentary of about two hundred pages appended. This commentary was in the form of some twenty essays—or "Remarks," as he called them—each Remark serving as note to some line or lines of the little rhymed allegory. This time he named his book *The Fable of the Bees: or, Private Vices Publick Benefits*. In 1723 he added several new passages, among them two long Prose essays (one of them an attack on charity schools) ; in 1724, he included a "Vindication" of his book from the attacks already accumulating; and in 1728 (by title-page, 1729) he published a Part II, of size equal to the first volume.

Obviously, such a framework gave Mandeville the opportunity of incorporating any thought he liked on any topic he liked; and he took advantage of the fact. An extraordinarily fertile speculator, he throws out original or suggestive opinions—some of much interest—on education, evolution, feminism, criminology, medicine, duelling, vegetarianism, public stews, psychology, economics, French literature, and theology. Among his educational conceptions, for example, is a foreshadowing of the Montessori system (*Fable*, II, 183-5 and 211). Then, too, Mandeville's theories in Part II of the *Fable* concerning the evolution of society were quite extraordinary.[2] He seems unique at the time in appreciation of the great slowness of the thing, the small part in it played by the individual, the unsteadiness of its progression, and its control by physical law. A similar anticipatory modernity will be found in Mandeville's embryonic feminism.[3] These, however, are side issues for this paper, and are noted merely in passing.

We shall be occupied here with Mandeville's influence in three fields only: literature, ethics, and economics.

I

Mandeville's purely literary influence was not considerable. The *Fable* had no direct imitators. Its influence was limited to the offering of tid-bits for amalgamation or paraphrase by other

writers. Such an influence, however, it did have, and on some big figures—chiefly, Pope, Johnson, Adam Smith, and Voltaire. Pope paraphrased the *Fable* both in the *Moral Essays* and in the *Essay on Man*.[4] The manuscript of the latter, it should also be noted, had, instead of the present line II, 240, this direct paraphrase of the sub-title of the *Fable of the Bees:*

And public good extracts from private vice.

It is just possible also that Pope derived the famous "To err is human, to forgive, divine" from a passage in another well-known book by Mandeville—the *Free Thoughts*.[5]—Dr. Johnson, who said that Mandeville opened his views into real life very much,[6] and whose economic theories were borrowed from Mandeville,[7] limited his literary indebtedness to a passage in one of his *Idlers* (No. 34), which is a paraphrase of a witty portion of the *Fable* (I, 106), and to some able discussions with Boswell about the book.—Adam Smith's literary obligation extends to at least one famous passage, but this matter will be considered later as incidental to Smith's debt to Mandeville in the field of economics.— The literary borrowings of Voltaire, whose great general indebtedness will also be touched on later, consisted in the paraphrasing in French verse of some seven pages of the *Fable* (I, 190–6), Voltaire's poem being called *Le Marseillois et le Lion* (Œuvres, ed. Garnier, 1877-85, X, 140-8) ; and of passages in *Le Mondain* and the *Défense du Mondain,* and in the *Observations sur MM. Jean Lass, Melon et Dutot; sur le Commerce,* which have parallels in the *Fable*.[8]

All this, however, constitutes an unimportant phase of Mandeville's influence. His great effect was on ethics and economics, and a very practical effect it was; no mere interchange of theories, but one bound up with the destinies of England and of France.

Before undertaking an analysis of this effect, however, I wish to give some impression of the enormous vogue of the *Fable,* and the eighteenth century's interest in it, for the light of this vogue points of relationship between the *Fable* and subsequent developments take on fuller significance.

The *Fable* first attracted attention in 1723, when Mandeville added to it his "Essay on Charity and Charity-Schools." Thereupon, the newspapers focussed on it at once, and within a year whole books began to be aimed at it. At the same time the public commenced to exhaust an edition a year.[9] Then it went into foreign editions.[10] Meanwhile, other books by Mandeville were being frequently printed in England and, translated, on the Continent.[11] Moreover, his works must have been made familiar to thousands who never saw the books by the many reviews of them (often of considerable length) in periodicals such as the *Bibliothèque Britannique* and the *Histoire des Ouvrages des Savans,*[12] in theological bibliographies like those of Masch, Lilienthal, and Trinius, and in encyclopedias like Chaufepié's and the *General Dictionary.* The many attacks, also, on the *Fable* not only illustrated the fame of the book, but diffused this fame still further—a celebrity often commented on by contemporaries.[13] The following is a partial list of some of the better known men who at some time gave him specific and often sustained attention: John Dennis, [14] William Law,[15] Reimarus,[16] Hume,[17] Berkeley,[18] Hutcheson,[19] Godwin,[20] John Brown,[21] Fielding,[22] Gibbon,[23] Diderot,[24] Holbach,[25] Rousseau,[26] Malthus,[27] James Mill,[28] Mackintosh,[29] Adam Smith,[30] Warburton,[31] John Wesley,[32] Herder,[33] Montesquieu,[34] Hazlitt,[35] and Bentham.[36] Some of these, such as Fielding, referred to him repeatedly, and some wrote whole books on him. William Law devoted a volume to him; so did John Dennis; and Francis Hutcheson, no mean figure in the history of philosophy, wrote two books against him; while Adam Smith allotted him half of a special article, and Berkeley, a dialogue.

Nor was this vogue merely academic. The *Fable of the Bees* made a public scandal, and reached through the resultant notoriety not only the public eye but the public emotion. Mandeville, with his teaching of the usefulness of vice, inherited the office of Lord High Bogey-man, which Hobbes had held in the preceding century. The *Fable* was twice presented by the Grand Jury as a public nuisance; minister and bishop alike denounced it from the pulpit.[37] The book, indeed, aroused positive consternation, ranging from the reprehension of Bishop Berkeley[38] to the horror of

John Wesley,[39] who protests that not even Voltaire could have said so much for wickedness. In France, the *Fable* was actually ordered burned by the common hangman.[40]

It would, in fact, be difficult to overrate the degree and extent of Mandeville's eighteenth-century fame. A letter of Wesley's,[41] in 1750, indicates that the *Fable* was current in Ireland. In France, in 1765, we find Diderot complaining that the tenets of the book had become so familiar as to be a conversational nuisance.[42] In 1768, the friend of Laurence Sterne, John Hall-Stevenson, thought a good title for one of his pieces would be "The New Fable of the Bees." As late, indeed, as 1787, and in America at that, the author of our first American comedy—a play meant for popular consumption[43]—refers to Mandeville as if the latter's theories were as well known to the audience as the latest proclamation of General Washington.

This outline of Mandeville's vogue will serve as a prelude to the search into his specific influence, and may also give some initial intimations of the justification for the claims I made at the outset concerning his importance.

II

Now, to understand the effect which Mandeville exercised on ethical theory, it will be necessary to sketch briefly his general philosophical position. A good part of Mandeville will escape in the process: the wit, humor, and worldly-wise cynicism which gave his thought its edge must be omitted; but that cannot be helped. — Mandeville called his book "Private Vices, Publick Benefits." Now, by that he did not mean that all evil has a good side to it, and that this good outweighs the ill. His paradox turned, instead, on a matter of definition. He adopted certain current ethical conceptions as to the prerequisites of morality. But when he came rigorously to apply the definition of virtue which he had thus derived he found that the world did not furnish any examples of people who lived up to the definition, and thus it became an obvious deduction that, since all is vicious, even matters beneficial to us arise from vicious causes, and private vices are public benefits.

The conception of virtue propounded by Mandeville pro-

claimed, first, that no action was really virtuous if inspired by selfish emotion; and this assumption, since Mandeville considered all natural emotion fundamentally selfish, implied the ascetic position that no action was virtuous if done from natural impulse. Secondly, Mandeville's definition of virtue declared that no action was meritorious unless the motive that inspired it was a "rational" one. As Mandeville interpreted "rational" to imply an antithesis to emotion and self-regard, both aspects of his ethical code—the ascetic and the rationalistic—alike condemned as vicious all action whose dominant motive was natural impulse and self-regarding bias—or, to put it from a different angle, his code condemned all such acts as were caused by the traits man shared with the animals.

This conception of morality was no invention of Mandeville's. He merely adopted the creed of two great popular groups of the period. The first group comprised the theologians who, from the orthodox belief in the depravity of human nature, concluded naturally that virtue could not be found except in such action as unselfishly denied or transcended the working of the nature they condemned.[44] To all logical inferences from Mandeville's position as to the moral necessity of unselfishness and the conquest of natural impulse these ascetics were also fairly committed. The other group comprised the rationalistic or "intellectualistic" ethical thinkers, who identified morality with such action as proceeded from rational motives. This group was committed to conclusions logically deducible from Mandeville's position only in so far as, like him, they made an antithesis between reason and emotion; but, since this antithesis was very commonly made, at least implicitly,[45] these thinkers too were largely implicated in Mandeville's conclusions. The implications, then, which Mandeville was to deduce from the rigorous application of his definition of virtue were such as could genuinely involve and provoke the thought of his day.

The conclusion reached by Mandeville that all human action is at bottom vicious was attained by a psychological analysis of human emotions and their relation to opinion never before equalled, except possibly by Spinoza, for scientific penetration and completeness. I shall not here attempt to detail the examina-

tion through which Mandeville reached the conclusions that
reason is not a determinant factor in men's actions, our most
elaborate and apparently detached ratiocination being basically
only a rationalizing and excusing of the demands of dominant
emotions; that all our acts—even those apparently most altruistic
and unselfish—are, traced to their source, due to some variety or
interplay of selfish emotion; that man, after all, is only "the most
perfect of animals" (*Fable*, I, 31) and, no matter how much
trained and preached at, can never transcend or contradict this
fact. It is enough to note that he found his ethical code impossible
of achievement, and, therefore, advised all pretenders to states-
manship not to worry about unselfishness and "rationality," but
to content themselves with so ordering things that there should
be such proper mixture of various self-counteracting selfish
passions as would produce harmonious results. For practical purposes, then, Mandeville offered, not rigorism, but utilitarianism[46]
as a guiding principle to the actual worldly world. And he felt it
a pretty good world, too, in which, although abstract virtue might
be absent, yet human self-seeking, properly controlled, could be
made to produce a prosperous and happy state of affairs.

But then came the paradox. All this actual scheme of things,
although it produces or can be made to produce such pleasant
results, is, he announced, wrong, because not in accord with the
demands of rigoristic morality. The passions are indispensable to
proper conduct, but they are wicked. Prosperity is a pleasant
thing, but it is evil. The utilitarian viewpoint is highly practical,
but it will send you to Hell. Indeed, all the things which Mandeville has shown so necessary and desirable he then rejects as
vicious. His philosophy, accordingly, has two aspects. First, he
presents the actual world and how to get along in it, and after
he has expounded the means of making it exceedingly pleasant,
he places a candle snuffer on his previous thought by declaring
that all these good things of the world are vicious because not
based and impossible of being based on the rigoristic demand for
unselfishness and rationally motivated action. *The Fable of the
Bees*, then, holds in solution two opposite points of view — the
utilitarian and the rigoristic or formalistic.

By juxtaposing these two in this manner, Mandeville has

achieved a latent *reductio ad absurdum* of the rigoristic point of view. But he never educed this *reductio ad adsurdum*. Although he spent most of his book in the demonstration that a life regulated by the principles of rigoristic virtue is not only impossible but highly undesirable, he continued to announce the sanctity of the formalistic creed. This paradoxical ethical duet which Mandeville carried on with himself is the point to note here, for it is this fact which gives the clue to the influence on ethics which he exerted.

The attacks on Mandeville focus on this paradox, but the type of attack varies according to the intellectual leanings of the particular polemicist. First there were the critics who, like William Law and John Dennis, adhered to the rigoristic school of ethics. On these the effect of the *Fable* was that of the insane root which takes the reason prisoner. William Law was almost alone in keeping his head, although not his temper. It was not merely the theories of Mandeville that caused this riot of reason, but the tone of the doctor's writing. Mandeville employed a humorously cynical downrightness of statement that made him so provocative that even now, after two hundred years, he has kept almost unimpaired his ability to irritate those who disagree with him. But, apart from their expression, there was enough in Mandeville's tenets to upset those who believed virtue necessarily unselfish and rational. Mandeville accepted their own position to argue them into unbearable predicaments. He agreed that only such behaviour is virtuous as is motivated not by selfish emotion but through the conquest of one's natural impulses or through sheer respect for a moral code; and then he demonstrated that there can be no such conduct in this world. He admitted that a state based on selfishness is corrupt and that luxury is contrary to the Christian religion, and then he proceeded to show that all society must be based on selfishness and that no state can be great without luxury. He agreed that men must transcend their animal nature, and then he proved that it could not be done. In other words, he took advantage of his opponents' own standards to show them that according to these ideals they had never done a virtuous action in their lives, and that, even if these standards could be lived up to, they would inevitably cause the total collapse of

society. Meanwhile Mandeville stood in the middle of this spectacle roaring with laughter; which did not help to soothe his critics.

The thing was like an argument between Bernard Shaw and a synod of revivalists. They lost their heads. If only Mandeville had accepted the *reductio ad absurdum* latent in his book and rejected the rigoristic system of ethics, things would have been simple for the William Laws. They would merely have rushed to the defense of their code, and been quite comfortable. But Mandeville didn't reject it; the force of his demonstration of the value of vice and impossibility of virtue rested on his accepting their position.

There were, therefore, only two rational[47] courses open to the rigorists. They could argue, first, that Mandeville's vivisection of human nature was faulty and that men really can act in a manner fundamentally unselfish and rational. This they tried.[48] But Mandeville's analysis had been so keen and thorough that few of his opponents dared claim that they had demonstrated more than that in some cases a man might conceivably be virtuous in their sense of the word. This was hardly very comforting, for it left them still drowning in a sea of *almost* undiluted iniquity.

The other method was to abandon the ascetic point of view and deny that only such actions were virtuous as were done from unselfish devotion to principle, and to call for another criterion of virtue. Now, the strange fact is that almost every rigorist who undertook to answer Mandeville did at some time or other in this fashion repudiate his own basal position.[49] William Law was perhaps as staunch and unmitigated an ascetic as ever urged his dogmas on other people; to Law an act done simply because a person wanted to do it was *ipso facto* a bad act.[50] Yet Law, in his answer to the *Fable*, at times approaches the utilitarian position, and approves natural impulse.[51]

Law was typical. Of the rigorists who attack the *Fable* with any insight, almost all[52] are driven at some point or other to turn upon their own rigorism and to set up instead some form of utilitarianism; that is, to maintain that moral laws are justly to be shaped and qualified according to the human ends to be served, and to measure the service of these ends in terms of human happiness.[53]

On the other hand, there was another class of critics of the *Fable*, comprising those men by intellectual bias anti-rigoristic, like Hume and Adam Smith. These men took the *Fable* more calmly. Not holding the formalistic premise, they were not upset by Mandeville's deductions therefrom. They agree with his analysis; but when he came to his rigoristic candle-snuffer and said, "All these good things are due to vice," they answered with Hume: If it be vice which produces all the good in the world, then there is something the matter with our terminology; such vice is not vice but good.[54] These critics then, simply accepted the *reductio ad absurdum* which Mandeville refused to educe, and, rejecting the formalism which gave rise to Mandeville's paradox, adopted instead a utilitarian scheme of ethics.

This may seem the simple and obvious thing to do. And it *is* simple and obvious now — after two hundred years. But in that simple and obvious step is the germ of the whole modern utilitarian movement; in that rejection of absolute *a priori* codes and that refusal to dissever man from the animals is the core of the modern scientific, empirical attitude. With the solving of Mandeville's paradox, indeed, is bound up our whole present-day intellectual atmosphere, the development of which the utilitarian movement has done so much to foster.

Now, recognition of the inexpediency of rigoristic codes, which recognition eventually led to the utilitarian movement, was to be found elsewhere than in Mandeville, and the Mandevillian paradox was to be found latent in every-day points of view; but it was in dealing with Mandeville's especially forceful statement of this paradox that the utilitarian leaders were first caused to solve it. It was Mandeville who furnished them with the specific stimulus. Their first statements of the utilitarian theory will be found in those books of theirs which deal with Mandeville, and were largely evolved through the controversy. This is true of three who wrote of him at considerable length — Francis Hutcheson, John Brown, and Adam Smith, while, of the other major leaders of the utilitarian movement, Hume was acquainted with Mandeville, Bentham and Godwin praised him, and James Mill strongly defended him.[55] And, turning from the leaders to the intellectual soil upon which they had to work, it should be recalled that contemporary anti- or non-utilitarian opinion had been qualified,

and thus prepared for change, by the insistent paradox of the *Fable,* the outstanding ethical irritant of its generation. The case might be put more formally: Mandeville's critics are forced in their consideration of him to adopt in common the utilitarian attitude. Yet these critics were very dissimilar thinkers. Their agreement, therefore, must in considerable measure have been due to the nature of the subject — the *Fable of the Bees.*

The paradox of the *Fable,* indeed, supplied a spur which, on contact, almost necessarily forced all groups toward utilitarianism; and the enormous vogue of the book, together with the facts that its paradox was based on dominant types of ethical theory and thus involved and affected their many adherents, and that the book was so studied and reacted to by the utilitarian leaders, is proof of how generally and efficaciously the spur was applied.

As a matter of fact Mandeville has an even fuller claim than this to be considered a prime mover in the development of modern utilitarianism: it is not only through forcing a solution of the paradox that private vices are public benefits that the *Fable* fathered the utilitarian philosophy; another salient feature of Mandeville's ethical scheme had effect of a similar sort. This feature can be equally well described as moral nihilism, philosophical anarchism, or pyrrhonism. In morals, declared Mandeville, there are no universally valid rules of conduct. No person believes one thing but someone professes the opposite; no nation approves one form of conduct but another nation as strongly condemns it. ". . . . hunting after this *Pulchrum & Honestum* is not much better than a Wild-Goose-Chace" *(Fable,* I, 380). "What Mortal can decide which is the handsomest, abstract from the Mode in being, to wear great Buttons or small ones? . . . In Morals there is no greater Certainty" *(Fable,* I, 377–9).

How Mandeville reconciled this pyrrhonism with the rigoristic ethics which he accepted superficially and the utilitarianism which was basic in his thought need not concern us here. The point is that he put his denial of general moral standards with his usual pungency, and that it produced noticeable reactions in a number of his critics.[56] It affected them in much the same way that his famous paradox had. It presented what was to them an intolerable scheme of things, which, for their peace of mind

and soul, they had to remodel. And this remodeling — the furnishing of those valid ethical standards whose existence Mandeville denied — led them either to assert some *a priori* code and to maintain a rigoristic scheme of ethics (in which case the other edge of Mandeville's blade — his paradox — drove them toward utilitarianism) ; or it caused them to appeal to the utility of actions to supply, for judging those actions, the moral criteria Mandeville denied.

Thus with a double lash Mandeville drove his critics toward utilitarianism. By making the rigoristic position intolerable and the anarchistic position plausible, he forced his readers to formulate a way out. He furnished the necessity which is the mother of invention.

Nor is this all; for not only did Mandeville have the effect of a horrible example by driving people away from the position he ostensibly supported; he must also have exercised the influence of a model to be copied. As I indicated earlier, he himself had adopted the utilitarian point of view, and his whole viewpoint and method is strongly empirical. Indeed, he gave the utilitarian principle one of its earliest statements in its modern form.[57] "If a Publick Act," he said, "taking in all its Consequences, really produces a greater Quantity of Good, it must, and ought to be term'd a good Act." And again, "No sinful Laws can be beneficial, and *vice versa*, . . . no beneficial Laws can be sinful."[58] Now, while I find no certain evidence of anyone's having copied directly after Mandeville's statements of the utilitarian philosophy, yet it is only rational to suppose that some of his myriad readers and students must have adopted such beliefs from the *Fable*.

Furthermore, considering the effect of the book on those who wrote about it, and its enormous vogue, it is only fair to assume that its influence was considerable on those who did not write about it. Such an influence would have been exerted not only through the *Fable* itself, but through the works of disciples and opponents. This last matter is not entirely conjectural. Bentham, for instance, said that one of the books which most affected him was the *De L'Esprit* of Helvétius.[59] Now, this book is in many ways simply a French paraphrase of the *Fable*.[60]

This unspecific influence might be much further enlarged upon, but it is hardly worth the while thus to elaborate conjecture when the positive facts already noted suffice to prove the *Fable of the Bees* one of the most fundamental and persistent influences underlying the whole modern utilitarian movement.

III

Let us consider now Mandeville's effect on the course of economic theory, where his dominance was perhaps at its greatest.

One aspect of Mandeville's effect on the history of economic thought was his association with the famous division of labor theory. It is generally known that Adam Smith made this principle into one of the foundation stones of modern economic thought, but it is not so well known that Adam Smith took this theory largely from Mandeville. Mandeville, in the *Fable of the Bees,* as early as the first edition in 1714, definitely developed this conception not only once but several times.[61] Now, of course, the mere fact that Mandeville anticipated Smith would not mean that Smith derived his tenets from Mandeville, for Smith had been anticipated by others besides Mandeville. But Mandeville has special claims to influence. We know that Smith was intimately acquainted with the *Fable of the Bees.* He gave a most able analysis of it in his *Theory of Moral Sentiments,* and devoted half an essay to the influence of Mandeville on Rousseau.[62] Moreover, Mandeville not only sets forth the divison of labor principle, but does so in the words that Smith was to make famous, speaking several times of "dividing" and "subdividing" "labour." Furthermore, one of the most famous passages in the *Wealth of Nations* — that about the laborer's coat — is only a padded paraphrase of a similar passage in the *Fable of the Bees.*[63] Finally, Dugald Stewart, who knew Smith personally, credits Mandeville[64] with having been Smith's inspiration. It does not seem that more need be said to indicate that considerable credit for putting the division of labor theory on its feet belongs to Mandeville.

But, though important, his influence on the establishment of this doctrine is a minor aspect of Mandeville's effect on economic tendencies. A more important phase was his place in the inter-

national discussion concerning the usefulness of luxury, one of the most widely agitated questions in the eighteenth century. The *Fable of the Bees* contains many passages — perhaps the best known passages in the book — in which Mandeville shows not only the inseparability of luxury from a flourishing state, but holds that the production and consumption of luxuries is necessary to make it flourishing. This opinion was in opposition not only to all the more ascetic codes of morality, but in contradiction to what might be called the classic economic attitude, which set forth the ideal of a Spartan state, exalted the simpler agricultural pursuits, and denounced luxury as the degenerator of peoples and impoverisher of nations. The question of the value of luxury was to be one of the great battlegrounds of Voltaire and the Encyclopedists.

Now, the *Fable of the Bees* was the practical starting place of the defense of luxury, and exerted an international effect, greatest, perhaps, in France. From Mandeville descend the chief exponents of this defense: Melon, Montesquieu,[65] Voltaire, and the Encyclopedists, and even defenders who were no economists, like Dr. Johnson.[66] Voltaire, perhaps the most influential of all the defenders, is especially indebted to Mandeville. The famous *Mondain* of Voltaire, one of the chief works which drove the defense of luxury into the public mind, is in large part simply a versification of some of the theories set forth in the *Fable of the Bees.*[67]

Nor was the *Fable* merely a potent influence in the works of other writers. It not only spurred on the others, but was itself in the van of the attack. In 1785, the learned Professor Pluquet, in a work approved by the *College Royal,* called Mandeville the first to defend luxury from the standpoint of economic theory;[68] and so thoroughly in the public mind was Mandeville conceived as spokesman for the defense of luxury that a popular American play[69] as late as 1787 apostrophized not Voltaire, not any of the well-known encyclopedists, but Mandeville as the arch-advocate for this defense.

We now come to perhaps the most important aspect of Mandeville's economic influence. In the *Fable of the Bees* Mandeville maintains, and maintains elaborately, the theory at present

known as the *laissez-faire* theory, which dominated modern economic thought for a hundred years and is still a potent force. This is the theory that commercial affairs are happiest when least regulated by the government; that things tend by themselves to find their own proper level; and that unregulated self-seeking on the part of individuals will in society so interact with and check itself, that the result will be for the benefit of the community. But unnecessary interference on the part of the state will tend to pervert that delicate adjustment. Mandeville develops this hypothesis in regard both to national and international matters. In national affairs, he says—and elaborates the thesis—"Proportion as to Numbers in every Trade finds it self, and is never better kept than when no body meddles or interferes with it" (*Fable,* I, 342). This advocacy of the *laissez-faire* theory he put into the most discussed part of the *Fable*—the notorious "Essay on Charity and Charity-Schools"; and the effect of his defense is evidenced by the number of replies directed specifically at this part of the *Fable.*

His application of the *laissez-faire* attitude to international concerns took the form of an attack on the then prevailing mercantile theory—the belief that a nation's wealth could be gauged by the amount of money in the country, and that, consequently, to keep bullion in the country, imports should be either limited or prohibited. In opposition to this, Mandeville, in keen analysis, demonstrated that a community's imports cannot be restricted without affecting the ability of other nations to buy that community's exports; and he developed, also, some of the disadvantages of a nation's possessing a disproportionate amount of the world's bullion.[70] This, of course, is a predominant phase of the philosophy underlying English free trade, and of the philosophy of free trade in general.

Some historians of economics have considered the *Fable of the Bees*[71] an effectual source of the doctrine; but here the case must be developed by other means than such definite citations as those which demonstrate Mandeville's relation to the division of labor theory and the defense of luxury. To begin with, considering the effect of Mandeville's other economic tenets, and the extraordinary popularity of the *Fable*; and in view also of the fact that

the great apostle of the *laissez-faire* theory (both in its national and international applications), Adam Smith, had such a knowledge of and such a debt to the *Fable of the Bees,* it becomes more than possible that as regards the *laissez-faire* theory also Mandeville's influence must have been considerable. And to these considerations must be added another more weighty. In the thought of the great leaders of the *laissez-faire* movement — Hume and Smith — economic theory is, as has been noted, the outgrowth of their ethical systems. They saw man as a mechanism of interacting passions which he cannot help indulging as they come uppermost. Fortunately, however, according to their belief, these passions, although at first sight their dominion might seem to threaten anarchy, are so composed and arranged that under the influence of society their apparent discords harmonize to the public good. This immensely complicated adjustment is not the effect of premeditated effort, but is the automatic reaction of man in society; premeditated effort could only bungle and interfere with the complex social harmony which the facts of man's nature have of themselves created and will maintain. Thus, from this conception of human nature, the *laissez-faire,* or individualistic, theory of economics naturally followed — a descendant of ethical speculation.

Now, as has been indicated above, the relations between Mandeville and the ethical philosophers of his age were very close, especially as to the conception of human nature which underlies the economic theory of Smith and of Hume. Indeed, this conception of human nature, without which there would have been no philosophy of *laissez-faire,* and with which there could hardly help but be, is specifically Mandeville's. It is Mandeville who describes man as a mechanism of personal interests, which, however, functions in society for the public benefit. Mandeville is the creator of the "economic man" about whom Smith and Hume built their system. The *laissez-faire* theorists who followed Mandeville, whatever they may have said about his terminology of "vice" and "virtue," accepted his analysis of human nature, and used it, without adding essentially to its completeness, as the foundation of their systems.[72]

This sketch of Mandeville's influence on economic thought

through the division of labor theory, the defense of luxury, and the *laissez-faire* philosophy does not exhaust his consequence in the field of economics; nor is our view of his general importance complete when we have added to his total effect on economics his commanding position in the development of the utilitarian movement. To complete our picture we should have to study the significance of that mass of fertile theory, embracing everything from anthropology to criminology, with which his work is crammed; we should have to analyze the possible effect of his other books, such as his once popular *Treatise on the Hypochondriack and Hysterick Diseases* and his *Enquiry into the Causes of the Frequent Executions at Tyburn,* which, according to J. M. Robertson, anticipated Howard's prison reforms;[73] we should need to consider the effect he exerted on outstanding figures like Hazlitt and Rousseau, and to add to our estimate a fact with which this paper has not been concerned – that the *Fable of the Bees* is the work of a literary genius. Only then should we have a full portrayal of the significance of a man who was perhaps among the half dozen English writers of the eighteenth century who most profoundly influenced the course of civilization.

NOTES

1 My page references apply equally to a number of editions—to those of 1724, 1725, 1728, and 1732 of the first part, and to the editions of 1729 and 1733 of Part II of the *Fable*.

2 There are, before Mandeville, only embryonic and fragmentary considerations of the growth of society from an evolutionary point of view. Of the ancients (Horace, *Satires*, I, iii, Lucretius, *De Rerum Natura*, book 5, and Aeschylus, *Prometheus Bound*, lines 442-506) Lucretius is the most elaborate. The moderns until Mandeville added nothing. There is either no or slight anticipation of Mandeville in Matthew Hale (*Primitive Origination of Man*), Bossuet (*Discours sur l'Histoire Universelle*, ed. 1845, pp. 9–10), or Temple (*Essay upon the Original and Nature of Government*); nor is he anticipated in such works as those of Giordano Bruno, Bodin, Thomas Burnet, Whiston, John Woodward, John Keill, or Vico.

3 See *Fable*, II, 187-9, and also the passage in Mandeville's *Virgin Unmask'd*, ed. 1724, pp. 115-7, beginning: "They have enslaved our Sex."

4 Elwin considers the following passages derived from Mandeville: *Moral Essays*, III, 13-14 and 25-26; *Essay on Man*, II, 129-30, 157-8, and 193-4. That

the *Essay on Man*, II, 129-30 and 157-8, owes anything to Mandeville, however, is doubtful, although the other lines are probably Mandevillian.

5 *Free Thoughts* (1729), p. 61: "If to err belongs to human fraility, let us bear with their errors."

6 Boswell, *Life*, ed. Hill, New York, 1889, III, 292.

7 See below, note 66.

8 Derivations from Mandeville in these three works are noted in André Morize's interesting dissertation, *L'Apologie du Luxe au XVIIIe Siècle et "Le Mondain" de Voltaire* (Paris, 1909).

9 New editions were published in 1724, 1725, 1728, 1729 and 1732 (all by Tonson), and of Part II in 1729, 1730, and 1733 (all by Roberts). Further editions appeared in 1734, 1755, 1772, 1795, and 1806.

10 French versions in 1740 and 1750; German versions in 1761 and 1818 and, possibly, 1817.

11 The *Treatise of the Hypochondriack and Hysterick Diseases* had three or four printings; the *Virgin Unmask'd*, at least five; the *Modest Defence of Publick Stews* at least six English editions and some nine French ones; the *Free Thoughts*, five English editions, one German edition, an edition in Dutch, and four in French.

12 For instance, the *Bibliothèque Angloise* for 1725 gave the *Fable* 29 pages and Bluet's reply to the *Fable* the same amount of space; the *Bibliothèque Raisonée* for 1729 reviewed the *Fable* in 44 pages; the *Bibliothèque Britannique* in 1733 gave 52 pages to Mandeville's *Origin of Honour;* *Maendelyke Uittreksels* for 1723 devoted 71 pages to the *Free Thoughts;* and the *Mémoires de Trévoux* (1740) allotted the *Fable* over a hundred pages.

13 For instance: "La Pièce... fait grand bruit en Angleterre" (*Bibliothèque Angloise* for 1725, XIII, 99); "Avide lectumest in Anglia et non sine lausu receptam" (Reimarus, *Programma quo Fabulam de Apibus examinat*, 1726); "The *Fable*... a Book that has made so much Noise" (*Present State of the Republick of Letters* for 1728, II, 462); "La Fables des Abeilles *a fait tant de bruit en* Angleterre" (preface to French version of *Fable*, ed. 1740, I.i); "Nicht nur die Feinde der christlichen Religion, sondern auch viele Christen zählen ihn unter die recht grossen Geister" (J. F. Jacobi, *Betrachtungen über die weisen Absichten Gottes*, 1749); "Such is the system of Dr. Mandeville, which once made so much noise in the world" (Adam Smith, *Theory of Moral Sentiments*, ed. 1759, p. 486); "La fameuse fable des abeilles... fit un grand bruit en Angleterre" (Voltaire, *Œuvres Complètes*, ed. Garnier, 1877-85, XVII, 29).

14 *Vice and Luxury Publick Mischiefs: or, Remarks on...the Fable of the Bees* (1724).

15 *Remarks upon...the Fable of the Bees* (1724).

16 *Programma quo Fabulam de Apibus examinat...* (1726).

17 *Essays*, ed. Green and Grose, I, 308-9.

18 *Alciphron: or, the Minute Philospher* (first and second dialogues); *Discourse Addressed to Magistrates*, 1736 (*Works*, ed. Fraser, Oxford, 1871, III, 424).

[19] Letter in *London Journal* for Nov. 14 and 21, 1724; *Inquiry into the Original . . . of . . . Virtue . . . In which the Principles of . . . Shaftesbury are . . . defended against . . . the Fable of the Bees* (1725); three letters in the *Dublin Journal*, Feb. 5, 12, and 19, 1726—reprinted as the latter half of *Reflections upon Laughter, and Remarks upon the Fable of the Bees* (Glasgow, 1750).

[20] *Political Justice*—ed. 1793, II, 815; ed. 1796, II, 484—5, note.

[21] *Estimate* (1758), II, 86; *On Honour* (1743), lines 176-9; *Essays on the Characteristics* (1751), in the second essay.

[22] *Tom Jones,* book 6, chap. I; *Amelia,* book 3, chap. 5; *Covent-Garden Journal,* ed. Jensen, New Haven, I, 258-263.

[23] *Memoirs,* ed. Hill, 1900, p. 23.

[24] *OEuvres,* ed. Assézat, Paris, X, 299 and IV, 102-3 (the latter sometimes attributed to Rousseau).

[25] *La Morale Universelle* (1820), I, xxi-xxiii.

[26] *Narcisse,* preface (*Œuvres,* ed. Petitain, 1859, 152). See Also Masson's edition of the *Profession de Foi du Vicaire Savoyard.*

[27] *Essay on . . . Population,* ed. Bettany, 1890, p. 553, note.

[28] *Fragment on Mackintosh* (1835). pp. 55-63.

[29] "Disertation Second," in *Encyclopædia Britannica,* ed. 1842, I, 323.

[30] Letter in *Edinburgh Review* (1755), No. 1, pp. 63-79; *Theory of Moral Sentiments* (1759), pp. 474-87 and 492.

[31] *Divine Legation of Moses* (1846), I, 156ff.

[32] Diary, entry for Apr. 14, 1756, and letter cited in Abbey's *English Church and its Bishops* (1887), I, 32.

[33] *Adrastea,* IV (2), 234-252.

[34] *De l'Esprit des Lois,* book 7, chap. 1.

[35] See index of Waller and Glover edition for some twenty-three references.

[36] *Works,* ed. Bowring, 1843, I, 49, note, and X, 73.

[37] Some of the sermons against it that got into print were *The True Christian Method of Educating the Children both of the Poor and Rich,* preached in 1724 by Thomas Wilson, Bishop of Sodor and Man; Chandler's *Doing Good . . . . on Answer to . . . the Fable of the Bees* (1728); a sermon delivered in 1727 by Isaac Watts (printed as *An Essay towards the Encouragement of Charity-Schools,* 1728); and Barnes's *Charity and Charity Schools Defended* (delivered 1724, printed 1727).

[38] *Works,* ed. Fraser, 1871, III, 424.

[39] *Journal,* ed. Curnock, IV, 157.

[40] G. Peignot, *Dictionnaire . . . des Principaux Livres Condamnés au Feu* (Paris, 1806), I, 282.

[41] Cited in Abbey's *English Church and its Bishops* (1887), I, 32.

[42] *Œuvres,* ed. Assézat. X, 299.

[43] Royall Tyler, *The Contrast,* III, ii.

[44] This was the respectable orthodox position. Thus Luther wrote, "All things in thyself are unrighteous, sinful, and damnable" (*Select Works,* trans. Cole, 1826, I, 13 and passim). And Calvin argued (*Institutes,* III, ix, 2), "For

there is no medium between the two things: the earth must either be worthless in our estimation, or keep us enslaved by an intemperate love of it. Therefore, if we have any regard to eternity, we must carefully strive to disencumber ourselves of these fetters"; and he speaks *(Institutes,* III, ix, 3) of the "contempt which believers should train themselves to feel for the present life." This belief in the corruption of human nature the Synod of Dort authenticated as the official Protestant doctrine. It is found in representative moral works of all sorts. For example, in his *Rule and Exercises of Holy Dying* (Temple Classics, p. 68), Jeremy Taylor wrote, "He that would die holily and happily, must in this world love tears, humility, solitude, and repentance." In 1722, in his *Conscious Lovers* (III, i), Steele satirized this attitude as if it were of general currency: "To love is a passion, 'tis a desire, and we must have no desires."

45 Rationalism, of one aspect or another, in seventeenth and eighteenth century ethics was, it is almost unnecessary to note, very marked, whether in a writer such as the Cambridge Platonist Culverwel, who states *(Of the Light of Nature,* ed. Brown, 1857, p. 66) that "the law of nature is built upon reason," or in a more systematic thinker like the "intellectualist" Samuel Clarke, who argues *(Works,* ed. 1738, II, 50-1): "From this first, original, and literal signification of the words, *Flesh and Spirit;* the same Terms have, by a very easy and natural figure of Speech, been extended to signify *All Vice* and *All Virtue* in *general;* as having their Root and Foundation, one in the prevailing of different *Passions and Desires* over the Dictates of *Reason,* and the other in the Dominion of *Reason and Religion* over all the irregularities of *Desires and Passions.* Every *Vice,* and every instance of *Wickedness,* of *whatever* kind it be; has its Foundation in *some unreasonable Appetite* or *ungoverned Passion, warring against the Law of the Mind."* And again—"All Religion and Virtue, consists in the Love of Truth, and in the Free Choice and Practice of Right, and in being influenced regularly by rational and moral Motives" *(Sermons,* ed. 1742, I, 457). Even so empirical a thinker as Locke holds, in contradiction to his main philosophy, that a complete morality can be derived by the exercise of pure ratiocination from general *a priori* principles, without reference to concrete circumstances; and Spinoza also, who had placed so great a stress on the dependence of thought upon feeling, nevertheless attempts to demonstrate his ethics "ordine geometrico."

However, although the general thought identified virtue with conduct in accord with "reason," "reason" was usually an ill-defined and contradictorily employed term. The ethical rationalism of the period implied, first, that the organization of the universe was a geometrically rational one, and that, therefore, moral laws were the "immutable and eternal" affairs whose disconnection with the facts of human nature Fielding was later to ridicule in *Tom Jones.* To such a conception the tastes and emotions in which men differed from one another were either irritating or negligible; and its stress was naturally laid upon the abstract, rational relationships which were true alike of all men. To this conception, therefore, "reason" tended to imply an antithesis to taste and individual impulse.

Secondly, the ethical rationalism of the day insisted that acts were virtuous only if their motivation was from "reason." It is at this point—the phase of rationalistic ethics of chief importance in relation to Mandeville—that current philosophy was most inchoate. No real attempt was usually made to define motivation by "reason." "Reason" sometimes implied any practical action, sometimes a proper blend of deliberation and impulse, and very often, indeed, it was used, as Mandeville used it, in connection with acts the decision to perform which was not determined by emotional or personal bias (which might, however, provided it did not determine the will to act, legitimately accompany the action). Again and again it is manifest upon analysis that action according to reason is thought of (even by thinkers who sometimes take a different position) as action done despite the insistence of natural impulses and self-regarding bias, in spite of one's animal nature. Sometimes the writer makes this antithesis comparatively obvious, as when Culverwel reasons: "Yet grant that the several multitudes, all the species of these irrational creatures [animals] were all without spot or blemish in . . . their sensitive conversation, can any therefore fancy that they dress themselves by the glass of a [moral] law? Is it not rather a faithfulness to their own natural inclinations? . . . A law is founded in intellectuals, in the reason, not in the sensitive principle" (*Of the Light of Nature*, ed. Brown, 1857, p. 62). The tendency of the rationalistic school to make reason a quite abstract function is illustrated in the work of Mandeville's contemporary Wollaston, whose rationalistic *Natural Religion Delineated* considered virtue simply as truth, and vice as untruth. The antithesis between reason and natural impulse is very sharp and explicit in Richard Price, who summed up the principles of the "intellectualist" school of which he was a belated member in the statement that "*instinctive benevolence* is no principle of virtue, nor are any actions flowing merely from it virtuous. As far as this influences, so far something else than reason and goodness influence, and so much I think is to be subtracted from the moral worth of any action or character" (*Review of the Principle Questions in Morals*, ed. 1787, pp. 323-4).

There were certain characteristics of the ethical rationalism of the day which explain and illustrate the tendency to disassociate reason and feeling. In the first place, rationalism was from one aspect transcendental. With its stress on "immutable and eternal laws" of right and wrong and its love of the formulable, it was largely an attempt to transcend the merely relative, and hence personal and individual emotions. Like the theological asceticism of its day (see above, note 44), it was a method of transcending concrete human nature. Secondly, it could hardly help being affected by this current theological asceticism and its condemnation of natural impulse, especially since so many rationalists were also theologians. The tendency to identify the theological and the rationalistic attitudes is evidenced in the prayer with which Thomas Burnet closed the second book of his *Theory of the Earth*: "*MAY we, in the mean time, by a true Love of God above all things, and a contempt of this Vain World which passeth away; By a careful use of the Gifts of God and Nature, the Light of Reason and Revelation, prepare our selves . . . for the*

great Coming of our Saviour." Note the paralleling of *"a contempt for this Vain World"* with *"the Light of Reason."* In the third place, because of the problem of the soul a sharp distinction was drawn between man and the animals. The belief that animals have no soul (rational principle) combined with the conviction that the soul is the ultimately important thing tended naturally to cause contempt for the animal functions and a belief that they could form no ingredient in virtue. Berkeley illustrates this tendency when, in his reply to Mandeville (*Alciphron*), he says, "Considered in that light [as he is an animal], he [man] hath no sense of duty, no notion of virtue" (*Works,* ed. Fraser, 1871, II, 81). Finally, to cause too sharp an antithesis between the conceptions of reason and feeling there was the all important fact of mental and literary inexactness, of failure to make and maintain proper distinctions. Since Mandeville's day philosophical speculation, to an appreciable extent on his account (see below, note 53), has become more precise as regards the distinction between reason and feeling, but in his time it so generally fell into assertions or implications of an antithesis between reason and impulse, even in the face of speculations in the same work maintaining an opposite position, that so great a thinker as Spinoza was not entirely exempt from the contagion, as is apparent in his *Ethica,* part 4, props. 53 and 56.

From the above it may be seen that, even though the position taken by Mandeville that no conduct can be virtuous unless the will to perform it was undetermined by natural impulse and selfishness may have been somewhat more extreme than the average, yet it is evident that his position was none the less in accord with a great body of contemporary theory. And, indeed, this close relation to his age is demonstrated by the violence of the popular reaction to his book.

⁴⁶ I use the term "utilitarian" in a looser sense than that in which specialists in philosophy ordinarily employ it. I use it as a blanket term for such teleological forms of ethics as eudaemonism and universal hedonism; and intend by it always an opposition to the insistence of rigoristic or formalistic ethics—rationalistic or ascetic—that not results but motivation by right principle determines virtuousness. To have used the technical vocabulary of the philosophical specialist would have needlessly hampered the reader trained in other fields; and, besides, my non-technical use of the term parallels the condition of ethical theory in Mandeville's day, when utilitarian theory had not yet taken to itself the specific connotation it now has, but was thought of simply as an ethics whose moral touchstone was results and not abstract principle.

⁴⁷ I say "rational" advisedly. Many of Mandeville's attackers simply misunderstood him. They took his terms quite literally, interpreting "vice" as something contrary to the welfare of the individual practising it. From this they proved "by rule demonstrative" that vice must therefore be injurious to society, the sum of individuals. But, of course, Mandeville meant by vice not something harmful to its devotees, but something contrary to the dictates of a strictly rigoristic morality. John Dennis is a good example of the literal-minded whose attack on the *Fable* was largely an excited attempt to prove that if a thing has a bad effect it has an effect which is bad.

And then, besides the logomachy arising from a too literal reading of the *Fable,* much of the controversy was mere vituperation, as in Hendley's *Defence of the Charity-Schools. Wherein the Many False, Scandalous and Malicious Objections of those Advocates for Ignorance and Irreligion, the Author of the Fable of the Bees . . . are . . . answer'd* (1725).

48 Notably Hutcheson (*Inquiry into . . . Beauty and Virtue*). But Hutcheson's attempt to prove the fundamental benevolence of humanity is not entirely an attack on Mandeville's psychological analysis; it is largely a giving of different names to the same emotions. Hutcheson, like Mandeville, denied the possibility of entirely dispassionate action; and Mandeville, like Hutcheson, admitted the reality of the compassionate impulses. Mandeville, however, insisted on terming all natural emotions selfish, whereas Hutcheson defined some of them as altruistic.

As to the effects of distinguishing between selfish and unselfish natural impulse, see below, note 53.

49 That is, if he did not indulge merely in vituperation or in the misunderstanding considered above, note 47.

50 See his *Serious Call to a Devout and Holy Life* (1727), *passim.*

51 *Remarks upon . . . the Fable of the Bees* (1724), pp. 33-37.

52 Examples of rigoristic critics thus forced to repudiate their position include Law, Dennis, Fiddes (*General Treatise of Morality,* 1724), and Bluet (*Enquiry whether Virtue tends to . . . Benefit . . . of a People,* 1725).

53 Of course there were ways for the rigorists to evade Mandeville's attack without quite giving up their position. Their very inconsistencies were a means of defense; and Mandeville, too, really had taken a rigoristic position more accentuated and bald than the average. But the devices by which the rigorists sought to defend themselves without shifting ground were a very incomplete defense. Thus, they argued that there was such a thing as morally neutral activity, and that, therefore, self-regarding action and natural impulse, while not sufficient by themselves for virtue, were not necessarily vicious. This destroyed Mandeville's demonstration that the rigoristic position implied everything to be necessarily vicious, but it left him able still to claim that nothing could be virtuous, moral neutrality being then the utter limit of moral achievement. This, of course, was hardly satisfactory to the rigorists. Similarly, the ascetics could and did argue that they did not deny the moral value of man's nature nor quite condemn selfishness—indeed, that, properly understood, man's real nature and greatest happiness is found only in obeying the *a priori* dictates of Heaven, and that, therefore, enlightened selfishness demands adherence to the rigoristic code. Not to notice the important shift of sense in the word "nature," it is enough to point out here that the "theological utilitarianism" here adopted is definitely an approach to more empirical utilitarianism, and, therefore, that here again Mandeville's pressure towards utilitarianism is only partially evaded. Again, the rigorists might deny, like non-rigorists such as Adam Smith, that all natural feeling was selfish, maintaining that some compassionate emotions were genuinely altruistic. But since they could not say this of all compassionate feeling (some of this being obviously a self-indulgence) they had to find a criterion to distinguish

between selfish and non-selfish compassionate emotion; and, a strictly rigoristic test being here not possible, a utilitarian criterion naturally forced itself upon them. And, waiving the efficacy of their replies to Mandeville, the very fact that they had to frame replies on profoundly significant ethical questions was itself a service to the progress of speculation. One may look long in pre-Mandevillian literature for such careful distinctions between reason and emotion and their respective virtuousness as Law, for example, is forced to make in his effort to show that Mandeville misunderstood the rigoristic position. Whether he misunderstood it or not, he forced its adherents to attempt a liberation of their creed from the contradictions and indefiniteness which by themselves had given enough ground for his satire.

And apart from the sheerly logical side of the matter, there was a psychological reason why the attempt to cope with Mandeville so weakened the power of the formalists. Formalism affirms its transcendence; it professes absoluteness. When, therefore, imperfection in a formalistic creed is sufficiently felt to induce a desire for modification, the impulsion to formalism —a craving for the absoluteness and perfection which the creed promised— is weakened at its source, for the creed is now seen to be somewhat a thing of uncertainty.

[54] See Hume, *Essays,* ed. Green and Grose, 1889, II, 178.

[55] For references see above, notes 19, 21, 30, 17, 36, 20, and 28.

[56] For instance, in Law (*Remarks,* section 3), Berkeley (*Works,* ed. Fraser, 1871, II, 76 and 82), Brown (*Essays,* second essay, section 4), Adam Smith (*Theory of Moral Sentiments,* ed. 1759, p. 474), and Fiddes (*General Treatise of Morality,* preface).

[57] Hutcheson's dictum that "*that Action* is *best,* which accomplishes the *greatest Happiness* for the *greatest Numbers*" (*Inquiry into . . . Beauty and Virtue,* ed. 1725, p. 164), was not pronounced till 1725.

[58] *Modest Defence of Publick Stews* (1724), pp. 68 and 69. Similar statements of the utilitarian position are found in the *Fable,* I, 274, II, 196, II, 333, and II, 335.

[59] See Leslie Stephen, *English Utilitarians* (1900), I, 177.

[60] Helvétius' derivation from Mandeville has been noted by Jodl, *Geschichte der Ethik* (Stuttgart, 1882), I, 189; Tabaraud, *Histoire Critique du Philosophisme Anglois* (1806), II, 186; Malesherbes (see Erdmann, *Grundriss der Geschichte der Philosophie,* ed. Berlin, 1870, II, 121); Morize, *L'Apologie du Luxe* (1909), p. 69; Sakmann, *Bernard de Mandeville* (Freiburg, 1897), p. 212; Schlosser, *History of the Eighteenth Century* (1843-52), I, 50; Guyot, *La Science Économique* (1907), p. 8; Hasbach, "Les Fondements Philosophique de l'Économie Politique" (in *Revue d'Économie Politique* for 1893, VII, 785); Buckle, *History of Civilization in England* (1872), II, 218; Robertson, *Short History of Freethought* (N. Y., 1906), II, 238. The Sorbonne blamed Helvétius' theories partly on Mandeville's teachings (see Sackmann, *Bernard de Mandeville,* p. 212).

[61] See *Fable,* I, 182-3, I, 411-4, II, 149, II, 335-6, II, 386, II, 391, and index to Part II under, "*Labour.* The usefulness of dividing and subdividing it."

62 See above, note 30.

63 Compare *Fable*, ɪ, 182-3 and 411-4 with *Wealth of Nations*, ed. Cannan, ɪ, 13-14. Cannan notes the parallel.

64 Stewart, *Collected Works*, ed. Hamilton, vɪɪɪ, 323. Cf. also vɪɪɪ, 311.

65 The indebtedness of Melon and Montesquieu is treated in Morize's *L'Apologie du Luxe*. Melon's debt is noted also by Espinas, "La Troisième Phase et la Dissolution du Mercantilisme" (in *Revue Internationale de Sociologie* for Mar. 1902, p. 166).

66 Johnson's economic tenets were apparently drawn from the *Fable*. Mandevillian passages abound; see *Works* (1825), xɪ, 349; Boswell, *Life*, ed. Hill, New York, 1889, ɪɪ, 170-1, ɪɪ, 217-9 (cf. *Fable*, ɪ, 118 ff.), ɪɪɪ, 56, ɪɪɪ, 265 (cf. *Fable*, ɪ, 108-10 and ff.), ɪɪɪ, 282 (cf. *Fable*, ɪ, 198-9), ɪɪɪ, 291-2, and ɪv, 173; *Lives of the English Poets*, ed. Hill, ɪ, 157 (Hill notes the origin of this in Mandeville.). Johnson himself practically admits his debt (*Life*, ɪɪɪ, 291): "He as usual defended luxury; 'You cannot spend money in luxury without doing good to the poor ...' Miss Seward asked, if this was not Mandeville's doctrine of 'private vices publick benefits.' " And Johnson responds with a brilliant criticism of the *Fable*, the statement that he read the book forty or fifty years ago, and the acknowledgement that it "opened my views into real life very much."

67 This is demonstrated in Morize's *L'Apologie du Luxe au XVIIIe Siècle*.

68 For the college's approval see Pluquet, *Traité Philosophique et Politique sur le Luxe (Paris,* 1786), ɪɪ, 501. Pluquet's statement concerning Mandeville's priority (*Traité*, ɪ, 16) is not quite accurate. Bayle had preceded Mandeville in defending luxury. However, the very error shows how closely Mandeville had become identified popularly with the defense of luxury.

69 Tyler, *The Contrast*, ɪɪɪ, ii.

70 For Mandeville's defense of free trade see especially *Fable*, ɪ, 110-4 and 284, and, for his theories concerning money, ɪ, 213-5 and 345.

71 Thus Hasback, "Les Fondements Philosophique de l'Économie Politique de Quesnay et de Smith" (in *Revue d'Économie Politique* for 1893, vɪɪ, 782); Lange, *Geschichte des Materialismus* (1887), p. 743; Laviosa, *La Filosofia Scientifica del Diritto in Inghilterra* (Turin, 1897), p. 683. Schatz calls it *(L'Individualisme Économique et Social,* ed. Paris, 1907, p. 62) "l'ouvrage capital ou se trouve tous les germes essentiels de la philosophie économique et sociale de l'individualisme."

72 Schatz has developed this matter in his "Bernard de Mandeville" (in *Vierteljahrschrift für Social- und Wirtschaftsgeschichte* for 1903, ɪ, 434-80).

Hume, it is true, came finally to assert the reality of benevolence, and Smith had always maintained this. However, their analysis of human nature really paralleled Mandeville's; they differed only in giving the same compassionate emotions contrary names, as Hutcheson did (see above, note 48). And, apart from that, in their economic writings they concentrated on man as a selfish mechanism, leaving his benevolence to be considered in more ethical works.

73 *Essays towards a Critical Method* (1889), p. 219.

Political Man

࿎

J. H. PLUMB

Most of the cultural and intellectual activities of Englishmen in the eighteenth century enjoyed an extension of public participation — art, music, literature, as well as theology, philosophy and history reached deeper into the nation: books, magazines, pamphlets, newspapers tumbled from the presses; and certainly there were far more literate men and women, aware of the great issues of the day, than there had been. Did, however, the political life of the nation run counter to this general development? Was the individual excluded more and more from political activity by the extension of the life of parliament from three to seven years, by the decline of party, and by growth of oligarchy? A narrow view of politics, a myopic concentration on the mechanics of parliamentary elections, might lead one to believe so, but politics and political issues still reached beyond the confines of Westminster. They were of paramount interest to a nation whose liberties, no matter how oddly institutionalised, were the object of envious admiration among the liberal philosophers of Western Europe. Consider for a moment the fury unleashed by the Excise Bill, or by the attempt to permit Jewish Naturalisation or even by the Cider Tax: to say nothing of Wilkes, America and the rest, and one cannot doubt the widespread participation of Englishmen in politics. True these outbursts were partly engi-

From Man Versus Society in Eighteenth-Century Britain, *ed., James L. Clifford (Cambridge: Cambridge University Press, 1968), pp. 1–21.*

neered, and they were but tornadoes that swept the surface, for
the basic structure of eighteenth-century politics was very stable,
steel-like in its strength, even if it bent in the wind. The political
experience of the seventeenth century was not obliterated over
night, either by the Glorious Revolution or the Septennial Act:
radical and Tories existed even in 1750. Politics was never merely
a matter for the politicians.

In the seventeenth century in order to win their victories
against the Crown, the gentry and their aristocratic allies had
called into being a large parliamentary electorate, and one which
from time to time exercised the powers of choice. Between 1700
and 1715, eight general elections for parliament were held, a far
greater number than have ever been held since in a comparable
time-span. Also, during this period only a handful of parliamentary boroughs avoided a contest, even those with very small
electorates.[1]

In order to understand the relationship of the individual to
the political institutions by which he was governed in the eighteenth century, it is very necessary to look at this early period
more closely, for it deeply influenced all subsequent political
history of the Hanoverian period.

There are a number of elementary factors to remember about
politics in the reign of Queen Anne which are sometimes overlooked. One I have already mentioned, the exceptional frequency
of general elections, and, at these elections, contests in all types
of constituency were rarely avoided for more than an election or
two. Counties went very frequently to a poll, involving, except
in such tiny counties as Rutland, thousands of freeholders. Some
counties where divisions went very deep, such as Essex, were
fought time and time again. As with the counties, so with the
great boroughs: Westminster, Bristol, Norwich, Coventry and
their like were battle grounds for — and I have no hesitation in
using the word — party. Nor did the tiny boroughs avoid contests:
a few did, but even some of the smallest corporations possessed
their party divisions, and often the defection of one or two voters
could swing the town from a Whig to a Tory patron. Frequent
elections, contests and party, Whigs versus Tories—these are the
three major ingredients of the politics of this period: factors

which enabled most gentlemen and a number of freeholders and burgesses to exercise a free political choice.[2] And this was England's vast singularity, a unique situation amongst the major powers of the world at this time.

The issues were clear, and understood by thousands of voters, if not all, and men in the heart of borough politics watched closely and with passion what was happening at Westminster. The choice of the Speaker of the House of Commons in 1705 was a vital test of party strength: John Smith was supported by the Whigs and the Court, William Bromley by the Tories.[3] Smith got home, in spite of a defection of seventeen Tory placemen to Bromley. (They paid for such insubordination later when fifteen of them lost their places.) [4] The contest had been avidly followed back in King's Lynn by Robert Walpole's Whig supporters. One of the leaders of the Lynn Whigs wrote off at once: 'the Choice of your Speaker is very pleasing to all honest men, but on the contrary a great Mortification to the High Church papists and atheists.'[5]

It was not only the great issues that these local politicians watched: they were keenly aware of the twists and turns of party tactics. Another Turner, John, the nephew of Charles, and Robert Walpole's least inhibited supporter in Lynn, wrote to him on 7 December 1705

I cannot tell what to judge of your condition when last Votes I saw[6] you were outmustered by 29 in the Agmondisham election.[7] I never thought to find Sr Edward Seymour [the Tory leader] a prophett, as our parsons will certainly represent him to be, for they encourage themselves with a saying of his that 205 volunteers will beat 248 prest men, so they still think to get the better of you.[8] But I cannot see they misse a man and I am sure you had a great many absent but if they will not apeare, they ought to be reckoned as cyphers. If you were not more hearty yesterday, I expect to heare you are baulkt at Norwich too.[9]

Politics mattered. And the number of people involved was very considerable. Take Norwich, which worried John Turner. In 1705, about 2,500 men voted: probably about 25 per cent of the active male population, and only 150 votes separated the Whig and Tory candidates. The principles were clear-cut: on the part

of the Whigs support for Marlborough's war (Turner had been terrified that there might be a reverse before the election), and opposition to the High Church party; dislike of high taxes, dissenters and courtiers on the part of the Tories.

Throughout the land, the electorate was divided. Small boroughs or large counties were both prone to attacks of party fever. So long as the Tories had prospects of office, their guineas could ring as true as a Whig's: in the pressure of circumstances, doubtful voters, wobblers uncertain of their own or the world's future, could float one way, then another, and often upset the certainties of machine politics. This is why, on occasion, the influence of Lord Wharton in quite small boroughs snapped and he found his candidates defeated and Tories returned. So long as power could come to the Tories — and it could and did for most of Queen Anne's reign, the factors which made for political stability — bribery and influence combined with open voting — were kept in check. Politics remained a game for two players.

Issues therefore counted; the gentry, who were very numerous, were divided sharply on questions of war and peace, on toleration of dissent and the succession to the Crown, matters which Elizabeth I thought should be reserved for princes. In Queen Anne's reign they were questions for the electorate, a remarkable development in a hundred years. But, of course, they were not the only questions. Politics have always been more than a question of issues: they imply the pursuit of power. By 1700, politicians were well aware that the freedom of the electorate could be a stumbling-block in their quest for power. Already determined and successful efforts had been made to eradicate party strife in the constituencies and to reduce them to subordination. Every art was used to secure control. Of course, there was much variety. Sometimes the personal, patriarchal and traditional authority of a great family, not necessarily very rich or very generous, was sufficient to dominate the small parliamentary borough that nestled against its estate: such was the authority of the Rashleighs at Fowey, the Burrards of Lymington or the Leighs of Lyme. But such corporations were getting rare by 1700. Most voters, no matter how loyal to a person or a party, knew that they possessed, in their parliamentary franchise, negotiable currency. Many of them liked to turn it into hard cash.

There has been too much evasion of the question of bribery: money played its part throughout the eighteenth century. Indeed, expenses steadily grew, particularly after the Septennial Act of 1716, which gave a seven years instead of a three years return on the investment. At Weobley in Herefordshire voters expected a minimum of £5 and often secured £20. And, as ever with bribery, they sometimes took money from both sides, but this was a dangerous practice when voting was open and gentlemen could break a mere tradesman's head with impunity. But bribery, like rich and lavish entertainment, seems to have been endemic in certain boroughs. Weobley, until most of the vote-houses were bought up, had a very bad name; so had Stockbridge and Great Bedwyn, where the poor weavers got what they could whilst the going was good. At Coventry, however, it was all drink, food and riot, usually organised by the innkeepers, that made its elections some of the most lurid of the eighteenth century. But it is as well to remember Coventry, along with Westminster, Middlesex and elsewhere, for they demonstrate that eighteenth-century politics could be savage and brutal with mobs roaring and rioting through the streets. Nor, as we shall see, was this violence necessarily confined to election times: political crisis too could unleash violence, and permit the individual to assuage his hatred of a system that more and more excluded him from power.[10]

But the political world of the Augustans did not consist merely in venal or riotous boroughs. Half the members of parliament came from boroughs with moderate or small electorates. Until the total defeat of the Tory party in 1715 and its obliteration from the serious world of politics, these boroughs were often very difficult to manage. Even small electorates, such as that of Buckingham, which only numbered thirteen, could be touchy. They expected entertainment; that was the *sine qua non* of politics throughout the century: a voter looked forward to gigantic binges at the candidates' or patrons' expense, not only at elections but also on other corporate occasions, such as the election of a mayor. They required more solid pledges: plate to adorn their guildhalls, schools and charities for their sons, water supplies to save themselves the expense, but, above all, jobs. The letter-bag of every M.P. with the slightest pretensions to influence was

stuffed with pleas and demands from voters for themselves, their relations or their dependents. Places in the Customs and Excise, in the Army and Navy, in the Church, in the East India, Africa and Levant Companies, in all the departments of state from door-keepers to clerks: jobs at Court for the real gentry or sinecures in Ireland, the diplomatic corps, or anywhere else where duties were light and salaries steady. These were the true coin of politics, the solvent that diminished or obliterated principle. And they worked faster once the Tory party had no hope of power. This was apparent to the meanest intelligence by the 1730s when Boling-broke finally threw in his hand and retired to France.[11]

Naturally with places comparatively scarce there were always more applicants than jobs, and this led the political managers to attempt to get rid of the electorate when they could, or discipline it when they could not. At first this may not have been a conscious process, but it rapidly became one.

In the small corporations the elimination of unwanted voters became a process of steady attrition: freemen, if they had the vote, ceased to be made, or the fee for admission to the freehold was pushed beyond the pocket of the small tradesman. In others, honorary freemen, usually reliable gentry from the surrounding countryside, were made in order to swing the electorate at the appropriate moment. More often than not, in an election disputed on petition, the House of Commons came down heavily on the side of the narrower franchise. To make the question of franchise more certain and therefore more manageable, the House passed in 1729 the Last Determinations Act, by which franchises were frozen to the last decision of the House on the question. Where votes went with property, it was bought up, at excessive cost maybe at the time, but future expensive contests could be eliminated. At Weobley in Herefordshire the electorate was quickly reduced from about 150 to 45 by such means.

Corporations with large electorates and the county constituencies posed different problems. Some voters in both types of constituency were controllable. It was rare, although not unknown, for a tenant to disobey his landlord and vote against his wishes; mostly they did as they were told. Nor could craftsmen be expected to disoblige rich and powerful merchant aldermen

living in their wards. Voting was open, and in these large constituencies it became common after 1700 for votes to be printed after the election in order that they could be analysed.[12] And, of course, there were loyalties — familial, territorial and political. Then, as now, men were born into the politics which they professed. All of this gave cohesion — at least to parties — but they did not diminish the enmity between them, whether these parties were political or factional or a mixture of both, particularly at a time when the gentry were both numerous and sharply divided. But contests in large constituencies became ruinously expensive, particularly after the Septennial Act of 1716.[13] In large counties such as Yorkshire with a numerous gentry, subscriptions could make even an expensive fight feasible, but, in smaller counties, the cost grew too high, so in county after county a treaty was made. Men sank their differences — the aristocracy sometimes taking one seat for a Whig, the gentry the other for a Tory: occasionally the gentry got both: in other counties the representation was divided geographically. After 1734 county contests became exceptionally infrequent. Twelve counties were not contested between 1754 and 1790, fifteen only once, so that it was a rare freeholder who exercised a vote more than once in his lifetime, and thousands never had even that once chance.[14] A marked contrast with the period between 1688 and 1725 when county elections were exceptionally common, and freeholders voted time and time again.

Hence, by the middle decades of the eighteenth century, a diminished electorate functioned only intermittently — with regularity at all elections only in about fifteen constituencies of which three, oddly enough, were in Kent.[15] Elsewhere contests were uncommon, often twenty years or more elapsing without a contest. Hence, the individual who possessed a political franchise very rarely had the opportunity to exercise it. Political power, both local and national, had been absorbed by groups of political managers whose ambitions, of course, varied as much as their own natures, but self-interest loomed larger than political principle. Indeed, principles might have died a total death but for the fact that the parliamentary system never became completely closed or the public without influence.

Politics, fortunately, are more than a matter of elections and the exercise of a franchise. Men were touched in their daily lives; often indeed knocked down by them. Although the volume of eighteenth-century legislation, in a public sense, was small; its private legislation was immense: and the eighteenth-century gentleman set about making a world to his own liking. Commercialisation of agriculture had begun centuries before, but the pace became headlong in the eighteenth century, which witnessed the near-elimination of the peasantry as a class. Enclosure bills rattled through the Commons. They were hated: throughout the country, the peasantry rioted against them. In 1710 the villagers rose at Bedingfield and the Norfolk Militia had to be called out to put them down.[16] Turnpikes were no better loved but they proliferated. The birds of the air, the rabbits of the heath, the fish in the streams were ferociously protected for the sport and sustenance of gentlemen. Property acquired the sanctity of life and theft meant death. Benefit of clergy was abolished and hanging as a punishment for crime increased.[17] Trivial crimes might mean transportation for life, first to America and then, after the Revolution, to Australia. The gentlemen merchants who ran the towns did not neglect themselves. In the 1760s and 1770s enabling acts permitted them to charge rates for many public services — paving, lighting, even police — which they supplied, although without notable efficiency. Politics was power, not only for individuals who manned the pumps and sluices of the parliamentary system, but also for the class which had come to dominate British life — commercially minded landowners with a sharp eye for profit.

In the earlier decades of the century the strains of the agrarian revolution had caused divisions within the landowning class; indeed this is the social basis of the cleavage between Whig and Tory, but the plight of the smaller gentry, still subject to vicissitude, had gradually eased and by the middle of the century a golden era was opening for them. This too helped to give solidity to the political system, which by 1750 had acquired a seemingly adamantine strength. What was increasingly obvious to the world at large was the development of a self-gratifying oligarchy that held power for its own profit.

The political nation, however, was always greater than those involved in the parliamentary system. It was growing throughout the eighteenth century both in size and in economic and social importance, and this aspect of politics was not affected by the setback of the Tory party. The seventeenth century, particularly its three periods of violent political struggle — the Civil War and Protectorate, the Exclusion Crisis and the Revolution of 1688 — had accustomed literate Englishmen to controversy: pamphlets, ballads, books were all used to influence political passion or to convince by argument. And the spread of the coffee house — viewed with alarm by Charles II and his ministers — had created, along with bookshops, not only centres for the dissemination of literature but also meeting grounds for men passionately interested in politics. Political literature spread to the provinces, to the country houses, to the taverns and inns of large country towns: provincial bookshops were more common than historians have allowed (after all, think of Johnson's father) : the citizens of London were not the only clubbable Englishmen: King's Lynn had a flourishing Whig dining club by Queen Anne's reign, if not before. By the time of Swift's first political pamphlet, there was a wide literate public, willing to spend its sixpence on a good piece of invective and to spread the copy around amongst like-minded neighbours.

Nor did this public diminish after 1715; indeed it grew: the public grew as the electorate diminished. The success of the *Craftsman* was due entirely to its existence. True the usual edition of the *Craftsman* was only about 3,000, and not infrequently below that figure; but issues which caught the public's attention soared to 6,000 and may have reached, on one or two occasions, 10,000.[18] And each copy was read by far more people than would read a present-day weekly. We know that the *Craftsman* was in great demand in the provinces.[19] But the *Craftsman* was but one paper, and there were many others from *Fog's Weekly* to the *London Evening Post* that were equally concerned with politics. And the newspaper was not the only means of propaganda. Pantomime, harlequinades, burlesques, Punch and Judy shows were given political twists. The London stage has never been more dominated by politics than it was between 1725 and 1737 when,

slandered beyond endurance, Walpole instituted a censorship of the theatre.[20] Whether he had a chance to vote or not, the literate and semi-literate Englishman had plenty of opportunity to jeer and scoff at his rulers. And at a more serious level he was exceptionally well informed.

Furthermore there was something of a cultural explosion in the middle decades of the eighteenth century, when literacy increased by leaps and bounds. Because of the decay of Oxford and Cambridge and some of the old-established grammar schools, there has been too ready an acceptance of the view that these years witnessed not only stagnation but retrogression in education. But schools were sprouting like mushrooms. Primarily they were started to provide elementary commercial training for boys, a veneer of middle-class polish for girls, and of course a fortune for the schoolmaster. As so frequently in eighteenth-century life, the fee was often more important that the service and schools could vanish overnight.[21] Nevertheless, many were good and stable. Something of the extent of this development may be assessed from the fact that 100 schools, most of them newly established, advertised in the *Northampton Mercury* between 1720 and 1760, and, even more impressive, the *Norwich Mercury* advertised sixty-three schools between 1749 and 1756.[22] And, a point which requires very little labouring, there was now a provincial press to advertise in. By 1760 there were forty provincial newspapers established in all the major towns of England. And, of course, the papers were not confined to the towns they were printed in — an elaborate system of itinerant pedlars, who often travelled forty or fifty miles in a day, disseminated them throughout the land. The *Northampton Mercury* was on sale in Sheffield, Cambridge, Warwick and Oxford — indeed throughout the East and West Midlands. Similarly the *Stamford Mercury* travelled up and down the Great North Road with the stage coaches.[23]

This new and growing literate public was also politically active. One has only to turn over the pages of Cowburne's *Liverpool Chronicle* for 1768 to discover that it is alive with political debate — letters urging freeholders how to vote in the coming general election, political information from Ireland and America, and curiously enough Wilkes's fortunes in the Middlesex election

were avidly followed, the sympathies of the paper being entirely with Wilkes. Fifty or sixty years previously there had been no such politically minded public in Liverpool: indeed there was not a public sufficient to run a newspaper, let alone two. There had been politicians, Whigs and Tories, a corporation well aware of political issues and a few hundred freeholders of varying political independence who were not unaware of the great issues at stake at Westminster, but now politics in Liverpool had moved into a different dimension. There were now thousands, not hundreds, of men and women alive to political issues and keen to debate them, even though they had no vote.[24]

The same was true not only of large and growing towns such as Liverpool, Bristol, Newcastle or Hull, but also of a new class of men and their skilled workers who were beginning to plant industry not in towns, but in the English countryside. Josiah Wedgwood at Etruria followed politics as keenly as his partner Thomas Bentley followed fashion in London.[25] And Jedediah Strutt over at Belper kept his eye on the political scene in London.[26] And, when the supporters in Middlesex of Wilkes are analysed, what do we find? The bulk of them are middling people — traders, craftsmen, petty manufacturers, men of small property.[27] Here was the public for whom Tom Paine was to write. His *Rights of Man* entranced Wedgwood. Here, indeed, is a political nation whom Namier and his followers have almost entirely ignored: as essential a part of the structure of politics at the accession of George III as the Cornish boroughs or the Shropshire gentlemen. Evidence of the political nation's size and vigour everywhere abounds. These are the people who roared for Chatham and hissed George III, who subscribed for comforts for American prisoners of British forces, who read and studied Paine, Priestley, Price and Cartwright. Were there then two worlds of politics in the eighteenth century — a tight political establishment, linked to small groups of powerful political managers in the provinces, who controlled parliament, the executive and all that was effective in the nation, and outside this an amorphous mass of political sentiment that found expression in occasional hysteria and impotent polemic, but whose effective voice in the nation was negligible?

Actually the political nation and the political establishment had never been completely divorced. Their relations certainly were strained and their contacts intermittent, but they existed. For one thing contests in the populous boroughs and counties sometimes took place and when they did more than the actual voters took part: mobs, processions, addresses and the like made those active at the hustings conscious of the popular will on political issues and those free from the strait-jacket of direct influence could be swayed by a sense of what they felt the nation wanted. Undoubtedly the enormous popular sympathy for Wilkes amongst the lower and middling classes affected those freeholders of the eastern and urban districts of Middlesex that were less prone to the influence of a landlord.

And there were Addresses. The right of a county or a corporation to address parliament was age-old. Although in the middle decades of the century the Commons was dominated by a single party, it was factionalised, and in the 1760s the factions were often at loggerheads on political issues of importance — America and Wilkes: later there were even more issues — reform of parliament, slave trade, Ireland, even commerce with France. Issues, *pace* Namier, abounded. And they divided counties and corporations. The Excise Bills even in 1733 had set the country aflame and Addresses rained on parliament.[28] During the War of American Independence the situation was equally intense. Again from the letters of Josiah Wedgwood we see how sharply Staffordshire was divided: some willing to support George III and Lord North in their intransigence, others driven frantic by it, and both sides addressing parliament from totally opposite standpoints in the name of the county as a whole. Such Addresses were usually initiated at so-called meeting of the county — gentlemen, substantial freeholders, office holders and Church dignitaries, that is men who belonged to the official political establishment. But they needed the political nation to back them, so Addresses required signatures and we know that copies were left in local taverns where men were solicited to sign. Such solicitations could only lead to argument and discussion and to a widening of political horizons. At Westminster, Addresses, except loyal ones, had very little effect, but they helped, perhaps, to moderate political pas-

sion. In the provinces they brought like-minded men into greater cohesion, and made them realise something of their own importance.

So by the 1760s there existed, in effect, two political nations in England, one growing, the other shrinking, with little contact between them. Had there been more, the grosser follies of handling both Wilkes and America could scarcely have taken place. The formal electorate was dwindling and called to execute its judgment less and less. Those who by education and interest might reasonably expect a political voice but were denied it, were steadily increasing. There were other factors, too, at work to help widen this cleavage: the dissenters. For decades their leaders had hoped against hope that their civic disabilities would be removed. Many, but by no means all, now felt that only a radical reform of political institutions could bring this about. Much of the aggressive criticism of parliament in the second half of the century came from dissent.[29]

Again in 1763, over twenty years of war came to an end. That war had been commercially aggressive: 'Commerce', in the words of Burke, 'had been made to flourish through war': both patriotism and profit had helped to still the voice of criticism. The dislocations of peace, however, combined with what seemed to many merchants a wanton return to France of commercial privileges seized during the war, helped to breed discontent. That is why they received George III at the Guildhall in stony silence. Demobilisation and unemployment added yeast to the dough. And, for once the professional politicians were in need of public issues. George III was young and there were no prospects of succession. Hence there were no 'futures' for them to dabble in. Some, like the duke of Newcastle, had played the 'in game' for so long that rousing the public had no charms for them, but Chatham possessed no inhibitions, and even Burke saw the necessity of exploiting the American grievances on behalf of the Rockinghams. Public protest, so long as it was skilfully handled, acquired a certain attraction for the Venetian oligarchy: they could now find a personal use for public discontent. It was the fusion of these circumstances which helped to create some of the great political debates of the 1760s and 1770s and provided

Chatham, Wilkes and Junius with their opportunities. The political establishment might ignore Wilkes and only give America a modicum of its attention, but it could not remain absolutely impervious to the criticisms and claims of the wider political nation. After all, John Wilkes did win his battle with parliament. Nor could the oligarchy remain deaf to threats to itself.

The demand for parliamentary reform in the 1770s and 1780s developed primarily in the towns. Even in the 1760s the Liverpool Debating Society was arguing whether politics could ever be purified without the introduction of the ballot box. It was the exclusion from the political power which they felt was rightly theirs because of their social and economic activity that led men such as Josiah Wedgwood to support annual parliaments, universal suffrage and the control of a member's actions by his constituents. The growing criticism of parliament as an institution swelled to a gale in the late seventies as disaster after disaster dogged North's American policies. It was not only the unrepresentative nature of Parliament which came in for the fury of attack, but also the graft which the political establishment lavished on itself. This new radicalism covered numerous shades of opinion from republican to Tory. Historians, I feel, never give sufficient emphasis to the prevalence of bitter anti-monarchical, pro-republican sentiment of the 1760s and 1770s. Sylas Neville's diary and papers demonstrate clearly enough that in the provinces, as well as in London, there were many men and women who were enthusiastic supporters of republican ideas, with strong sympathies towards America, men and women who possessed as much hatred of George III as the most dedicated Boston radicals. After all, Neville never had the slightest difficulty in collecting a few cronies on 30 January to toast the execution of Charles I.[30] And Tom Paine's books, it must be remembered, sold in far greater quantities than those of any other political commentator. Indeed Paine and his readership cry aloud for further investigation.

This powerful radicalism was strongest in London, the big seaport towns and the growing manufacturing districts of Lancashire, the West Midlands and the West Riding of Yorkshire, but it combined with, and indeed was itself infused with, the

ideas of the Tory radicalism of the earlier decades of the century which had called, not for fundamental reform, but for the purification of political institutions. The country-squire's old panacea of annual parliaments and the exclusion of placemen from parliament acquired in the hands of the Reverend Christopher Wyvill and the Yorkshire Association fresh vigour. Even their suggestion that the number of Knights of the Shire should be increased in order to strengthen the independent element in parliament was no novelty. It had been adumbrated in the first year of the century.[31]

There is no need here to trace the course of the first strong movement for parliamentary reform or even to discuss whether or not this brought England to the very edge of revolution. For my purpose it is enough to indicate the width of political interest and to underline the conflict which existed between the political establishment and the political nation: a conflict which did not begin with Junius or end with the failure of the Association movements. It origins lie in the seventeenth-century emergence of the electorate and the division was not healed until the late nineteenth century, for the growth of the political nation was always far faster than the spread of representative government. What are of interest, in the context of this paper, in the last two decades of the eighteenth century are two developments. One is the even more rapid growth of the political nation which began to acquire new leadership and a more sophisticated organisation, and the effect of patriotism in helping the establishment defeat its aspirations. Nor were these two factors dissociated. Fears for property proved a strong stimulant to loyalty.

Interest in politics penetrated deeper into society during the last two decades of the eighteenth century, although in London, at least, political interest amongst the working classes may have been more extensive than historians have allowed. A Swiss traveller, César de Saussure, was highly amused in 1726 to see shoeblacks reading newspapers for the foreign news.[32] And craftsmen were well aware that parliament's legislation affected their interests — usually adversely.[33] By 1750 what was essentially a lower-middle-class debating society — the Robin Hood (well-named) — had achieved notoriety. There were a number of deist and politi-

cal clubs operating in a twilight world of mechanics and intellectuals. The part played by the humbler freemasons in starting and
maintaining such clubs, which were partly educational as well as
political, needs investigating, but the connection may be close.
After all, Thomas Hardy was an active member of the pseudo-
masonic organisation called the Gregorians.[34] Lower-middle-class
radicalism grew during the 1780s and 1790s and received further
impetus from the early phases of the French Revolution. Tom
Paine's *Rights of Man* is reputed to have sold 400,000 copies,
a prodigious figure, even allowing for a considerable margin
of error.[35] And contemporaries were quick to notice who was
reading it. 'Our peasantry now read the *Rights of Man* on
mountains and moors and by the wayside' wrote T. J. Mathias in
1797.[36] Radicalism was getting out of hand. The expensive books
and pamphlets of Priestley and Price, the dilettante leadership of
Horne Tooke, Major Cartwright, Earl Stanhope and the like
could be tolerated, but Thomas Hardy's organisation was beginning to take on the unwelcome air of a revolutionary movement
of *sans-culottes*. And the example of France was not beguiling.
The solid bourgeois wing of the political nation read its Burke
and drew far closer to the political establishment in sentiment.
It did not want revolution; nevertheless it still desired power. So
it entered into a more direct competition with the oligarchy over
seats in parliament. After 1790 contested elections begin to increase rapidly again, and the cost of elections soared to new
heights. There was a definite push by the richer commercial and
manufacturing interests to buy their way into political power.
Few such men as Beckford, Townsend or Sawbridge, city million-
aires who supported Wilkes, were to be found consorting with the
aggressive radical movement that took Paine for its hero. The
French Revolution did not only close the ranks of the professional
politicians. It did more than this. It drove deep fissures into the
political nation itself. Whereas in the 1770s reform had not
seemed to threaten property or status, it now reeked of revolution. As politics became national, they sharpened class division.
And the terrible spectacle of a literate, politically minded, working class began to stalk the land. But it is not only the French
Revolution that added a fresh dimension to the complexities of

politics, divided as they were into this twofold world of political establishment and political nation. Patriotism became an issue as well as property.[37]

Of course patriotism is a highly complex matter, involving self-interest, aggressive economic appetites, xenophobia and a host of disreputable and semi-disreputable motives; it is a singularly powerful emotion. However, I am concerned not with causes, but with effects. We can see patriotism influencing radicalism in the later stages of the American War of Independence. Support for America had been very widespread in both London and the provinces, but, as soon as the American war became a general war, involving France and Spain, that support began to wither. Bristol, from being pro-American, became pro Lord North.[38] Even that ardent supporter of all things American, Josiah Wedgwood, began to have his doubts. If victory for America meant defeat of Britain by France and Spain, he was not at all sure that he could face such an outcome and he felt that he might have to support North. Although his radicalism remained firm, he was confused and baffled by the issues which *patriotism in the time of war* raised.[39] And, of course, the long wars against Revolutionary France and Napoleon in which armies were lost, invasion threatened and hundreds of ships sunk, posed a graver threat. It enabled Pitt and his supporters to denigrate radicalism as Jacobin, alien, antipatriotic. In other countries — America, Russia, China — radical attitudes to society have joined with patriotism and been immensely strengthened by it. In England radicalism was seriously weakened first by the American War of Independence and afterwards by the wars against France.

By the end of the eighteenth century, the political nation had grown until it had begun to embrace some of the lowest classes of society. The true working class, however, that is the unskilled labourers in town and countryside, were, in spite of Tom Paine, still largely outside politics. They were stirring: increasingly they were beginning to realise that their condition in life depended on the political institutions by which they were governed and the men who ran them. The threat of a possible fusion between the lower middle classes and the working population, inspired by revolutionary ideas of political and social justice, spurred the

richer leaders of the political nation and the political establishment to find a *modus vivendi.*

The division between the two, which had steadily grown during
the eighteenth century, was, however, still deep in 1800. Provincial bankers and merchants, men such as Pares and Biggs
of Leicester, felt that they lacked power both locally and nation-
ally commensurate with their social and economic status. So long
as such men did so, there was always a danger of a revolutionary
situation. But they were as terrified as Hannah More of a politically conscious proletariat, and between 1800 and 1832 they
fought their way into power through the old methods of the
establishment—money and the unreformed system of parliamentary representation.[40] By the 1820s, some of the old-established
conservative forces were losing the battle and running short of
cash: for example, Leicester corporation, a bulwark of traditional
oligarchy, had to mortgage its estates in 1826 to fight off the
radical threat to its parliamentary representation. By 1831 it
could not afford the money necessary to outbid the Leicester
manufacturers who clubbed together to get their reform candidates in.[41] This was a far safer method of prising open the gates
of political power than manning the barricades. The Reform Bill
of 1832 marks the realignment of political forces: the powerful
and rich leaders of the political nation, men who had used public
issues and public agitation, forced the old political oligarchy to
accommodate them — at a price. The old landowning and farming interests were strengthened by the large increase in the county
membership. Politics remained, as it had been since the middle of
the eighteenth century, an affair of two nations. But, as in the
eighteenth century, they were not divorced: those who controlled
the political machinery were susceptible to opinion. Europe was
to give them lesson after lesson of the folly of ignoring the political hopes and aspirations of the mass of the people: and Britain's
increasing riches permitted the extension of franchise without
undue fear for the traditional institutions. So a process begun in
the seventeenth century, and only temporarily checked in the
eighteenth, was brought to fruition in the nineteenth. The process
was the spread of politics to embrace the entire population. It was
done with such skill that the conservative forces continued to

dominate English life in spite of universal suffrage. Not until 1945 did Britain have a really radical government.

The eighteenth century opened with a large parliamentary electorate accustomed to exercising its powers; it was divided and organised into parties that were separated by sharp political issues. The total collapse of the Tories after 1715 permitted the development of oligarchy which both diminished and disciplined this electorate, although never to the point of extinction. This process was counterbalanced by a steady growth in the political consciousness of the nation at large, and by the development of strong economic and social interests that demanded political power. And the conflicts and struggles that ensued gave a life and vitality to eighteenth-century politics which steadily engulfed larger sections of the population. Political life in the eighteenth century was therefore always richer, freer, more open than the oligarchical nature of its institutions might lead one to believe. And this gave Englishmen in this century a political experience that was unique. The richness and variety of that experience has received recently all too little attention. As far as the eighteenth century is concerned, political decisions and the turmoil they aroused are the heart of politics, not elections. It is time we returned to their study.

NOTES

[1] For a fuller discussion of the growth of the electorate in the seventeenth century and its consequences for the politics of the period 1689–1715 see J. H. Plumb, *The Growth of Political Stability in England, 1675–1725* (London, 1967), pp. 34–47.

[2] *Ibid.* 66–97.

[3] John Smith (1655–1723) of South Tedworth, Hants. A leading Whig, a friend of the Junto who was a Lord of the Treasury from 1694 to 1702; Chancellor of the Exchequer 1699–1701, 1708–10; Commissioner of the Union with Scotland 1706; Speaker 1705–8. A close friend of Sir Robert Walpole, he sat in parliament 1679–81, 1691–1723. (*Dictionary of National Biography*.) William Bromley (1664–1732) of Bagington, Warwickshire, a leading Tory who was Commissioner of Public Accounts 1696–1705; Speaker 1710–13; Secretary of State 1713–14. M.P. 1689–98, 1701–32. (*Dictionary of National Biography*.)

[4] W. A. Speck, 'The Choice of a Speaker in 1705', *Bulletin of the Institute of Historical Research,* xxxvii (1964), 20–35.

⁵ Camb. Univ. Lib. C(holmondetey) H(oughton) MSS, Charles Turner to Robert Walpole, 31 October 1705.

⁶ The votes of the House of Commons were printed; totals of divisions were given, not names of voters.

⁷ A seat at Amersham (Bucks.) was under dispute. This is described as a pocket borough of the Drakes (Tories) by Walcott (Robert Walcott, *English Politics in the Early Eighteenth Century* (Oxford, 1956), pp. 13, 40). However, in 1705 party division reared its head. Sir Samuel Garrard, one of the Tory members, afterwards the Lord Mayor of London who invited Sacheverell to preach in 1710, had supported the Tack, and Sir Thomas Webster, an ardent and rich Whig, decided to oppose him. Two polls were taken because Webster insisted that all inhabitants not receiving alms had the right to vote: the Tories maintained only those paying church rates had the right. The two polls were:

	Inhabitants	Ratepayers
Viscount Newhaven (T)	90	58
Sir Samuel Garrard (T)	84	54
Sir Thomas Webster (W)	91	41

The interesting fact here is the very considerable support given to Sir Thomas Webster in a town dominated by the great estate and house of Shardeloes which belonged to the Drakes. Doubtless Webster's money helped to strengthen some Whig sentiments, but he also possessed a solid voting base. This is an excellent illustration of the strength of party in a closed borough (see *Hist. MSS Comm.* xv, app. 4, 180), but there are many others.

⁸ These figures refer to the division on the choice of Speaker: Smith won by 248 to 205. Seymour had led the opposition to Smith.

⁹ C(holmondeley) H(oughton) MSS, John Turner to Robert Walpole, 7 December 1705.

¹⁰ For these and further examples, see J. H. Plumb, *The Growth of Political Stability in England, 1675–1725* (London, 1967), pp. 66–97; L. B. Namier, *The Structure of Politics at the Accession of George III* (2nd ed., London, 1961), pp. 102–4; G. Rudé, *The Crowd in History* (New York, 1964), pp. 47–64.

¹¹ Plumb, *op. cit.* pp. 78 f. For Buckingham, F. P. and M. M. Verney, *Memoirs of the Verney Family during the Seventeenth Century* (London, 1907), ii, 380–8.

¹² For the way votes were carefully scrutinised, see J. H. Plumb, *Sir Robert Walpole* (London, 1960), ii, 322.

¹³ In 1784 Chester cost the Grosvenors £8,500 for food and drink for 3,000 electors: Gervas Huxley, *Lady Elizabeth and the Grosvenors* (London, 1965), pp. 85–6. Essex in 1763 is said to have cost both sides over £30,000: L. B. Namier and J. Brooke, *History of Parliament 1754–90* (London, 1964), 1, 4.

¹⁴ L. B. Namier and J. Brooke, *op. cit.* 1, 9. At six general elections during this period there were only 37 county contests out of a possible 240.

¹⁵ *Ibid.* 1 *passim.*

¹⁶ C(holmondeley) H(oughton) MSS, John Wrott to Robert Walpole, 31 May 1710; G. Rudé, *The Crowd in History*, p. 35. He cites riots in South Yorkshire and Nottinghamshire in 1791 and 1798 respectively.

17 Leon Radzinowitz, *A History of English Criminal Law* (London, 1948), I, 4–5. 'Broadly speaking, in the course of the hundred and sixty years from the Restoration to the death of George III, the number of capital offences had increased by about one hundred and ninety.'

18 L. W. Hanson, *The Government and the Press* (Oxford, 1936), p. 85. Also, C(*holmondeley*) H(*oughton*) *MSS*, 74, folios 12, 13, 64.

19 J. H. Plumb, *Sir Robert Walpole*, II, 142.

20 John Loftis, *The Politics of Drama in Augustan England* (Oxford, 1963), pp. 63–127.

21 Nicolas Hans, *New Trends in Education in the Eighteenth Century* (London, 1951).

22 G. A. Cranfield, *The Development of the Provincial Newspaper, 1700–1760* (Oxford, 1962), pp. 215–16.

23 *Ibid.* pp.168–206.

24 The only copy of this newspaper is in my possession. Many issues contain detailed reports from America, for example 4 August 1768, which prints three and a half columns on riots in Boston; pro-American arguments were printed and so too were the arguments of 'Scrutator', who followed 'the Pennsylvanian Farmer's insidious epistles' and wrote to refute them (4 August 1768). The paper was much more strongly biased towards Wilkes than towards the American colonies, although again the paper was careful to print an occasional satirical thrust at Wilkes himself (e.g. 18 August 1768—the Strutter to J. Wilkes, Esq.). There were at least two debating societies in Liverpool at this time, the Conversation Club and the Debating Society, which concerned themselves with politics, the latter being the more radical. A similar awareness of political issues and widespread public interest in politics existed throughout the West Midlands, particularly Birmingham.

25 Ann Finer and George Savage, *The Selected Letters of Josiah Wedgwood* (London, 1965).

26 R. S. Fitton and A. P. Wadsworth, *The Strutts and the Arkwrights* (Manchester, 1958).

27 G. Rudé, *Wilkes and Liberty* (Oxford, 1962), pp. 220–3. Also 'The Middlesex Electors', *EHR* (1960), pp. 601–17.

28 J. H. Plumb, *Sir Robert Walpole*, II, 251–67; E. R. Turner, 'The Excise Crisis', *EHR* (1927), pp. 34–57.

29 Anthony Lincoln, *English Dissent, 1763–1800* (Cambridge, 1938); Eugene Charlton Black, *The Association* (Cambridge, Mass., 1963), pp. 174–212.

30 *The Diary of Sylas Neville 1767–1788*, ed. Basil Cozens-Hardy (Oxford, 1950), pp. 90–1, 149. See also Caroline Robbins's pioneer work, *The Eighteenth Century Commonwealthman* (Cambridge, Mass., 1959).

31 Black, *op. cit.* pp. 31–130; H. Butterfield, *George III, Lord North and the People 1779–80* (London, 1949), pp. 229–68.

32 César de Saussure, *A Foreign View of England in the Reigns of George I and George II* (London, 1902), p. 162.

33 G. Rudé, *The Crowd in History 1730–48*, particularly chapter IV, 'Labour

Disputes in Eighteenth-Century England'.

³⁴ Nicolas Hans, *New Trends in Education in the Eighteenth Century* (London, 1951), p. 177.

³⁵ P. S. Foner, *The Complete Writings of Thomas Paine,* ed. P. S. Foner (New York, 1945), II, 910. 'At least one hundred thousand copies of the cheap edition were sold in England, Ireland, and Scotland' (*ibid.* I, xxx).

³⁶ Quoted by James T. Boulton, *The Language of Politics in the Age of Wilkes and Burke* (London, 1963), p. 138. Also M. G. Jones, *Hannah More* (Cambridge, 1952), p. 133, where it is reported that pt II was found 'lurking at the bottom of mines and coalpits'. And A. Temple Patterson, *Radical Leicester* (Leicester, 1959), p. 72.

³⁷ Of course some rich men stayed loyal to their reformist principles, more it would seem in the provinces than the metropolis. Josiah Wedgwood welcomed the French Revolution, as did Thomas Walker of Manchester to his cost. See Frida Knight, *The Strange Case of T. Walker* (London, 1957).

³⁸ *The American Correspondence of a Bristol Merchant 1766–1776,* ed. G. H. Guttridge (Berkeley, Calif., 1934), p. 6; Namier and Brooke, *History of Parliament 1754–1790,* I, 206–7; W. E. Minchinton, *Politics and the Port of Bristol in the Eighteenth Century* (Bristol, 1963), p. xxxi.

³⁹ *Wedgwood MSS* (Barlaston). Josiah Wedgwood to Thomas Bentley 7 August 1779. Wedgwood remained unconvinced by those radicals who opposed raising a regiment of militia in Staffordshire in order to free troops for America. 'I am not at present fully convinced by them, that it is better to fall a prey to a foreign enemy rather than defend ourselves under the present ministry. Methinks I would defend the land of my nativity, my family and friends against a foreign foe, where conquest and slavery were inseparable, under any leaders —the best I could get for the moment, and wait for better times to displace an obnoxious minister, and settle domestic affairs, rather than rigidly say, I'll be saved in my own way and by people of my own choice, or perish and perish my country with me.' I owe this quotation to Mr. Neil McKendrick.

⁴⁰ For Hannah More, see M. G. Jones, *Hannah More* (Cambridge, 1952). For the growth of working-class literacy, R. K. Webb, *The British Working Class Reader 1790–1848* (London, 1955); Donald Read, *Press and People 1790–1850* (London, 1961).

⁴¹ Temple Patterson, *op. cit.* pp. 146–55, 186–8.

Literature and Religion in Eighteenth-Century England

⟆

A. R. HUMPHREYS

I. An Active Interest

We know, and what is better we feel inwardly that religion is the basis
of civil society, and the source of all good and of all comfort.

BURKE

Reflections on the Revolution in France, in *Works*, iv. 98

For several decades the reputation of Augustan religion has
been rising. Where the Victorians saw on the whole only apathy
and even cynicism, their successors have found that the sober
good will, rising at times to a luminous devotion, which characterises much Hanoverian worship still makes an appeal. At
first sight, indeed, there is little colour or spectacle in the Hanoverian panorama, except where it displays the Methodist or
Evangelical revivals (themselves protests against apathy), or
certain great but exceptional volumes like Law's *Serious Call to
a Devout and Holy Life* (1728), Butler's *Analogy* (1736), and the
works of Berkeley. Even these, standing out against an apparently
widespread unbelief, seem to witness rather to the strength of the
tide against which they strain than to any general faith. It is true
that certain merits have long been recognised; since Leslie
Stephen's *English Thought in the Eighteenth Century* (1876)

From *A. R. Humphreys*, The Augustan World *(London: Methuen and Co. Ltd.,
1954), pp. 138–178.*

and Abbey and Overton's *English Church in the Eighteenth Century* (1878), the Church has been vindicated from intellectual sloth and indeed found rich in controversial distinction, and the publication of ecclesiastical records and biographies is weakening the charge of spiritual sloth. Yet even the better Churchmen and Dissenters, with a few exceptions, seem to lack spiritual poetry, and prompt us to accept the Victorian judgment. How far was the judgment true?

This chapter aims not at epitomising Augustan religious history but at discovering how religion influenced writers and their public. Whatever apathy there may have been, men of letters were greatly concerned about religion and many of them, including some not usually credited with spiritual interest like Waller and Roscommon in the Restoration years and Pomfret and Prior among the Augustans, tried their hands at religious themes. Prior indeed is characteristic; brilliant in social verse, he yet looked on *Solomon* (1718) as his most important poem. The public too was interested: 'there is not any where, I believe, so much Talk about Religion as among us in England' *The Guardian* (No. 65) asserted in 1713. Three decades later Young's *Night Thoughts* echoed the comment—'Few ages have been deeper in dispute about Religion that this' (book vi, preface). As Swift put it in *Thoughts on Various Subjects,* 'we have just enough Religion to make us hate, but not enough to make us love one another', and Defoe's *True-Born Englishman* mocked at disputants fertile in dogma and barren in charity:

> *In their Religion they are so unev'n,*
> *That each Man goes his own By-way to Heaven.*
> *Tenacious of Mistakes to that degree*
> *That ev'ry Man pursues it sep'rately,*
> *And fancies none can find the Way but he.*

Hanoverian religion was anything but unbroken torpor: a Churchman, in the eyes of a Methodist or 'freethinker', was a Laodicean; a Methodist, in the eyes of a Churchman or freethinker, was a fanatic; and a freethinker, in the eyes of a Churchman or Methodist, was a coxcomb.

The appetite for polemics and morality was remarkable. Addison's Saturday lay sermons in *The Spectator* were widely read (though Berkeley's 'grave discourses' in *The Guardian* were not so popular), Butler's austere *Analogy* went into three editions in its year of publication (1736), and Young's *Night Thoughts,* almost ten thousand lines of inexpressible tedium, had ten editions in five years. Sermons flowed from the printers: controversies filled the land with gesticulating contestants. Leslie Stephen once observed that nobody could recall the causes of the eighteenth century's wars save examinees whose knowledge had not yet had time to leak out, and the same is true of its religious quarrels. Yet in their own day, as Johnson said of the Bangorian affair, they 'filled the press with pamphlets, and the coffee-houses with disputants' *(Life of Savage)*. A fertile press and reverberating coffee-houses are unmistakable signs of popular interest.

The Bangorian controversy exploded from a sermon by Hoadly, Bishop of Bangor, in 1717, alleging that no earthly institution (such as an organised church) properly represents the spiritual kingdom of Christ. From a bishop this was a startling doctrine and the consequences were violent; it has been reckoned that fifty-three writers fired off two hundred pamphlets on the subject, and forty years later Goldsmith in *The Bee* (17 November, 1759) complained that clergymen were still bemusing their long-suffering congregations with it. Another storm arose over the Arian doctrines of William Whiston, Newton's successor in the Lucasian professorship at Cambridge, who was deprived of his Chair in 1710 for disbelief in the Trinity. Incidentally he also held that clergymen should marry once only, and it was the Vicar of Wakefield's devotion to this doctrine that jeopardised his son's marriage, since the bride's father was about to take a fourth wife. On Arianism and Deism something will be said later.

When tempers were fired with political as well as religious fuel the blaze was particularly fierce. This was evident in the famous trials of Sacheverell and Atterbury. The former so immoderately denounced the toleration of Dissenters that he was impeached by Parliament in 1709 and to the accompaniment of anti-Dissenter riots found guilty in 1710. If the pillory, said Defoe in *A Hymn to the Pillory,* held all who deserved it,

> *There would the Fam'd* S[achevere]ll *stand*
> *With Trumpet of Sedition in his Hand,*
> *Sounding the first* Crusado *in the Land.*
> *He from a Church of* England *Pulpit first*
> *All his Dissenting Brethren curst:*
> *Doom'd them to Satan for a Prey,*
> *And first found out* the shortest way

(an allusion to Defoe's own parody of High-Church fury, *The Shortest Way with the Dissenters,* which had landed him in the pillory). Yet Sacheverell's sentence was so light as to seem a moral victory and to be wildly celebrated by his Tory friends and the hotheaded citizenry.

The trial of Atterbury, Bishop of Rochester, was not dissimilar, though the Whigs now won outright. Found guilty of Jacobite intrigues he was exiled in 1723 and died abroad in 1732. As at Sacheverell's trial tumults broke out in his favour, and both affairs illustrate the dangers of religious inflammation, which blazed at intervals until the Gordon riots of 1780 provided a tragic climax.

Polemics can flourish while spirituality decays. Yet spirituality if often absent from these disputes was not always so. Law's first work arose out of the Bangorian turmoil and Butler's out of his criticism of Deism, the *Analogy* being its culmination. And in non-controversial matters there was steady respect for religion sometimes deepening into real devotion. Burke throws an unexpected light on this in commenting on a custom — the Grand Tour — not often associated with faith. Youths on their travels, he says, have clergymen-tutors

not as austere masters, nor as mere followers, but as friends and companions of a graver character, and not seldom persons as well born as themselves. With them, as relations, they most commonly keep up a close connection through life. By this connection we conceive that we attach our gentlemen to the church; and we liberalize the church by an intercourse with the leading characters of the country.

Reflections, in *Works,* iv. 109

On a deeper level Burke often asserts with earnest passion the integral nature of religious reverence to the whole organism of

Church and State. The Augustans were often enough worldly, but they often also encouraged devotion, sometimes prosaic but reliable as with Parsons Cole and Woodforde, sometimes complacent yet genuine, as with Addison, sometimes troubled as with Butler, Johnson and Cowper, and sometimes passionate and joyful as with Berkeley and Law.

II. Modes of Faith

In the Shops and Warehouses the prentices stand some on one side of the Shop and some on the other (having Trade little enough) and there they throw *High Church* and *Low Church* at one another's Heads like battledore and shuttlecock.

DEFOE

Reasons Against the Succession of the House of Hanover (1713), 5

For modes of faith, Pope thought, only graceless zealots could fight. Two centuries of anger had taught the folly of dissension. Yet dissension itself reflected the importance attaching to faith, and Burke's pronouncement that religion was the basis of civil society would have been echoed by each of the three main parties — Churchmen, Papists and Dissenters. The lines of eighteenth-century division must now be drawn, with the proviso that they grew gradually less harsh.

Over the Roman Catholics it is unnecessary to linger. Excluded by the Test Act of 1673 from civil and military office they were suspect of Jacobitism and drew as little attention to themselves as possible. 'I had my beginnings among men of a proscribed religion', Pope told Joseph Spence, and he spoke of his private boyhood and youth. Popular distrust was always simmering; the Monument (which, Pope wrote in the third *Moral Essay*, 'like a tall bully lifts its head and lies') bore an inscription that Papists had caused the Great Fire; the '15 and '45 rebellions threatened a Stuart restoration; and even Horace Walpole smelt Papal machinations in a most improbable quarter — 'the Methodists', he surmised, 'are secret Papists and no doubt they copy, build on, and extend their rites towards [Rome]' (*Memoirs of the reign of George III*, 1894, iii. 35). A Relief Bill in their

favour caused an upheaval in Scotland (1778) and the still more violent Gordon Riots in England (1780), when London had a week's reign of terror and the mob besieged Parliament, menaced the Bill's promoters, and burnt Papist chapels and the formidable Newgate Prison. Yet the frenzy died away; another Relief Bill became law in 1791 and granted a fair measure of toleration. All in all, the Roman Church loomed in English eyes (with some reason) as a bogy, but its adherents were a small and peaceable minority.

The relations of Church and Dissent were more intricate. The two were not always in sharp antithesis, any more than were the two ill-defined political parties, and as with the political parties the split of allegiances was accepted with some dismay. Before the Restoration the main division — between Episcopalians and Presbyterians — had been within the Church, between the advocates of prelacy, ritual and temporate reform, and those of presbyterianism (organisation by presbyteries of clergy and people), austerity and thorough change. The Act of Uniformity (1662), however, caused a break by enforcing episcopal ordination, and drove from the Church those who 'dissented'. Even so, the more Latitudinarian Churchmen, towards the end of the seventeenth century, hoped for renewed comprehension within a tolerant Church, and this hope is interestingly presented in Dr. Carpenter's *Thomas Tenison* (1948). Because it failed, many able men were lost to the Church, universities and crown offices, though with corresponding benefit to chapels, trade and industry.

Within the Church there was much variety. On one wing came the Non-Jurors like Archbishop Sancroft, Bishop Ken, Thomas Hearne and Jeremy Collier, loyal to the divine right of James II, unprepared to swear allegiance to William and Mary, and the centre of vigorous pamphlet polemics. Colley Cibber's comedy *The Non-Juror* (1718) is a stoutly Whiggish view of 'the stiff Non-Juring Separation Saint' Sir John Woodvil, seduced by a 'vile Non-juring Zealot, Dr. Wolf, and reclaimed by a sensible son. This, it need hardly be said, is a caricature of a devoted body of men faithful to a lost cause. Apart from this small minority (gradually lost to view as time passed) there were the High- and

Low-Church parties which prompted Swift's High- and Low-Heel satire in 'Lilliput'. The former upheld Caroline traditions of Church power and prerogative, the latter the Latitudinarian rationalism which played down dogma and privilege and preached mainly a reasonable faith and the social virtues. The 'men of Latitude' found their programme in Locke's *Letters Concerning Toleration* (1689—1706) and *The Reasonableness of Christianity* (1695), and their leader in Archbishop Tillotson. Their faith seems now to have an ethical rather than a religious flavour, yet it was then a matter of high humanity and of Christian charity, certainly not the less admirable for seeing Christian faith in the light of divine mercy and human brotherhood. From the time of the Cambridge Platonists through the eighteenth century and into the nineteenth it diffused a spirit, at best of extensive charity, at worst of prosaic reason, which was the best possible antidote to sectarian strife.

Of Dissent it is harder to generalise. Strictly speaking, one needs to distinguish, as Tenison's *Argument for Union* (1683) says, between

Presbyterians, Arians, Socinians, Anabaptists, Fifth-Monarchy Men, Sensual Millenaries, Behmenists, Familists, Seekers, Antinomians, Ranters, Sabbatarians, Quakers, Muggletonians [and] Sweet Singers.

Ignoring these niceties of fission, the main divisions were between Presbyterians, Independents and Baptists. All went back to Elizabethan times or the early Stuarts. The Presbyterians had cherished from the later sixteenth century the idea (triumphant in Scotland) of a national Church organised not under bishops but under the more democratic system of presbyteries, and had for a while in Commonwealth days accomplished their dream. The Independents, descended from Elizabethan Separatists, had also known their hour of glory as Cromwell's strongest supporters, but unlike the Presbyterians they looked not for a national Church but for independent congregations gathered by the magnetism of direct religious experience. The Baptists, originating in the early seventeenth century, prizing adult bap-

tism as the hallmark of the true Christian, were fired with a zeal which later brought many of them into sympathy with Methodism. Theirs is the credit of having introduced the eighteenth century's great innovation in worship — the supplementing of metrical psalms by congregational hymns, and the establishment thereby of a profoundly important body of popular poetry.

Such was the main, original, constitution of Dissent. Fewer but increasingly influential were the Quakers and Unitarians. The latter, followers of Arius or Socinus in denying Christ's equality with the Father ('silver-tongued anti-Christs', John Wesley called them), gained ground gradually as 'the reasonableness of Christianity' encroached on dogmatic faith; Milton, Newton and Locke were touched with Arianism, and Samuel Clarke and William Whiston imbibed it deeply. The most notable of eighteenth-century Unitarians were Richard Price the minister of Old Jewry whose radicalism provoked Burke into his *Reflections on the French Revolution*, Joseph Priestley the chemist-philosopher, and Josiah Wedgwood. Like the Quakers they were a small sect but comprised an intelligent and public-spirited body of Dissent, and their ethical Christianity bore fruit out of proportion to their numbers, in England and New England alike.

Methodism has hardly yet been mentioned, for though it is now perhaps the most characteristic example of Nonconformity it was not, originally, Dissent. It arose long after the dissenting sects of 1662, it was frowned on as hysterical by many Hanoverian Dissenters (now sober citizens), and its founders did not mean to secede from the Church, which they wished only to revitalise. Yet in effect Methodism became a form of Dissent, casting its spell on thousands whom the Church did not touch, and the greatest religious movement of the time fell largely outside the Establishment.

There are few greater Englishmen than John Wesley, and to compress his achievement into a paragraph is like trying to see the world in a grain of sand and eternity in an hour. From his father's High-Church devotion and from William Law's religious passion he and his brother Charles drew a spirit which instilled into England and the American colonies a profound emotion,

breaking up ignorance and apathy and bringing their followers the most personal sense of religious experience. Churchmen and Dissenters had every excuse for suspicion; convulsions and apocalyptic frenzies seized the early congregations as if with a consuming fire. Yet there was hardly any other channel for the sense Methodism brought — that of the soul's condition — and fortunately this happened on the whole not (as it might have done) under the severity of Calvinism but under the charity of Arminianism, which preached salvation to all men. The Wesleys' hymns will be considered later; their spirit recalls Blake (influenced by them) when, to the question whether he did not see the sun like a disk of fire, he answered 'O no, no, I see an innumerable company of the heavenly host crying: "Holy, Holy, Holy is the Lord God Almighty!" ' George Whitefield, it is true, was a Calvinist, and it was the Calvinistic side of Evangelicalism which so afflicted Cowper, but the Wesleys announced the comforting faith of salvation for all, and their influence is perhaps the most remarkable social phenomenon of the later eighteenth century. Yet the movement was not entirely their doing; there was evangelicalism apart from and indeed prior to Methodism, as in Cornwall under Samuel Walker of Truro; men like John Berridge of Everton, John Newton (Cowper's friend), William Wilberforce and Charles Simeon at Holy Trinity, Cambridge, were moved by an independent though similar spirit. By the end of the century, Evangelicalism both within and without the Church united Churchmen and Nonconformists in that powerful religious emotion which meant so much to the future.

Though sympathy between the different denominations grew by degrees it was not very conspicuous in the early years of the century. The controversial violence of Queen Anne's reign is reflected in Swift's *Journal to Stella* and *Examiner* papers, in Defoe, and in his adversary Ned Ward's *Hudibras Redivivus.* The more vehement sectarians entertained feelings such as Blake was to epitomise in *The Everlasting Gospel:*

> *Both read the Bible day and night,*
> *But thou read'st black where I read white.*

Swift and Defoe represent this state of affairs, though not in an extreme form. Swift held by a consolidating Toryism of Church and State; most Englishmen, he thought, were for uncompromising churchmanship and the belief that

the Church of England should be preserved entire in all Her Rights, Powers and Priviledges; all Doctrines relating to Government discouraged which She condemns; all Schisms, Sects and Heresies discountenanced and kept under due Subjection . . .; Her open Enemies (among whom I include at least Dissenters of all Denominations) not trusted with the smallest Degree of Civil or Military Power; and Her secret Adversaries, under the Names of Whigs, Low-Church, Republicans, Moderation-Men and the like, receive no Marks of Favour from the Crown, but what they should deserve by a sincere Reformation.

Free Thoughts Upon the Present State of Affairs, in *Political Tracts 1713–1719* (1953), 88

He was strong for unity around a reverenced Church and Crown; like the Vicar of Bray in his Tory phase,

> *Occasional Conformists base*
> *[He] damn'd, and Moderation;*
> *And thought the Church in danger was*
> *From such Prevarication.*

When 'faction' is suppressed and 'things return to the old course', he says in the 43rd *Examiner,* then 'mankind will naturally fall to act from principles of reason and religion'. That reason could lead rather to dissent than to assent was a thing he apparently could never understand; though far less extreme than many Churchmen he stood stoutly to the right of centre and thought all virtue stood with him.

He loathed Dissent and tolerant cosmopolitan Whiggery:

These men take it into their imagination that trade can never flourish unless the country becomes a common receptacle for all nations, religions and languages. Such an island as ours can afford enough to support the majesty of a crown, the honour of a nobility, and the dignity of a magistracy; we can encourage arts and sciences, maintain our bishops and clergy, and suffer our gentry to live in a decent hospitable

manner; yet still there will remain hands sufficient for trade and manufactures.

The Examiner, No. 22

It is an illiberal passage in some ways, prompted by fear of an influx of European Protestants if the Whigs were allowed to admit them, but its basis is an emotional attachment to the poetry of Church and state shared, in different ways and without Swift's limitations, by Shakespeare, Johnson, Burke and Coleridge.

It was not shared, however, by Defoe, patriotic though he was, for his attachments were to Dissent, toleration and trade. No more than Swift does he show any real religious experience — each is devoted rather to religious politics, Anglican or non-conformist. But his devotion, like Swift's, was sincere, and though he gave Harley some time-serving advice on the way to discourage Dissent he remained a Dissenter himself for his soul's good. In face of High-Church fury he and his fellows robustly cried down the High-flyers and Jacobites, and naturally they provoked their enemies:

> *They made a fearful Acclamation,*
> *And loudly cry'd up Moderation . . .*
> *The Low-Church are Prevaricators,*
> *Proud of the Name of Moderators:*
> *By subtle Arts made factious Tools,*
> *In short, they're the Dissenters' Fools.*

So did Ward's *Hudibras Redivivus* deride them. But Defoe's pleas for toleration and his support of the Low-Church and Hanoverian parties were anything but fractious. In a group of pamphlets — *An Answer to the Question, 'What if the Queen should Die?', What if the Pretender should Come?,* and the ironical *Reasons Against the Succession of the House of Hanover* (all 1713) he campaigned against Jacobitism, as in *The Storm* he had turned the tempest of 1703 into a divine judgment on intolerance. These quarrels are remote now, but then they were matters of life and death — men convicted on religious grounds could die in the pillory, and an attempt was made to assassinate Defoe's friend William Colepepper. The reign of Anne cannot

be understood without a knowledge of the violent winds still blowing from the storm-centres of the seventeenth century.

Yet the Augustans gradually learned the middle way. Defoe's fine apologia for his propagandist work — *An Appeal to Honour and Justice* (1715) — sounds a note of reconciliation:

It is and ever was my Opinion, that Moderation is the only Vertue by which the Peace and Tranquillity of this Nation can be preserv'd. I think I may be allow'd to say, a *Conquest of Parties* will never do it! *A Ballance of Parties* MAY.

The mob was sometimes dangerous, but reason slowly prevailed. The old prepossessions, it is true, survived in a modified form; Johnson was a Tory and a Churchman and thundered against the American colonies for their dissidence, while Burke was a Whig and admired the Protestantism of the Protestant religion which animated them. Yet Burke and Johnson were warm friends, and the latter was even sympathetic, late in life, with the new evangelicalism. In the 1790s, unfortunately, a chasm opened between rationalist Dissenters and the great body of Churchmen and others, on the subject of radical politics; in this case Burke who had moved to the right stormed against radical Dissent as an ally of 'atheism'. But during most of the eighteenth century the lessons of forbearance were learned, and antipathies brought within reasonable bounds.

III. Attack and Defence

My friend Sir Roger told them, with the air of a man who would not give his judgment rashly, that much might be said on both sides.

ADDISON

The Spectator, No. 122

Moderation, however, may look like apathy; it may originate less in charity than in carelessness. Was religion apathetic, heedless and dull? Is the indictment correct which condemns the Church as sycophantic and complacent, Dissent as drab or hysterical, and the public as ignorant and irresponsible? The devil's

advocate must be heard, though with the proviso that most of what he says comes from worried clerics who were anything but advocates of the devil.

The first objection might be that dull preaching went on in dull churches. Postponing the question of preaching, one may admit that many people find neoclassic buildings less rich in religious emotion than mediaeval or even pseudo-mediaeval, and indeed often as pagan as the fashionable chapel which Pope describes in the *Epistle to Burlington* (141–8) :

> *And now the Chapel's silver bell you hear,*
> *That summons you to all the Pride of Pray'r;*
> *Light Quirks of Musick, broken and uneven,*
> *Make the Soul dance upon a Jig to Heaven.*
> *On painted Cielings you devoutly stare,*
> *Where sprawl the Saints of Verrio or Laguerre,*
> *On gilded Clouds in fair expansion lie,*
> *And bring all Paradise before your eye.*

Gothic churches are taken to symbolise ages of faith, classical churches nothing but humanism. We see too clearly in these well-lit, symmetrical structures. Like Milton we may prefer 'storied windows richly dight'; like Gray, we desire 'the long-drawn aisle and fretted vault'; like Burke, we feel that the clear and the sublime do not go together. And the services in these buildings were, we deduce, too prosaic: mediaeval murals had disappeared under a coat of whitewash, and poetic faith under that of plain reason.

To these objections there are reasonable answers. The church had become an auditory for hearing the service rather than a setting for ritual, a development influenced perhaps by Inigo Jones's St. Paul's in Covent Garden, a simple rectangle with galleries to provide more seats. Wren planned his churches similarly, so that each worshipper could actively participate in the whole service. The spatial unity emphasised the unity of priest and people, and the intention was far from one of pagan pomp — it was the desire that the act of worship should be felt intimately by each person. The best study of these questions (Addleshaw and Etchells's *Architectural Setting of Anglican Worship*,

1948) describes the better churches as 'a perfect expression of eighteenth-century Anglicanism, its lucidity, its classical view of life, its freedom from cant and humbug, its objectivity'. The Augustans' religious emotions were different from ours but not necessarily inferior, and they found a style congruous to their needs, spacious, dignified and thoughtful. Berkeley likened St. Paul's Cathedral to the whole spirit and purpose of Anglicanism (*The Guardian*, No. 70):

The Divine Order and Economy of the one seemed to be emblematically set forth by the just, plain and majestic Architecture of the other. And as the one consists of a great Variety of Parts united in the same regular Design, according to the truest Art and most exact Proportion; so the other contains a decent Subordination of Members, various sacred Institutions, sublime Doctrines, and solid Precepts of Morality digested into the same Design, and with an admirable Concurrence tending to one View, the Happiness and Exaltation of Human Nature.

Speaking of the happiness and exaltation of human nature Berkeley is not making humanity self-sufficient; as little as anyone in his age did he forget spirituality, and it is a religious happiness and exaltation he has in mind. Defoe too found St. Paul's 'the beauty of all the churches in the city, and of all the Protestant churches in the world', and correlated its dignity with the plainness of Protestant doctrine (*Tour*, i. 336). St. Paul's, it is true, is the masterpiece of English classical buildings but its idiom is the language of the time and the Augustans found it abundantly reverent, as indeed it is. Nor did Dissenters think their meeting-houses too prosaic, those plain brick boxes or severe stucco-and-Doric-columned halls for the direct service of God, such as still placate the eye in country towns and indeed, though sadly grimed, in most industrial cities.

The twin-objection, of dull services, must be admitted to be more valid. Latitudinarianism was the spirit of prose. Swift found the normal Anglican preacher tedious, and by contrast exhibited an abnormal Anglican ('little parson Dapper', *i.e.* Joseph Trapp, High-Church-and-Sacheverell partisan) and a Dissenter (Daniel Burgess of Covent-Garden Meeting-House), both

famous for their vehemence (*The Tatler,* No. 66). Church services, Wesley complained, were perfunctory, and Goldsmith even
lamented the vogue of Tillotson's much-praised style, under
whose influence 'the spruce preacher reads his lucubration without lifting his nose from the text and never ventures to earn
the shame of an enthusiast' (*The Bee,* 17 November, 1759). Dissenting sermons were not always better; in mid-century both
Church and Dissent were respectable, and generally dull. The
evangelical revival of course made a difference; on 30 July, 1763,
as Johnson and Boswell sailed down to Greenwich and talked
of preaching styles, Johnson praised the Methodists and Scots
Presbyterians for their vivacity, as 'the only way to do good to
the common people', and in 1764 Goldsmith's essay *On the
English Clergy and Popular Preachers* contrasted the polite
tedium of the one party with the zeal of the other. In extenu-
ation one might plead that Church and Dissent by forfeiting
some poetry had acquired more reason, that clerical duties were
often done well, and that dull sermons are not one age's monopoly. But that hardly refutes the persistent charge.

There remains, however, a worse accusation — that of worldli-
ness. Some accounts show the clergy as worse than worldly: Swift
drew his vicar-schoolmaster in the 71st *Tatler,* a coarse figure
who sometimes played bowls while his curate conducted his
services, and sometimes slept 'sotting in the desk on a hassock'
while the curate preached. Crabbe was mordant about the sport-
ing parson in *The Village* who scorned a pauper's funeral, or
the reprobate in *Inebriety* (177–82):

> *The reverend wig, in sideway order plac'd,*
> *The reverend band, by rubric stains disgrac'd,*
> *The leering eye, in wayward circles roll'd,*
> *Mark him the pastor of a jovial fold,*
> *Whose various texts excite a loud applause,*
> *Favouring the bottle, and the good old cause.*

Fielding has his repulsive Trulliber in *Joseph Andrews* and
Thwackum in *Tom Jones,* Hogarth his grotesques in *An Election
Entertainment* and *The Sleeping Congregation,* and Churchill

his 'Atheist Chaplain of an Atheist Lord'. In actual life there were men like Churchill himself, the strongest satirist between Pope and Byron, and drawn by Hogarth as a bear in clerical bands grasping a club and a tankard of ale — a hit at his dissipations. Sterne, consumptive and of an electrical sensibility, was not perhaps strictly accountable for his dubious morals, but *Tristram Shandy* is a Rabelaisian novel for a clergyman and it is not surprising that Warburton came to think him 'an irrevocable scoundrel' and that Wesley, as he told Sophie von la Roche, hoped 'never to have a Sterne amongst the seven hundred clerics of his community'. Less erratic but still hardly praiseworthy were easy-going men like Edmund Pyle, royal chaplain and prebendary of Winchester, who remarked that 'the life of a prebendary is a pretty easy way of dawdling away one's time; praying, walking, visiting, and as little study as the heart could wish', or Cornwallis, a man of the world whose lavish entertainments were reproved by George II as 'levities and vain dissipations' yet who became Archbishop in 1768. As for men like Swift, Hoadly and Warburton, those characteristic Augustan figures, though they clearly felt they were doing their duty by the Church they conceived it to lie rather in controversy than in spiritual enlightenment.

The higher preferments were part of politics and Whig and Tory alternation swayed the bench of bishops this way and that, a condition which, when the Whigs established something like a monopoly, Johnson described as 'no better than the politics of stockjobbers and the religion of infidels'. Behind this partisanship there was something religious — a concern for the Church's honourable estate on the Tory side, and for liberalism towards Dissent on the Whig. But in the foreground these decent motives were hidden by opportunism. A striking instance of religious politics was the help Walpole received from his Whig bishops in 1733, when in two critical divisions twenty-four of the twenty-five bishops who voted supported him, giving him victory by a single vote. Such a performance might conceivably reflect a conscientious conviction but it could also look remarkably like venality.

Preferment was unsystematic, with favouritism on one hand and neglect on the other. Hoadly, by propagating the principles of 1688, flattering George I, and taking a strong line against Atterbury, garnered from successive Whig ministries the sees of Bangor (1715) which he never visited, Hereford (1721), Salisbury (1723) and the valuable Winchester (1734). More remarkable was the career of Brownlow North, younger half-brother of Lord North who was Prime Minister from 1770 to 1781, and as Lord North was a Tory it cannot be said that only the Whigs took their responsibilities lightly. Brownlow became a canon in 1768 at twenty-seven, Dean of Canterbury at twenty-nine, and Bishop of Coventry at thirty. Even an unsqueamish age was surprised at this, and Lord North is said to have rejoined that Brownlow was indeed rather young but that if he were kept waiting he might no longer have a Prime Minister for his brother. Lord North in fact conveniently held on to office and continued his fraternal care: Brownlow was translated to Worcester in 1774 and in 1781 to Winchester, the wealthiest see after Canterbury and Durham, where his income of £5,000 was worth in modern terms about four times as much. Surviving there for thirty-nine years he netted in all, in modern values, well over £750,000. Happily he was a good and generous man; he founded charities and raised large sums for church building. But no more than Lord North was he averse from favouritism; he made his elder son master of St. Cross Hospital, his younger son prebendary of Winchester, and the latter's son (another Brownlow) registrar of the diocese (a sinecure) at the somewhat remarkable age of seven.

At the other extreme there were poor curates, poor parsons, and even poor bishops. In the 22nd *Examiner* Swift spoke of the clergy as 'groaning everywhere under the weight of poverty, oppression, contempt and obloquy' until Queen Anne's bounty relieved them. Soon afterwards *The Guardian* (No. 65) felt compelled to ask

How is it possible for a Gentleman under the Income of fifty Pounds a Year, to be attentive to sublime Things? *Power and Commandment to*

his Ministers to declare and pronounce to his People is mentioned with
a very unregarded Air, when the Speaker is known in his private Condition to be almost an Object of their Pity and Charity.

Curates received in general from £30 to £40 a year — Fielding's
Abraham Adams has £23 for himself, his wife and six children.
Even benefices were often miserable: in the early eighteenth
century more than half were under £50 a year. Goldsmith's parson
in *The Deserted Village* is, we recall, 'pasing rich on forty
pounds a year', and the Vicar of Wakefield holds one living of
£35 and then moves to another of £15 which he supplements by
farming. Churchill spoke of himself in *The Author* (347–50) as

> *Condemn'd (whilst proud and pamper'd sons of lawn,*
> *Cramm'd to the throat, in lazy plenty yawn)*
> *In pomp of rev'rend beggary to appear,*
> *To pray, and starve, on forty pounds a year.*

Poor stipends had often to be raised by the holding of plurali-
ties, but the normal Augustan cleric remained in moderate position at best, respected in the varying degrees which his own worth
merited and the civility or boorishness of his parishioners
prompted. The ordinary clergy were truly a part of their times,
not markedly above their fellows in social standing, somewhat
superior in learning and conduct but, for both evil and good,
little separated from the mass of the people. They fished, shot,
hunted, farmed and marketed with their neighbours, and on
Sunday assumed a degree of extra dignity and preached to them.
They were often ill-paid or ill-qualified, but if not always invested
with the reverence which the nineteenth century thought proper
(and which prevailed in Scotland from the days of John Knox)
yet they included many good parish priests and Dissenting
ministers, and an unspecialised relationship of church and people
has its merits.

The clergy, on the whole, spread a touch of civilisation: is it
not a good thing, Swift asks ironically in the *Argument Against
Abolishing Christianity,* 'to have one literate man in each parish?'
Thomas Percy, famous for the *Reliques of Antient English Poetry,*
observed to Johnson that one could tell 'whether or no there was a

clergyman resident in a parish by the civil or savage manner of the people', and Johnson quoted the remark to a discouraged young parson who sought his advice. 'A clergyman's diligence', Johnson added, 'always makes him venerable' (Boswell, *Life of Johnson,* 30 August, 1780). The 112th *Spectator* is a pleasant picture of social civility; the villagers, 'with their best faces and in their cleanliest habits', meet every Sunday 'to converse with one another upon indifferent subjects, hear their duties explained to them, and join together in adoration of the Supreme Being.' Country Sundays have changed but little. Sir Roger de Coverley's clergyman is the true shepherd of such a flock, sensible, sound in scholarship, handy at backgammon, and judicious in choosing his sermons from the published works of eminent divines. Good instruction is what he purveys, with no nonsense about original composition. The Vicar of Wakefield is equally companionable with his parishioners, and when he moves from his first to his second cure the neighbourhood comes to greet him, 'dressed in their finest clothes and preceded by a pipe and tabor'. In actual life diaries such as William Cole's, of Bletchley, and Parson Woodforde's, record honest lives devoted to their country charges; and Pastor Moritz describes a Sunday at Nettlebed in Oxfordshire in words which recall the life of Hardy's Wessex (*Travels,* 1924, 135–6) :

The service was now pretty well advanced, when I observed some little stir in the desk; the clerk was busy, and they seemed to be preparing for something new and solemn; and I also perceived several musical instruments. The clergyman now stopped and the clerk said, in a loud voice, 'Let us sing to the praise and glory of God, the forty-seventh psalm'. I cannot well express how affecting and edifying it seemed to me, to hear this whole, orderly and decent congregation, in this small country church, joining together, with vocal and instrumental music, in praise of their Maker. It was the more grateful, as having been performed not by mercenary musicians, but by the peaceful and pious inhabitants of this sweet village. I can hardly figure to myself any offering more likely to be grateful to God.

Through Augustan worship there runs the feeling which still rules in quieter districts, a steady element in normal life, not unworldly or intense, but taken naturally and for granted. It has

its limitations, admittedly, as Parson Adams found when he questioned the innkeeper about salvation. 'Faith, master,' replied the host, 'I never once thought of that; but what signifies talking about matters so far off? (*Joseph Andrews*, II. 3). The answer, however distressing to Adams, is as natural as any that Hardy's countrymen might give; it reflects a religious life as normal as the process of the crops, and sunshine and rain in due season.

Yet this sensible religion, it may be objected, omits everything of importance; it impresses neither those to whom religion means much nor those to whom it means little. Neither hot nor cold, like the Laodiceans it knows not that it is 'wretched, and miserable, and poor, and blind, and naked'. Was Georgian religion mere complacency?

It did certainly anticipate Talleyrand's warning against zeal, but stability was newly-won and still precarious. "Enthusiasm' did indeed seem, in Bishop Butler's phrase to Wesley, 'a horrid thing, a very horrid thing', and Samuel Butler and Abraham Cowley, those forerunners of the Augustans, flayed the extremists, the former in the Puritan Hudibras, the latter in *The Character of a Holy Sister*. So did Dryden, and so did Addison, denouncing 'false zealots in religion', including those whose zeal was for atheism (*The Spectator*, Nos. 185–6). Fielding, through the mouth of Adams, equated 'nonsense and enthusiasm'; John Shebbeare's *Letters on the English Nation* (1756) denounced 'swivel-headed bigots or fallacious free-thinkers'; and Johnson deplored Milton's polemics, wrote of Puritan fervour in the *Life of Butler* as an almost incomprehensible thing, and in the *Dictionary* defined enthusiasm as 'a vain confidence of divine favour or communication'. Some of this was regrettable but all of it was natural; to be moderate was not to shirk but to seek the truth. William Law was anything but a Latitudinarian, yet he like others lamented that sectarian zeal split the Church (*Address to the Clergy* 1764, 58) :

Christendom, full of the nicest Decisions about Faith, Grace, Works, Merits, Satisfaction, Heresies, Schisms, &c., is full of all those evil Tempers which prevailed in the Heathen World.

Latitudinarian tolerance seemed the dawn of a saner age, purged

only of the inessentials of faith. The Augustans were often self-satisfied in their beliefs, but the terms in which such men as Swift, Fielding (in his anti-Stuart *Champion* and *Jacobite's Journal*) and Burke (in the *Reflections* and the *Speech on the Army Estimates*) defend their position are those of confident men to whom extremes, not moderation, were wretched, miserable, poor, blind and naked aberrations.

One more charge must now be considered, that Hanoverian religion suffered from widely-testified spiritual anaemia and stands convicted by its own defenders. Swift's *Argument Against Abolishing Christianity* is a virtuoso's exercise in irony, but its tenour cannot, one feels, be entirely discounted. Swift does not intend, he explains, to advocate real Christianity—that would be 'a wild Project'; it would 'destroy at one Blow all the Wit, and half the Learning, of the Kingdom'. He pleads only for nominal Christianity, which deters no-one from his vices and even heightens their relish by the sauce of hypocrisy. Religion keeps the masses obedient, gives free-thinkers an easy butt and gratifies our Continental allies; surely this convenient veneer is worth preserving? This is ironic but its diagnosis is not reassuring. The 21st *Guardian* speaks of a 'prevailing Torrent of Vice and Impiety', and Berkeley's *Principles of Human Knowledge* (1710) of 'the absurdities of every wretched set of Atheists' (section xcii). John Byrom told his sister Phoebe, in February 1729, that he had bought Law's *Serious Call* but that 'Mr. Law and the Christian Religion . . . are mightily out of fashion at present'. And Bishop Butler's 'Advertisement' to the *Analogy* (1736) is a sombre comment:

It is come, I know not how, to be taken for granted, by many persons, that Christianity is not so much as a subject of enquiry; but that it is now at length discovered to be fictitious. And accordingly they treat it as if, in the present age, this were an agreed point among all people of discernment, and nothing remained but to set it up as a principal subject of mirth and ridicule, as it were by way of reprisals, for its having so long interrupted the pleasures of the world.

In 1737 Butler's friend Secker became Bishop of Oxford, and it is hardly coincidence that his first charge to his clergy (1738) is

almost an echo of these words. Butler's own charge to the clergy
of Durham in 1751 speaks of a positive zeal for infidelity, 'truly
for nothing, but *against* everything that is good and sacred
amongst us'.

These protests sound serious, but any age might be proved
irreligious with no more trouble than has gone to the collecting
of them — that is, with very little trouble at all. Was spiritual
decay then unduly prominent? On the whole, the ordinary man
at any time is neither very religious nor very irreligious, and one
would expect this to be so with the Augustans also. In his
Evidences of Christianity (1794: pt. iii, ch. vii) Paley sensibly
remarks that religion is a private thing and

operates most upon those of whom history knows the least; upon fathers
and mothers in their families, upon men-servants and maid-servants,
upon the orderly tradesman, the quiet villager, the manufacturer at his
loom, the husbandman in his fields.

Among such people the variations from age to age will not be
spectacular. The trouble lay not in the middle levels but on the
lowest and the highest: two classes were perceptibly at fault.

One was the very poor. Developing a social conscience as they
did, the Augustans came to realise the brutal misery in which the
destitute lived: Wesley found the Kingswood colliers 'one remove
from the beasts that perish'. In such circumstances religious ignorance was natural, and the century's awakening to the consequences of poverty is not to its religious discredit.

The other class was that of the social sophisticate, sometimes
but not always identical with the "freethinker'. Polite society is
seldom very religious, and as polite society under the Georges was
prominent its indifference was a source of concern. In the 6th
Spectator Steel declares that 'the affectation of being gay and in
fashion has very near eaten up our good sense and religion'. Law
writes the *Serious Call*, he avers, because 'this polite age of ours'
has scared men away from devotion, and Swift's *Letter of Advice
to a Young Poet* speaks of the current distaste for anything so
unmodish as faith, for 'our Poetry of late has been altogether
disengag'd from the narrow Notions of Virtue and Piety'. Young's
Night Thoughts (book viii) also recommends the orthodoxy of

'sense' as against the heterodoxy of 'wit', though making much heavier weather of it than Swift.

The polite world being supercilious, religion had to be presented in terms it might understand. It might appear, for instance, as a matter of good taste — as it does in Steele's *Christian Hero* (1701), his and Addison's periodicals, and Shaftesbury's *Characteristicks* (1711). *The Guardian* (No. 21) recalls that the infallible Tillotson had found the Bible's style better than Virgil's, and No. 86 raises *The Book of Job* above the classical epics, and anticipates the day

when it shall be as much the Fashion among Men of Politeness to admire a Rapture of St. *Paul,* as any fine expression in *Virgil* or *Horace;* and to see a well-dressed young Man produce an Evangelist out of his Pocket and be no more out of Countenance than if it were a Classick printed by *Elzevir.*

The connoisseur might read his Bible without harm to his taste.

Religious and moral truths, moreover, were to be conveyed by the politest of means, urbane ridicule of irreligion. Shaftesbury advocated this manner and Addison followed him. The heretic would be bantered into faith, the profligate reformed through laughter. So, said Addison in *The Spectator* (No. 445), 'I have set up the immoral man as the object of derision.' Ridicule, it is true, was a weapon the infidel could use too, and Mandeville, Hume and Gibbon did so with disturbing skill. 'The truth' was not a monopoly. But the store set by ridicule was the sign both of less vehement tempers and of the civilised taste which preferred rapiers to cudgels. And if it were fashionable to be a sceptic, it was still a fashion with drawbacks even in worldly terms; Chesterfield himself, the virtuoso of the graces, was severe upon infidelity and polite towards religion, though in suavely ambiguous terms which relegated it rather to the status of a social guarantee (*Letters,* 8 January, 1750) :

Depend upon this truth, That every man is the worse looked upon, and the less trusted, for being thought to have no religion; in spite of all the pompous and specious epithets he may assume, of *esprit fort,* freethinker or moral philosopher; and a wise atheist (if such a thing there

is) would, for his own interest and character in the world, pretend to some religion.

Despite the tone of this, we need not conclude that Chesterfield is merely recommending hypocrisy as the tribute vice pays to virtue; he is also urging a serious truth in language attuned to the man of society. Social irreverence was not widely approved, though it was current enough to seem dangerous, and was to be laughed out of its presumption.

As troublesome as the atheist was the 'freethinker', a polymorphous nightmare. The 'Advertisement' to Berkeley's *Alciphron, or the Minute Philosopher* (1732) undertook to consider him 'in the various Lights of Atheist, Libertine, Enthusiast, Scorner, Critic, Metaphysician, Fatalist and Sceptic'. Almost any accusation could hit so large a target, and the whole matter reflects the difficulty of replacing dogma by a 'reasonable' faith. The main freethinkers were Deists, who tried to determine the elements of religion independently of the Bible and Revelation, since a benevolent Deity would surely not have concealed the great truths from all but a small proportion of mankind. There were pre-Augustan Deists but the main trouble came with Toland's *Christianity not Mysterious* (1696), Wollaston's *Religion of Nature Delineated* (1724), Tindal's *Christianity as Old as the Creation* (1730), and Chubb's *The True Gospel of Jesus Christ* (1738). Despite the references to Christianity in these titles the Deists were devising not Christian apologetics but proofs that unaided reason could find out the essentials of faith.

There is no room here for detail but Deism naturally shocked the orthodox, who rallied strongly, and whose reaction is reflected in the Vicar of Wakefield's outburst — 'No freethinker shall ever have a child of mine.' Law's *Case of Reason* is an answer to Tindal, Berkeley's *Alciphron* is intelligent satire, and Butler's *Analogy* replies to Deism though without mentioning it. That 'free thought' should venture to discuss faith seemed impertinence; Addison reprimanded 'bigoted infidels' who spread scepticism (*The Spectator*, No. 185), Horace Walpole listened to the Parisian *philosophes* and then told George Montagu, on 22 September, 1765, that there is 'as much bigotry in attempting con-

versions from any religion as to it', and Burke, infuriated by the radicals, wrote in the *Reflections* that 'if our religious tenets ever want a further elucidation we shall not call on atheists to explain them' (*Reflections, in Works,* iv. 99). Deists were not, indeed, atheists; they believed in a benevolent God. But their rejection of Revelation and their universalising of religious belief seemed tantamount to atheism. When Herbert Croft was gathering materials for the *Life of Young* Johnson passed him information about Tindal, Young's dialectical adversary at All Souls. 'Don't forget that rascal Tindal, Sir,' he would vociferate, 'Be sure to hang up the Atheist' (A. Chalmers's *English Poets,* 1810, xiii. 341 fn.). Such was the general sentiment. The Deists were raked (though not without effective reply) by guns far heavier than their own. The orthodox blazed away with all they could muster — Swift, Berkeley, Addison, Steele, Law, Butler, Warburton, Fielding, Johnson, Young and Burke. Through the reigns of Anne, George I and George II there were intermittent tremors, with a quake of exceptional force in 1754 when Mallet published the works of Bolingbroke. These, said the 9th *Connoisseur,* gave new life and spirit to free thinking, and Garrick thrust a strongly anti-Bolingbroke stanza into his poem on Lord Pelham's death. Deism caused long-lasting concern — indeed, in 1760 Goldsmith had to suggest that it was time to give up the controversy for something fresher (*On the English Clergy and Popular Preachers*).

But the dispute passed away or changed gradually into different forms. Despite the outcry against infidelity, Johnson told Boswell on 14 April, 1775, 'there are in reality very few infidels'. 'Who now reads Bolingbroke?' Burke asked in the *Reflections,* 'Who ever read him through?' (*Works,* iv. 98). The new alarm centred rather on the scepticism of men like Hume and Gibbon and the rationalism of the radicals. Johnson frowned when the name of Priestley was mentioned, and walked out of company when Richard Price entered it. But the monument to the late-Augustan phase of the battle is not Johnson's but Burke's. With deep emotion the *Reflections* upholds the fundamental connection between Christianity and national life; Church and State are connected in a sacramental bond and the commonwealth is 'con-

secrated' by the Church establishment. All who minister in
Church and State, therefore, have 'high and worthy notions of
their function and destination', and an eye

> not to the paltry pelf of the moment, nor to the temporary and tran-
> sient praise of the vulgar, but to a solid, permanent existence, in the
> permanent part of their nature, and to a permanent fame and glory, in
> the example they leave.

Britons are conservative by nature, Burke explains, and prefer
rather to maintain an imperfect religion than to tinker with it:

> there is no rust of superstition with which the accumulated absurdity of
> the human mind might have crusted it over in the course of ages that
> ninety-nine in a hundred of the people of England would not prefer to
> impiety.
>
> *Reflections,* in *Works,* iv. 99

Allowing for rhetorical fervour that was largely true. 'Free-
thinkers' and radicals argued an unpopular case and extended
the horizons of thought; they were grossly misrepresented and
their courage deserves gratitude. But the ordinary man held by
his ordinary notions, whether in church or chapel, and sympa-
thised with the old rather than the new.

The 'truth' about Hanoverian religion will not go in a sentence, but the more that religion is understood the less it need be
broadly condemned. Its weaknesses were recognised then as they
are now. Yet neither Church nor Dissent should be judged merely
by its defects; if they were prosaic and cautious they were served
by many labours of worth and devotion. Vulnerable to attack,
and sometimes despondent about their influence, their defense
still evoked from the ablest men of the age more passion than
was shown on any other subject.

IV. *'An Inward Chearfulness'*

Whether amid the gloom of night I stray,
Or my glad eyes enjoy revolving day,

> *Still Nature's various face informs my sense*
> *Of an all-wise, all-pow'rful Providence.*
>
> GAY
>
> *Contemplation on Night*, 1-4

The characteristic Augustan belief is in the mercy of God and the duty of beneficence in man. This, though no new invention, is markedly different in tone from the characteristic belief of the century before, which had produced so much emotion. Individuals like Cowper, convinced of their sins by apparent revelation, could still suffer as excruciatingly as Bunyan had done, but in general the age was, like Johnson's hermit in *Rasselas*, 'cheerful without levity'. It felt in its faith not so much the ecstatic joy that Cowper felt when he thought himself saved as the steady joy of descrying God's beneficence displayed at large. Religion, Thomson assures us in *Liberty*, has now become a thing of joy and confidence:

> *Nor be Religion, rational and free,*
> *Here pass'd in silence, whose enraptur'd eye*
> *Sees Heav'n with Earth connected, human things*
> *Link'd to divine; who not from servile fear,*
> *By rites for some weak tyrant incense fit,*
> *The God of Love adores, but from a heart*
> *Effusing gladness.*
>
> (iv. 561–7)

The stars, in Addison's hymn, sing in their God-given paths, and their bright constancy betokens a divine assurance.

The new spirit encouraged a new optimism: God, as Locke said, was actively interested in his creatures' happiness. This faith, too, was anything but a new discovery; the Christian tradition has cherished love as often as it has feared judgment. But so much stress on happiness was novel; so well-designed a universe must have good ends, and what end better than universal happiness? Shaftesbury followed Locke: so did Addison: Pope declared happiness (rather than, though certainly not instead of, salvation) to be 'our being's end and aim': the preface to Akenside's

Pleasures of the Imagination (1744) celebrated 'the benevolent intention of the Author of Nature in every principle of the human constitution', and introducing William King's *Origin of Evil* (1731) the Reverend John Gay, an early Utilitarian, said that man's happiness is 'the criterion of the will of God'. The old fears might still be felt — the names of Law, Butler, Johnson and Cowper remind us that orthodoxy could still oppress the believer. But characteristically it was optimism which the Augustans cherished, optimism not without precedent but increasingly dominant over the fear of God, and expressing itself in the soul's calm sunshine and the heartfelt joy.

Perhaps the belief that the universe was ruled not by an autocrat but by a constitutional monarch observing the comprehensible laws of reason was not an unmixed blessing, since it might remove God to a distance, as a power working not directly as a First Cause but indirectly through natural laws, second causes discoverable by science. 'Philosophy that lean'd on Heav'n before', Pope observed as a symptom of impending intellectual night, 'Shrinks to her second cause and is no more' (*Dunciad*, iv. 644), and Berkeley protested against this shrinking, this loss of the sense of the numinous, by which the very uniformity God observes in presenting the universe to our minds is misread as the mere mechanical working of physical laws (*Principles of Human Knowledge*, sec. xxxii) :

This consistent, uniform working, which so evidently displays the goodness and wisdom of that governing Spirit whose will constitutes the laws of Nature, is so far from leading our thoughts to him, that it rather sends them a-wandering after second causes.

Yet in many cases, perhaps most, an enlargement of mind and elevation of spirit followed the scientific 'proof' of what Addison calls 'the exuberant and overflowing goodness of the Supreme Being whose mercy extends to all His works' (*The Spectator*, No. 519). It did so in Berkeley's own case; for him, man's steady sense of the external world is the mark of God's unwearying creative care. Asking how an immaterial mind can know the material universe Berkeley answers that all perceptions (including the

evidence the senses seem to give of the world around) are directly presented to the mind by God, who perpetually creates our world for us in its beauty and order. The ironic result is that men take this very order as the sign of an automatic universe; only in calamities and interruptions of order (what insurance companies unfortunately call 'acts of God') do they see evidence of divine power. For Berkeley God is manifested not so much in prodigies as in the perpetual stability of things, in the fact that every time the eyes look in a certain direction they see a certain tree, and every night is succeeded by the following morning. The passages in which Berkeley praises this divine dispensation, this spiritual motivation, this unremitting fostering care, are among the finest prose of the century. Other writers too, without Berkeley's almost mystical intelligence, found reason for joy. Gay and Thomson have been quoted; Shaftesbury, following the Cambridge Platonists, spoke of man's duty to be in the 'sweetest' disposition whenever he thinks of spiritual things, and Addison recurrently echoed the advocacy of happiness:

I cannot but look upon it [a cheerful mind] as a constant habitual gratitude to the great Author of Nature. An inward chearfulness is an implicit praise and thanksgiving to Providence under all its dispensations. It is a kind of acquiescence in the state wherein we are placed, and a secret approbation of the divine will.

The Spectator, No. 381

Eccentric beliefs therefore were not only unorthodox but a forfeiture of happiness. Freethinkers, it was argued, must be morose because they reject a personal God and lose the believer's truest joy, which only a sense of guilt and atheism (Addison thinks) can banish. Berkeley's 27th *Guardian* speaks of 'those gloomy Mortals who by their Unbelief are rendered incapable of feeling those Impressions of Joy and Hope'. It was a retort to the claim that wit and confidence were the marks of free thought and sourness and gloom those of faith. When Methodism brought back the introspection of an earlier age Churchmen could still claim that they were the happy ones and only 'enthusiasts' miserable (an idea the Wesleyans would fervently have rebutted) — Goldsmith has a

pleasant *Citizen of the World* paper (No. 111) relating how the new sect 'weep for their amusement and use little music except a chorus of sighs and groans', and how lovers 'court each other from the Lamentations'. It need hardly be said that an Irish imagination is at work here, but at least the stress put on the happiness of the accepted faith and the misery of deviations from it is significant.

To imply that for no orthodox person was the world a vale of tears would be absurd: moods are controlled by temperament and circumstances as well as by the trend of the time. Butler's *Analogy* is shadowed with the darkness of life, which reason interprets no better than revelation; it speaks of 'the present state of vice and misery', and admits that neither religion nor reason can afford satisfaction, since 'satisfaction in this sense does not belong to such a creature as man' (*Works,* ed. W. E. Gladstone, 1896, i. 364). Johnson too felt the mood of religious dread, and reviewing Soame Jenyns's *Free Inquiry into the Nature and Origin of Evil* (1757) he demolished the argument that because pain and evil seem to be ordained by God man should pretend they are a form of good. Young too was gloomy; most of the earth, he declared, is savage wilderness, a symbol of fallen man (*Night Thoughts,* i. 285). And when in 1750 London experienced a combination of storm, earthquake, and Aurora Borealis (acts of God in the popular but not Berkeleyan sense), the citizens forgot that the Deity was the Prime Mover of an Age of Reason, and gathered in the fields expecting the doom of Sodom and Gomorrah, just as if Enlightenment had not dawned.

Yet an earthquake is one thing, and normal life another. At ordinary times men paid a reasonable obedience to moral duty, cheered by a sense of God's approval and that 'sweet contemplation' of which Gay speaks (*Rural Sports,* i. 107–20) :

> *Now night in silent state begins to rise,*
> *And twinkling orbs bestrow th'uncloudy skies ...*
> *Millions of worlds hang in the spacious air,*
> *Which round the sun their annual circles steer;*
> *Sweet contemplation elevates my sense*
> *While I survey the works of Providence.*
> *O could the muse in loftier strains rehearse*

The glorious author of the universe,
Who reins the winds, gives the vast ocean bounds,
And circumscribes the floating worlds their rounds,
My soul should overflow in songs of praise,
And my Creator's name inspire my lays.

Such sentiments were typical of their time, and they inspired, if less of earnest passion than did the sense of mystery and dread, both personal serenity and an expansive goodwill towards others.

V. Religion and Literature

A reasonable life, and a wise use of our proper condition, is as much the duty of all *men,* as it is the duty of all *Angels,* and *intelligent* beings. These are not *speculative* flights, or *imaginary* notions, but are *plain* and *undeniable laws,* that are founded in the *nature* of rational beings, who as such are obliged to live by reason, and glorify God by a continual right use of their several talents and faculties.

WILLIAM LAW
A Serious Call to a Devout and Holy Life (1728), 77

How then did the muse 'rehearse The glorious author of the universe'? Was literature influenced by the instinct for faith?

To ask this is to ask whether writers were affected by some of the themes that most deeply concerned them, and the answer must clearly be that they were, that in this supposedly indifferent age religion provided a standard of judgment and a mode of expression both consciously and subconsciously important. Tillotson and *The Guardian,* we have seen, showed even the venerated classics to be 'faint and languid' by the side of the Bible. Familiarity with the Bible did as much as anything, even familiarity with Shakespeare, to nourish the imagination. This influence was partly rhythmical (no other source could so have affected Law and Burke, for instance), and partly concerned with diction and imagery, with a willingness to break through the 'polite' modes and be passionate and elaborate. Its effect on Thomson was described by an early editor, Patrick Murdock, as follows:

It is certain he owed much to a religious education; and that his early acquaintance with the sacred writings contributed greatly to that *sublime,*

by which his works will be for ever distinguished. In his first pieces, the *Seasons*, we see him at once assume the majestic freedom of an Eastern writer, seizing the grand images as they rise, cloathing them in his own expressive language, and preserving throughout the grace, the variety, and the dignity, which belong to a just composition, unhurt by the stiffness of formal method.

Works of James Thomson (1762), introduction, iv

In particular it was hymnody which showed this influence, and the eighteenth century, rapidly developing the congregational hymn, was 'the Century of Divine Songs' (the phrase is from George Sampson's *Seven Essays*, 1947). This is not the place to compete with Sampson's admirable discussion or with Bernard Manning's *Hymns of Wesley and Watts* (1942), yet even a brief inspection must see in the better hymns a range of feeling and wealth of imagery which other poems of the time hardly approach. The hymn as we know it is the child of Dissent and its first great writer — Isaac Watts — a Congregationalist. It partakes, then, of the fervour of early Dissent and it amplifies this enormously when the Wesleys set to work. Methodist hymns are often thought to be gloomy and even morbid, but this strain (with a few exceptions) belongs rather to the Calvinist than the Arminian side, which delights to celebrate divine mercy. William Law speaks of the joys of psalm-singing, and these joys the Wesleys preserve in their hymns, Charles in particular abounding in images of spacious, radiant and infinite things like oceans, rivers, water, fire and light, and commanding too a concise, firm utterance, strongly observant of line and rhyme, which is part of his Augustan inheritance. Unlike the polite connoisseur the hymn-writer needed no prompting to admire the Bible; the force of its contents impressed upon him its vigour, its concrete and picturesque phrasing, its lyrical and dramatic power. From it there flowed an oriental wealth of colouring, into hymns like Watts's 'We are a garden wall'd around' or Newton's 'Glorious things of thee are spoken', or a passion of joy, in Byrom's 'Christians, awake!' (which shows what the heroic couplet could be besides satire), Olivers's 'The God of Abraham praise', Doddridge's 'Hark the glad sound', Perronet's 'All hail the power of Jesus' name', and many hymns by Watts and the Wesleys, Newton and

Cowper. Others were grave, like Toplady in 'Rock of Ages', or confident, like Addison in 'The spacious firmament' and 'When all Thy mercies, O my God'.

This is a sparse account of a large topic, and it ignores — an inviting theme — the question whether literary criteria are relevant to the judgment of hymns. Still, amenable or not to literary criticism, the hymn reveals a good deal about its time, and its character extends into other poems not themselves hymns, which include Watts's vehement *Ode on the Day of Judgment* (the most passionate sapphics in English) and pre-eminently Smart's *Song to David*, which peals like the clash of bells, or organs played at a thanksgiving. Smart is often spoken of as *sui generis*, and so he is in the degree in which his imagination rises, his verse throbs with excitement and his images have a Biblical majesty. But his poem is only the crown of a flourishing mode and nothing in it is surprising except its genius.

In less directly Biblical ways religion enriches literature with a sense of values which writers and readers were readier to recognise than some conceptions of the age might suggest. Sophisticated breakfast-tables, one might imagine, would hardly welcome in their periodicals such things as versified Biblical texts, Addison's and Watts's hymns, and Pope's *Messiah* (which Steele introduced as being 'by a great genius who is not ashamed to employ his wit in the praise of his Maker' — *Spectator,* No. 378). Yet *The Spectator* did not hesitate to print these and other religious compositions. The journals abounded in lay sermons and moral discourses, and Addison in particular made it his business to promote religion. For this above all Swift and Pope praised him, Somervile asserted that 'presumptuous Folly blush'd and Vice withdrew' before him (*To Mr. Addison*), and Tickell, in verses *To the Supposed Author of The Spectator,* averred that as a result

> the rash fool who scorn'd the beaten road
> Dares quake at thunder, and confess his God.

The essays which produced this gratifying effect are not all palatable, but some are still persuasive and dignified. They plead the social virtues — good nature, benevolence, forbearance — and the

Christian virtues — faith, hope, charity. The 413th *Spectator,* for
example, one of Addison's 'Pleasures of the Imagination' series,
takes on a characteristic illumination of religious gratitude. God
encourages man to explore the universe by giving him pleasure in
novelty, makes the sexes mutually attractive, and inspires a general enjoyment of beautiful things, in order

> that he might render the whole creation more gay and delightful. He
> has given almost everything about us the power of raising an agreeable
> idea in the imagination, so that it is impossible for us to behold his
> works with coldness or indifference, and to survey so many beauties
> without a secret satisfaction or complacency.

Such themes recur — themes of the soul's improvement, of divine
beneficence, and of immortal happiness. Berkeley too rises to
admirable eloquence by religious meditation, by his faith that
'all the choir of heaven and furniture of the earth, in a word all
those bodies which compose the mighty frame of the world' are
thoughts in the mind of God (*Principles of Human Knowledge,*
section vi), and in Law there coexist the religious senses of sin
and ecstatic happiness:

> If any one would tell you the shortest, surest way to all happiness, and
> all perfection, he must tell you to make a *rule* to yourself, to *thank and
> praise God for every thing that happens to you.* For it is certain that
> whatever seeming calamity happens to you, if you thank and praise
> God for it you turn it into a blessing. Could you therefore work mira-
> cles you could not do more for yourself than by this *thankful spirit,* for
> it *heals* with a word speaking, and turns all that it touches into
> happiness.
>
> *Serious Call,* 279

In such writing there is a particular dimension, that of a scale
of supramundane values. It is the background against which Swift
pillories hypocrisy in the *Argument Against Abolishing Christianity,* and it inspires that underthrob of rhythm which brings
Addison's Westminster-Abbey *Spectator* (No. 26) to an end. It
appears gravely in Cowper, in his sense that the world is being
weighed in the balance of religion and that its cares — commerce,

politics, diversion — distract man from his fundamental search. It develops in Johnson's criticism a magnificence of evaluation which convinces him that neither criticism nor literature is the most important thing in life — nor, indeed, are the daily experiences of life itself. The most important thing for Johnson goes beyond criticism and literature; it is that man's real concern is religious. Divine themes, he declares, are indeed often too high for poetry; in the *Life of Waller* he speaks of the poet's difficulties when faced with higher subjects than poetry can attain. In the *Life of Young* he accounts for the failure of Young's *Last Day* on the grounds that its very subject 'makes every man more than poetical' and inspires 'a general obscurity of horrour that disdains expression'. *Paradise Lost,* however, he admits to have risen to the height of its great argument, and his emotions on its theme are expressed in a passage which rings with something of the seventeenth century's power and shows what resonance could be sounded in the eighteenth by the enormous prospect of religious beliefs:

We all, indeed, feel the effects of Adam's disobedience: we all sin like Adam, and like him must all bewail our offences; we have restless and insidious enemies in the fallen angels, and in the blessed spirits we have guardians and friends; in the Redemption of mankind we hope to be included; in the description of heaven and hell we are surely interested, as we are all to reside hereafter either in the regions of horrour or of bliss.

One of his finest meditations is the end of the last *Idler,* in the Holy Week of 1760. It is one single magnificent sentence which must be quoted despite its length; indeed, in its length sustained by its majestic deliberation lies its very quality:

As the last *Idler* is published in that solemn week which the Christian world has always set apart for the examination of the conscience, the review of life, the extinction of earthly desires and the renovation of holy purposes; I hope that my readers are already disposed to view every incident with seriousness, and improve it by meditation; and that, when they see this series of trifles brought to a conclusion, they will consider that, by outliving the Idler, they have passed weeks, months and years

which are no longer in their power; that an end must in time be put to
everything great, as to everything little; that to life must come its last
hour, and to this system of being its last day, the hour at which proba-
tion ceases and repentance will be vain; the day in which every work of
the hand, and imagination of the heart, shall be brought to judgment,
and an everlasting futurity shall be determined by the past.

Nothing in Johnson's journalism became him like the leaving it;
the commonplace idea rises into fresh power in that stately
gravity which relates the recurrence of daily work to the passage
of time and the imminence of eternity.

That same sense of great significance sounds throughout the
century. In Berkeley, Law, and Goldsmith's earnestness as he
composes Dr. Primrose's sermon (*The Vicar of Wakefield,* ch.
29), the age's reason rises into something of poetry, which comes
not as an overtone of fear but from a desire that men shall realise
their spiritual selves. This desire in this degree could come only
from a religious sense of life (though not necessarily an orthodox
or even a Christian one), and whether coloured by the gloomy
dignity of Bishop Butler or Johnson, the rapture of Berkeley or
Law, or the various tones of Cowper and the hymn-writers it
reveals a dimension of life of which the Augustans are too often
thought heedless.

In Law this dimension is particularly prominent; life for him
is consecration. In the *Address to the Clergy,* finished just before
his death in 1761, he speaks earnestly of 'the *one Thing* needful,
the one Thing *essential* and only *available* to our Rising out of
our fallen State' — that is, participation in the divine spirit. He
rejects creeds 'not wholly built upon this *Supernatural Ground*'
but based wholly on human reason, and denies that his spiritual
zeal is gross 'enthusiasm' (*Address to the Clergy,* 2nd ed.
1764, 89):

Poor miserable Man! that strives with all the Sophistry of human Wit,
to be delivered from the immediate continual Operation and Government of the Spirit of God, not considering that where God is not, there
is the Devil, and where the Spirit rules not, there is all the Work of the
Flesh, though nothing be talked of but Spiritual and Christian Matters.
I say talked of: for the best ability of the natural Man can go no further

than Talk, and Notions and Opinions about Scripture Words and
Facts; in these he may be a great Critic, an acute Logician, a powerful
Orator, and know everything of Scripture except the Spirit and the Truth.

The *Serious Call* reclaimed Johnson from being, as he put it to
Boswell, 'a lax *talker* against religion': picking it up casually at
Oxford, and 'expecting to find it a dull book (as such books generally are)', he found himself outmatched by Law's passion and
reason. To include the *Serious Call* in the province of literature
as well as of religion is not stretching the point, for in a lucid
and supple style it conveys the true illumination of the time, the
high value given to reason as man's distinctive faculty, the
alliance between reason and intuition, and the sense of life as a
perfecting of man's better qualities (*Serious Call*, 75):

If we had a Religion that consisted in absurd superstitions, that had no
regard to the perfection of our nature, People might well be glad to
have some part of their life excused from it. But as the Religion of the
Gospel is only the refinement, and exaltation of our best Faculties, as
it only requires a life of the highest Reason, as it only requires us to
use this world as in reason it ought to be used, to live in such *tempers*
as are the glory of intelligent beings, to walk in such *wisdom* as exalts
our nature, and to practise such *piety* as will raise us to God; who can
think it grievous to live *always* in the spirit of such a Religion, to have
every part of his life full of it, but he that would think it much more
grievous, to be as the Angels of God in heaven?

If Law's 'vigorous mind', said Gibbon judiciously in his *Autobiography,* had not been 'clouded by enthusiasm, he might be
ranked with the most agreeable and ingenious writers of the
times'. One might safely go further; Law shows that the 'reason'
to which his age appealed was not always mere intellectual abstraction but could be (as with the Cambridge Platonists in the
seventeenth century) a faculty of spiritual light.

The Augustan writer, then, gained from religion an emotion
which no other subject so strongly inspired. Even on themes not
specifically religious he benefited from what was, despite controversy, a stable frame of accepted values. In Fielding, for instance,
there is little about religious fundamentals though much about

clergymen good and bad, deists and (in *Amelia*) moral conduct; yet his characteristic air of assurance owes much to the settled Hanoverian Protestantism which enabled him unquestioningly to 'place' these debatable matters. Much the same is true of Pope, though he was by birth a Roman Catholic and by friendship a Deist. He shows little sense of personal religion, or indeed of ability to philosophise deeply for himself, yet the current metaphysical certainty enables him to feel at home in life and to answer its problems, impregnable in ultimate conviction. Johnson, though sombre where Pope is confident, trusts no less in the established 'truths'; *Rasselas,* with little explicit reference to religion, is a deeply religious book. And Gray's *Elegy,* though its ostensible theme is the lot of the poor, has behind it the acceptance of Augustan faith, a ceremonial of feeling which unrebelliously submits to the settled order. With few exceptions the Augustans show as little uncertainty over fundamentals as architects did over style; whether orthodox or not they know the right solutions.

Did literature, finally, gain or lose in passing from seventeenth- to eighteenth-century religious feeling? As the emotional temperature dropped something precious was indeed lost. 'They say miracles are past', Shakespeare's Lafeu had already complained in *All's Well,*

and we have our philosophical persons to make modern and familiar, things supernatural and causeless. Hence is it that we make trifles of terrors, ensconsing ourselves into seeming knowledge, when we should submit ourselves to an unknown fear.

Ensconsing itself into seeming knowledge the eighteenth century sometimes found the world too intelligible. If, with Pope, one thought all discord harmony not understood, all partial evil universal good, it was a cause for satisfaction but it denied the convictions of human experience. One could be blinded by excess of light. For great poetry a sense of the tragic is nearly essential, a sense of the mystery of things without too much of that 'irritable reaching after fact and reason' which Keats deplored in Coleridge. From Chaucer to Yeats and Eliot the finest poetry has come from

those who have recognized evil as firmly as good. Among the Augustans the real poetry came from those in whom optimism wore thin (as with Pope), or was missing entirely (as with Johnson), or alternated with melancholy (as with Gray's *Elegy*, Goldsmith's *Deserted Village*, Cowper and Crabbe), or was eclipsed by a variety of moods outside the rational vogue (as with Smart, Collins, Burns and Blake). In much Augustan writing, despite its competence, good sense and good taste, we miss the sense of the numinous. Feeling may not be lacking, yet it often fails to move us; the *Hymn* Thomson appended to *The Seasons* is not without passion and clearly Thomson was full of exultation and awe, yet the awe arises from the thought of a universe designed to awaken man's unmitigated admiration, and the exultation inspires only a heavy rhetoric. Parnell's *Night-Piece on Death*, with tomb-stones, shrouded spirits, croaking raven and similar apparatus, has a theme that would have stirred the seventeenth century to an emotional crisis, yet it is a calm discourse reproving death for frightening men instead of seeming a natural state in the transition to heaven. Young is equally calm about the great mysteries (*Night Thoughts*, ix. 2049–50):

> *What's* Vice?—*Mere want of compass in our thought.*
> Religion *what?*—*The proof of* Common-Sense.

Religion was too often the proof of common sense; it was so for the Deists ('I banish all hypotheses from my philosophy', Toland observed); it was so for Pope's *Essay on Man* and for rationalistic divines like Bishop Watson of Llandaff, who rejected 'dark disquisitions concerning necessity and liberty, matter and spirit' in favour of what he thought the plain contents of the Bible (*Anecdotes of the Life of Richard Watson*, 1817, i. 15).

As in architecture, order and clarity were prevailing over complexity and mystery: such a process is valuable especially after an age of dispute. The Augustan simplification reduced but did not nullify the emotional nourishment which literature drew from religion, just as the rational order of Augustan church architecture did not mean an absence of religious feeling though its feeling was less complex than that of preceding ages. The rational

order of Augustan faith made the intimacy and variety of the
seventeenth century's faith unattainable, yet it inhibited neither
the tenderer moods nor the expression of deep and steady belief.
Of the former kind there are, for instance, Isaac Watt's *Horae
Lyricae* (1706), *Hymns and Spiritual Songs* (1707–9), and
Divine Songs (1715), Charles Wesley's verses for children, and,
supremely, Blake's *Songs of Innocence* (1789). Poems like *The
Lamb, The Little Black Boy, Holy Thursday, The Divine Image*
and *Night* are exquisitely 'innocent', and touched with mystical
penetration. Blake it is true differed profoundly from current
fashion; there is in him no lack of mystery, which haunts *The
Tyger, Jerusalem* and the prophetic books. He was a law to himself. Yet he had his religious affiliations within the century
(Smart's *Jubilate Agno* is a striking anticipation of his 'possessed'
manner and rapt perception), referred warmly to Methodism,
and was affected by the mystical element in Evangelicalism.
Not everything in Georgian religion was plain and orderly.

And even when it was plain and orderly, it might not lack in
feeling. A verse in the *Dies Irae*, Mrs Thrale relates, would
reduce Johnson to tears. The verse was that weighty one:

> *Quaerens me, sedisti lassus;*
> *Redemisti, crucem passus;*
> *Tantus labor non sit cassus!*[1]

Cowper too experienced and expressed both the agony and the
devotion of belief, and John Newton was redeemed from slave-
trading to share in writing the Olney hymns. Religion inspired
dignified and reverent styles and a tone of steadiness and gravity.
Its preference for the settled order prolonged injustices and it too
easily assumed a divine sanction for remediable evils. Yet against
this may be set the labours of many who from religious motives
fought against injustice at home and abroad. If they were not
revolutionary it was because they saw no reason to be so; stability
was too recent a gain, the mob (as France was to prove) was too
easily inflamed, and reforms could come quietly.

---

[1] "You have been weary, seeking me; suffering on the cross, you have redeemed me; let not such labor be in vain."

The religious background, then, was characteristically English, in the earnest dignity of the old order (conservative Anglican or Dissenting) and the fervent conscientiousness of the new (Evangelical). There is much to praise in it. As the last example of its quality let Tickell furnish some lines of his poem *On the Death of Mr. Addison,* which express its union of the personal and the social, a control and decorum which do not obscure the genuine emotion, and which foreshadow Gray's *Elegy*:

> *Can I forget the dismal night that gave*
> *My soul's best part for ever to the grave?*
> *How silent did his old companions tread,*
> *By midnight lamps, the mansions of the dead;*
> *Through breathing statues, then unheeded things,*
> *Through rows of warriors, and through walks of kings.*
> *What awe did the slow solemn knell inspire,*
> *The pealing organ, and the pausing choir;*
> *The duties by the lawn-rob'd prelate pay'd;*
> *And the last words, that dust to dust convey'd!*
> *While speechless o'er thy closing grave we bend,*
> *Accept these tears, thou dear departed friend.*

That, as much as anything in English, has the moving solemnity of the ceremony of death. Its quality is hardly imitable in any other period, and as clearly as *The Guardian's* praise of St. Paul's, it indicates that the Augustans were not deficient in religious feeling.

Retrospect: The Beautiful, The Sublime, and The Picturesque

༄

WALTER JOHN HIPPLE, JR.

If a history, a literal history, of the aesthetic thought of the eighteenth century were attempted, its purpose must be to educe from the facts a summary proposition, or set of summary propositions, which would distill the essence of a narrative, a narrative of changes in subject, in principle, in method, and in purpose within the discussion of aesthetics. The materials would be organized to display the parts of those changes — their stages or their aspects — and the data selected would be those most indicative of the progression studied, or which were causes of that progression. Yet a system of thought, if considered as a logical entity, is an indissoluble crystal, fixed, out of time and change. It is only the minds of the authors and students of those systems — their tastes, associational patterns, predominant passions, habits of inquiry, convictions and conjectures — which can change. A literal intellectual history, then, is really a history of the choices — choices of subject, of principle, of method — made by the authors of systems, and of the causes of those choices; it is an examination of systems taken not as logical entities but as psychological products. My concern, however, has been not with the history either of speculation or of taste in eighteenth-century

From *Walter John Hipple, Jr.*, The Beautiful, The Sublime, and the Picturesque in Eighteenth-Century British Aesthetic Theory *(Carbondale: Southern Illinois University Press, 1957), pp. 302–320. An introductory paragraph has been omitted here.*

292

Britain, but with those sets and systems of ideas which were then crystallized, to examine their facets, to compare their lusters, and to note the various refractions of the same light as it is transmitted through them.

For though reality may be one, the reflections of it in thought are many; we see only the image of reality through the prism of our own thought, an image which depends more directly on the nature of that prism of concepts and distinctions and patterns of inference through which we look than upon the object of our view. It is not more in our power after examining twenty systems of aesthetics than before to answer the naive and natural question, "What, then, *is* beauty after all?" What beauty is in itself, outside *all* system of thought, is indeterminable; we see only the image of it through the terms in which we describe it, the categories to which we refer it, the inferences by which we interpret it. The purpose which leads us to the objects of our contemplation, the presuppositions which have equipped us with a vocabulary and prepared us to distinguish some aspects of the object and to pass over others, our habits of reasoning — these circumstances make up that prism or lens through which we view reality; what our lens brings into focus, we see. Different lenses are of use for different purposes, to be sure, and we can grind our lens to fit the application; but dispense with it, we can not.

The problem in giving an account of a variety of systems of thought is to establish a set of terms and distinctions sufficiently comprehensive that the concepts and arguments of the systems discussed can be compared without prejudice in the terms of the analyst. Where the systems compared have many and major features in common — as with these British systems of the eighteenth century — this task is of course simpler. R. S. Crane has observed that the neo-classical tradition in literary criticism was not a body of doctrine; it was "a large but historically distinguishable aggregate of commonplace distinctions, of a highly flexible and ambiguous kind, out of which many variant critical systems and doctrines could be constructed"[1] — distinctions such as general and particular nature, instruction and pleasure, uniformity and variety, sublime and pathetic, and the like. A critic within this tradition might employ such of these distinctions as were

useful for solution of the problems to which he addressed himself, giving the various concepts the interpretation and emphasis appropriate to the structure of his thought. The tradition which we are here examining is confined to a more narrowly defined subject — the beautiful, sublime, and picturesque — than the miscellaneous critical tradition which Crane describes, and the discussions form a more closely integrated tradition; yet here too there is a great variance of doctrine within a common manner.

The common features of that manner, then. The aestheticians of this period all found their subject to be psychological: the central problem for them was not some aspect of the cosmos or of particular substances, nor was it found among the characteristics of human activity or of the modes of symbolic representation; one and all, they found their problem to be the specification and discrimination of certain kinds of feelings, the determination of the mental powers and susceptibilities which yielded those feelings, and of the impressions and ideas which excited them. For this reason, "taste" is their fundamental concern. Numerous inquiries were devoted to the faculty itself; and when this faculty was found to be derivative, consequent on special modes of action and interaction of other faculties, such inquiry could be complex enough. Even when the faculty of taste was not itself the major subject, it was still fundamental to every inquiry. Addison had declared that the arts were "to deduce their Laws and Rules from the general Sense and Taste of Mankind, and not from the Principles of those Arts themselves";[2] and though his "Pleasures of the Imagination" papers were not devoted to analyzing the operation of taste and imagination (for he considered the efficient causes inexplicable), his attention was merely shifted to those qualities, the beautiful, great, and uncommon, which were sensed and judged by those faculties. Hutcheson's "internal sense," likewise, is a kind of taste; and his overarching purpose in the "Inquiry concerning Beauty" was to establish the existence of such a discriminating sense as propaedeutic to his examination of morals in terms of similar senses. Gerard's *Essay on Taste* is only the most elaborate and analytical of a class of works common enough in this period, works having as their chief subject analysis of the faculty itself. Hume contributes his neat essay, "On

the Standard of Taste." The treatises of Burke, Lord Kames, and Blair, those of Reid, Alison, and Knight open with accounts, some of them elaborate, of taste and associated faculties as a natural preliminary to examination of its objects. Stewart and Reynolds are exempted, one by his dialectical, the other by his philosophical, method from beginning with taste; yet one devotes a discourse, the other an essay to it subsequently. Price and Repton, too, disclose their views, though the fragmentary nature of Repton's works prevents a connected account, and Price takes the views of Burke for granted, merely introducing additions and alterations at need.

Granted, then, that though Gerard alone of the writers here studied devotes the greater part of his treatise to this as his central theme, all the writers of the century begin with presuppositions about, and most with explicit discourses on, taste. The psychology of taste which all these writers employed was genetic rather than *a priori*: their analysis of mental phenomena was essentially historical, depending always upon determination of original impressions and the reduction of more complex ideas and feelings to combinations of these primary materials. *An Inquiry into the Original of Our Ideas of Beauty and Virtue, A Philosophical Inquiry into the Origin of Our Ideas of the Sublime and Beautiful*: such titles are testimony. And when Payne Knight entitled his work *An Analytical Inquiry into the Principles of Taste*, the implication was the same: this *analysis* is the breaking down of the complicated phenomena to simpler elements and principles of combination. It is this trait of the eighteenth-century British systems, I take it, which is so often called "empirical." Continental rationalisms, and those British systems of the next century which were modeled on the German, also find their principles in psychology. But they were not genetic or historical; they appeal instead to *a priori* principles and categories of thought. It is the habit of the eighteenth-century British philosophers to analyze those principles and categories, to find explicable what the rationalists take as primary givens; and this analysis, these experiential explanations, are a major feature of what is called empiricism. Such empiricism is, to be sure, a very different thing in the writings of a Hume or Alison from what

it is in a Reid or Kames; but even those Scots who took issue with the systematic reductions of Hume, who asserted a host of primary and original sensibilities and powers, still used their greater number of principles as Hume used his more simple and elegant postulates — used them, that is, as simple elements into which the parts of more complex phenomena could be resolved, and from the effects of which the effects of those more complex phenomena could be calculated.

The notion of an unanalyzable *gestalt* would be a fiction to these writers; the whole is resolvable into and explicable by its elementary parts and the relations connecting them. Alison's theory is the type of this mode of philosophizing in aesthetics, both in the simplicity of its principles and in the intricacy of its analyses. Reynolds — and Shaftesbury, too — is exceptional to this generalization, for his dialectical way of thinking requires neither such a set of elementary notions nor such analysis of complexes; the analogical principle of generality and particularity applies in one fashion or another to every branch of his subject. Yet most of Reynolds' dicta lend themselves readily to statement in the more conventional mode; Reynolds, too, is psychologically oriented, and only gives the faculty psychology of his age an unusual dialectical twist.

That taste should be the fundamental concept in the aesthetics of the eighteenth century is a consequence of the philosophizing of criticism. One of the tendencies Crane has noted in the evolution of neoclassical literary criticism is "an important shift of emphasis in the critical writing of the mid-eighteenth century — a shift that exalted the philosopher (in the current sense of an inquirer into the operations of the mind) over the artist or the mere critic as the expert best qualified to determine the rules of art and that served, hence, to bring about, within criticism, a sharper separation between criticism itself, considered as a codification of past artistic experience, and the 'demands of nature,' on which its precepts and judgments, if they are to be valid, must ultimately rest."[3] The subject of the present book has automatically selected for comment those writers of whom this new method was most characteristic: for to extract and refine the sublime and beautiful wherever they are imbedded in nature or

in art requires some "tincture of philosophy" in those who would mine such ore. The rules and conventions of literary criticism might enable many a criticaster to pronounce on particular works with no more painful consequence than triteness, and even that might be redeemed by novelty of subject; but in the more abstract and philosophical examination of the beautiful, to be trite is to be worthless — only the logic of system is of value here. In aesthetics, accordingly, some degree of philosophic system was present from the first; the new character noted by Crane in the literary criticism of mid-century began in the "philosophical criticism" with Hutcheson. After Hutecheson's *Inquiry*, no writer could pretend to importance as an aesthetician without credentials as a philosopher, or at any rate without a native bent for analysis and systematization.

Not only, then, was this mode of aesthetics founded on psychology, but upon an empirical, genetic, and usually associationist psychology: philosophic principles were sought in human nature, philosophic method was found in a mental atomism of elements and laws of combination. Such an orientation directs attention away from the technical aspects of artistic construction and towards the universal properties of natural or artificial objects which affect the perceiving mind. It is the perceiving mind, moreover, not the mind as creative, from which principles are drawn. Any psychology accounts of course for both perception and creation, taste and genius; but there may still be a difference of priority and emphasis. It would be plausible to argue that one difference between neo-classical literary criticism and that of the Romantic period is that in neo-classical criticism the principles of examination and evaluation are drawn ultimately from the nature of the audience, in Romantic criticism from the powers of the artist. It is true equally of the aesthetics of the eighteenth century as of its criticism that principles are derived from the mind beholding beauty or sublimity, the mind in which these characters subsisted as feelings. The artist's powers, as represented in his works, are considered as among the sources of aesthetic pleasure, and, like the technical problems of artistic construction, are treated subordinately to the emotions of taste. Gerard, to be sure, authored a lengthy and closely reasoned *Essay*

on Genius, a work which, like Alison's *Essays on Taste,* works
out in detail a mental atomism; but this essay has little to the
purpose on the beautiful or the sublime. And so with the other
studies of genius in the period; except for generalizations on
the connection of original genius, the sublime, and primitive
society where human nature shoots wild and free, or on the
correlation of powers of imagination with a vague Longinian
sublimity, there is little attempt to bring such studies into
relation with the beautiful, sublime, picturesque.

Indeed, the chief discussion of the artist's work in this tradition
(setting aside Reynolds' *Discourses,* and even these tend to resolve
genius into taste) is in the controversy on the picturesque. But
although Gilpin might write essays on sketching landscape, his
central concern is the cultivation of the perceiving taste through
the knowledge, and practice, of art; and his picturesque traveler,
though he sets out on his rambles to find scenes of art from the
hand of nature, returns preferring nature unimproved to the
tinsel efforts of art. Repton, as a practicing artist concerned to
justify his art and himself as a professor of it, uses his status only
to authorize his analyses of taste. Price and Knight, again, have
to do with genius or art only to the extent that they wish, partly
by study of the works of art, to form a taste which will both
guide artists and gratify amateurs.

The beautiful, sublime, and picturesque being feelings raised
up in the mind from impressions and associated ideas, it was
natural that the mind as perceiving rather than creating should
have been the focus of discussion. At the same time, another
circumstance in the nature of the subject militated against extensive consideration of art itself. Beauty, sublimity, and picturesqueness are found in nature as well as in art. A transcendental
aesthetician, acknowledging this fact, might see in it only an
excellent reason for beginning with, and largely confining himself
to, art: for the whole includes the part, and to determine the
beauty of art necessarily determines also that simpler and less
complete beauty of nature. But this reasoning is plausible only
if method is not analytic and genetic: for if we are to resolve the
beauty of the complex into the beauties of its components and
their relations, we will not be tempted to start with the whole.

We will begin instead with the elementary and original — the elements being original not only in a logical but also in a chrono-logical sense. What is it in colors which fascinates the child? What is the taste of men uncorrupted by artificial society — the primitives of an heroic age, the untutored but feeling rustic, the country gentleman remote from the fashions of London, or the sophisticated connoisseur whose very sophistication enables him to allow for the effects of custom, education, and vogue? What is the etymology of "picturesque"? To what objects was the epithet "beautiful" first applied? Questions such as these come naturally to the mind which habitually thinks in this vein. Since nature is prior to art both in the history of our experience and in the order of creation, and since nature is the simpler, we begin with nature — or, when we do employ art works as data, we are likely to ignore or minimize in them those characteristics dis-tinctively artificial. In nature, then, and increasingly in natural scenery — in the gilded colors of sunsets, the tangled intricacies of wooded glens, the formless might of stormy oceans — we find our problems and data. When these data have yielded to our analyses, when we have in hand our principles of unity in variety, of the association of moral traits with line and color, or what-ever they may be — then, and only then, may we approach the complicated and derivative products of art. From them we derive additional principles: we discern the influence of design and of fitness (or, if we have seen design and fitness in the works of nature, we see them here in a new relationship) ; we uncover the effects of imitation; and we one by one account for the differentiae of art from nature.

It remains a constant characteristic of these aestheticians — Reynolds excepted — that their analyses apply to natural objects first, or to artificial objects not distinguished from natural, and only by secondary elaboration to art works as differentiated from natural things. There is yet another common characteristic con-sequent on their taking as fundament human nature: that nature, being common to all men, or at any rate having common poten-tialities, implies that there is a normal taste. To exhibit the standard of taste is an object at which all these writers aim. Crane has noted that in neo-classical literary criticism there was

a shift in emphasis between the age of Dryden and that of Johnson, that the standard was at first rested chiefly on rules induced
from the works sanctioned by universal consensus, that as
criticism became more philosophical the standard came to be
grounded more on theories of human nature.[4] The aetheticians
we are here studying put the standard from the first on the basis
of human nature; though some still laid stress on the argument
from consensus as well (Blair, for instance, or Reynolds, whose
principle of generality naturally accords with that argument),
others skeptically eschew it. Gerard and Knight are as aware as
any modern relativist made skeptical by excess of knowledge, that
there is no consensus except within a cultural tradition, that even
taken over many ages the judgment of Peking and Tokyo does
not coincide with that of Athens and London. Indeed, so long
as taste is considered merely as a species of sensation it does not
admit of a standard; not only do cultures vary, but each man's
constitution and experience determine his peculiar likings and
aversions, and these are for him preferable to any other's.

Yet each of our writers owed allegiance to the standard, or to a
standard; and many — Burke, Gerard, Hume, Lord Kames, Reynolds, Knight, Stewart — devised explicit arguments to demonstrate a rightness in taste. Each might justify the standard by his
own peculiar principles — Hume by shifting the argument from
the impressions of sensibility to the idea of critical competence,
Kames by appealing to original senses which testify to the universality and perfection of human nature, Reynolds by using
his contrary of the one and the many, Burke by examining the
common basis of human faculties in the external senses. But
their works were all (in the language of Hogarth's subtitle)
"Written with a View of Fixing the Fluctuating Ideas of Taste."
For it is possible to examine the causes of our preferences and
aversions, to determine which are unavoidable, which accidental;
which universal to all men, which common to our culture, our
era, or our class, which peculiar to ourselves. The effect on us
of a complex whole can be analyzed, reduced to the operation
of simple causes. Our response to these simple elements may be
a matter of feeling, and the common feelings of mankind may
for these be a standard; but the proper response to the complex

whole becomes a matter of computation after such analysis. Taste as judgment is referred to principles and is conscious of grounds; it is (as Blair put it) "a sort of compound power, in which the light of the understanding always mingles, more or less, with the feelings of sentiment."[5] All the treatises of the century are implicitly determinations of the standard: if (for instance) the sublime be what Burke or Kames or Alison avers, and produced by the causes assigned, and we feel it not — then we feel amiss. The analytic method of this tradition is the method *par excellence* not merely of showing that there is a standard, but of determining what that standard is. The dialectic method of Shaftesbury and Reynolds pronounces with equal force that there is a true Taste, a true Beauty, but the showing forth of that taste and that beauty depends less on cold precision of analysis, more on the cultivation and eloquence of the dialectician.

So far, I have been concerned with traits common to all, or almost all, systems of the century. Was there, then, no change, no progress? Certainly there is no simple and straightforward development, no progress from shadowy intuition to the blaze of full illumination. Neither the characteristic subject matter, the philosophic principles, the prevailing method, nor even the doctrines changed in any way lending itself to ready generalization. Intellectual history, like biological, is a record of haphazard mutation and opportunistic development. In just this random way the century had opened with a triad of aesthetic characters: Addison's uncommon, great, and beautiful. Novelty, which is not co-ordinate with the great and the beautiful, remained in the discussion for a time: Hutcheson mentions it, Akenside adopts it in the first edition of his *Pleasures of Imagination*, Gerard allows it to stand as one of the internal senses. But Hume and Hogarth ignored it, and Burke struck it out, one would think for once and all, as a co-ordinate character; but there is no system in the history of systems, and Reid — in 1785! — again introduces novelty as an organizing topic, though very properly rejecting its claims to independent status.

The division of this book into two parts implies a more important shift in subject matter: beautiful and sublime become beautiful, sublime, and picturesque. Yet note: Alison, even in

1811, devotes scarcely a paragraph to the picturesque, nor is picturesqueness a major topic for Stewart. We can say truly, only that the picturesque is a topic introduced by Gilpin, and which was with some later writers a major focus of interest. Whether a writer after Gilpin finds the picturesque a topic of engrossing importance and co-ordinate with beauty and sublimity (like Price), or though important not co-ordinate (like Knight), or not important (like Allison) — these variations are functions of the systems, and the systems do not fall into a chronological pattern. The analyst can note that it was the predominance of Burke's special view of beauty which led to the distinction of the picturesque by Gilpin, and that the inadequacies of Gilpin's analysis opened the way to fresh explorations by Price and Knight: but these are the vagaries of historical accident, or at any rate the effects of extra-philosophical causes, not the inevitable rush of intellectual orthogenesis.

Another shift accompanies the evolution of the picturesque, perhaps partly causes it. Discussion of scenery and gardening runs through the century — Addison is eloquent on these topics. But as the picturesque came into favor as a taste and as a topic, the discussion of landscape and of landscape gardening came to occupy a far larger, often an overwhelmingly predominant, place in the discussion. The works of the end of the century abound alike with detached analysis of the forms, colors, and textures of scenery, with practical rules for arranging Nature to suit man's convenience or for disarranging her to suit his wilder fancy, and with poetical rhapsodies on the delights, aesthetic, moral, or religious, which Nature affords.

The philosophic method employed throughout this tradition of discussion of the beautiful, sublime, and picturesque was, as I have suggested, analytic and genetic;[6] yet some writers within the tradition performed but superficial analyses, others pursued more searching inquiries; and various authors resolved the gross phenomena into different elemental principles. A sketch of the varieties of causal explanation adduced has been included in my Introduction; but a recapitulation in different terms may not be useless here. Shaftesbury and Reynolds, it should be noted, stand pretty much outside the tradition methodologically, for

though they, like the more literal and differential writers, grounded their systems on psychological principles, their method of inquiry was dialectical and organic, and their Beauty one, not a set of related beauties. Considering, however, the other writers —

Addison distinguished the three characters, great, uncommon, and beautiful, and noted some of the leading components of these characters — that, for instance, there is beauty of color, of proportion, of arrangement. Yet there is little further analysis of these components; other obvious physical varieties both of sublimity and beauty are omitted; and the complicated interconnections between the physical and mental worlds are quite ignored, even though Addison had available a rudimentary associational theory.

Hutcheson's far more philosophical theory pursued the analytic approach much further. His purpose, the demonstration of an internal sense of beauty, led him to adopt a single analytical device — the notion of uniformity in variety — with which to reduce all forms of beauty, including that beauty of mind which Addison had left out of account, to a single formula. But though physical, moral, and intellectual beauties are all treated by Hutcheson, his system (in which association plays a limited role, and often one of interference with the perception of beauty) does not lend itself to penetrating investigation of their commingling and reciprocal influence; nor does it encourage exploration of the sublime alongside that of beauty.

In the philosophy of Hume, an associationism is employed to analyze most of the phenomena of human nature to their ultimate constituents; but Hume's aesthetic is sketchy. Rather disappointingly, he does not find much connection between physical and moral beauty, has little to say on those beauties immediately pleasing, makes no effort to separate design and fitness from utility; these and other negligences are, of course, the consequence of Hume's always mentioning beauty incidentally to some other object of analysis — beauty itself was never the focus of his attention. Disappointing, too, is the fragment of a theory of sublimity which Hume invented, suggestive, like the essays on taste and tragedy, of the subtle analysis which his powerful psychology could have yielded had it been turned upon such subjects.

The method of Hume was developed by Gerard, and more rigorously and elaborately by Alison; but before Gerard published, Hogarth's theory was brought forward, employing a method very different from Hume's but equally characteristic of this tradition. Hogarth resolves beauty into a half-dozen elements — fitness, variety, &c. — all which, however, are reduced to traits of lines: line becomes the element into which all manner of beauty is analyzed. Like Hutcheson, Hogarth does not develop a distinct aesthetic of the sublime, for this his linear analysis would not readily allow; rather, he reckons greatness only an excellence supervening to beauty. And for Hogarth, as for all analytic writers, moral and intellectual beauty is different from physical; though some dispositions of lines can signify moral traits, they are not beautiful by reason of this signification.

In the theory of Gerard, eclectic though it is, Hume's method is that largely pursued; the analysis is carried out in terms of ideas, impressions, and operations of imagination. Though Gerard (like most eighteenth-century writers) uses the term "association" to designate the less close, even the capricious or disruptive, linkages among ideas and impressions, his system is, in a wider sense of the term, associational; and its breadth of scope, flexibility of analysis, and subtlety of argument are partly attributable to Gerard's use of this powerful analytical tool. As in Hume, the connection of physical and moral beauty consists in the dependence of both taste and virtue on operations of imagination, in the similarity of the pleasures from these two kinds of excellence, and in the reciprocal influence of character and taste. Such connections of resemblance and of cause and effect are the marks of a system which essentially differentiates ethics from aesthetics. All of the analytic systems make such differentiation, for even in Hutcheson, in Reid, and in Alison the beauty of virtue is distinct from the virtue.

The system of Burke, more radically than most of the theories of this school, treats beauty and sublimity in terms of constituent elemental qualities, each producing its own part of the total effect without interaction: the beauty of an object has so many quanta of the beauty of smoothness, and so forth. Burke's logic, designed to separate the components of complex objects, and

with a strong bias towards the discovery of simple natural causes operating directly upon our sensibility, is well adapted to such a system. And although Burke makes use of association, his more distinctive analysis is into physiological stimuli; since the separate elements of beauty act individually upon the nervous system without being blended, as it were, in the mind, Burke's atomism comes to lay a good deal more stress on the atoms than on the relations among them, which are largely reduced to a matter of addition and subtraction. This trait of the system produces a certain dogmatic inflexibility and a negligence of context in assessing the aesthetic effects of the simple properties. All of those theories, in fact, which suppose distinct responses by external or internal senses to separate aesthetic elements necessarily share this inflexibility, for the sense is always prepared to respond to the appropriate stimulus. The physiological apparatus of Burke's system, and of Hogarth's too, makes it especially liable to this defect. The defect can be minimized by choice of a single principle capable of many kinds of applications — as in Hutcheson — or by development of a large number of senses — as in Kames. Nonetheless, the more purely associational analyses have an inherent capacity for modulations and contextual adjustments which the systems reposing on a sense or senses lack.

Burke's postulated physiological mechanism enables him to draw the sharpest of separations between beauty and sublimity, and precludes him from admitting novelty, the picturesque, or any third character into his system. So definite was Burke's division of beauty and sublimity that even those later writers who wished to deny any absolute contrariety of the two characters — Knight, or Stewart, or (outside the analytic group) Reynolds — still often used the terms as if they constituted an exclusive and exhaustive distinction, or employed the concepts as organizing principles for their discussions.

The distinguishing feature of the system of Lord Kames, and one which he derived from, or as a member of, that sect of Scottish philosophy which arose to combat the reductive analyses of Hume, is the assertion of a multitude of original perceptions through separate senses provided by Providence for their reception. The consequence of this bent is, of course, that aesthetic

phenomena are readily broken down into a variety of atomic elements, each class perceived through a special sense. The components are so varied that analyses of very considerable complexity can be worked out, and the results are sufficiently precise that Kames can build from them a synthetic system of criticism, elaborate for the literary arts, less so for gardening and architecture.

Blair's purpose is very like that of Lord Kames: to work out an analysis the results of which can be put to use in synthesis of a theory of the literary arts. But Blair's interest is more literary and less philosophical than that of Kames; his principles are fewer, his results more general, his synthetic theory more detached from the preceding analysis. Clearly inferior to Kames in connecting his aesthetic with his criticism, and kept by his eagerness to get on with the criticism from penetrating very far in the aesthetic, Blair nonetheless has one advantage: he is free of Kames's penchant for finding special senses and final causes, and he not only keeps open the investigation of efficient causes but even makes some effort to resolve the various modes of sublimity into one by association of ideas (though allowing beauty to be one only through association of like feelings from the different modes of it). His deficiency in middle principles of analysis, however, his tendency to leap from first principle to particular instance, leaves Blair's system poorly verified and somewhat meager.

With Reid, the sublime and beautiful were brought within the framework of a philosophic system, and both the merits and defects of Reid's aesthetic follow from that system. Because of Reid's theory of direct perception of the outer world, he finds that beauty and sublimity subsist as real and objective excellences in things; and since matter itself can not be "excellent" except as connected with mind by some relation, beauty and sublimity must ultimately derive from mind. But Reid brings forward little evidence to support this position; it rests on deduction from the principles of his metaphysics, which is in turn established intuitively. Neither Reid's purpose in treating beauty nor his characteristic method of thought lead him to undertake detailed or subtle analysis, and his aesthetic system,

saving only the principle that all beauty is from mind, contains little novelty either in doctrine or in demonstration.

The analytic and genetic method is given its most systematic, its most exhaustive, development by Alison. Employing an associational psychology, operating wholly in terms of ideas and habits of imagination, Alison develops an aesthetic both comprehensive and subtle, equally adapted to formulating broad principles and to making delicate adjustment to particular contexts. Not only does Alison work out all the permutations of the elements of his system — the component ideas and the modes of their combination — but he employs the most rigorous inductive method, consciously organizing data and contriving experiments to meet the requirements of inductive logic. Hume, Gerard, and Alison had, of these writers, the most complete grasp of the kind of logic appropriate to an analytic system, recognizing that neither deduction from principles of human nature (whether these be indemonstrable or established inductively) nor induction from the raw data of taste is alone adequate for proof in aesthetics, wherein plurality of causes and intermixture of effects abound. Both deductive and inductive inference must be used, and their consilience alone constitutes proof. But since the powers and sensibilities of human nature which enter into aesthetic response are several, and their operations more than ordinarily subtle, the deductive process can not be pursued safely without some view of the law towards which demonstration is to be directed; and such view is afforded by empirical generalization from the data of taste. Here is the use of consensus: to suggest empirical laws which can serve as hypotheses towards which the ratiocinative part of the process can be oriented. The ratiocination is the principal part of the proof, and that part from which the bulk of the doctrine will be evolved. Gerard lays perhaps too much emphasis on successively ascending inductions rising to more and more general laws, and tends to see the deduction as only verificative of results already arrived at inductively; and yet he does not select his data (in the *Essay on Taste* at any rate) to meet express conditions for such induction. Alison's concern is to establish the most general laws of taste, those from which the more particular rules of judgment

and criticism can be deduced; and such first principles must be proved, if they are proved at all, inductively. It is in the perfection of inductive techniques for establishing these most general laws that Alison is distinguished beyond any other writer of this tradition, beyond even Hume, from whom much of the technique may have been borrowed.

It might be argued that one line of development within this tradition is in this very matter: the perfecting of inductive technique and the co-ordination of inductive and deductive procedures in the process of proof. But there is no consistent evolution. Hume, well before mid-century, had in hand such a logic; Gerard and Alison advance beyond him in applying it to aesthetic subjects; but contemporary with these men are Gilpin, Repton, and Price, with little conception of it — or, if it be judged unfair to cite men without pretensions to philosophy, Blair and Reid will serve as well. Even Payne Knight, though he is a systematic writer, has less grasp of inductive procedure than Alison. All that can be argued, I think, is that three major writers at the end of the century — Alison, Knight, and Stewart — had a more philosophic command of logic as applied to aesthetics than did any earlier cluster of writers. This is negligible as a generalization, especially if we reflect that Alison, in 1790, had advanced beyond the later writers.

Addison had set in progress the inquiry concerning the sublime and beautiful by discriminating the characters without explaining the mode of their operation; his very abandonment of the quest for efficient causes opened the question to other writers. In much the same way, Gilpin initiated a new phase of the discussion by introducing the character of the picturesque without finding any plausible explanation of its influence upon us. Addison had few predecessors and no adequate tools of analysis; Gilpin, though numerous systems lay ready to his hand, yet failed so signally to define his problem with accuracy, and performed his inductions with so little care, that his effort served chiefly as an incitement to later inquirers infected with his taste but disappointed in his analysis of its objects.

The theory of Price, brought forward shortly after, displays an interesting shift in the technique of analysis; for though Price

stands forth as the champion of Burke, he defends Burke's theory mostly in foreign terms. For Burke the essential device used to explain the sublime and beautiful was a physiological hypothesis; but though Price does affirm allegiance even to this, it is not easy to justify the picturesque by the theory of Burke. The real, though but half-acknowledged, basis of Price's theory is associational. Burke, too, of course, had employed associational psychology; but in Price, what was subordinate in Burke has become predominant. The shift is real; but it is an imperfect indication of a general transformation of aesthetic theory into purely associational terms. Hume had been an associationist before Burke; Knight, writing after Gerard and Alison, after Price had attenuated the physiological part of Burke's theory, still re-introduces into the discussion a new physiological hypothesis to account for the picturesque.

The special merit of Price's method is his skilful comparison and opposition of the aesthetic characters, of beauty, sublimity, picturesqueness, and their opposites, through detailed analyses of the elements of line, texture, light, and color, and of the composition of these elements into distinct characters. But his theory was left exposed to much misunderstanding because of the confusion in which, after all, the psychological mechanisms were left, the wavering between a notion of direct action upon the nervous system and an associational theory the reaches of which were not fully explored. Knight's major work, the *Analytical Inquiry*, left nothing to conjecture, for it is organized faculty by faculty, the analysis moving by stages from simple sensation to refined judgment and complicated passion. It is in the clarity with which the beautiful, sublime, and picturesque are related to these faculties that Knight's acuteness and originality is displayed. The ambiguities of the terms "beautiful" and "picturesque" are resolved with unusual elegance through Knight's theory of transitive meanings, which permits him to assign the different meanings to the objects and operations of the different faculties.

Repton's aesthetic is more applied than theoretic; his general principles, repeatedly though not always consistently enumerated, are never systematically evolved either from empirical induction

or from a theory of human nature. Taken as topics of argument, however, they allow Repton to draw up rules for the practice of his art, though the rules do not follow so inevitably from the principles as to prevent Repton's taste from undergoing considerable change in the course of his career. But Repton's aesthetic is too much an *ad hoc* justification of his style in gardening and architecture to dwell upon his method.

Stewart, however, introduces a novelty in method. Still more than the analyses of other writers of this tradition, his is historical and genetic. Alison had been content to trace each of the various modes and forms of beauty separately to its mental root; Knight to rest each upon an appropriate faculty and to treat the faculties in a sequence corresponding to the order of their development; and so with other writers — each traced the kinds of beauty individually to their origins. Stewart, however, and Stewart alone, takes the progress of the mind to be in principle like a chain, and he follows it link by link. The analytic device by which he traces the chain is the theory of transitive meanings which he adopted from Knight; the progress he studies is a progress in the wider and more various applications of terms. Stewart's view that inductive method in mental philosophy may concern itself with the laws describing the connections of matter and mind, but not with the manner of that union, allows him freedom from the rigidities imposed by physiological hypotheses or the postulation of internal senses; but his own conception of linear and stepwise development along a thread of transitive meanings imposes its own restrictions.

My partial review of the writers of this school does not disclose marked tendencies or striking improvements; rather, it presents, within the limits of a broad common method, a scattered variety of particular systems. The different purposes of the authors partly account for this variety — whether the purpose is to complete a philosophical system (as with Stewart) or to prepare a prolegomenon to some other branch of philosophy (as with Hutcheson), whether to treat the nature and conditions of an art (as with Reynolds) or to justify a particular style in an art (as in Repton), whether to find the roots of the principles of taste (as with Alison) or to form a new taste (as with Gilpin).

The philosophic allegiance of the authors is a factor too — whether they are dialecticians (like Shaftesbury and Reynolds), thorough analysts (like Hume and Alison), or intuitionists (like Kames and Reid). Each system, again, reflects the state and momentum of current discussion: a writer may introduce a new problem — this Addison did; or may add a new dimension to discussion already in progress — which Gilpin did; may incorporate previous efforts into a more comprehensive theory — as Burke did Hogarth's, or Price Burke's; or may demolish false views which had gained currency — as did Knight. And doubtless each system reflects the tastes of its author and of its age; Hogarth's theory might be used to justify one set of preferences, Price's another. But after all these causes, philosophical and extra-philosophical, are allowed for, there is still, as it appears to me, an element of surprise and originality; the different habits of thought arise from causes too subtle to be categorized. There is perhaps an analogy with mutations in the biological world: causes presumably exist, but all except the grossest escape us. There is little pattern, even in retrospect; and no prediction.

NOTES

[1] R. S. Crane, "On Writing the History of English Criticism, 1650–1800," *University of Toronto Quarterly*, XXII (July, 1953), 385.

[2] *The Spectator*, No. 29 (April 3, 1711), I, 109.

[3] Crane, "English Neoclassical Criticism: An Outline Sketch," in *Critics and Criticism, Ancient and Modern* (Chicago: University of Chicago Press, 1952), p. 383.

[4] *Ibid.*, pp. 382–84.

[5] Blair, *Lectures,* ii, ed. cit., I, 40.

[6] The method which I have called "analytic and genetic" appears to be similar to the "logistic" method which Richard P. McKeon describes in his intricate "Philosophy and Method," *JP*, XLVIII, No. 22 (October 25, 1951), 653–82.

Towards Defining an Age of Sensibility

ᨀ

NORTHROP FRYE

The period of English literature which covers roughly the second half of the eighteenth century is one which has always suffered from not having a clear historical or functional label applied to it. I call it here the age of sensibility, which is not intended to be anything but a label. This period has the "Augustan" age on one side of it and the "Romantic" movement on the other, and it is usually approached transitionally, as a period of reaction against Pope and anticipation of Wordsworth. The chaos that results from treating this period, or any other, in terms of reaction has been well described by Professor Crane in a recent article in the Toronto Quarterly. What we do is to set up, as the logical expression of Augustanism, some impossibly pedantic view of following rules and repressing feelings, which nobody could ever have held, and then treat any symptom of freedom or emotion as a departure from this. Our students are thus graduated with a vague notion that the age of sensibility was the time when poetry moved from a reptilian Classicism, all cold and dry reason, to a mammalian Romanticism, all warm and wet feeling.

As for the term "pre-romantic," that, as a term for the age itself, has the peculiar demerit of committing us to anachronism before we start, and imposing a false teleology on everything

From ELH, *vol. 23, no. 2, June 1956 (Baltimore: The Johns Hopkins Press), pp. 144–52.*

we study. Not only did the "pre-romantics" not know that the Romantic movement was going to succeed them, but there has probably never been a case on record of a poet's having regarded a later poet's work as the fulfilment of his own. However, I do not care about terminology, only about appreciation for an extraordinarily interesting period of English literature, and the first stage in renewing that appreciation seems to me the gaining of a clear sense of what it is in itself.

Some languages use verb-tenses to express, not time, but the difference between completed and continuous action. And in the history of literature we become aware, not only of periods, but of a recurrent opposition of two views of literature. These two views are the Aristotelian and the Longinian, the aesthetic and the psychological, the view of literature as product and the view of literature as process. In our day we have acquired a good deal of respect for literature as process, notably in prose fiction. The stream of consciousness gets careful treatment in our criticism, and when we compare Arnold Bennett and Virginia Woolf on the subject of Mrs. Brown we generally take the side of Virginia Woolf. So it seems that our age ought to feel a close kinship with the prose fiction of the age of sensibility, when the sense of literature as process was brought to a peculiarly exquisite perfection by Sterne, and in lesser degree by Richardson and Boswell.

All the great story-tellers, including the Augustan ones, have a strong sense of literature as a finished product. The suspense is thrown forward until it reaches the end, and is based on our confidence that the author knows what is coming next. A story-teller does not break his illusion by talking to the reader as Fielding does, because we know from the start that we are listening to Fielding telling a story — that is, Johnson's arguments about illusion in drama apply equally well to prose fiction of Fielding's kind. But when we turn to *Tristram Shandy* we not only read the book but watch the author at work writing it: at any moment the house of Walter Shandy many vanish and be replaced by the author's study. This does break the illusion, or would if there were any illusion to break, but here we are not

being led into a story, but into the process of writing a story: we wonder, not what is coming next, but what the author will think of next.

Sterne is, of course, an unusually pure example of a process-writer, but even in Richardson we find many of the same characteristics. Johnson's well-known remark that if you read Richardson for the story you would hang yourself indicates that Richardson is not interested in a plot with a quick-march rhythm. Richardson does not throw the suspense forward, but keeps the emotion at a continuous present. Readers of *Pamela* have become so fascinated by watching the sheets of Pamela's manuscript spawning and secreting all over her master's house, even into the recesses of her clothes, as she fends off assault with one hand and writes about it with the other, that they sometimes overlook the reason for an apparently clumsy device. The reason is, of course, to give the impression of literature as process, as created on the spot out of the events it describes. And in the very beginning of *Boswell in London* we can see the boy of twenty-one already practising the art of writing as a continuous process from experience. When he writes of his adventure with Louisa he may be writing several days after the event, but he does not use his later knowledge.

In poetry the sense of literature as a finished product normally expresses itself in some kind of regularly recurring metre, the general pattern of which is established as soon as possible. In listening to Pope's couplets we have a sense of continually fulfilled expectation which is the opposite of obviousness: a sense that eighteenth-century music also often gives us. Such a technique demands a clear statement of what sound-patterns we may expect. We hear at once the full ring of the rhyming couplet, and all other sound-patterns are kept to a minimum. In such a line as:

> And strains from hard-bound brains eight lines a year,

the extra assonance is a deliberate discord, expressing the difficulties of constipated genius. Similarly with the alliteration in:

> Great Cibber's brazen, brainless brothers stand,

and the fact that these are deliberate discords used for parody indicates that they are normally not present. Johnson's disapproval of such devices in serious contexts is written all over the *Lives of the Poets.*

When we turn from Pope to the age of sensibility, we get something of the same kind of shock that we get when we turn from Tennyson or Matthew Arnold to Hopkins. Our ears are assaulted by unpredictable assonances, alliterations, inter-rhymings and echolalia:

> Mie love ys dedde,
> Gon to hys death-bedde ...

> With brede ethereal wove,
> O'erhang his wavy bed ...

> The couthy cracks begin whan supper's o'er,
> The cheering bicker gars them glibly gash ...

> But a pebble of the brook
> Warbled out these metres meet ...

In many of the best-known poems of the period, in Smart's *Song to David,* in Chatterton's elegies, in Burns's songs and Blake's lyrics, even in some of the Wesley hymns, we find a delight in refrain for refrain's sake. Sometimes, naturally, we can see the appropriate literary influences helping to shape the form, such as the incremental repetition of the ballad, or Old Norse alliteration in *The Fatal Sisters.* And whatever may be thought of the poetic value of the Ossianic poems, most estimates of the value parrot Wordsworth, and Wordsworth's criticisms of Ossian's imagery are quite beside the point. The vague generalized imagery of Ossian, like the mysterious resonant names and the fixed epithets, are part of a deliberate and well unified scheme. *Fingal* and *Temora* are long poems for

the same reason that *Clarissa* is a long novel: not because there is a complicated story to be told, as in *Tom Jones* or an epic of Southey, but because the emotion is being maintained at a continuous present by various devices of repetition.

The reason for these intensified sound-patterns is, once again, an interest in the poetic process as distinct from the product. In the composing of poetry, where rhyme is as important as reason, there is a primary stage in which words are linked by sound rather than sense. From the point of view of sense this stage is merely free or uncontrolled association, and in the way it operates it is very like the dream. Again like the dream, it has to meet a censor-principle, and shape itself into intelligible patterns. Where the emphasis is on the communicated product, the qualities of consciousness take the lead: a regular metre, clarity of syntax, epigram and wit, repetition of sense in anti-thesis and balance rather than of sound. Swift speaks with admiration of Pope's ability to get more "sense" into one couplet than he can into six: concentration of sense for him is clearly a major criterion of poetry. Where the emphasis is on the original process, the qualities of subconscious association take the lead, and the poetry becomes hypnotically repetitive, oracular, incantatory, dreamlike and in the original sense of the word charming. The response to it includes a subconscious factor, the surrendering to a spell. In Ossian, who carries this tendency further than anyone else, the aim is not concentration of sense but diffusion of sense, hence Johnson's remark that anybody could write like Ossian if he would abandon his mind to it. Literature as product may take a lyrical form, as it does in the sublime ode about which Professor Maclean has written so well, but it is also the conception of literature that makes the longer continuous poem possible. Literature as process, being based on an irregular and unpredictable coincidence of sound-patterns, tends to seek the brief or even the fragmentary utterance, in other words to centre itself on the lyric, which accounts for the feeling of a sudden emergence of a lyrical impulse in the age of sensibility.

The "pre-romantic" approach to this period sees it as de-veloping a conception of the creative imagination, which be-came the basis of Romanticism. This is true, but the Romantics

tended to see the poem as the *product* of the creative imagination, thus reverting in at least one respect to the Augustan attitude. For the Augustan, art is posterior to nature because nature is the art of God; for the Romantic, art is prior to nature because God is an artist; one deals in physical and the other in biological analogies, as Professor Abrams' *Mirror and the Lamp* has shown. But for the Romantic poet the poem is still an artefact: in Coleridge's terms, a secondary or productive imagination has been imposed on a primary imaginative process. So, different as it is from Augustan poetry, Romantic poetry is like it in being a conservative rhetoric, and in being founded on relatively regular metrical schemes. Poe's rejection of the continuous poem does not express anything very central in Romanticism itself, as nearly every major Romantic poet composed poems of considerable, sometimes immense, length. Poe's theory is closer to the practice of the age of sensibility before him and the *symbolistes* after him.

In the age of sensibility most of the long poems, of course, simply carry on with standard continuous metres, or exploit the greater degree of intensified recurrent sound afforded by stanzaic forms, notably the Spenserian. But sometimes the peculiar problems of making associative poetry continuous were faced in a more experimental way, experiments largely ignored by the Romantics. Oracular poetry in a long form often tends to become a series of utterances, irregular in rhythm but strongly marked off one from the other. We notice in Whitman, for instance, that the end of every line has a strong pause — for when the rhythm is variable there is no point in a run-on line. Sometimes this oracular rhythm takes on at least a typographical resemblance to prose, as it does in Rimbaud's *Saison en Enfer,* or, more frequently, to a discontinuous blend of prose and verse in which the sentence, the paragraph and the line are much the same unit. The chief literary influence for this rhythm has always been the translated Bible, which took on a new impetus in the age of sensibility; and if we study carefully the rhythm of Ossian, of Smart's *Jubilate Agno* and of the Blake Prophecies, we can see three very different but equally logical developments of this semi-Biblical rhythm.

Where there is a strong sense of literature as aesthetic product, there is also a sense of its detachment from the spectator. Aristotle's theory of catharsis describes how this works for tragedy: pity and fear are detached from the beholder by being directed towards objects. Where there is a sense of literature as process, pity and fear become states of mind without objects, moods which are common to the work of art and the reader, and which bind them together psychologically instead of separating them aesthetically.

Fear without an object, as a condition of mind prior to being afraid *of* anything, is called *Angst* or anxiety, a somewhat narrow term for what may be almost anything between pleasure and pain. In the general area of pleasure comes the eighteenth-century conception of the sublime, where qualities of austerity, gloom, grandeur, melancholy or even menace are a source of romantic or penseroso feelings. The appeal of Ossian to his time on this basis needs no comment. From here we move through the graveyard poets, the Gothic-horror novelists and the writers of tragic ballads to such *fleurs du mal* as Cowper's *Castaway* and Blake's Golden Chapel poem in the Rossetti MS.

Pity without an object has never to my knowledge been given a name, but it expresses itself as an imaginative animism, or treating everything in nature as though it had human feelings or qualities. At one end of its range is the apocalyptic exultation of all nature bursting into human life that we have in Smart's *Song to David* and the ninth Night of *The Four Zoas*. Next comes an imaginative sympathy with the kind of folklore that peoples the countryside with elemental spirits, such as we have in Collins, Fergusson, Burns and the Wartons. Next we have the curiously intense awareness of the animal world which (except for some poems of D. H. Lawrence) is unrivalled in this period, and is expressed in some of its best realized writing: in Burns's *To a Mouse,* in Cowper's exquisite snail poem, in Smart's superb lines on his cat Geoffrey, in the famous starling and ass episodes in Sterne, in the opening of Blake's *Auguries of Innocence.* Finally comes the sense of sympathy with man himself, the sense that no one can afford to be indifferent to the fate of anyone else, which underlies the pro-

tests against slavery and misery in Cowper, in Crabbe and in Blake's *Songs of Experience.*

This concentration on the primitive process of writing is projected in two directions, into nature and into history. The appropriate natural setting for much of the poetry of sensibility is nature at one of the two poles of process, creation and decay. The poet is attracted by the ruinous and the mephitic, or by the primeval and "unspoiled" — a picturesque subtly but perceptibly different from the Romantic picturesque. The projection into history assumes that the psychological progress of the poet from lyrical through epic to dramatic presentations, discussed by Stephen at the end of Joyce's *Portrait,* must be the historical progress of literature as well. Even as late as the preface to Victor Hugo's *Cromwell* this asumption persists. The Ossian and Rowley poems are not simple hoaxes: they are pseudepigrapha, like the Book of Enoch, and like it they take what is psychologically primitive, the oracular process of composition, and project it as something historically primitive.

The poetry of process is oracular, and the medium of the oracle is often in an ecstatic or trance-like state: autonomous voices seem to speak through him, and as he is concerned to utter rather than to address, he is turned away from his listener, so to speak, in a state of rapt self-communion. The free association of words, in which sound is prior to sense, is often a literary way of representing insanity. In Rimbaud's terrifyingly accurate phrase, poetry of the associative or oracular type requires a "déreglement de tous les sens." Hence the qualities that make a man an oracular poet are often the qualities that work against, and sometimes destroy, his social personality. Far more than the time of Rimbaud and Verlaine is this period of literature a period of the *poete maudit.* The list of poets over whom the shadows of mental breakdown fell is far too long to be coincidence. The much publicized death of Chatterton is certainly one of the personal tragedies of the age, but an easier one to take than the kind of agony which is expressed with an almost definitive poignancy by Smart in *Jubilate Agno*:

For in my nature I quested for beauty, but God, God, hath sent me to sea for pearls.

It is characteristic of the age of sensibility that this personal
or biographical aspect of it should be so closely connected with
its central technical feature. The basis of poetic language is
the metaphor, and the metaphor, in its radical form, is a statement of identity: "this is that." In all our ordinary experience
the metaphor is non-literal: nobody but a savage or a lunatic
can take metaphor literally. For Classical or Augustan critics
the metaphor is a condensed simile: its real or common-sense
basis is likeness, not identity, and when it obliterates the sense
of likeness it becomes barbaric. In Johnson's strictures on the
music and water metaphor of Gray's *Bard* we can see what
intellectual abysses, for him, would open up if metaphors ever
passed beyond the stage of resemblance. For the Romantic critic,
the identification in the metaphor is ideal: two images are
identified within the mind of the creating poet.

But where metaphor is conceived as part of an oracular and
half-ecstatic process, there is a direct identification in which the
poet himself is involved. To use another phrase of Rimbaud's,
the poet feels not "je pense," but "on me pense." In the age
of sensibility some of the identifications involving the poet seem
manic, like Blake's with Druidic bards or Smart's with Hebrew
prophets, or depressive, like Cowper's with a scapegoat figure,
a stricken deer or castaway, or merely bizarre, like Macpher-
son's with Ossian or Chatterton's with Rowley. But it is in this
psychological self-identification that the central "primitive"
quality of this age really emerges. In Collins's *Ode on the
Poetical Character,* in Smart's *Jubilate Agno,* and in Blake's
Four Zoas, it attains its greatest intensity and completeness.

In these three poems, especially the last two, God, the poet's
soul and nature are brought into a white-hot fusion of identity,
an imaginative fiery furnace in which the reader may, if he
chooses, make a fourth. All three poems are of the greatest
complexity, yet the emotion on which they are founded is of
a simplicity and directness that English literature has rarely
attained again. With the 1800 edition of *Lyrical Ballads,*
secondary imagination and recollection in tranquillity took over
English poetry and dominated it until the end of the nineteenth
century. The primitivism of Blake and Smart revived in France

with Rimbaud and Gérard de Nerval, but even this development had become conservative by the time its influence reached England, and only in a few poems of Dylan Thomas, and those perhaps not his best, does the older tradition revive. But contemporary poetry is still deeply concerned with the problems and techniques of the age of sensibility, and while the latter's resemblance to our time is not a merit in it, it is a logical enough reason for re-examining it with fresh eyes.

Suggestions Toward a Genealogy
of the "Man of Feeling"[1]

෴

R. S. CRANE

We may take, as a convenient starting-point for our inquiry, two passages from works published respectively in 1754 and 1755. In the first of these the Scottish moralist David Fordyce is attempting to enumerate the emotional satisfactions peculiar to the benevolent man:

His Enjoyments [he writes] are more numerous, or, if less numerous, yet more intense than those of bad Men; for he shares in the Joys of others by Rebound; and every Increase of *general* or *particular* Happiness is a real Addition to his own. It is true, his friendly *Sympathy* with others subjects him to some Pains which the hard-hearted Wretch does not feel; yet to give a loose to it is a kind of agreeable Discharge. It is such a Sorrow as he loves to indulge; a sort of pleasing Anguish, that sweetly melts the Mind, and terminates in a Self-approving Joy. Though the good Man may want Means to execute, or be disappointed in the Success of his benevolent Purposes, yet . . . he is still conscious of good Affections, and that Consciousness is an Enjoyment of a more delightful Savour than the greatest Triumphs of successful Vice.[2]

In the other passage an anonymous essayist writes in a somewhat similar vein on the subject of "moral weeping":

Moral weeping is the sign of so noble a passion, that it may be questioned whether those are properly men, who never weep upon any

From E L H, *vol. 1, 1934 (Baltimore: The Johns Hopkins Press), pp. 205–30.*

occasion. They may pretend to be as heroical as they please, and pride themselves in a stoical insensibility; but this will never pass for virtue with the true judges of human nature. What can be more nobly human than to have a tender sentimental feeling of our own and other's [*sic*] misfortunes? This degree of sensibility every man ought to wish to have for his own sake, as it disposes him to, and renders him more capable of practising all the virtues that promote his own welfare and happiness.[3]

That these two passages sum up fairly well between them the peculiar moral doctrine which lay back of the mid-eighteenth-century cult of the "man of feeling" no one familiar with the popular literature of that period will be disposed to deny. The identification of virtue with acts of benevolence and still more with the feelings of universal good-will which inspire and accompany these acts; the assumption that such "good Affections" are the natural and spontaneous growth of the heart of man uncorrupted by habits of vice; the anti-stoical praise of sensibility — "it may be questioned whether those are properly men, who never weep upon any occasion"; the complacent emphasis on the "pleasing Anguish, that sweetly melts the Mind, and terminates in a Self-approving Joy": these, it will be readily granted, were the distinguishing "notes" of the philosophy which found expression, between the seventeen-thirties and the seventeen-nineties, in the sentimental heroes and heroines of countless English novels, plays, and poems.

We may leave to others the task, still far from completed, of tracing the fortunes of this philosophy in the days of its triumph and especially of describing the varied forms of opposition which it provoked and the reaction which set in against it in the closing decades of the century. Our immediate concern in this paper is rather with the question how it ever came to triumph at all. For it was not a philosophy which the eighteenth century could have derived full fledged, as it derived its primitivism, for example, from ancient or Renaissance tradition. It was something new in the world — a doctrine, or rather a complex of doctrines, which a hundred years before 1750 would have been frowned upon, had it ever been presented to them, by representatives of every school of ethical or religious thought. Neither in antiquity, nor in the Middle Ages, nor in

the sixteenth century, nor in the England of the Puritans and
Cavaliers had the "man of feeling" ever been a popular type.

It is true that a solution of the problem has been offered us —
a solution which in recent years has won wide acceptance among
students of English literature. It has been observed that most if
not all of the distinctive elements of the sentimental benevolism
of the mid-eighteenth century already existed at the beginning of
the century in the writings of the third Earl of Shaftesbury, and
it has been noted that the aristocratic author of the *Characteristics*, for all the suspicions which could be cast on his religious
orthodoxy, enjoyed a very considerable vogue in intellectual
circles during the four or five decades following his death; from
these facts the conclusion has been drawn that it was mainly
from Shaftesbury and his immediate disciples that the impulses
came which affected both the literary creators of the "man of
feeling" and his admirers among the public.[4]

The chief difficulty with this explanation is that it begins too
late. If we wish to understand the origins and the widespread
diffusion in the eighteenth century of the ideas which issued in
the cult of sensibility, we must look, I believe, to a period considerably earlier than that in which Shaftesbury wrote and take
into account the propaganda of a group of persons whose opportunities for moulding the thoughts of ordinary Englishmen
were much greater than those of even the most aristocratic of
deists. What I would suggest, in short, is that the key to the
popular triumph of "sentimentalism" toward 1750 is to be
sought, not so much in the teaching of individual lay moralists
after 1700, as in the combined influence of numerous Anglican
divines of the Latitudinarian tradition who from the Restoration
onward into the eighteenth century had preached to their congregations and, through their books, to the larger public essentially the same ethics of benevolence, "good nature," and "tender
sentimental feeling" as was expressed in the passages from Fordyce and his anonymous contemporary quoted at the beginning
of this paper.[5]

In order to make this clear it will be necessary to consider
somewhat at length four principal aspects of the ethical and

psychological propaganda of these divines during the period from about 1660 to about 1725.

1. *Virtue as universal benevolence.* — That the teaching of the Latitudinarian clergy should have assumed from the first a strongly humanitarian bent is not surprizing in the light of the purposes which animated the earliest leaders of the movement. Along with other aims which need not concern us here, it was the fervent hope of the "Latitude-men" that they might succeed in freeing the religion of the English people from those errors concerning the nature of God and the value of human works which had been spread by the Puritans. Their characteristic views on both these questions were clearly summarized by Joseph Glanvill, himself an adherent of the party, in an essay published in 1676.

They took notice [he wrote], what *unworthy* and *dishonourable Opinions* were publish'd abroad concerning *God,* to the disparagement of all his Attributes, and discouragement of vertuous Endeavours, and great trouble and dejection of many pious Minds; and therefore here they appear'd also to *assert* and *vindicate* the Divine Goodness and *love of Men* in its *freedom* and *extent,* against those Doctrines, that made his *Love, Fondness;* and his *Justice, Cruelty,* and represented God as the Eternal Hater of the far greatest part of his reasonable Creatures, and the designer of their Ruine, for the exaltation of *meer Power,* and *arbitrary Will:* Against these sowr and dismal Opinions They stood up stoutly, in a time when the Assertors of the Divine Purity and Goodness, were persecuted bitterly with nicknames of Reproach, and popular Hatred. . . . They shew'd continually how impossible it was that *Infinite Goodness* should *design* or delight in the misery of his *Creatures:* . . . That *Goodness* is the Fountain of all his Communications and Actions *ad extra:* That to *glorifie* God, is rightly to apprehend and celebrate his Perfections, by our Words, and by our Actions: That *Goodness* is the *chief* moral Perfection: That *Power* without Goodness is *Tyranny;* and *Wisdom* without it, is but *Craft* and *Subtilty;* and *Justice, Cruelty,* when *destitute* of Goodness: . . .

By *such* Principles as *These,* which are wonderfully fertile, and big of many great Truths, they undermined, and from the bottom overthrew the fierce and churlish *Reprobatarian Doctrines.* . . .[6]

Nor were they any less hostile, Glanvill goes on to say, to the Puritan dogma of justification solely by faith in the imputed righteousness of Christ, with its corollary of the worthlessness of "our *Good Works* and Christian *Vertues*":

And because *Morality* was despised by those elevated Fantasticks, that talked so much of *Imputed Righteousness,* in the false sense; and accounted by them, as a *dull,* and *low* thing; therefore those Divines labour'd in the asserting and vindicating of this: Teaching the *necessity* of *Moral* Vertues; That *Christianity* is the *highest improvement* of them; . . . That the *power* of it consists in subduing *self-will,* and ruling our *passions,* and moderating our *appetites,* and *doing* the *works* of real Righteousness towards God, and our Neighbour.[7]

For this reason, Glanvill further tells us, what chiefly distinguished their teaching was its practical temper and aim. Vigorous upholders of the rights of human reason in matters of religion, they nevertheless attached much more importance to the moral ends of Christianity than to the speculative content of its theology. "Their main Design was, to make Men *good,* not *notional,* and knowing; and therefore, though they *conceal'd* no *practical* Verities that were proper and seasonable, yet they were sparing in their *Speculations,* except where they tended to the necessary vindication of the *Honour* of *God,* or the directing the Lives of Men. . . ."[8] "They cared for no mans *wit,* that wanted *goodness*; and despis'd no mans *weakness,* that had it."[9]

And finally, as a consequence both of their faith in God's impartial benevolence toward all men and of their belief in the primacy of practice over doctrine, they set themselves to break down sectarian prejudices and to proclaim the Catholic principle of "*universal* Charity, and Union," holding, as Glanvill again expressed it, that "the *Church* consists of all those that agree in the profession, and acknowledgement of the Scripture, and the *first* comprehensive, *plain Creeds,* however scatter'd through the World, and distinguish'd by names of Nations and Parties, under various degrees of light, and divers particular models, and forms of Worship, as to circumstance, and order: That every lover of God, and of the Lord Jesus Christ in sincerity, who lives according to the few, great acknowledg'd Doctrines, and Rules of a ver-

tuous and holy life, is a *true Christian*, and will be happy; though
he be ignorant of many points that some reckon for Articles
of Faith, and err in *some*, which others account *sacred*, and
fundamental. . . ." [10]

The purposes and doctrines which Glanvill here attributes
to the original "Latitude-men" met with increasingly wide acceptance, in the years following the Restoration, among the more
influential clergy of the Establishment, especially, it would seem,
among those who had been educated at Cambridge. We may
trace them in the sermons and other writings of prominent
divines like Isaac Barrow, Robert South, John Tillotson, Richard Cumberland, Samuel Parker, Hezekiah Burton, Richard
Kidder, John Scott, Edward Pelling, William Sherlock, Gilbert
Burnet, Richard Bentley, Samuel Clarke, as well as in the discourses of many lesser men who yet occupied important livings
in the days of the later Stuarts and the early Hanoverians.
Whatever differences there may have been among these clergymen, they were all united in their detestation of the darker
aspects of the Puritan creed, in their insistence on the religious
value of human works, in their exaltation of "goodness" over
doctrine, in their zeal for "universal Charity and Union." [11]

With this general outlook, it was natural that they should become great preachers of the social virtues. And few things, indeed,
were more characteristic of these Latitudinarian divines than
the assiduity with which they exhorted their hearers and readers
to benevolent feelings and acts as the best means at once of
actualizing the beneficent designs of God for man and of realizing
the aim of religion to perfect human nature. Charity was one of
their favorite themes: not the charity which was primarily love
of God; not charity merely to the parish poor or to fellow Chris-
tions, but a "general kindness" to all men because they are
men, an active desire to relieve their sufferings, if not to alter
the social conditions in which they live; the kind of charity best
described by the words — more common in the eighteenth century, but already coming into use — "humanity," "good nature,"
"universal benevolence."

Of this strain in their preaching numerous illustrations could
be given from the Restoration onward. The sermons of Isaac

Barrow (d. 1677) were particularly rich in expressions of the theme, and his discourse on *The Duty and Reward of Bounty to the Poor* (1671) remained a classic with readers of humanitarian sympathies for nearly a hundred years.[12] To Tillotson likewise the subject had a strong appeal: "How much better it is," he wrote in a typical passage, "to do good, to be really useful and beneficial to others, and how much more clearly and certainly our Duty, than to quarrel about doubtful and uncertain Opinions."[13] For Samuel Parker, as for his master Cumberland, the principle to which all the laws of nature could be reduced was "universal Justice or Humanity, or so much love and goodwill to all Mankind, as obliges every man to seek the welfare and happiness of the whole Community and every Member of it, as well as his own private and particular Interest."[14] For William Clagett, writing in 1686 *Of the Humanity and Charity of Christians,* the obligation to do good to all men derives its force not merely from the fact that charity is enjoined upon us by Christ and his apostles; the obligation also has its basis in common humanity, since to *"Man* only of all Creatures under Heaven, God has given this quality, to be affected with the Grief and with the Joy of those of his own kind; and to feel the Evils which others feel, that we may be universally disposed to help and relieve one another."[15]

In the early eighteenth century the current of this humanitarian homiletic was flowing more strongly than ever. It was not necessary to read the works of the Earl of Shaftesbury to learn that "to love the public, to study universal good, and to promote the interest of the whole world, as far as lies within our power, is surely the height of goodness, and makes that temper which we call divine";[16] the same lesson was being taught from hundreds of pulpits in London and the provinces by clergymen who had inherited the benevolistic spirit of their Latitudinarian predecessors of the generation before. Typical of these was Samuel Clarke, preaching in 1705 on *The Great Duty of Universal Love*:

The true End and Design of Religion, is manifestly this; to make Men wiser and better; to improve, exalt, and perfect their Nature; to teach them to obey, and love, and imitate God; to cause them to extend their

Love and Goodness and Charity to all their Fellow-Creatures, each in their several Stations, and according to the measure of their several Abilities; in like manner as the universal Goodness of God, extends it self over all his Works through the whole Creation....[17]

Typical also was Francis Squire, rector of Exford in Somerset and author in 1714 of a sermon on *Universal Benevolence: or, Charity in its Full Extent*, "humbly dedicated to Richard Steele," the climax of which was this rhapsody on the peculiar merits of the benevolent man:

Who can sufficiently express the *Dignity* of such a Person? What Trophies does he deserve? What endless Monuments of Praise and Glory belong unto him? He is in an implicit League of Philanthropy with the Guardian Angels, he carries on the great Cause of the Saviour of Mankind, he is the honourable Distributer of his *Creator's* Blessings, he wears more emphatically the *Image* of his God, and shares with him in an universal Reverence, and (I was going to say) Adoration. For indeed, there are few that can withhold a Veneration from such a one; and for those impious Wretches who offer Violence to their Nature and their Consciences to detract from him, we have the Pleasure to observe they are forc'd to belye him before they can dishonour him; they must first maliciously hide the Vertue, before they can obscure those Beams of Glory that arise from it.[18]

Of the same school, finally, was George Stephens, author of *The Amiable Quality of Goodness as Compared with Righteousness, Considered* (1731):

Compare [he exclaims] the Characters of the Just and Good Man as already drawn before you: Set them in Contrast one against the other. *That* indeed strikes us with Awe and Reverence: *This* attracts our Love and Admiration.

It may, I conceive, be of Service to Religion, if we pursue this Reflexion a little farther. Moral Writers have well observed, that Justice is a Virtue of the greatest Consequence to Society, the very Cement, that binds it firmly together. And is it not equally true, that Goodness is the Ornament and Pleasure of it? Do not the Comforts and mutual Endearments of Life all flow from Goodness? Will not he, that is only guided by Justice, be led to many hard and cruel Things? And is not

Extremity of Justice proverbially call'd the utmost Injury? Let us then
learn indeed, and study to be just; but let us at the same time *love
Mercy,* and hearken to the softer Dictates and Whispers of Humanity.[19]

2. *Benevolence as feeling.* — For most of the divines who were
thus helping to set the tone of eighteenth-century humanitarian
exhortation, the words "charity" and "benevolence" had a double
sense, connoting not only the serviceable and philanthropic
actions which the good man performs but still more the tender
passions and affections which prompt to these actions and constitute their immediate reward. For this emphasis they had, it is
true, an excellent warrant in various New Testament texts.[20]
But there was more to their frequent statements of the idea than
merely a development of I Corinthians 13, and an adequate
explanation must also take into account the pronounced strain
of anti-Stoicism which throughout the period characterized their
ethical thought.

How consciously in revolt they were against the distrust of
the passions and the exaggerated assumptions concerning man's
rationality which they attributed to the Stoics can be seen in
numerous places in their writings.[21] The passions, they insisted
with Aristotle, are neither good nor evil in themselves; they
may, however, be ordered to virtue, and when so ordered they
have a positive value, since they and not our weak reason are
the forces which make it possible for us to act at all; to wish
to eradicate them from our nature is not only a futile but a
misguided desire. "The *Stoicks,*" wrote James Lowde in 1694,
"would make Man so wholly rational, that they will scarce
allow him to be sensible, and would wholly exclude all natural
affections and bodily passions out of humane Nature. . . . The
Designs . . . is, *First,* impossible; *Secondly,* it would be preju-
dicial thereunto, were it feisible; for these when duly regulated,
become the subject matter of moral Vertue, and also add Vigour
and Wings to the Soul in its pursuits of Vertue."[22] George
Stanhope, in translating Epictetus in 1694, made the same point:
"I think it cannot fairly be denied," he remarked, "that in their
Way of Treating the Passions and Powers of the Soul, they [the
Stoics] much overshot the Mark, and have quite mistaken the

Case. . . . These are indeed the secret Springs that move and actuate us; and all the Care incumbent upon the Governing Part of the Mind, is to set them right. . . . So that in truth, the main, I might say the whole of our Duty and Happiness, consists, not in stifling these Affections, and condemning them to a State of utter Inactivity, but in moderating and regulating them."[23] And Charles Hickman, who became Bishop of Derry under Queen Anne, devoted some fifteen pages in one of his sermons (1700) to a formal refutation of the Stoic notion that because the passions lead us into dangers and betray us into sin, " 'tis fit they should be rooted out."

'Tis certain [he concluded] that when our passions are well regulated and reformed, they are great assistances and encouragements to Vertue. Our Reason is a cold and heavy principle, that moves us but slowly to our Work; but Passion puts an eagerness into our Desires, and a warmness into our Prosecutions, and makes the work go chearfully and vigorously on. . . .

Our Reason has but little to do in the forming of our minds, and bringing us to a vertuous Religious Life; 'tis our Passions and Affections that must do the work, for till they begin to move, our Reason is but like a Chariot when the Wheels are off, that is never like to perform the Journey.[24]

So widely prevalent, indeed, were views like these in the later seventeenth and early eighteenth centuries that it is difficult to understand how it could ever have been supposed by modern students that the moral ideal of that age was one of "cold intellectuality."[25]

Such in any case was not the ideal preached by these Latitudinarian divines. And in nothing was their revolt against "the Stoic's pride" more evident than in their repudiation of the notion that though the good man must relieve the distresses of others he must not allow himself to be emotionally affected by the misfortunes he sees.

The doctrine against which they protested was familiar to the seventeenth century in the pages of Seneca[26] and of his

various modern disciples.[27] It was stated with unusual explicitness by the Frenchman Antoine Le Grand, whose compendium of Stoic teaching was translated into English in 1675 under the revealing title of *Man without Passion: or, The Wise Stoick, According to the Sentiments of Seneca:*

For as these generous Philosophers [Le Grand wrote] strip their wise man of all the maladies of his Soul, they allow not that other mens misfortunes should be his miseries: they will have him as little concerned for his Neighbors afflictions as for his own disasters: They will have him to be fortune proof; and that that which discomposeth others, should teach him Constancy, and an even temper, What say they, doth Vertue consist in infirmity? Must we be guilty of effeminacy, to perform Acts of Generosity? Can we not be charitable without being afflicted? And can we not relieve those that are in misery, unless we mingle our Sighs with their Sobs and Groans, and our Cries with their Tears? A wise man ought to consider the Poor for their Relief, and not himself to share in their Calamities; he ought to protect them from oppressions, and not to be inwardly disturbed for them; he ought to endeavour their comfort, and not to be a Partner in their misfortunes.[28]

To this creed of "stoical insensibility" our divines opposed what they insisted was the true Christian idea of a charity which derives both its force and value from the fact that the good man does permit himself to be "inwardly disturbed." There can be no effective benevolence, they declared again and again, that does not spring from the tender emotions of pity and compassion, and so far from suppressing these emotions we ought rather to look upon them as the marks which distinguish men of genuine goodness from those who are merely righteous or just. Not the Senecan wise man, relieving but not pitying, but the tenderhearted Christian, pitying before he relieves, was the ideal which they preached to their generation; and as time went on their emphasis tended more and more to dwell on those elements of "softness" and quick emotional response to the spectacle of human misery which were to constitute for the eighteenth century the peculiar traits of the "man of feeling." Of the many clergymen of the half century following the Restoration who helped to disseminate this kind of "sentimentalism" —

a "sentimentalism" still distinctively Christian in its backgorund and expression — it is possible to consider only a few. Let us begin with Robert South, commenting in a sermon of 1662 on the difference between the moral teaching of Christians and that of the Stoics:

Sorrow in their esteem was a sin scarce to be expiated by another; to pity, was a fault; to rejoice, an extravagance. . . . To us let this be suffi- cient, that our Saviour Christ, who took upon him all our natural infirmities, but none of our sinful, has been seen to weep, to be sorrow- ful, to pity, and to be angry: which shows that there might be gall in a dove, passion without sin, fire without smoke, and motion without disturbance.[29]

The essential doctrine is here, but the tone and emphasis are still those of the seventeenth century rather than the eighteenth. This can also be said of a development on the same theme in Richard Kidder's *Charity Directed* (1676) :

The Doctrine of the *Stoicks* allowed the good man to *help,* but forbad him to *Pity* and *Compassionate* the *Needy.* [A note here refers to "Senec. de Clement. *l. 2. c. 5.*"] But we learn to do both from the Example and the Precepts of our Lord. Our Alms must be the Off- spring of our Charity and Kindness: and if we were allowed to be void of Pity and Compassion, 'tis to be feared our Relief would be but small. He is most likely to help his Neighbour that hath a great sense of his Misery. And Christianity hath provided better for the Poor than the Philosophy of the *Stoicks.* . . .[30]

From the middle of the next decade a change in tone becomes perceptible, manifesting itself, for example, in this passage on the duty of tenderheartedness in a sermon of Gregory Hascard (1685):

[Tenderheartedness consists in] being extremely sensible of the com- mon troubles and miseries of our Christian Brethren; this is the spring and original, the proper Source and cause of our Charity and Meekness, our Love and Relief of our fellow Beings. When our tempers are soft and sensible, and easily receive impressions from the Sufferings of

others, we are pain'd within, and to ease our selves, we are ready to succour them, and then Nature discharging her Burthen and Oppression, creates both her own pleasure and satisfaction, and performs her Duty. The multitude of miserable Persons will not upon this account produce a continued trouble in your breast, for if the generality of mankind had this fellow-feeling, it would lessen the number; and as it is, the pleasure of doing good far surpasseth the pain in pittying. . . .[31]

The same note is sounded in a sermon preached in 1697 by William Sherlock, Dean of St. Paul's:

A Charitable Mind is very easy to receive the Impressions of Charity; and the more charitably it is disposed, still the more easy. Every pitiable Object moves and affects such Men; and they are no more able to resist the silent Oratory of meagre Looks, naked Backs, and hungry Bellies . . . than to deny themselves what is necessary to Life. . . . A soft and tender Mind, which feels the Sufferings of others, and suffers with them, is the true Temper and Spirit of Charity; and Nature prompts us to ease those Sufferings which we feel. . . . An inward Principle is more powerful than all external Arguments; and Sense and Feeling is this Principle, and Charity is this Sense.[32]

In much the same vein, again, were the reflections of Charles Hickman in his sermon, already quoted, against the Stoic distrust of the passions (1700):

It is not a sign of *Goodness* in Man, to have no Passion in him, for such a Man is apparently Good for nothing at all. He does not hate his Brother, 'tis true: But then he does not love him neither. He does not oppress his Neighbour perhaps; but withal, he neither pities, nor relieves him. . . .
[In the character of the "good" man there is a certain] softening quality. 'Tis that which our Language very happily expresses by Good Nature. . . .

Indeed, goodness is the only excellence in Man, that deserves to be belov'd or priz'd. Good nature is all that a Man is good for in the World; without which, his riches only make him insolent, and his knowledge will but make him vain, and all his other admired qualities, render him the more dangerous, and suspected, and unfit for humane conversation. Nay, without this Goodness, and benignity of Mind,

Righteousness is nothing else but Interest, and Vertue nothing but design, and Religion it self will dwindle either into frowardness, or formality.[33]

The word "sensibility," when these passages were written, had not yet come into fashion in the sense in which it was chiefly to be used by the writers and public of the mid-eighteenth century. It is clear, however, that the quality of mind later eulogized under the name of "sensibility" or "moral weeping" by the sentimentalists of the 1740's and 1750's was no other than the quality which was already being recommended so warmly as the distinguishing sign of the benevolent man by these anti-Stoic preachers of the later 1600's. "Humanity, in its first and general Acceptation," wrote an essayist of 1735 in what was certainly one of the earliest formal definitions of "sensibility" in its new sense, "is call'd by Holy Writers, *Good-will towards Men*; by Heathens, *Philanthropy*, or *Love* of our *Fellow Creatures*. It sometimes takes the Name of *Good-nature*, and *delights* in *Actions* that have an *obliging* Tendency in them: When strongly *impress'd* on the *Mind*, it assumes a *higher* and nobler Character, and is not satisfy'd with *good-natured* Actions alone, but *feels* the *Misery* of others with *inward Pain*. It is then deservedly named *Sensibility*, and is considerably increased in its intrinsick Worth. . . ."[34] What was this but the doctrine of the "soft and tender mind" made widely familiar over a generation before by our divines?

3. *Benevolent feelings as "natural" to man.* — When Shaftesbury in 1698 praised Benjamin Whichcote for his defence of "Natural Goodness" and bestowed on him the title of "Preacher of Good-nature,"[35] he was using phrases which might have been applied, with little qualification, to most of the leading divines and many of their followers in the movement of which Whichcote had been an early pioneer. Without shutting their eyes to the great amount of actual selfishness and inhumanity in the world, they devoted much effort, nevertheless, to picturing the heart of man as "naturally" good in the sense that when left to its own native impulses it tends invariably to humane and sociable feel-

ings — and this "without the Discipline of Reason, or the Precepts of Religion."[36]

There can be little question that this optimistic appraisal of human nature was in part a manifestation of the revolt against Puritanism which we have already observed in the early leaders of the Latitudinarian group. It would hardly have been possible had it not been for their vigorous insistence, against the one-sided Augustinianism of the Lutheran and Calvinistic traditions, that man was not completely depraved as a result of the Fall, that he has still some natural power of doing good, that "nature" can cooperate with "grace" to the end of his salvation.[37] But this is only part of the story; and what chiefly provoked them to their frequent declarations of man's "natural goodness" was undoubtedly not so much their enmity to the Puritans as their zeal for combatting the dangerous political and moral doctrines of Thomas Hobbes.

Of the many important issues raised for them by the publication of the *Leviathan* in 1651 we need concern ourselves with only one: the issue involved in Hobbes' contention, which was indeed central to his whole political theory, that without a government possessed of complete power the natural passions of man would lead to a state of constant social war. The "Lawes of Nature," he had written, " (as *Justice, Equity, Modesty, Mercy,* and (in summe) *doing to others, as wee would be done to,*) of themselves, without the terrour of some Power, to cause them to be observed, are contrary to our naturall Passions, that carry us to Partiality, Pride, Revenge, and the like."[38] And the reason is, as he said in another passage, that "men have no pleasure, (but on the contrary a great deale of griefe) in keeping company, where there is no power able to overawe them all. For every man looketh that his companion should value him, at the same rate he sets upon himselfe: And upon all signes of contempt, or undervaluing, naturally endeavours, as far as he dares (which amongst them that have no common power to keep them in quiet, is far enough to make them destroy each other,) to extort a greater value from his contemners, by dommage; and from others, by the example." So that it is manifest, Hobbes concluded, "that during the time

men live without a common Power to keep them all in awe,
they are in that condition which is called Warre; and such a
warre, as is of every man, against every man."[39]

It is easy to understand why this doctrine should have aroused
the opposition of our divines. By reducing all human motivation to egoistic passions of pride and self-esteem, Hobbes, it
seemed clear to them, had gone far toward making not only
political justice but morality itself a purely arbitrary thing,
dependent wholly upon the will of those in power. To offset so
distasteful a conclusion it was obviously necessary to show the
falsity of the conception of human nature upon which it rested.
They devoted themselves, therefore, with much energy, to maintaining, against the *Leviathan,* that the nature of men is such
that even without government they can be trusted to live
together peacefully in sympathetic and helpful mutual relations. Our divines were not the first, of course, to uphold this
thesis, and they made much of the fact that in Aristotle, in
Cicero, in Juvenal, to say nothing of other classical and patristic
authors, the capacity of human beings for amicable social living
had been set in a much fairer light than in the writings of the
cynical philosopher of Malmsbury.[40] But this did not prevent
them from frequently giving to the old commonplaces a new
turn and force or from developing them in some directions far
beyond anything contained in the ancient texts.

From the point of view of the present study the most significant result of their efforts was the dissemination of the idea
that man is essentially a gentle and sympathetic creature, naturally incline to society not merely by his intellect, which
tells him that kindness to others is the best means to the end
of his own private happiness, but still more by "those passions
and inclinations that are common to him with other Creatures"
and which, like everything in his nature, have "a vehement
tendency to acts of love and good-will."[41]

Among the anti-Hobbesist preachers of "natural goodness"
in the years immediately following the Restoration, one of the
most important was Isaac Barrow. In a number of sermons on
the theme of charity delivered in the 1660's and early 1670's
he protested vigorously against the "monstrous paradox, cross-

ing the common sense of men, which in this loose and vain
world hath lately got such vogue, that all men naturally are
enemies one to another."[42] The truth is, he insisted, that if
the practice of benevolent acts is our duty it is in part because
such acts are in accord with, and not, as Hobbes had said, contrary to, our natural passions.

We are indispensably obliged to these duties, because the best of our
natural inclinations prompt us to the performance of them, especially
those of pity and benignity, which are manifestly discernible in all, but
most powerful and vigorous in the best natures; and which, questionless,
by the most wise and good Author of our beings were implanted therein
both as monitors to direct, and as spurs to incite us to the performance
of our duty. For the same bowels, that, in our want of necessary sustenance, do by a lively sense of pain inform us thereof, and instigate us
to provide against it, do in like manner grievously resent the distresses
of another, and thereby admonish us of our duty, and provoke us to
relieve them. Even the stories of calamities, that in ages long since past
have happened to persons nowise related to us, yea, the fabulous reports
of tragical events, do (even against the bent of our wills, and all resistance of reason) melt our hearts with compassion, and draw tears from
our eyes; and thereby evidently signify that general sympathy which
naturally intercedes between all men, since we can neither see, nor hear
of, nor imagine another's grief, without being afflicted ourselves. Antipathies may be natural to wild beasts [here he refers in a note to a well-
known passage in Juvenal's fifteenth satire]; but to rational creatures
they are wholly unnatural.[43]

Another expounder of the same doctrine was Samuel Parker,
whose *Demonstration of the Divine Authority of the Law of
Nature* (1681) was designed in the main as a reply to Hobbes.
All our "natural desires," he wrote, "are not only just and
reasonable in themselves, but they incline us to such designs
and actions, as naturally tend to the good and welfare of mankind."[44] To this end in particular we have been endowed by
the Creator with the passions of "Natural Pity and Compassion,"
the operation of which, when they have not been overlaid by
contrary habits, is almost mechanical:

... as for the generality of Men their hearts are so tender and their

natural affections so humane, that they cannot but pity and commiserate the afflicted with a kind of fatal and mechanical Sympathy; their groans force tears and sighs from the unafflicted, and 'tis a pain to them not to be able to relieve their miseries. . . .[45]

Tillotson, likewise, among the divines of this generation, was given to frequent pronouncements of the same anti-Hobbesist sort. "So far is it," he wrote in one of his sermons, "from being true, which Mr. *Hobbes* asserts as the fundamental *Principle* of his *Politicks, That Men are naturally in a State of War and Enmity with one another*; that the contrary *Principle*, laid down by a much deeper and wiser Man, I mean *Aristotle*, is most certainly true, *That Men are naturally a-kin and Friends to each other.*"[46] And the basis of this kinship, he explained elsewhere, is to be found in "the mere propensions and inclinations of their nature" – propensions comparable to "those instincts, which are in brute creatures, of natural affection and care toward their young ones."[47]

From the middle of the 1680's the number of such declarations would seem to have perceptibly increased; it had now become part of the recognized duty of the preacher of a charity sermon to picture human beings in an amiable light as creatures naturally disposed to impulses of pity and benevolence. The result was a long series of amplifications on the theme of man's essential "good nature," of which the following may serve as representative samples. From a sermon of 1686:

Tho *Nature* inclines us to Humanity, yet *Custom* and *bad Principles* may give us another *Bias,* and make us unconcern'd what others feel. But Nature, without Art and Force used upon it, seldom proves cruel; and we see that they which have the least of that we call *Breeding,* are prone to Pity and Commiseration. Men of a simple and rustick Education, and of mean Professions, easily fall into Compassion; and seldom fail of relieving one another, if the consideration of their own Interest does not prevail against it.[48]

From one of 1700:

For our Incitement [to benevolence] . . . there are natural Motions

wrought within us, and moulded into our very Frame: For when we
see a miserable Object, Nature it self moves our Bowels to Compassion,
and our Hands to give; and those of the finest Temper are soonest
affected with the Distresses of other Men.[49]

From one of 1701:

Nature has implanted in us a most tender and compassionate Sense
and Fellow-feeling of one anothers Miseries, a most ready and prevailing propension and inclination to assist and relieve them; insomuch
that pity and kindness towards our Brethren have a long time, passed
under the name of Humanity, as properties essential to and not without
Violence to be separated from humane Nature....[50]

From another of 1708:

But if we are thus slenderly furnish'd for Speculative Knowledge, we
are manifestly framed and fashion'd for Acts of divine *Worship,* and the
Practise of *social* Vertues. Nature has endu'd us with the tenderest
Passions: We are all Counterparts one of another: The Instruments
tun'd Unison: the doleful Cry of one in extreme Distress, makes the
Strings to tremble at our very Hearts....

You have an Instance of this in the most Ancient History, *Gen.* 44 and
45, when Men follow'd closer the unsophisticated Dictates of Nature.
[Then follows the story of Joseph and his brethren, after which the
preacher concludes:] This is not alledg'd as an Instance of his Vertue,
it was the Voice of Nature, *charity of the Machine,* and Formation. A
Man must be disciplin'd into hardness of Heart, and neild into
Cruelty....[51]

From one, finally, preached some time before 1720:

God has implanted in our very Frame and Make, a compassionate Sense
of the Sufferings and Misfortunes of other People, which disposes us
to contribute to their Relief; so that when we see any of our Fellow-
Creatures in Circumstances of Distress, we are naturally, I had almost
said, mechanically inclined to be helpful to them ... [And] as all the
Actions of Nature are sweet and pleasant, so there is none which gives
a good Man a greater, or more solid, or lasting Pleasure than this of
doing Good.... Where Men follow Nature in those tender Motions of

it, which incline them to Acts of Kindness and Charity, they will not
be easy, except they lay hold of the proper Occasions of exerting
them. . . .

So strongly is this natural Tenderness, where Nature is not one Way
or another corrupted, apt to operate in us; and which therefore, from
the *Greeks*, we very significantly render *Philanthropy;* from the *Latins,
Humanity;* and which in the Language of our own Nation, and with a
particular respect to the Genius of it, we express by *good Nature.* . . .[52]

It is no wonder that the deist Tindal in 1730, in referring to the
doctrine that man is "a social creature, who naturally loves his
own species, and is full of pity, tenderness & benevolence,"
should have prefaced his statement of it by the phrase "as our
Divines maintain against *Hobbs*."[53]

The significance of their assiduous preaching of this doctrine
for the problem with which we are here concerned scarcely
needs to be pointed out. For clearly if a capacity for "pity,
tenderness & benevolence" is what principally distinguishes man
from other creatures, and if, as was generally assumed in the
seventeenth and eighteenth centuries, it is man's duty to live
in conformity with his nature, then it follows that he does
this most completely who not only practices an active benevolence toward all men but cultivates and makes manifest the
"good Affections" of his heart. In a striking sentence by Isaac
Barrow, written as early as the 1670's, this association between
the psychology of "natural goodness" and the ethics of "sensibility" was already clearly expressed. "Since nature," wrote
Barrow, ". . . hath made our neighbour's misery our pain, and
his content our pleasure; since with indissoluble bands of
mutual sympathy she hath concatenated our fortunes and affections together; since by the discipline or our sense she instructs
us, and by the importunity thereof solicits us to the observance
of our duty, let us follow her wise directions, and conspire with
her kindly motions; let us not stifle or weaken by disuse, or
contrary practice, but by conformable action cherish and confirm the good inclinations of nature."[54]

4. *The "Self-approving Joy."* — In still another way, finally,
the preaching of the Latitudinarian clergy contributed to the

formation of the state of mind which was later to be reflected in the popular conception of the "man of feeling." This was through their frequent exhortations to their hearers and readers to consider how enjoyable the benevolent emotions may be to the individual who allows himself to feel them. From the Restoration into the eighteenth century there came from Anglican pulpits a steady stream of such exhortations, varying in tone from simple developments on the Aristotelian topic of the inherent pleasantness of virtue to eloquent reminders of the "pleasing Anguish, that sweetly melts the Mind, and terminates in a Self-approving Joy"[55] which is the chief earthly reward of persons who indulge their naturally good inclinations.

The theme, as we might expect, was a favorite one with Barrow. "As nature," he wrote in 1671, in a passage which was long after to be quoted with approval by Fielding,[56] "as nature, to the acts requisite toward preservation of our life, hath annexed a sensible pleasure, forcibly enticing us to the performance of them: so hath she made the communication of benefits to others to be accompanied with a very delicious relish upon the mind of him that practises it; nothing indeed carrying with it a more pure and savoury delight than beneficence. A man may be virtuously voluptuous, and a laudable epicure by doing much good; for to receive good, even in the judgment of Epicurus himself (the great patron of pleasure), is nowise so pleasant as to do it. . . ."[57]

Many others in the seventeenth century wrote in a similar strain. "There is no sensual Pleasure in the World," said Tillotson, "comparable to the Delight and Satisfaction that a good Man takes in doing good."[58] "He that shews Mercy to a Man in his misery," remarked Richard Kidder, "does a double kindness at once (and 'tis hard to say which is the greater) one to his Brother, and another to himself. There is a Delight and Joy that Accompanies doing good, there is a kind of sensuality in it."[59] "The first Reward of Vertue," Samuel Parker wrote, "is its own natural and intrinsick Pleasure," and he proceeded to bring out with remarkable frankness the strain of egoistic hedonism which the conception involved:

Acts of Love and Kindness are in themselves grateful and agreeable to
the temper of humane Nature; and all Men feel a natural Deliciousness
consequent upon every Exercise of their good-natur'd Passions; And
nothing affects the Mind with greater Complacency, than to reflect
upon its own inward Joy and Contentment. So that the Delight of every
vertuous Resolution doubles upon it self; in that first it strikes our
Minds with a direct Pleasure by its suitableness to our Natures, and
then our Minds entertain themselves with pleasant Reflections upon
their own Worth and Tranquility.[60]

Here, in 1681, was the whole philosophy of the "man of
feeling"! By the beginning of the eighteenth century the theme
had become a commonplace of nearly every charity sermon,
and preachers exhausted the resources of their rhetoric in
depicting the exquisite pleasure which the good man feels in
contemplating his own benevolent deeds. One example will
suffice — a particularly illuminating one. The rewards of benevolence, Charles Brent told his congregation at Bristol in 1704,
are not to be looked for merely in the life to come.

There is for certain, even now, a most Divine and Heavenly Pleasure
in doing Good; a Pleasure that is suited to the truest Movings of
Humanity, that gratifies the purest of all our natural Inclinations, that
Delights and Comforts even to the cherishing of our own Flesh, that
runs along with our Affections and our Bowels so very sympathetically,
that some good Men have indulged and epicuriz'd in it, till they have
tempted to call it downright *Sensuality:* And yet a Pleasure without
the least Abatement or Allay. A Pleasure too, that doth not lye linger-
ing in the Futurities of a World to come, but commences with our very
Act, nay before it; beginning even with our very Intensions: For we
are no sooner entering upon a Design of serving Mankind, but we take
up great Sums of Delight and Alacrity upon it, before-hand; and one
Advantage here is, that the Pleasure does not leave us as soon as the
Work is done, but lasts as long and lively upon our Minds, as our
Memories will serve us to recollect it. . . .[61]

In these passages — and many more like them could be quoted
from the sermon literature of the late seventeenth and early
eighteenth centuries[62] — one can see a clear foreshadowing of

that curious type of hedonism — the often frankly avowed pursuit of altruistic emotions for egoistic ends — which was to characterize most of the representative "men of feeling" of the next two generations. Sir Charles Grandison might have been a parishioner of Parker or Brent, and Parson Yorick their successor.

The hypothesis I have tried to suggest in this paper is not intended to be taken as an adequate or in any way exclusive explanation of the rise of the mid-eighteenth-century mode of sensibility in England. There is always the influence of Shaftesbury to be considered — a very real and important influence especially after 1725 when it was reinforced by that of his disciple Hutcheson. Even in the later seventeenth century, moreover, the ideas we have been discussing were not the exclusive property of writers of sermons. Mr. Ustick has recently called attention to their appearance in certain courtesy books of the 1680's,[63] and to the examples he gives others could doubtless be added. By 1714, as every one knows, they had begun to find their way into the popular literature of essays and plays.

My intention has not been to minimize these other factors in the preparation for sentimentalism, but merely to consider whether the whole movement does not become somewhat more intelligible historically than it has hitherto seemed when we bring into the picture, also, the propaganda of benevolence and tender feeling carried on with increasing intensity since the Restoration by the anti-Puritan, anti-Stoic, and anti-Hobbesian divines of the Latitudinarian school.

NOTES

[1] This paper was prepared for presentation before the Language and Literature Club of the University of Wisconsin in April, 1934. I have inserted many additional references, but have not otherwise greatly altered the exposition. It goes without saying that I have not attempted an exhaustive study of any aspect of the subject.

[2] *The Elements of Moral Philosophy*, 1754, pp. 263-4.

[3] *Man*, No. 43, October 22, 1755 (in a letter signed "A. B.").

[4] The best statement of the case for Shaftesbury is still that of C. A. Moore in

PMLA 31 (1916). 264-325. Cf. also W. E. Alderman, *ibid.* 46 (1931). 1087-94, and *Transactions of the Wisconsin Academy of Sciences, Arts and Letters* 26 (1931). 137-59.

5 I have brought together some of the evidence in the *Philological Quarterly* 11 (1932). 204-06. See also Rae Blanchard, *The Christian Hero, by Richard Steel,* Oxford, 1932, pp. xvii-xxv, and Lois Whitney, *Primitivism and the Idea of Progress in English Popular Literature of the Eighteenth Century,* Baltimore, 1934, pp. 21-6. Shortly before his death my friend, the late F. B. Kaye, had projected a study of the question which, had he lived to complete it, would have made the present essay superfluous. Though my own conclusions differ in some particulars from his, I am heavily indebted to him both for interpretative suggestions and for materials.

6 *Essays on Several Important Subjects in Philosophy and Religion,* 1676, Essay 7, pp. 21-2. The essay purports to be a continuation of Bacon's *New Atlantis.*

7 *Ibid.,* pp. 24-5.

8 *Ibid.,* p. 15. Cf. pp. 26, 30, 45.

9 *Ibid,* p. 51.

10 *Ibid.,* p. 31. A characterization of the Latitudinarians similar on most points to Glanvill's is given in Edward Fowler's *The Principles and Practices of Certain Moderate Divines of the Church of England Abusively Called Latitudinarians,* 1670. See the 2d ed., 1671, pp. 18, 115, 117, 120, 126, 129, 194, 199, 228, 234-7, 347.

11 Cf., e. g., Isaac Barrow, *Theological Works,* 1830, 6. 541: "It is a peculiar excellency of our religion, that it doth not much employ men's care, pains, and time about matters of ceremonial observance; but doth chiefly (and in a manner wholly) exercise them in the works of substantial duty, agreeable to reason, perfective of man's nature, productive of true glory to God, and solid benefit to men"; Robert South, *Sermons,* Philadelphia, 1844, 1. 462: "Believing without doing good is a very cheap and easy, but withal a very worthless way of being religious"; John Tillotson, *Works,* 4th ed., 1728, 2. 167: "When we come to die we can call nothing our own but the good works which by the grace of God we have been enabled to do in this life."

12 See below, n. 56. The discourse is printed in *Theological Works,* 1830, 2. 169-258.

13 *Works,* 1728, 1. 155. Cf. also *ibid.* 1. 160-1, 169-71; 2. 513, 595.

14 *A Demonstration of the Divine Authority of the Law of Nature,* 1681, pp. 17-18; cf. *ibid.,* pp. 24-5.

15 Ed. 1687, p. 4. Cf. also pp. 8-9, 14.

16 *Characteristics,* ed. Robertson, 1. 27.

17 P. 2.

18 P. 25. Cf. pp. 6-7.

19 Pp. 13-14. In addition to the texts quoted or referred to above, see the following: Samuel Parker, *A Free and Impartial Censure of the Platonick Philosophie,* 1666, pp. 23-7; Thomas Hodges, *The Creatures Goodness,* 1675, p. 43, and *passim;* William Gould, *The Generosity of Christian Love,* 1676, pp. 12-13; Richard Kidder, *Charity Directed,* 1676, pp. 4-13, 22-5; Thomas Willis, *The*

Excellency of Wisdom, 1676, pp. 27-30; Adam Litteton, *A Sermon ... June 24, 1680*, 1680, p. 29; John Scott, *The Christian Life*, 1681, pp. 178, 186-7; Joseph Glanvill, *Some Discourses, Sermons and Remains*, 1681, pp. 101-02, 125-8; Robert South, "Sermon Preached May 3, 1685," in *Twelve Sermons*, 5th ed., 1722, pp. 436-8; Hezekiah Burton, "Of Doing Good to All Men," in *A Second Volume of Discourses*, 1685, pp. 491-4, 498-500, 518-26, 546-52, 604; Thomas Wagstaffe, *A Sermon Preached ... Novemb. 24, 1687*, 1688, pp. 20, 26, 28; John Norris, *The Theory and Regulation of Love*, 1688, pp. 85-6; Henry Waring, *The Rule of Charity*, 1690, pp. 4, 21-2; Edward Pelling, *A Practical Discourse upon Charity*, 1693, pp. 3-5; Francis Atterbury, *The Power of Charity to Cover Sin ... Preach'd ... August 16, 1694*, 1708, p. 13; Robert Grove, *Profitable Charity*, 1695, pp. 12-14; William Sherlock, "The Nature and Measure of Charity" (1697), in *Sermons Preached upon Several Occasions*, 1719, pp. 211-12; Edward Synge, *A Gentleman's Religion*, Part 3 (1697), pp. 157-61; Benjamin Whichcote, *Select Sermons*, 1698, pp. 218-19, 272; John Smith, *An Essay on Universal Redemption*, 1701, p. 5; Thomas Lynford, *The Charitable Man Bears Much Fruit*, 1712, p. 12; William Lupton, *The Necessity ... of ... Charity*, 1713, p. 10; Gilbert Burnet, *Some Sermons Preach'd on Several Occasions*, 1713, pp. 224-7; Richard Bentley, "A Sermon Preached before King George I on February the Third, 1716-17," in *Works*, ed. A. Dyce, 3 (1838), 266-7; William Beveridge, "The Chain of Evangelical Graces" (1720), in *Theological Works*, 1845, 6. 114; John Leng, *A Sermon Preach'd ... April 6, 1724*, 1724, pp. 6-8, 11; Alured Clark, *A Sermon Preached ... January the 25th, 1725*, 1726, pp. 6-7; Samuel Wright, *Charity in All Its Branches*, 1732, pp. v-ix.

20 Cf. Richard Kidder, *Charity Directed*, 1676, p. 19; Anthony Horneck, *The Nature of True Christian Righteousness*, 1689, p. 20; Charles Hickman, *Fourteen Sermons*, 1700, Sermon 11; Richard Crossing, *Practical Discourse Concerning the Great Duty of Charity*, 1722, p. 7.

21 See, in addition to the texts given above, Richard Baxter, *A Treatise of Self-Denyall*, 1660, p. 279; Henry More, *An Account of Virtue*, 1690, pp. 34-42 (originally published in Latin as *Enchiridion ethicum*, 1666); H. Lukin, *The Chief Interest of Man* (1670), 3d ed., 1718, pp. 55-69; Matthew Hale, *Contemplations Moral and Divine*, 1682, Part 1, pp. 104-06; Part 2, p. 71; John Hartcliffe, *A Treatise of Moral and Intellectual Virtues*, 1691, pp. 294-6; M. Burghope, *The Government of the Passions*, 1701, pp. 3-5; Francis Bragge, *A Practical Treatise on the Regulation of the Passions*, 1708, pp. 4-5, 6-7, 17-19; John Tottie, *A View of Reason and Passion*, 1736, pp. 6-8.

22 *A Discourse Concerning the Nature of Man ... with an Examination of Some of Mr. Hobb's Opinions*, 1694, p. 24.

23 *Epictetus His Morals*, 2d ed., 1700, Preface, sigs. [A 5]-[A 6].

24 *Fourteen Sermons*, 1700, pp. 271-2.

25 Many similar statements could of course be collected from the secular writers of the period. See, e.g., Meric Casaubon, *Marcus Aurelius ... His Meditations*, 4th ed., 1673, Preface; Sir William Temple, "Of Gardening" (1685), in *Works*, 1814, 3. 208-10; Sir Thomas Pope Blount, *Essays on Several Subjects*,

3d ed., 1697, pp. 195-200; Tim. Nourse, *A Discourse upon the Nature and Faculties of Man*, 1697, pp. 104-09; Richard Steel, *The Christian Hero* (1701), ed. Blanchard, 1932, p. 74; Charles Gildon, *The Deist's Manual*, 1705, pp. 120-30; *Spectator*, No. 408, June 18, 1712; *Lover*, No. 32, May 8, 1714; Pope, *Essay on Man*, 1733, 2. 101-22.

26 Cf., e. g., *The Workes of . . . Seneca*, trans. by Thomas Lodge, 1620, pp. 608, 609, in "Of Clemencie," Book 2, chap. 5, 6: "For it is nought else but a basenes of the heart which melteth in beholding another mans miseries. . . . He [the wise man] will assist his Neighbour that weepeth, without weeping himself. . . . He will not . . . be mooued, but will helpe, will profit, as being borne for the common good and the seruice of the Commonweale."

27 E. g., Justus Lipsius. See *A Discourse of Constancy*, trans. by Nathaniel Wanley, 1670, 1. 12, pp. 67-70.

28 Pp. 277-8.

29 "Of the Creation of Man in the Image of God," in *Sermons*, Philadelphia, 1844, 1. 28. Cf. also 1. 431.

30 P. 19.

31 *A Sermon*, 1685, pp. 7-8.

32 "The Nature and Measure of Charity" (April 6, 1697), in *Sermons*, 3d ed., 1719, 1. 214-15. Cf. also *ibid.*, pp. 206-08.

33 *Fourteen Sermons*, pp. 265, 321, 328-9. For other texts on the same theme see: Thomas Watson, *A Plea for Almes*, 1658, pp. 14-15; John Tillotson, *Works*, 1728, 1. 170 (preached December 3, 1678); John Scott, *The Christian Life*, 1681, pp. 184-5; Anthony Horneck, *The Nature of True Christian Righteousness*, 1689, p. 20; Edward Pelling, *A Practical Discourse upon Charity*, 1693, pp. 6-8; George Stanhope, *Epictetus His Morals* (1694), 2d ed., 1700, Preface, sig. [A 6ᵛ]; E. Young, *Sermons on Several Occasions*, 1703, 2. 365-6; Richard Crossing, *Practical Discourse Concerning the Great Duty of Charity*, 1722, p. 7; R. Skerret, *Alms-giving without Charity Unprofitable*, 1723; Alured Clarke, *A Sermon Preached . . . January the 25th, 1725*, 1726, p. 16.

34 *Prompter*, No. 63, June 17, 1735.

35 Preface to *Select Sermons of Dr. Whichcot*.

36 The phrase occurs in *A Sermon*, 1739, by Thomas Herring, Bishop of Bangor. See pp. 5-6: "It is the Property of Mercy to pity the Infirmities of other Men; . . . to cultivate a Tenderness and Humanity of Temper, a quick and ready Feeling of each others Wants and Pains. . . . And this is what indeed we are naturally carried to without the Discipline of Reason, or the Precepts of Religion.—There is something in the Human Constitution that naturally melts at Human Misfortunes. . . ."

37 Cf., e. g., Isaac Barrow, "Sermon XXVI," in *Theological Works*, 1830, 2. 36; 3. 533; Joseph Glanvill, *Some Discourses*, 1681, pp. 6-7, 29, 55-6; Sir Matthew Hale, *A Discourse of the Knowledge of God, and of Our Selves*, 1688, pp. 54, 276; Edward Synge, *A Gentleman's Religion*, Part 2 (1697), pp. 54-5, 62. See E. Gilson, "Le Moyen Age et le naturalisme antique," *Archives d'histoire doctrinale et littéraire du Moyen Age* 7 (1932). 5-37.

[38] Chap. 17.

[39] *Ibid.*, chap. 13. Cf. also chap. 11, beginning.

[40] For Aristotle see, e. g., Barrow, *Theological Works* 2. 37, 80; Tillotson, *Works*, 1728, 1. 305; Samuel Parker, *A Demonstration of the Divine Authority of the Law of Nature*, 1681, p. viii; for Cicero, *ibid.*; for Juvenal, Barrow, *Theological Works*, 2. 141, 224. Many of the most important classical and patristic texts had been assembled by Grotius in his *De jure belli ac pacis*, 1625, Prolegomena, sects. 6-7, and Book 1, chap. 1.

[41] The phrase is Samuel Parker's in *A Demonstration of the Divine Authority of the Law of Nature*, p. 29.

[42] *Theological Works*, 1830, 2. 79.

[43] *Ibid.* 2. 140-1. Cf. also *ibid.*, pp. 36-7, 78-80, 224-5. The theme is present in Barrow's "First Sermon" (preached at Cambridge, June 30, 1661); see *Sermons Preached upon Several Occasions*, 1678, pp. 24-5.

[44] P. 50.

[45] P. 55. Cf. pp. 21-2, 25-6, 29-30.

[46] *Works*, 1728, 1. 305. The date of the sermon was March 8, 1689.

[47] *Ibid.* 2. 298-9.

[48] William Clagett, *Of the Humanity and Charity of Christians, A Sermon Preached . . . Nov. 30, 1686*, 1687, p. 5. Cf. the same author's *A Paraphrase, with Notes . . . upon the Sixth Chapter of St. John . . .* , 1693, p. 76.

[49] Z. Isham, *A Sermon*, 1700, pp. 4-5.

[50] Sir William Dawes, *Self-love the Great Cause of Bad Times*, 1701, p. 9.

[51] Knightly Chetwood, *A Sermon Preach'd before the . . . Lord Mayor . . .* , *April 5, 1708*, 1708, pp. 8-9.

[52] Richard Fiddes, *Fifty-Two Practical Discourses on Several Subjects*, 1720, pp. 112-13.

I append here references to other texts of the period in which similar ideas are expressed: William Pike, *Observations, Censures and Confutations of Divers Errors . . . of Mr. Hobs*, 1657, pp. 91-2; Thomas Tenison, *The Creed of Mr. Hobbes Examined*, 2d ed., 1671, pp. 140-1; Robert South, "Of the Origin, Nature, and Baseness of the Sin of Ingratitude" (1675), in *Sermons*, 1844, 1. 179; Richard Cumberland, *A Treatise of the Laws of Nature*, trans. 1727, p. 164 (the Latin original appeared in 1672); John Scott, *The Christian Life*, 1681, pp. 175-6; Thomas Mannyngham, *A Sermon Preached at the Hampshire Feast*, 1686, pp. 16 ff.; J. Lowde, *A Discourse Concerning the Nature of Man*, 1694, sigs. A4-A4ᵛ, pp. 164-6; Jeremy Collier, "Of General Kindness," in *Miscellanies*, 1694; H. Downes, *The Excellency of Publick Charity*, 1697, p. 3; Benjamin Whichcote, *Select Sermons*, 1698, pp. 92-3, 181-2, 217, 381-2, and *Works*, Aberdeen, 1751, 4. 257-8; Edmund Calamy, *A Sermon Preach'd before the Societies for Reformation of Manners*, 1699, pp. 12-13; W. Sherlock, "The Nature and Evils of a Vicious Self-love" (c. 1700), in *Sermons*, 3d ed., 1719, 1. 368-70, 379; Stephen Chapman, *A Sermon Preach'd before the Free-born Citizens of Bristol*, 1703, pp. 1-2; Samuel Clarke, *The Great Duty of Universal Love*, 1705, pp. 4-5; Andrew Snape, *A Sermon Preach'd before the Princess Sophia*, 1706, pp. 19-22;

Benjamin Loveling, *The Best Use of Riches, A Sermon*, 1706, p. 14; William Colnett, *A Sermon Preach'd before the Societies for Reformation of Manners*, 1711, pp. 5-6; Gilbert Burnet, *Some Sermons*, 1713, pp. 232-3; Henry Grove, *Spectator*, Nos. 588, 601, Sept. 1, Oct. 1, 1714; Richard Bentley, *A Sermon Preach'd ... Feb. 3, 1716-17* (1717), in *Works*, ed. Dyce, 3 (1838). 269; George Smalridge, *Twelve Sermons*, 1717, p. 199; Alured Clarke, *A Sermon Preached ... January the 25th, 1725*, 1726, pp. 4-10; Samuel Wright, *Charity in All Its Branches*, 1732, pp. 2-3; T. Rundle, *A Sermon Preached ... Feb. 17, 1733-34*, 1734, pp. 5-6.

[53] *Christianity as Old as the Creation*, 8vo ed., 1731, p. 49.

[54] *Theological Works* 2. 142.

[55] See above, p. 205.

[56] *Covent Garden Journal*, No. 29, April 11, 1752, ed., Jensen, 1. 308.

[57] *Theological Works* 2. 255. Cf. also 2. 141-2.

[58] *Works*, 1728, 1. 156. Cf. also 2. 599.

[59] *Charity Directed*, 1676, p. 12.

[60] *A Demonstration of the Divine Authority of the Law of Nature*, p. 64.

[61] *Persuasions to a Publick Spirit*, 1704, pp. 15-16.

[62] See, e. g., H. Lukin, *The Chief Interest of Man* (1670), 3d ed., 1718, pp. 46-50; Hezekiah Burton, *Several Discourses*, 1684, p. 80, and *A Second Volume of Discourses*, 1685, pp. 564-72; Gregory Hascard, *A Sermon*, 1685, p. 5; Edward Pelling, *A Practical Discourse upon Charity*, 1693, p. 25; Edmund Calamy, *A Sermon Preach'd before the Societies for Reformation of Manners*, 1699, p. 18; E. Young, *Sermons on Several Occasions*, 1702, 1. 391-2; Samuel Clarke, *The Great Duty of Universal Love*, 1705, p. 4; Daniel Waterland, "The Duty of Doing Good" (1712), in *Works*, 1823, 8. 372; Gilbert Burnet, *Some Sermons*, 1713, pp. 246-8; Francis Squire, *Universal Benevolence: or, Charity in its Full Extent*, 1714, pp. 12-13; Henry Grove, *Spectator*, No. 588, Sept. 1, 1714; Alured Clarke, *A Sermon Preached ... January the 25th, 1725*, 1726, p. 5.

[63] *Modern Philology* 30 (1932). 161-6.

A Chronology of Eighteenth-Century Cultural History 1687-1799

Events	Births, Deaths	Publications in England	Publications outside England
1687	d. Waller (b. 1606)	Dryden, Song for St. Cecilia's Day; Newton, Principia	
1688 Glorious Revolution	b. Pope d. Bunyan		
1689 English Bill of Rights		Purcell, Dido and Aeneas	
1690		Locke, Essay Concerning Human Understanding; Treatises of Civil Government; Temple, Essay upon the Ancient and Modern Learning	Perrault, Parallèles des anciens et des modernes (to 1697)
1692 Salem witchcraft executions		Locke, Some Thoughts Concerning Education	
1693		Newton, Method of Fluxions	

Events	Births, Deaths	Publications in England	Publications outside England
1694 Bank of England founded		Wotton, *Reflections upon Ancient and Modern Learning*	
1695		Congreve, *Love for Love*; Locke, *Reasonableness of Christianity*	Leibnitz, *Système nouveau de la nature*
1697		Dryden, *Alexander's Feast*; Sergeant, *Solid Philosophy*	Bayle, *Dictionnaire historique et critique* (to 1706)
1698		Collier, *A Short View of the Immorality and Profaneness of the English Stage*	
1700 Berlin Academy of Science founded	*d.* Dryden (*b.* 1631) *b.* Thomson	Congreve, *The Way of the World*	
1701 War of Spanish Succession (to 1714)			

Events	Births, Deaths	Publications in England	Publications outside England
1702 Reign of Queen Anne (to 1714) *Daily Courant* (first English daily newspaper) founded			
1703	*b.* John Wesley		
1704 Battle of Blenheim		Swift, *Tale of a Tub* and *Battle of the Books* Newton, *Opticks*	
1705 Steam engine invented by Newcomen		Mandeville, *The Grumbling Hive*	
1707 Union of British and Scottish Parliaments	*b.* Fielding *b.* Charles Wesley	Watts, *Hymns and Spiritual Songs*	

Events	Births, Deaths	Publications in England	Publications outside England
1709	d. John Phillips (b. 1676) b. Johnson	Rowe's edition of Shakespeare Pope, Pastorals Steel, Tatler (to 1711) Berkeley, An Essay towards a New Theory of Vision	
1710 Handel's arrival in England			
1711		Swift, Journal to Stella (to 1713) Berkeley, Treatise Concerning the Principles of Human Knowledge Addison & Steel, Spectator (to 1712) Pope, Essay on Criticism Shaftesbury, Characteristics of Men, Manners, Opinions, Times, etc.	Leibnitz, Théodicée Cotton Mather, Essays to Do Good
1712	b. Rousseau	Addison, Spacious Firmament on High	Wolff, Gedänken von den Kräften des menschlichen Verstandes

Events	Births, Deaths	Publications in England	Publications outside England
1713 Treaty of Utrecht		Pope, *Windsor Forest* Addison, *Cato* Berkeley, *Hylas and Philonous*	Increase Mather, *A Plain Discourse Showing Who Shall and Who Shall Not Enter Heaven*
1714 Reign of George I (to 1727)	*b.* Shenstone	Gay, *The Shepherd's Week* Pope, *The Rape of the Lock* Mandeville, *The Fable of the Bees*	Leibnitz, *Monadologie*
1715 Death of Louis XIV Jacobite Revolt		Pope, *Iliad* translation (to 1720)	Fénelon, *Traité de l'existence de Dieu*
1716	*b.* Gray	Gay, *Trivia*	
1717	*b.* Horace Walpole	Pope, *Eloisa to Abelard*	Penn, *Religion Professed by the Quakers*
1719	*d.* Addison (*b.* 1672)	Defoe, *Robinson Crusoe* Watts, *Psalms of David*	Wolff, *Gedänken von Gott, Welt, und Seele*

Events	Births, Deaths	Publications in England	Publications outside England
1720 South Sea Bubble			
1721	d. Prior (b. 1664)	Parnell, *Night Piece on Death*	
1722	b. Akenside b. Collins	Defoe, *Moll Flanders* Wollaston, *Religion of Nature*	
1723			Voltaire, *Henriade*
1724	b. Kant (d. 1804)	Swift, *Drapier's Letters* Burnet, *History of my own Time* (to 1734)	Vico, *Principi di una scienza nuovo* (to 1730)
1725		Pope's edition of Shakespeare Hutcheson, *Inquiry into Beauty and Virtue*	

Events	Births, Deaths	Publications in England	Publications outside England
1726 Voltaire in England (to 1729)		Swift, *Gulliver's Travels* Thomson, *Seasons* (to 1730) Dyer, *Grongar Hill*	
1727 Reign of George II (to 1760)		Gay, *Fables* (to 1738)	
1728	*b.* Goldsmith	Gay, *Beggar's Opera* Pope, *Dunciad* (first version)	
1729	*d.* Congreve (*b.* 1670) *b.* Burke	Swift, *Modest Proposal* Law, *Serious Call*	
1730 Methodist Society established at Oxford			Tindal, *Christianity as Old as Creation*
1731 *Gentleman's Magazine* founded	*d.* Defoe (*b.* 1660) *b.* Cowper		

Events	Births, Deaths	Publications in England	Publications outside England
1732 Covent Garden Theatre built	d. Gay (b. 1685)	Berkeley, Alciphron	
1733 Georgia founded by Oglethorpe	d. Mandeville (b. 1670?)	Pope, Essay on Man Theobald's edition of Shakespeare Berkeley, Theory of Vision	
1734 1st English translation of La Fontaine			Voltaire, Lettres philosophiques
1735		Pope, Epistle to Arbuthnot Hogarth, A Rake's Progress	Linnaeus, Systema natura
1736 Repeal of English statutes against witchcraft		Butler, Analogy of Religion . . . to the Constitution of Nature	
1737 Theatre Licensing Act	b. Gibbon	Shenstone, Schoolmistress	

Events	Births, Deaths	Publications in England	Publications outside England
1738 Conversion of John Wesley; beginning of Methodist Revival		Johnson, *London* Bolingbroke, *Letters on the Study of History*	
1740 Reign of Frederick the Great (to 1786)		Richardson, *Pamela* Thomson and Mallet, *Alfred*	
1741		Fielding, *Joseph Andrews* Charles and John Wesley, *Psalms and Hymns*	J. Edwards, *Sinners in the Hands of an Angry God*
1742 Fall of Walpole		Handel, *Messiah* Young, *Night Thoughts*	
1743		Pope, *Dunciad* (final version)	D'Alembert, *Traité de Dynamique*
1744 First Methodist Conference	d. Pope	J. Warton, *The Enthusiast* Akenside, *The Pleasures of Imagination*	

Events	Births, Deaths	Publications in England	Publications outside England
1745 Jacobite Rebellion	d. Swift		
1746		Hogarth, *Marriage à la Mode*	Condillac, *Origine des connaissances humaines* Diderot, *Pensées philosophiques*
		Collins, *Odes*	
1747 Battle of Culloden H. Walpole acquires Strawberry Hill		Warburton's edition of Shakespeare	
1748 Treaty of Aix-la-Chapelle	d. Watts (*b.* 1674) d. Thomson	Richardson, *Clarissa* Hume, *Philosophical Essays Concerning Human Understanding* Thomson, *Castle of Indolence*. Smollett, *Roderick Random*	Montesquieu, *L'Esprit des lois*
1749	d. Ambrose Phillips (*b.* 1675?) b. Goethe (*d.* 1832)	Fielding, *Tom Jones* Johnson, *Vanity of Human Wishes* Hartley, *Observations on Man*	Swedenborg, *Arcana celesta* (to 1756) Buffon, *Histoire naturelle* (to 1788)

Events	Births, Deaths	Publications in England	Publications outside England
1750		Johnson, *Rambler* (to 1752)	Rousseau, *Discours sur les sciences et les arts*
1751		Gray, *Elegy Written in a Country Churchyard*	B. Franklin, *Experiments and Observations in Electricity* Diderot & D'Alembert, *Encyclopedie*, Vol. I & II
1752 Gregorian calendar adopted		Smart, *Poems on Several Occasions*	
1753 British Museum founded	*d.* Berkeley (*b.* 1685)		Linnaeus, *Species Plantarum*
1754	*d.* Fielding *b.* Crabbe	Hume, *History of Great Britain, Vol. I*	Condillac, *Traite des sensations* J. Edwards, *Freedom of the Will*
1755		Johnson, *Dictionary of the English Language* Hutcheson, *System of Moral Philosophy*	Voltaire, *La Pucelle* Rousseau, *Sur l'origine de l'inégalité* Kant, *Allgemeine Naturgeschichte*

Events	Births, Deaths	Publications in England	Publications outside England
1756 Seven Years' War (to 1763)		Burke, *On the Sublime and the Beautiful* Warton, *Essay on the Writings and Genius of Pope*	
1757 Battle of Plassey	*b.* Blake	Gray, *The Bard* and *The Progress of Poesy* Hume, *Natural History of Religion*	Haller, *Elementa physiologiae* (to 1760)
1758		Johnson, *Idler* (to 1760)	Franklin, *Poor Richard's Almanac* Helvetius, *De l'Esprit*
1759 Capture of Quebec by General Wolfe	*d.* Collins *b.* Burns	Johnson, *Rasselas* Adam Smith, *Moral Sentiments*	Voltaire, *Candide*
1760 Reign of George III (to 1820)		Sterne, *Tristram Shandy* Macpherson, *Ossian*	Rousseau, *Nouvelle Héloïse*
1761	*d.* Richardson	Churchill, *Rosciad*	

Events	Births, Deaths	Publications in England	Publications outside England
1762 Reign of Catherine the Great (to 1796)		Macpherson, *Fingal* Goldsmith, *Citizen of the World*	Rousseau, *Le contrat social* Gluck, *Orfeo*
1763 Canada ceded to Britain	d. Shenstone	Smart, *A Song to David*	
1764 Literary Club established in London by Dr. Johnson & others		Goldsmith, *The Traveller*	Voltaire, *Dictionnaire philosophique* Winckelmann, *Geschichte der Kunst des Altertums*
1765 Stamp Act Watt's steam engine	d. Young	Walpole, *Castle of Otranto* Johnson's edition of Shakespeare Blackstone, *Commentaries on the Laws of England* (to 1768) Percy, *Reliques*	
1766		Goldsmith, *Vicar of Wakefield*	Lessing, *Laokoön*

Events	Births, Deaths	Publications in England	Publications outside England
1768 Spinning machine invented Royal Academy founded		Priestley, *First Principles of Government* Sterne, *Sentimental Journey*	
1769		Burke, *Observations on the Present State of the Nation*	Diderot, *Le rêve de d'Alembert*
1770	d. Akenside b. Wordsworth	Burke, *Thoughts on the Present Discontents* Goldsmith, *The Deserted Village*	Holbach, *La système de la natur* Kant, *De mundi forma et principiis*
1771	d. Gray b. Scott	Beattie, *The Minstrel*, Book I	
1772 First partition of Poland	b. Coleridge		
1773		Goldsmith, *She Stoops to Conquer* Monboddo, *On the Origin and Progress of Language*	Herder, *Von deutscher Art und Kunst*

Events	Births, Deaths	Publications in England	Publications outside England
1774	d. Goldsmith b. Southey	Warton, *History of English Poetry* (to 1781)	Goethe, *Werther* Gluck, *Iphigenie en Aulide*
1775	b. Lamb b. Jane Austen	Sheridan, *The Rivals*	Kant, *Anthropologie*
1776 American Declaration of Independence		Adam Smith, *Wealth of Nations* Gibbon, *Decline and Fall of the Roman Empire* (to 1788)	T. Paine, *Common Sense*
1777		Cook, *A Voyage toward the South Pole* Priestley, *A Disquisition on Matter and Spirit*	Gluck, *Iphigenie en Aulide*
1778	d. Rousseau d. Voltaire b. Hazlitt	F. Burney, *Evelina*	Freneau, *American Independence*

Events	Births, Deaths	Publications in England	Publications outside England
1779			
1781		Cowper, *Olney Hymns* Johnson, *Lives of the Poets* (to 1781) Hume, *Dialogues Concerning Natural Religion*	Buffon, *Epoques de la natur* Kant, *Kritik der reinen Vernunft* Schiller, *Die Räuber* Rousseau, *Confessions*
1782		Priestley, *History of the Corruption of Christianity*	Crevecoeur, *Letters from an American Farmer*
1783		Blake, *Poetical Sketches* Crabbe, *The Village* Blair, *Lectures on Rhetoric and Belles Lettres*	N. Webster, *Grammatical Institute of the English Language* (to 1785)
1784	d. Johnson b. Leigh Hunt		

Events	Births, Deaths	Publications in England	Publications outside England
1785	*b.* De Quincey	Cowper, *The Task* Paley, *Moral Philosophy*	
1786		Burns, *Poems*	
1787			Mozart, *Don Giovanni* Goethe, *Egmont*
1788 U. S. Constitution ratified	*d.* Charles Wesley *b.* Byron		Kant, *Kritik der praktischen Vernunft*
1789 French Revolution		Blake, *Songs of Innocence* E. Darwin, *The Loves of the Plants* Bentham, *Principles of Morals and Legislation*	Lavoisier, *Traité élémentaire de chemie*
1790		Blake, *Marriage of Heaven and Hell* Malone's edition of Shake-speare Burke, *Reflections on the French Revolution*	Kant, *Kritik der Urteilskraft*

Events	Births, Deaths	Publications in England	Publications outside England
1791	d. John Wesley	Boswell, *Life of Johnson*	Paine, *The Rights of Man* De Sade, *Justine*
1792	b. Shelley	M. Wollstonecraft, *Rights of Women*	
1793 Louvre established		Godwin, *Political Justice*	
1794 Whitney patents cotton gin Slavery abolished in French colonies		Blake, *Song of Innocence and Experience* Paley, *A View of the Evidences for Christianity*	Condorcet, *Esquisse d'un tableau historique des progrès de l'esprit humain*
1795	b. Keats b. Carlyle	Hutton, *Theory of the Earth*	Goethe, *Wilhelm Meister's Lehrjahre*
1796	d. Burns	Coleridge, *Poems on Various Subjects*	Laplace, *Exposition du système du monde*

Events	Births, Deaths	Publications in England	Publications outside England
1797	d. Horace Walpole d. Burke		Goethe, *Hermann und Dorothea*
1798 Irish rebellion		Wordsworth and Coleridge, *Lyrical Ballads*	
1799		Malthus, *Principles of Population*	Schleiermacher, *Reden über die Religion*

A Selected Bibliography

❧

I. General Studies, Collections
and Bibliographies

II. Political and Social History

III. Science

IV. Religion

V. Philosophy

VI. The Arts, Aesthetics, and
Critical Standards

I. General Studies, Collections, and Bibliographies

Barber, W. H., ed. *The Age of the Enlightenment: Studies Presented to Theodore Besterman.* London: Oliver and Boyd, 1967.

Bredvold, Louis I. "Some Basic Issues of the Eighteenth Century," *Michigan Alumnus Quarterly Review* LXIV (1957), 45-54.

Brissenden, R. F., ed. *Studies in the Eighteenth Century.* Toronto, University of Toronto Press, 1969.

Clifford, J. L. "The Eighteenth Century," *MLQ* XXVI (1965), 111-34.

———— *Early Eighteenth-Century English Literature: A List of Reference Works and Selected Reading.* New York: Columbia, 1959, 1962.

———— *Later Eighteenth-Century English Literature: A List of Reference Works and Selected Reading.* New York: Columbia, 1960.

Clifford, J. L. and Louis A. Landa, eds. *Pope and his Contemporaries: Essays Presented to George Sherburn.* Oxford: Clarendon, 1949.

Davies, Hugh Sykes and George Watson, eds. *The English Mind: Studies in the English Moralists presented to Basil Willey.* Cambridge: Cambridge University Press, 1964.

Essays on the Eighteenth Century Presented to David Nichol Smith. Oxford: Clarendon, 1945.

McCutcheon, Roger P., ed. *The Present-Day Relevance of Eighteenth-Century Thought.* Washington, D.C.: A.C.L.S., 1956.

Mollenauer, Robert, ed. *Introduction to Modernity: A Symposium on Eighteenth-Century Thought.* Austin, Texas: University of Texas, 1965.

Moore, Cecil Albert. *Backgrounds of English Literature, 1700-1760.* Minneapolis: University of Minnesota Press, 1953.

Schilling, Bernard N., ed., *Essential Articles for the Study of English Augustan Backgrounds.* Hamden, Conn.: Archon, 1961.

Tucker, Susie I. *Protean Shape: A Study in Eighteenth-Century Vocabulary and Usage.* London: Athlone, 1967.

Wasserman, Earl R., ed. *Aspects of the Eighteenth Century.* Baltimore, Md.: John Hopkins, 1965.

II. Political and Social History

Beattie, John M. *The English Court in the Reign of George I.* Cambridge: Cambridge University Press, 1967.

Cobban, Alfred. *Edmund Burke and the Revolt against the Eighteenth Century.* London: George Allen & Unwin, 1960.

Collins, A. S. "The Growth of the Reading Public During the Eighteenth Century," *RES* II (1926) 284-94 & 428-38.

Dickson, Peter G. M. *The Financial Revolution in England: A Study in the Development of Public Credit, 1688-1756.* London: Macmillan, 1967.

Flinn, M. W. *The Origins of the Industrial Revolution.* London: Longmans, 1966.

Harris, R. W. *England in the Eighteenth Century: A Balanced Constitution and New Horizons.* London: Blandford, 1963.

Harrison, Wilfrid. *Conflict and Compromise: History of British Political Thought, 1593-1900.* New York: Free Press, 1965.

Hearnshaw, F. J. C., ed. *The Social and Political Ideas of Some English Thinkers of the Augustan Age, 1650-1750.* New York: Geo. G. Harrap, 1928.

Holmes, Geoffrey. *British Politics in the Age of Anne.* London: Macmillan, 1967.

Humphreys, A. R. "The 'Rights of Women' in the Age of Reason," *MLR* XLI (1946), 256-69.

Kramnick, Isaac. *Bolingbroke and his Circle; the Politics of Nostalgia in the Age of Walpole.* Cambridge, Mass: Harvard University Press, 1968.

Marshall, Dorothy. *Dr. Johnson's London.* New York: Wiley & Sons, 1968.

Mingay, G. E. *English Landed Society in the Eighteenth Century.* London: Routledge and Kegan Paul, 1963.

Natan, Alex, ed. *Silver Renaissance: Essays in Eighteenth-Century English History.* London: Macmillan, 1961.

Plumb, J. H. *England in the Eighteenth Century.* London: Penguin, 1950.

——— *Men and Places.* London: Cresset Press, 1963.

Rude, George. "The London 'Mob' of the Eighteenth Century," *The Historical Journal* II (1959), 1-18.

Thomson, M. A. *Some Developments in English Historiography during the Eighteenth Century.* London: H. K. Lewis, 1957.

III. Science

Bush, Douglas. *Science and English Poetry: A Historical Sketch, 1590-1950.* New York: Oxford, 1950.

Carré, Meyrick H. "Doctrines of Creation and the Rise of Science," *London Quarterly and Holborn Review* CLXXXIV (1959), 54-9.

Crum, Ralph B. *Scientific Thought in Poetry.* New York: Columbia University Press, 1931.

Dijksterhuis, Eduard J. *The Mechanization of the World Picture.* trans. C. Dikshoorn. Oxford: Clarendon Press, 1961.

'Espinasse, Margaret. "The Decline and Fall of Restoration Science," *Past and Present* #14 (November, 1958), 71-89.

Grange, Kathleen M. "Pinel and Eighteenth-Century Psychiatry," *Bulletin of the History of Medicine* XXXV (1961), 442-53.

Hall, A. Rupert. *From Galileo to Newton.* New York: Harper and Row, 1963.

Hesse, Mary B. *Science and the Human Imagination: Aspects of the History and Logic of Physical Science.* New York: Philosophical Library, 1955.

Jones, William Powell. "The Idea of the Limitations of Science from Prior to Blake," *SEL* I (1961), 97-114.

———— "Science in Biblical Paraphrases in Eighteenth-Century England," *PMLA* LXXIV (1959), 41-51.

Kovacevich, Ivanka. "The Mechanical Muse: the Impact of Technical Inventions on Eighteenth-Century Neoclassical Poetry," *HLQ* XXVIII (1965), 263-81.

Koyre, Alexandre. *From the Closed World to the Infinite Universe.* Baltimore: Johns Hopkins, 1957.

Kuhn, Albert J. "Glory or Gravity: Hutchinson vs. Newton," *JHI* XXII (1961), 303-22.

Nicolson, Marjorie Hope. *Newton Demands the Muse: Newton's OPTICKS and the Eighteenth-Century Poets.* Princeton: Princeton University Press, 1946.

———— *Science and Imagination.* Ithaca, N.Y.: Cornell University Press, 1956.

IV. Religion

Colie, Rosalie L. "Spinoza and the Early English Deists," *JHI* XX (1959), 23-46.

Cragg, Gerald R. *The Church and the Age of Reason, 1648-1789*. New York: Atheneum, 1961.

———— *Reason and Authority in the Eighteenth Century*. Cambridge: Cambridge University Press, 1964.

Curtis, L. P. *Anglican Moods of the Eighteenth Century*. Hamden, Conn.: Archon, 1966.

Davies, Horton, *Worship and Theology in England from Watts and Wesley to Maurice, 1690-1850*. Princeton: Princeton University Press, 1961.

Fairchild, Hoxie Neale. *Religious Trends in English Poetry. Volume II: 1740-1780. Religious Sentimentalism in the Age of Johnson*. New York: Columbia University Press, 1942.

Greene, Donald. "Augustinianism and Empiricism: A Note on Eighteenth-Century English Intellectual History," *Eighteenth Century Studies* I (1967), 33-68.

Knox, R. A. *Enthusiasm: A Chapter in the History of Religion*. Oxford: Clarendon, 1950.

Linker, R. W. "English Catholics in the Eighteenth Century: An Interpretation," *Church History* XXXV (1966), 288-310.

Macdonald, Alastair. "Enthusiasm Resurgent," *Dalhousie Review* XLII (1962), 352–63.

Manuel, Frank E. *The Eighteenth Century Confronts the Gods*. Cambridge, Mass.: Harvard University Press, 1959.

Odom, Herbert H. "The Estrangement of Celestial Mechanics and Religion," *JHI* XXVII (1966), 533-48.

Routley, Erik. *English Religious Dissent*. Cambridge: Cambridge University Press, 1960.

Stromberg, Roland, "Lovejoy's 'Parallel' Reconsidered," *Eighteenth Century Studies* I (1968), 381–95.

Sykes, Norman. *Church and State in England in the Eighteenth Century*. Hamden, Conn.: Archon, 1962.

Wasserman, Earl R. "Nature Moralized: Divine Analogy in the Eighteenth Century," *ELH* XX (1953), 39–76.

V. Philosophy

Baker, John T. "Space, Time, and God: A Chapter in Eighteenth-Century English Philosophy," *Philosophical Review* XLI (1932), 577–93.

Becker, Carl L. *The Heavenly City of the Eighteenth-Century Philosophers.* New Haven: Yale University Press, 1932.

Brehier, Emile. *The Eighteenth Century.* trans. Wade Baskin. Chicago: University of Chicago Press, 1930.

Gay, Peter. *The Enlightenment: An Interpretation. The Rise of Modern Paganism,* New York: Knopf, 1966.

Humphreys, A. R. " 'The Eternal Fitness of Things': An Aspect of Eighteenth-Century Thought," *MLR* XLII (1947) 188–98.

James, D. G. *The Life of Reason: Hobbes, Locke, Bolingbroke.* London: Longmans, Green, and Co., 1949.

Letwin, Shirley R. *The Pursuit of Certainty.* Cambridge: Cambridge University Press, 1965.

Lovejoy, A. O. *Essays in the History of Ideas.* Baltimore: Johns Hopkins Press, 1948.

Price, Martin. *To the Palace of Wisdom: Studies in Order and Energy from Dryden to Blake.* New York: Doubleday, 1964.

Rostvig, Maren-Sofie. *The Happy Man: Studies in the Metamorphoses of a Classical Ideal.* Vol. II, 1700–1760. Oslo: Oslo University Press, 1958.

Sampson, R. V. *Progress in the Age of Reason.* Cambridge, Mass.: Harvard University Press, 1956.

Suckling, Norman. "The Enlightenment and the Idea of Progress," *Studies on Voltaire and the Eighteenth Century* LVIII (1967), 1461–80.

Tuveson, Ernest Lee. *Millennium and Utopia: A Study in the Background of the Idea of Progress.* Berkeley: University of California Press, 1949.

————— "Space, Deity and the 'Natural Sublime'," *MLQ* XII (1951), 20–38.

Vereker, Charles. *Eighteenth-Century Optimism: A Study of the Interrelations of Moral and Social Theory in English and French Thought between 1689 and 1789.* Liverpool: University Press, 1967.

Warnock, G. J. *Berkeley*. London: Penguin, 1953.

Whitney, Lois. *Primitivism and the Idea of Progress in English Popular Literature of the Eighteenth Century*. Baltimore: Johns Hopkins, 1934.

Willey, Basil. *The Eighteenth Century Background: Studies on the Idea of Nature in the Thought of the Period*. London: Chatto & Windus, 1940.

VI. The Arts, Aesthetics, and Critical Standards

Bredvold, Louis I. *The Natural History of Sensibility*. Detroit: Wayne State University Press, 1962.

Brett, R. L. *The Third Earl of Shaftesbury: A Study in Eighteenth-Century Literary Theory*. London: Hutchinson, 1951.

Bullough, Geoffrey. *Mirror of Minds: Changing Psychological Beliefs in English Poetry*. Toronto: University of Toronto Press, 1962.

Clough, Wilson O. "Reason and Genius: an Eighteenth-Century Dilemma: Hogarth, Hume, Burke, Reynolds," *PQ* XXIII (1944), 33–54.

Cohen, Ralph, "Association of Ideas and Poetic Unity," *PQ* XXXVI (1957), 465–74.

———— "David Hume's Experimental Method and the Theory of Taste," *ELH* XXV (1958), 270–89.

Crane, R. S. "English Neoclassical Criticism: An Outline Sketch," *Critics and Criticism*. Chicago: University of Chicago Press, 1952.

Elledge, Scott. "The Background and Development in English Criticism of the Theories of Generality and Particularity," *PMLA* LXII (1947), 147–82.

Fitzgerald, Margaret M. *First Follow Nature: Primitivism in English Poetry, 1725–50*. New York: Columbia, 1947.

Frazer, Ray. "The Origin of the Term 'Image'," *ELH* XXVII (1960), 149–61.

Gothein, Marie Louise. *A History of Garden Art*. Vol. II. trans. Archer-Hind. New York: Hacker Art Books, 1966.

Hadfield, Miles. *Gardening in Britain*. London: Hutchinson, 1960.

Hagstrum, Jean H. *The Sister Arts: The Tradition of Literary Pictorialism and English Poetry from Dryden to Gray*. Chicago: University of Chicago Press, 1958.

Havens, Raymond D. "Simplicity, a Changing Concept," *JHI* XIV (1953), 3–32.

Hussey, Christopher. *English Gardens and Landscapes 1700–1750*. London: Country Life Ltd., 1967.

———— *The Picturesque: Studies in a Point of View*. 2nd edition. Hamden, Conn.: Archon, 1967.

Hyams, Edward S. *The English Garden*. New York: Harry N. Abrams, 1964.

Irwin, David. *English Neoclassical Art: Studies in Inspiration and Taste*. London: Faber and Faber, 1966.

Kallich, Martin. "The Argument against the Association of Ideas in Eighteenth-Century Aesthetics," *MLQ* XV (1954), 125–36.

Kliger, Samuel. "The 'Goths' in England: an Introduction to the Gothic Vogue in Eighteenth-Century Aesthetic Discussion," *MP* XLIII (1948), 107–17.

Kristeller, Paul Oskar. "The Modern System of the Arts:A Study in the History of Aesthetics, II," *JHI* XIII (1952), 17–46.

Lees-Milne, James. *Earls of Creation: Five Great Patrons of Eighteenth-Century Art*. London: Hamish Hamilton, 1962.

Lovejoy, A. O. "The First Gothic Revival and the Return to Nature," *MLN* XLVII (1932), 419–46.

———— " 'Nature' as Aesthetic Norm," *MLN* XLII (1927) 444–50.

Malins, Edward G. *English Landscaping and Literature*. London: Oxford University Press, 1966.

Manwaring, Elizabeth Wheeler. *Italian Landscape in Eighteenth-Century England: A Study Chiefly of the Influence of Claude Lorrain and Salvator Rosa on English Taste, 1700–1800*. New York: Russell and Russell, 1925, 1965.

Monk, Samuel H. *The Sublime: A Study of Critical Theories in Eighteenth-Century England*. Ann Arbor: University of Michigan Press, 1960.

Ong, Walter J. "Psyche and the Geometers: Aspects of Associationist Critical Theory," *MP* XLVIII (1951), 16–27.

Rogerson, Brewster. "The Art of Painting the Passions," *JHI* XIV (1953), 68–94.

Schueller, Herbert M. "Correspondences between Music and the Sister Arts, According to Eighteenth-Century Aesthetic Theory," *JAAC* XI (1953) 334–59.

———— Literature and Music as Sister Arts: An Aspect of Aesthetic Theory in Eighteenth-Century Britain," *PQ* XXVI (1947), 193–205.

———— "The Use and Decorum of Music as Described in British Literature: 1700–1780," *JHI* XIII (1952), 73–93.

Stolnitz, Jerome. "Beauty: Some Stages in the History of an Idea," *JHI* XXII (1961), 185–204.

———— "On the Origins of 'Aesthetic Disinterestedness'," *JAAC* XX (1961), 131–43.

D0877850